Interest Rate Markets

Founded in 1807, John Wiley & Sons is the oldest independent publishing company in the United States. With offices in North America, Europe, Australia, and Asia, Wiley is globally committed to developing and marketing print and electronic products and services for our customers' professional and personal knowledge and understanding.

The Wiley Trading series features books by traders who have survived the market's ever-changing temperament and have prospered—some by reinventing systems, others by getting back to basics. Whether the reader is a novice trader, a professional, or somewhere in between, these books will provide the advice and strategies needed to prosper today and well into the future.

For a list of available titles, visit our Web site at www.WileyFinance.com.

Interest Rate Markets

Markets

A Practical Approach to Fixed Income

SIDDHARTHA JHA

WILEY

John Wiley & Sons, Inc.

Published by John Wiley & Sons, Inc., Hoboken, New Jersey.
Published simultaneously in Canada.

For general information on our other products and services or for technical support, please contact our Customer Care Department within the United States at (800) 762-2974, outside the United States at (317) 572-3993 or fax (317) 572-4002.

Wiley also publishes its books in a variety of electronic formats. Some content that appears in print may not be available in electronic books. For more information about Wiley products, visit our web site at www.wiley.com.

Library of Congress Cataloging-in-Publication Data:

Jha, Siddhartha, 1984–
    Interest rate markets : a practical approach to fixed income / Siddhartha Jha.
      p. cm. – (Wiley trading series)
    Includes bibliographical references and index.
    ISBN 978-0-470-93220-9 (cloth); ISBN 978-1-118-01777-7 (ebk);
    ISBN 978-1-118-01778-4 (ebk); ISBN 978-1-118-01779-1 (ebk)
  1. Interest rates.   2. Fixed-income securities.   3. Bonds.   I. Title.
    HG1621.J43 2011
    332.63′2044–dc22

                                  2010043312

Printed in the United States of America

10 9 8 7 6 5 4 3 2 1

To my parents

Contents

Acknowledgments   xiii

Introduction   xv

CHAPTER 1   Tools of the Trade   1

Basic Statistics   2
Regression: The Fundamentals   6
Regression: How Good a Fit?   11
Principal Components Analysis   14
Scaling through Time   15
Backtesting Strategies   16
Summary   17

CHAPTER 2   Bonds   19

Basics of Bonds   19
Risks Embedded in Fixed Income Instruments   22
Discounting   27
Bond Pricing   28
Yield Curve   32
Duration   34
Convexity   37
Repo Markets   42
Bid Offer   44
Calculating Profit/Loss of a Bond   45
Carry   45

Forward Rates   47
Rolldown/Slide   51
Curves and Spreads   53
Butterfly Trades   55
Summary   56

CHAPTER 3   Fixed Income Markets   59

Federal Reserve   60
Treasuries   67
STRIPS   70
TIPS   71
Mortgages   73
Agency Debt   77
Corporate Bonds   79
Municipal Bonds   82
Summary   84

CHAPTER 4   Interest Rate Futures   85

Basics of Futures Transactions   86
Eurodollar Futures   89
Convexity (or Financing) Bias   92
Creating Longer-Dated Assets Using
    Eurodollar Futures   93
Treasury Futures   94
Fed Funds Futures   101
Futures Positioning Data   104
Summary   105

CHAPTER 5   Interest Rate Swaps   107

Basic Principles   108
Duration and Convexity   111
Uses of Swaps   112
Counterparty Risk   115
Other Types of Swaps   115
Summary   124

**CHAPTER 6 Understanding Drivers of
              Interest Rates**   **125**

Supply and Demand for Borrowing   126
Components of Fixed Income Supply and Demand   141
Treasury Supply   141
Other Sources of Fixed Income Supply   145
Fixed Income Demand   148
Short-Term Yield Drivers   157
Summary   172

CHAPTER 7 Carry and Relative Value Trades   **173**

Carry Trades   173
Carry Trade Setup and Evaluation   175
Pitfalls of the Carry Trade   178
Carry-Efficient Directional Trades   182
Relative Value Trades   183
Setting Up Relative Value Trades   185
Treasury Bond Relative Value—Par Curve   191
Other Treasury Relative Value Trades   193
Summary   194

**CHAPTER 8 Hedging Risks in Interest
              Rate Products**   **197**

Principles of Hedging   198
Choices of Instruments for Hedging   202
Calculating Hedge Ratios   210
Yield Betas   215
Convexity Hedging   218
Summary   223

CHAPTER 9 Trading Swap Spreads   **225**

How Swap Spreads Work   225
Why Trade Swap Spreads?   230
Directionality of Swap Spreads to Yields   240
Futures Asset Swaps   241

Spread Curve Trades   243
Summary   245

**CHAPTER 10   Interest Rate Options and
                Trading Volatility**   **247**
_____

Option Pricing and Fundamentals   249
Modifications for the Interest Rate Markets   254
Quoting Volatility   256
Measuring Risks in Option Positions   257
Put/Call Parity   266
Implied and Realized Volatility   268
Skew   270
Delta Hedging   270
Interest Rate Options   275
Embedded Options and Hedging   280
More Exotic Structures   283
Yield Curve Spread Options   284
Forward Volatility   285
Volatility Trading   286
Interest Rate Skew   293
Volatility Spread Trades   294
Caps versus Swaptions   297
Summary   298

**CHAPTER 11   Treasury Futures Basis
                and Rolls**   **299**
_____

The Futures Delivery Option   299
Calculating the Delivery Option Value   309
Option-Adjusted and Empirical Duration   311
Treasury Futures Rolls   313
Summary   318

CHAPTER 12   Conditional Trades **319**

Conditional Curve Trades 320
Conditional Spread Trades 324
Summary 328

References **329**

About the Author **331**

About the Web Site **333**

Index **335**

Acknowledgments

This work is the outcome of inspiration, training, and support I received from so many colleagues, friends, and family. Much as I am deeply indebted to them, I cannot possibly mention them all in the short space here. To name just a few, Pavan Wadhwa and Srini Ramaswamy helped me understand markets in a thorough and logical manner throughout my career. I would like to thank Ross Jackman and Russ Mannis for their encouragement at the start of my career in municipals. My discussions about finance with colleagues such as Manas Baveja and Anthony Heading over the years have been instrumental in addressing any doubts in my thought process. I also want to acknowledge Kelly for her unwavering support.

A number of individuals took the time to perform the arduous task of editing and offered advice on content. Specifically, I want to express my gratitude to my dad and to Hitomi Kimura for their assistance.

Last, but definitely not least, I would like to thank the editing staff at Wiley who took the time to thoroughly edit my manuscripts. In particular, I thank Laura Walsh, Judy Howarth, and Laura Cherkas for their assistance with the whole publication process.

Introduction

The U.S. fixed income market, with securities worth trillions of dollars traded yearly, is one of the largest in the world. It attracts a wide variety of borrowers and investors, from individuals and corporations to governments. The market offers an array of instruments such as bonds, swaps, futures, and options for trading or managing risk. As the size and sophistication of the U.S. fixed income market have increased over the past two decades, so have the challenges and opportunities that come along with these instruments. Managing interest rate risk has become a crucial task for portfolio managers. Indeed, the various crises that punctuated the financial markets over the past two decades have underscored the importance of this task. Therefore, given the complexity of interest rate products and the range of macroeconomic factors that affect them, participants in the fixed income markets need to have frameworks for logical and in-depth analysis of trades and embedded risks.

Such a framework needs to be based on the principles of mathematical modeling as well as an intuitive grasp of the economy and monetary policy. Mathematical models are important because the contemporary fixed income market has numerous complex products that require quantitative foundations. Likewise, the knowledge of fundamentals is indispensable because markets are more integrated than ever before. However, the current literature on the U.S. fixed income market lacks the balance of these essential elements. Some works rely on a qualitative approach, whereas others exaggerate the significance of quantitative models. The overemphasis on models, as is well known, was a part of the problem in recent financial crises.

This book breaks a new, middle ground. It begins with the essential mathematical tools needed to objectively analyze data and financial instruments. These instruments can be thought of as packages of different types of risks that on one hand provide opportunity to trade, and on the other hand involve careful management. Such management requires both mathematical skills and an intuitive grasp of the economy and financial markets.

To this end, this book analyzes fundamentals and financial flows and identifies the optimal instruments for a trade using quantitative tools.

This book is meant for both newcomers and experienced professionals in fixed income markets. For newcomers, it builds an understanding of bonds and more complex products such as interest rate swaps, futures, and options. Subsequently, it describes the driving factors behind fixed income markets and explains how to use these products to express views on interest rates and their spreads. For experienced professionals, the book describes economic fundamentals and the behavior of market participants in order to explain short-term as well as long-term drivers of interest rates. As an important companion to trading, the book discusses hedging. The details include its general principles as well as the choice of instrument for a hedge. The information is meant to enable effective risk management and construction of market indicators. Finally, the limitations and pitfalls of each type of trade are discussed; the lessons of past financial crises show there is no such thing as a safe trade.

To summarize, the framework of the book includes:

- Quantitative tools that form the foundations of market analysis
- Mechanics of interest rate products, both bonds and derivatives, including swaps, options, and futures
- Thought processes for forming a view on interest rates and related variables, such as swap spreads
- Types of trades commonly done by professionals in the market to express views and detailed discussions of methods to accurately set up the trades
- The importance of quantitatively managing risks inherent in interest rate trades
- Common pitfalls and risks facing popular interest rate trades

Interest Rate Markets

CHAPTER 1

Tools of the Trade

To understand markets in a logical and objective manner, it is important to employ tools from mathematics and statistics in an appropriate way to unearth relevant patterns. This chapter highlights some of the basic tools used by practitioners to understand the volumes of data produced on a daily basis by financial markets. The tools described here allow an understanding of data in relatively simple terms and help forecast the direction of seemingly random series. The focus here is on the intuition behind mathematical tools rather than a deep dive into the formulas. Often finance books and academic papers rely on complex mathematical models to explain market behavior. As markets are constantly evolving, elaborate quantitative constructs can rapidly become irrelevant and provide false signals about market movements.

The frequent failure of complex quantitative models to forecast markets is not intended to discourage market investors from using mathematics; instead, *misuse* of math is to be avoided. Indeed, mathematics is crucial for objective analysis of market movements and for appropriately controlling risks. Although overuse of mathematics can be a problem, the opposite is just as dangerous. Market participants who only use qualitative assessments to trade markets may be exposed to numerous hidden risks. In the paragraphs to come, we consider some statistical techniques useful in finance, the appropriate situations in which to use them, and their embedded assumptions. These techniques are building blocks; creative thinking and building on the ideas behind these methods can lead to the discovery of new trading patterns as well as a more thorough evaluation of market behavior. This chapter purposefully avoids mathematical proofs; instead, the focus is on developing a practical and intuitive grasp of the concepts. Readers are encouraged to consult mathematics or statistics texts for more detailed analysis of the concepts.

BASIC STATISTICS

Knowledge of basic statistics is a prerequisite for understanding today's markets, and especially the rates markets, where there is a preponderance of mathematically adept investors. We use the term "basic stats" to refer to initial descriptive statistics used to understand the data quantitatively. We build on these initial descriptions of the data using more advanced statistical techniques. To begin with, we consider the time series of a simple and commonly traded security: the 2-year Treasury yield. Figure 1.1 shows the 2-year Treasury yield time series over the past 20 years. We refer to this series repeatedly as we build our tools to think about how to trade this security. The figure also shows the average value and increments of

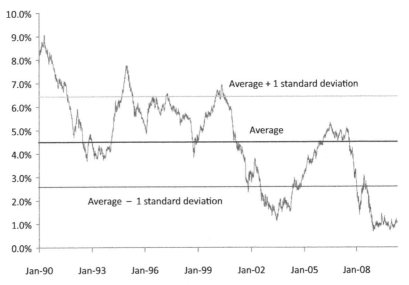

FIGURE 1.1 Two-Year Treasury Yield along with Average Value and One–Standard Deviation Bands
Source: Board of Governors of the Federal Reserve.

one standard deviation (SD) from the average value over the entire period shown. These quantities are discussed in more detail later in the chapter.

For a time series, basic descriptive statistical quantities are akin to descriptions of people's height and weight. In the realm of time series, the crucial descriptions are mean (or average), standard deviation, minimum, maximum, and, to a lesser extent, median. (Note: Mode is a commonly used descriptor in some fields but tends to have limited application in finance.) The median refers to the point in the middle when the data is sorted. The median tends to be less useful than the average since it is very resistant to outliers while profit and losses (P/Ls) are not. The mean of a string of data is the sum of the data series divided by the number of data points. The mean is susceptible to outliers since unusually high or low points can drag the average in either direction. Figure 1.1 shows the mean of the 2-year Treasury yield, which is 4.5% over the long run. This average, though, is susceptible to extreme values of the 2-year yields. At times, to deal with series where outliers can misrepresent data, outlying data can be trimmed, referred to as a trimmed mean. An example of this methodology is the calculation of the London Interbank Offered Rate (LIBOR) by the British Bankers' Association (BBA), where 16 banks submit their estimates for short-term rates and the top four and bottom four submissions are discarded to arrive at a trimmed mean. Frequently, averages are considered on a rolling basis over a fixed number of days; these are referred to as moving averages. Here, each point in the modified time series represents the average of a fixed number of preceding points from the original time series. A related concept to the average value is the weighted average. The simple average essentially multiplies each variable with an equal weight of $1/n$, where n is the number of elements. However, the weights on the average do not need to be equal, but can instead be altered based on different criteria. For example, the weight could be altered based on how close the data point is to today if more recent data points need to be given more weight.

Since most financial market entities are not deterministic, a concept called a random variable is useful. A random variable can be thought of as a variable that can take on a range of values, such as the commonly used x in algebra. However, the difference here is that instead of having a set value in an equation, a random variable essentially is a "package" of values, with each value occurring with some probability. The range of values of the random variable as well as the probabilities associated with the variable is known as its probability distribution (or just distribution). For a random variable, a special type of weighted average is known as the expected value. The expected value is calculated as the average payoff of the random variable weighted by the probability of its occurrence. For example, if the payoff from a dice roll is the rolled value, then the expected value is $1 \times 1/6 + 2 \times 1/6 + 3 \times 1/6 + 4 \times 1/6 + 5 \times 1/6 + 6 \times 1/6 = 3.5$, since each roll has 1/6 probability of taking place. Note that given the equal probability of each roll, the expected value is the same as the simple average of the payoffs. The notation for expected value of a random variable is generally $E(X)$.

Probability distributions as with the dice are known as discrete distributions because the payoffs occur in discrete amounts. In the finance field, continuous distributions, which have continuous payoffs, are used more frequently. One common probability distribution used in finance and other fields is the normal distribution, which represents the familiar bell curve. The center of the distribution, and also the most likely scenario, is the average. A continuous probability distribution's description is generally given through a mathematical function known as a probability density function. The probability density function gives the chance of an event occurring for this distribution around a single point—it can be approximately thought of as equivalent to the 1/6 probability of a given dice roll in a discrete distribution. For example, for the normal distribution, the probability density function (pdf) is

$$\text{pdf}(x) = 1/\sqrt{(2\pi\sigma^2)} \times e^{-(x-\mu)^{\wedge}2/(2\sigma^{\wedge}2)}$$

where σ = standard deviation
         μ = mean of the distribution

Taking this one step further, we arrive at a cumulative distribution function (cdf), which gives the probability of the random variable taking values *less than* a given value. For example, for a normal distribution, this would be denoted as $\Phi(k)$, which is the probability of a random normal variable x taking values less than k. Unlike the pdf, the normal distribution cdf does not have a closed-form formula, but instead numerical methods are needed to calculate the value. Geometrically, it is the area under the bell curve to left of the k point. The details of probability distributions are beyond the scope of this text, but the idea of a cumulative distribution arises in pricing options, which we discuss in Chapter 11. The concept behind the terminology is the important bit, as these functions can be calculated using software packages.

The expected value can be thought of as the average level of a random variable. The variance can be thought of as movement of the variable around its average. The variance is calculated as the sum of squared deviations of each data point from the average normalized by the number of data points. For the die described earlier, the variance would be calculated as $1/6 \times [(3.5-1)^2 + (3.5-2)^2 + (3.5-3)^2 + (3.5-4)^2 + (3.5-5)^2 + (3.5-6)^2]$.

In expected value notation, variance $= E(X - \mu)^2 = E(X^2) - E(X)^2$. The standard deviation, a related and more commonly considered measure, is defined as the square root of the variance. Variance and standard deviations are measures of dispersion in a data set; since they sum up squares of deviation, a negative or positive deviation is irrelevant in this case. Regardless of whether it is positive or negative, the size of the deviation is what matters. The weight of each deviation grows rapidly by how "unusual" it is (i.e., how far away it is from the average value). Figure 1.1 shows increments of one standard deviation above and below the average 2-year Treasury yield since 1990; the standard deviation here is 1.9%. Due to the link between standard deviation and dispersion, it is also used commonly as a risk measure in finance, and is commonly referred to as *volatility*. For example, volatility of a series of historical returns may be represented as 10% per year. If market returns are assumed to follow a normal distribution, the volatility has a further interpretation. For each standard deviation away from the mean in either direction, the chance of being outside the range drops off successively. For 1 standard deviation on either side of the mean of a normal distribution, the chance of an occurrence in that range is about 68.3% and 95% for 2 standard deviations. Therefore, a volatility of 10% per year implies that next year's return is likely to be 10% above or 10% below the average return about 68% of the time. Furthermore, the return has a 95% chance of being within $10\% \times 2 = 20\%$ of the average. Of course, if the distribution was different than normal, then the likelihood of outsized returns could be lower or higher. One area of continuing research in academic and market circles deals with the fact that normal distributions make "unlikely" events much rarer than reality (i.e., the frequency of multi–standard deviation moves in markets is higher than would be the case if markets were truly normal). There are other types of distributions that have "fat tails" (i.e., incorporate a higher likelihood of large moves), but the mathematics related to such distributions tends to be more complex, making them less prevalent in models.

The concept of volatility applies to a single variable and can be extended further to covariance between two or more variables. The covariance conveys how much two quantities move with respect to each other. In expected value notation, the covariance between two variables X and Y is calculated as $E(X \times Y) - E(X) \times E(Y)$. If two variables are independent, that is, they have no relation to each other, the covariance is 0. These expected values depend on the distributions of the two variables. Covariance also is used to calculate the variance of the sums of two variables. The variance of a sum of random variables A and B, expressed as $\text{Var}(A + B) = \text{Var}(A) + \text{Var}(B) + 2 \times \text{Cov}(A, B)$. The covariance is closely related to the concept of correlation, which will be discussed in more detail when we cover regression.

REGRESSION: THE FUNDAMENTALS

Now that the basic statistics have been covered, we move on to regression, which is one of the most extensively used, and at times misunderstood, tools to analyze empirical data. The purpose of regression is not really to price the instruments, but rather to analyze time series data and deduce relationships between them to predict their future behavior. The basic statistics discussed in the previous section concern a single time series. However, as might be expected, the financial world is full of intersecting relationships between variables, with various factors coming in and out of importance. Regression analysis provides a logical way to analyze such relationships.

The most commonly used type of regression is linear regression, which fits a "best-fit" line between the scatterplot of data points of two variables. By "scatterplot," we mean a graph that conveys this information: "the value of y when the value of x was __." Another way to think about this scatterplot is the value of a variable y at time t versus the value of a variable x also at time t (although time does not have to be the only common factor). An example of such a relationship would be between inflation and unemployment rate. Figure 1.2 shows the relationship from 1975 to 1977; the linear relationship between the two is evident. The y-axis on the figure is the inflation rate, the x-axis is the unemployment rate, and each point on the figure is the inflation rate that existed for a given level of unemployment rate. The points do not have to be unique—for example, at an unemployment level of 8%, we may see inflation at 2% in one time period and at 10%

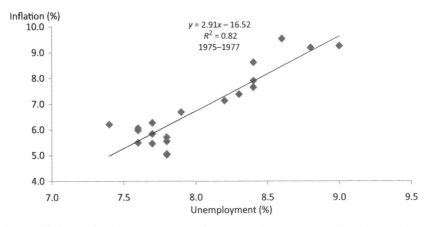

FIGURE 1.2 Inflation Regressed against Unemployment from 1975 to 1977
Source: Federal Reserve Bank of St. Louis.

in another time period, which would lead to two vertical points at 2% and 10% corresponding to 8% on the x-axis in the graph.

Once we have our data set defined, the regression line is fitted by finding a line such that the sum of squared distances from the line across the scatterplot points is minimized. This process is known as the least squares method and forms the basis for many simpler-fitting algorithms. The linear regression process results in an equation of the form:

$$y_{\text{model}} = \text{alpha} + \text{beta} \times x_t \qquad (1.1)$$

where   alpha and beta = constants (explained below)
            x_t = explanatory variable at time t

The equation here can be thought of as the "average" relationship between y and x. Thus, by inputting an x value, we can arrive at a model y value. The meaning of the term "linear regression" becomes apparent, since our model equation is that of a straight line in geometry. The model y value is the best prediction of y *given* a value of x, which is referred to as a conditional expectation or conditional mean. Recall that earlier we referred to the mean of a series as a first-order prediction, but now we are conditioning that mean on the value of an explanatory variable, which we hope will improve prediction results. Given that Equation 1.1 is a best-fit line through the data, most data points will tend to lie at some distance from the line. This leads to the concept of the error, which can be found by considering a particular value of x. Now we consider the y value on the same day as x, referred to as the "actual" value, and subtract out the model value of y, which is found by plugging in x into Equation 1.1. To summarize:

$$y_{\text{model}} = \text{alpha} + \text{beta} \times x_t$$

$$\text{error}_t = y_t - y_{\text{model}}$$

where error_t = error at time t

Before we analyze the errors in further detail, what are the alpha and beta in Equation 1.1? The alpha is referred to as the intercept, and it is the value of y if the value of x is 0. The alpha can be thought of as the "default" value of the dependent variable in case of lack of effect from x. Occasionally, the intercept can be forced to be 0 in situations when it is known beforehand that the default value of y when x is 0 is also 0, which is an option that is not commonly used. The beta here, as the reader may recall from geometry class, is the slope of the best-fit line. The slope's intuitive interpretation is the sensitivity of y to x; that is, the change in y for a unit change in x. The beta is a crucial variable to understanding relationships between variables, which in turn is an important factor when offsetting risks in trades (discussed in detail in Chapter 8). The error$_t$, shown as the difference between the actual value and the model value, is also known as the residual. The residual gives a quantitative measure of how effective the regression is at predicting the actual values for any given explanatory variable value. Of course, the smaller the residual, the more accurate the regression. Since the residual varies for each explanatory variable, a combined measure known as the standard error can give a quantitative measure of how well the regression works at fitting the data. The standard error is essentially the standard deviation of the residuals. It gives an indication of the average error for the regression's predictions—the larger the standard error, the less accurate the regression.

Finally, given the linear nature of this relationship, the fact that beta is constant implies that the sensitivity of y to changes in x remains the same regardless of the level of x; at times, this may be a desirable characteristic, but at other times, this may be too simplistic a model, and nonlinear methods may need to be considered (discussed later). In Figure 1.2, for example, the alpha is shown to be -16.52 and beta is 2.91. This beta implies that as unemployment rises 1%, the inflation rate in this period rises 2.91%.

The stylized example in Figure 1.2 focuses on the basic case of a single-variable linear regression. However, as the reader may have guessed, financial variables are rarely driven by a single factor, but instead are complex interactions of many factors. To consider a more realistic case, Equation 1.2 may be easily extended to the case of many variables:

$$y_{\text{model}} = \text{alpha} + \text{beta}_1 \times x_{1t} + \text{beta}_2 \times x_{2t} + \ldots + \text{beta}_n \times x_{nt} \qquad (1.2)$$

where   alpha and beta$_{1\ldots n}$ = constants
        $x_{1t}, x_{2t}, \ldots x_{nt} = n$ explanatory factors at time t

As with the one-variable case, the predicted y is linear with respect to its factors, but in this case, more than one explanatory variable is being used to predict y. The error here is computed using a similar calculation, by subtracting the actual value of y and the model value of y. The alpha, or intercept, also has the same interpretation, which represents the value of y if none of the factors had any contribution to the prediction. In multiple regression, the betas take on a slightly more subtle interpretation. Each beta is the *partial* sensitivity of y with regard to the corresponding factor (i.e., beta$_1$ is the partial sensitivity of x_1). The partial sensitivity can be thought of as the effect of one particular factor on y *after* controlling for the effects of all other variables considered. An example of this would be in the case of a medical study to consider the effect of weight on blood pressure, where it may not be enough to know the average increase in blood pressure for each one-pound gain in weight. Instead, other factors, such as family history or job stress levels, may need to be added. Once these other factors are added in the regression, the partial beta of weight will change since other relevant factors are being considered; the new, partial sensitivity of blood pressure to weight gives a more accurate relationship between the two. In the context of finance, knowledge of partial sensitivities is essential for hedging risks and accurately setting up trades. When important factors are missing from a model, a trader/researcher can have an inaccurate sense of the impact of various market factors on a trade, which can of course lead to large losses.

Multiple regressions are difficult to visualize given the multidimensional nature of the modeling. For a two-variable regression, for example, a three-dimensional figure would be required with two axes for the independent variables and an axis for the dependent variable. While impractical in a two-variable regression, for higher-order regressions, the figures are even less practical. To display multiple regressions on two-dimensional figures, the concept of a partial regression is used. Consider Equation 1.2. To display the relationship of the y variable to x_{1t}, the regression to display would be $y - (\text{beta}_2 \times x_{2t} + \ldots + \text{beta}_n \times x_{nt})$ regressed against x_{1t}. This *partial* regression would preserve the same pattern and strength of association as multiple regression. To view the regression versus other x variables, the same procedure is repeated while keeping the target variable on the right-hand side of the equation.

So far we have considered only linear regression, in both single and multivariate settings. The linear aspect can be deduced by looking at the equations (they resemble the equations of a line in geometry) and also follows from the fact that the sensitivity of y to any factor x is a fixed constant beta. This constant beta does not have to be the case. In fact, linear regression is a very special case of general regression methods, and nearly any function may be used to relate x and y. The introduction of more complicated functions beyond a straight line vastly increases the complexity of the problem being considered, and should be used only if there is a compelling case to do so. As we will see in the goodness-of-fit section, an overly complicated model may improve the explanatory power of a model, but also subjects it to an increased risk of overfitting, which can actually lead to poor subsequent predictions.

Although general nonlinear regressions are a complex topic, there is a relatively simple extension of the linear regression just considered. Here, the alphas and betas are similar to the linear regression case (i.e., fixed constants), but the variables themselves may be squared, cubic, or higher powers of the factor variables. Why would we consider such a case? Generally, polynomials are considered when the relationship between y and x

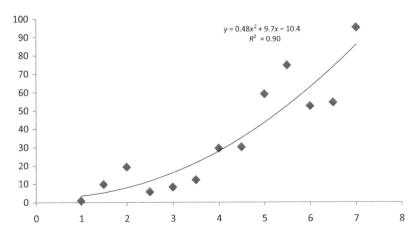

FIGURE 1.3 Example of a Quadratic Regression

is very plainly not a straight line, as seen in Figure 1.3, which shows two fictitious data sets with a quadratic relationship. It may be that the sensitivity of y grows as x grows, which would be the case in the quadratic regression depicted in Equation 1.3:

$$y_{\text{model}} = \text{alpha} + \text{beta}_1 \times x + \text{beta}_2 \times x^2 \tag{1.3}$$

Here, the equation is similar to the ones we covered earlier, but the dependence of y is on the square of x. The consequence of this is that y does not grow at a fixed beta rate as x grows; instead the growth in y becomes more rapid as x grows. Another way to think about a quadratic regression is that the *sensitivity of y to x itself grows in a linear fashion*, making y linked to x in a square relationship. For example, if we assume alpha $= 0$ and beta $= 2$, the value of y at $x = 1$ is $0 + 2 \times 1^2 = 2$; at $x = 2$, the value of y is $0 + 2 \times 2^2 = 8$. Here, the value of y rose by 6 when x increased from 1 to 2.

To explore these ideas in more concrete terms, we consider a simplified case of explaining the 2-year yield, which we considered earlier in examples of the mean and standard deviation. These quantities describe the series. In fact, if we were asked to predict the 2-year yield, we may use the long-term mean of 4.5% as our first guess. Although simple to compute, as Figure 1.1 shows, the mean is also a very poor predictor of future movements, given that deviations from the mean can be very large. How can we improve on this? To answer this question, we must first hypothesize which other, more fundamental variables may be driving the 2-year yield. As a matter of terminology, the 2-year yield then is referred to as the "dependent" variable while our mystery variable to explain the 2-year yield would be an "explanatory" or "independent" variable. By incorporating at least some of the vast amount of information available to us about related variables, we may greatly improve the accuracy of our predictions. We explore drivers of interest rates in subsequent chapters and use regressions often to improve on forecasting as well as to understand which drivers matter more than others.

REGRESSION: HOW GOOD A FIT?

Although we can easily come up with a line to fit the data, not all fits are alike. We discussed the standard error earlier in relation to residuals as a way to quantitatively determine the prediction error for a regression. Although the standard error is a useful metric to understand the magnitude of errors to expect from a model, it can be difficult to compare standard errors across models, especially if the models are not very similar. Furthermore, when relying on linear regressions, the standard error measure does not easily tell us whether the linear regression model is appropriate to begin with—some data sets resemble linear patterns more closely than others. To quantify a goodness of fit, one of the most common, and also misunderstood, metrics is correlation. Correlation can be thought of as the closeness of association between two variables. It is a normalized measure allowing comparison of linear fit across different models. Correlation varies between –1 and 1. A correlation of –1 implies strong negative association, and a correlation of 1 implies strong positive association. A correlation of 0 implies little or no association. Correlation may be familiar from daily usage as a way to convey association, but in mathematical terms, the formula is:

$$\text{Correlation} = \text{cov}(X, Y)/[\text{stdev}(X) \times \text{stdev}(Y)]$$

where   cov = covariance
            stdev = standard deviation

Although covariance calculates association between variables X and Y, it is difficult to compare covariance across different data sets since it is dependent on their individual volatility levels. Essentially, correlation is a way of normalizing covariance for the volatilities of the individual series and results in a more easily comparable number. Correlation is not order dependent; that is, the y and x variables can be interchanged without affecting the measure.

A measure related to correlation is the R^2, which, as the name may imply, is the square of the correlation calculation above. The R^2 denotes the percentage of variation in the y variable explained by the x (or vice versa). Since it is the square of a number, it is always positive. Therefore, R^2 does not specify the direction of the association, only the strength. There is no magic level of R^2; it is completely situation dependent, and for different models, different levels are tolerated. For example, for a model that is supposed to trade the market, a 50% R^2 would be poor. R^2 can also be increased by merely adding more variables, which is generally suboptimal. Therefore, an adjustment is made to the R^2 that inserts a penalty for inserting additional variables. The penalty for excess variables makes the adjusted R^2 the more commonly used metric. The R^2 can also determine the value of a variable in a model. A rough method is to remove a variable from a multiple regression and determine the impact on the overall R^2; if the R^2 does not change, the variable was likely not too important.

For the 2-year yield example, probably the most fundamental driver would be the prevailing Federal Reserve target interest rate. One point to note here is that we need to select an explanatory variable about which we may be able to form reasonably accurate predictions or use lags (more on this later); more importantly, we have a reasonable expectation of causality of the variable. We would not want to use a variable such as the lunar cycle in our prediction for 2-year yields; however, one can expect the federal funds rate, on the other hand, to have a direct causal relation to interest rates of farther out maturities. After the explanatory variable has been selected, we can calculate the correlation between the 2-year yield and the federal (fed) funds target rate, possibly using a software package. Another variable that may be relevant for the 2-year Treasury could be the Standard & Poor's (S&P) 500 index since money tends to flow between equities and Treasuries depending on risk appetite. Figure 1.4 shows the

FIGURE 1.4 Path of Fed Funds, Treasury Yields, and Equities over Time
Source: Board of Governors of the Federal Reserve.

three variables alongside each other; the close relationship among the three variables is clear. The correlation between the 2-year Treasury yield and the fed funds target is 85%, while the correlation between the 2-year Treasury and S&P 500 is 61%. As a multiple regression, the combined R^2 for the multiple regression is 86%. Note that in the pairwise regressions, the fed funds versus 2-year Treasury regression is 85%; adding the S&P 500 increases it only to 86%, which means that the S&P 500 adds less "new information" in addition to the fed funds rate. Although this description is mathematically vague, this is a quick way to roughly figure out which variables matter in a multivariable regression.

The concept of correlation is relatively simple to grasp, and given the proliferation of computers, one rarely has to calculate it by hand. However, issues can arise when using correlation inappropriately in financial markets. Since understanding relationships between market variables is very important to understanding markets overall, misinterpreting correlation can be quite risky. One issue with correlation is that it is susceptible to erroneous signals in *nonstationary* variables. Stationary variables are those whose average and variance roughly stay the same over time. If a variable is trending higher consistently, for example, it is not stationary. Figure 1.5 shows a regression of two variables, the 2-year Treasury yield and the Japanese yen currency. The R^2 of the regression of the levels of the two variables is 70%, suggesting a strong link between the variables. To be sure, there may be some relationship between the variables dealing with cross-border flows and the search for higher interest rates. However, this correlation may arise in part from pure trending in the 2007 to 2008 time

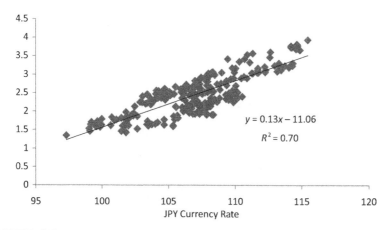

FIGURE 1.5 2Y Treasury Yield Level Regressed against the Japanese Yen Level
Sources: Board of Governors of the Federal Reserve, Bloomberg LP.

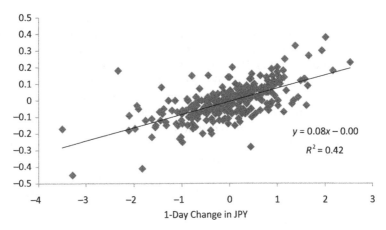

FIGURE 1.6 2Y Treasury Yield Changes Regressed against Japanese Yield Changes
Sources: Board of Governors of the Federal Reserve, Bloomberg LP.

period used for the regression, since the economic turmoil at the time caused many variables to move in similar trends even if they had little causal link. To test the link between the yen and 2-year yields in a more rigorous way, a better regression is between daily changes of the two variables. The use of daily changes reduces the chance of spurious trends creating false correlations. Figure 1.6 shows the regression of daily changes between the yen and 2-year Treasury yield. Now the R^2 is at 42%, which is still relatively high but significantly lower than the 70% in the levels regression. This suggests that some of the relationship in the levels of the two variables is due to trending and some to causality; in general for regressions, it is always prudent to check regressions between changes or percentage changes to control for spurious trends.

PRINCIPAL COMPONENTS ANALYSIS

Principal components analysis (PCA) is a statistical technique used to simplify multidimensional data sets that are highly correlated. In informal terms, PCA calculates a few underlying variables that describe complicated systems where the variables are closely related. PCA has become increasingly common in the rates market lately as it is an ideal technique to simplify the interest rate market. After all, the interest rate market is composed of interest rates of different time frames, such as 2-year, 5-year, and 10-year maturities, all of which move closely with each other. Instead of using regressions of each of these rates, PCA breaks down the system into a simpler two to three variables that describe the system almost as well as using the whole set of factors. The principal components are ranked in order of how much they explain the system. For example, the first principal component is the linear combination of interest rates, which describes the maximum amount of variation of the interest rate market; the second principal component describes the maximum amount of variation after the effect of the first principal component is taken out; and so on. These reduced variables tend to be linear weighted averages of the full set of variables, such as the weighted average of the 2-, 5-, 10-, and 30-year rates. By using PCAs to describe the various interest rates in the market, investors can also find those rates that seem unusually high or low, thus pointing to opportunities for profit. Thus, PCA can be used as a first step to find mispriced trades; once these are found, the fundamental and technical factors behind them are needed to eliminate trades that are mispriced for a good reason. A detailed discussion of the mathematics underlying PCA is beyond the scope of this book; for more information on PCA and other multivariable statistical methods, see *Applied Multivariate Statistical Analysis* by Härdle and Simar.

SCALING THROUGH TIME

A common assumption behind financial mathematics is that returns follow a Brownian motion. A random series of returns can be thought of as a random walk—that is, movements up or down based on an outcome from a probability distribution. Without digging deeply into the mathematics, Brownian motion can be understood as the random walk stemming from a normal distribution. One of the ideas that stems from the theory of Brownian motion is that variance scales with time; for instance, the passage of time grows the variance of the process by a proportional factor. Thus, the standard deviation grows with the square root of time. For example, if the daily standard deviation of a Brownian motion series is 1%, the three-month standard deviation would be $1\% \times \sqrt{60}$ since three months is 60 business days, while the one-year standard deviation is $1\% \times \sqrt{251}$, or 15.84% (since there are 251 business days in one year). These are the standard deviation scales for a Brownian motion—for example, if the one-year standard deviation is greater than 15.84%, the series is trending, while a one-year standard deviation less than 15.84% implies a stronger mean reversion tendency.

BACKTESTING STRATEGIES

Statistical tools can help formalize trading rules to provide objective signals. Even if signals produced by trading rules are not implemented blindly, they can provide a useful way of verifying whether certain rules have resulted in effective profits in the past. One very simple rule, for example, can be formulated as: "If bond prices fell yesterday, sell bonds today with the expectation of a further decline." Such a strategy is very simplistic and unlikely to be very effective, but it is an example of a trading rule whose performance can be tested in the past. Various statistical methods, such as regressions, combined with relevant fundamental driving factors, can be useful in building models that eventually may give trading signals. These signals can be tested in the past. Once a trading rule is used to generate past results, various statistical quantities can measure how good the rule is in producing profits. The simplest way to evaluate the results of an existing strategy or a prospective series of signals is to use average return. However, it is possible that two strategies with the same average return could have very different risks. For example, two strategies with 3% per year return could have 10% per year and 30% per year standard deviation, making the second one much less attractive due to its higher volatility. To account for this, a common metric is to take the ratio of the average to the standard deviation. In the example, the ratios are 3%/10% and 3%/30%, or 0.3 and 0.1, making the first one more attractive. In general, any profit or return needs to be scaled by volatility as it removes the "luck" factor, since increasing risk can generally increase returns. The ratio of average return to standard deviation is known as a Sharpe ratio. At times, the ratio is annualized using the frequency of the trades or observations of returns to enable better comparison with other strategies. For example, if a trading strategy gives a signal once a week, the annualized ratio would use $\sqrt{52}$ for 52 weeks in a year. Most often, at least a Sharpe ratio over 1.0 is needed to consider the strategy as viable, although this threshold can vary depending on the type of trade and risk tolerance. Furthermore, combining different strategies with relatively low individual Sharpe ratios can produce higher Sharpe ratio combinations. What determines how additive new strategies are? In short, it is correlation. Highly correlated strategies combined together will not be very additive for the combined Sharpe ratio, but combining strategies with low correlation can result in the Sharpes adding up, even if the individual ones are low.

The Sharpe ratio is just the starting point in evaluating a trading strategy. Even strategies with relatively high Sharpes can have large drawdowns. *Drawdown* refers to the largest peak-to-trough decline in returns and measures a sort of worst-case scenario for the strategy. A trader may not be willing to accept a high Sharpe strategy with a large drawdown that can deplete capital, leaving little for the strategy. In addition to the overall drawdown, periods where the strategy does poorly must be analyzed closely. In such periods, it is necessary to understand the driving factors contributing to the poor performance; regressions of strategy returns versus market variables can help determine these problem factors. Overall, building trading strategies is as much about thinking of trading rules as it is about controlling risk in an effective way. To do this, a variety of statistical measures should be employed to understand all aspects of a strategy's risk.

SUMMARY

This chapter covered the basic mathematical tools needed to understand data in a somewhat objective manner. In the end, statistics and mathematics are just tools to help understand and forecast relationships between different variables. Methods such as regression can help analyze relationships between multiple variables and to assess the strength of such relationships. Since financial variables tend to be increasingly linked with each other, statistical tools are indispensable in understanding markets. Statistical tools such as Sharpe ratios can also help to separate out the "luck" factor and enable a more objective assessment of the performance of a trading strategy. Finally, each mathematical tool is associated with a set of assumptions and flaws. It is important to be cognizant of these flaws and assumptions to use these tools effectively in analyzing data.

CHAPTER 2

Bonds

B onds are the starting point for understanding the fixed income market. They represent a standardized form of loan between investors and debt holders and form the foundation of the fixed income market. Although bonds are traded in massive volume daily, they are less known to the general public than the stock market. Unlike stocks, which have indefinite maturity and uncertain dividends that can be withdrawn at will by the issuer, bonds have a fixed maturity and fixed interest at inception (or interest that changes according to an agreed-on formula). Furthermore, while stocks are issued mainly by corporations, bonds have a tremendous variety of issuers, including governments, corporations, and homeowners. This chapter introduces the basic characteristics of bonds, their valuation, and the risks of investing in them. Even if the borrower of the debt is sure to repay the loan, there are other risks to consider if bonds are bought and sold in the market. We quantify and attempt to control them, especially when initiating trades beyond simply buying or selling a single bond.

BASICS OF BONDS

To understand the details of bonds, first consider a simple case where you lend your friend $5 for a week. In the case of such micro-loans, most of the time the $5 is returned after a week with no adjustment made for interest. However, let's take the example to a larger scale. Assume that you have lent money not to a good friend, but to an institution, such as the government. Also, instead of $5, suppose you have lent $1 million. Finally, instead of a week, suppose the term of the loan is 10 years. In this case, the government promises to return your $1 million after 10 years, probably using it for purposes like defense or social welfare in the meantime. Although lending without interest was okay with the $5 to your friend for a week, this case is obviously very different. With the government, you are unlikely to just hand over $1 million today and be satisfied with getting it back after 10 years. To see why this is so, consider what else could have been done with the $1 million. To be sure, you could choose to consume it now rather than wait 10 years. Or you could invest the money in a stock and, perhaps, realize large gains if the stock market rises. Finally, if choosing a safe route, you could have saved it in a bank and earned interest in a savings account. Given all these different choices, it is then not unreasonable for the investor to demand that interest be given in return for lending the $1 million to the government.

A bond can be thought of as a loan with standardized terms regarding repayment and interest. This standardization allows larger institutions to borrow from a diverse pool of lenders without having to renegotiate terms with each one. However, standardization generally extends to a particular issue; it does not hold for bonds across markets and sometimes even for different bonds issued by the same institution. For example, bonds issued by some companies may have interest payments that change with market conditions (known as floating rate bonds), while bonds of other institutions may pay their principal over time instead of all at once. Even if the interest rate is fixed, the interest could be paid in different ways: It could be given out at fixed intervals, or the "fixed" interest rate could be zero and an amount larger than $1 million could be given at the end of 10 years with no payments in the interim. We consider the different features in this chapter. To avoid confusion, we first consider examples from the Treasury bond market, which is the debt market for the U.S. government. This is one of the world's largest bond markets and also has straightforward terms that serve as a good starting point. Afterward we consider exceptions and differences across markets.

To understand bonds, consider the $1 million loan to the government for 10 years just mentioned. The $1 million here would be known as the *notional*. Given the government's massive borrowing needs, it would not be feasible for it to negotiate a loan with every investor. Instead, the government sells bonds, which investors buy with cash. The cash is sent to the Treasury, and, as with any other loan, the Treasury uses the cash for the purposes deemed necessary. At the end of the term of the bond, in this case 10 years, the Treasury is supposed to return the $1 million. There are three initial attributes to keep in mind when considering a bond: coupon rate, maturity, and price. *Coupon rate* refers to the interest rate of payments made by the issuing entity (in this case, a Treasury bond) and is expressed as a percentage. While the government has the $1 million it was lent, it will pay interest every six months. Treasury bonds are fixed rate bonds, which, as the name implies, means that the coupon payments stay constant through the life of the bond. If the coupon rate of our bond was 3%, the yearly payment of interest would be $3 per $100 of the bond, or in the case of $1 million, $30,000 per year. As the interest is paid out every six months, it means a payment of $15,000 every six months. These payments are made until the term of the bond, at which time the principal is also returned. In our example, the bond is supposed to last for 10 years, which is referred to as the *maturity* of the bond, listed in MM-YY format as a date. This is an important distinction between bonds and equities: In bonds, there is a fixed date after which the bond no longer exists. The fixed maturity date in turn prompts considerations that an investor in equities does not have to consider; for example, when the bond is bought, it is 10 years in maturity, but after a year, *it is only a 9-year bond.* If interest rates for 10-year loans differ from interest rates for 9-year loans, the investor may realize profit or loss just from the aging effect, which is known as rolldown (discussed in more detail later in this chapter).

The $1 million here is known as the *face value* of the bond, which can be thought of as the amount of the loan to the government. However, even if the face value is $1 million, the value or price of the bond may not be equal to the face value. Indeed, bonds get traded between investors all the time, and if you are purchasing a bond from another investor, you are essentially taking on the loan. In that case, since the interest payments by the Treasury remain fixed during the life of the bond, in different circumstances, the interest rate may be more or less attractive. For example, if other, similar Treasury bonds are offering 5%, the 3% bond looks much worse, while if other Treasury bonds are offering 1%, the 3% bond would be a great coupon. Therefore, given changes in interest rates, you may want to pay more or less than the face value for the bond, and this amount is known as the price of the bond. Since face value can differ across bonds, price is generally quoted in per-$100 terms. For example, a bond priced at $99 implies that the bond trades at 99% of its face value. Therefore, to lend $100 to the issuing institution, you only have to pay $99. This would generally be the case if the fixed interest rate being offered by this bond is worse than that of similar new bonds in the market.

The bond market is full of terminology that can confuse a newcomer. Given the usual movement in rates, the common unit of change is basis points (bps), which represent 1/100 of 1%. Therefore, a change in interest rate on a bond from 3.53% to 3.54% represents a change of 0.01%, or 1 bp. Numerous units in the fixed income market quote changes and even levels in basis points. In the bond space, changes in yield require a bit of care. When a change in a 5-year bond yield is mentioned, the change may not be referring to the same 5-year bond. This is because new bonds are issued at regular intervals, and essentially a new 5-year bond exists as soon as it is auctioned. A fresh 5-year bond in this case is called an *on-the-run* bond, while the older bond is an *off-the-run* bond. For example, if a 5-year bond is issued monthly, in January 2010, the on-the-run bond would be the January 2015 maturity bond, while the December 2014 maturity bond would be the off-the-run bond. The November 2014 maturity bond would be the double off-the-run, and so on. In February 2010, when the February 2015 bond is issued, it becomes the on-the-run bond while the January 2015 becomes the off-the-run.

RISKS EMBEDDED IN FIXED INCOME INSTRUMENTS

Bonds can be thought of as a package of fixed cash flows for a certain period of time and then repayment of initial principal. In financial settings, it is generally equally, if not more, constructive to think of securities and contracts as packages of risks rather than just as cash flows. These risks can range from the mundane to minute hidden ones, and each deserves time and management—sometimes the smallest source of risk can expand to cause catastrophic losses when stress periods arrive. Any fixed income instrument can also be decomposed into a set of standard types of risk exposure. For any given instrument, some risks may be especially important. Other instruments may exist solely to offset certain classes of risks. These classes of risks include:

- Interest rate risk
- Credit risk
- Inflation risk
- Financing/liquidity risk
- Tax risk
- Regulatory risk

Interest Rate Risk

This is perhaps the starting point when considering the risk embedded in any fixed income instrument. Any security—such as a bond, loan, or any other contract with *fixed* cash flows over a certain period of time—is exposed to interest rate risk. Interest rate risk stems from fixed cash flows being received or paid, and therefore changes in the broader market interest rates can make these fixed cash flows seem more or less attractive. As this attractiveness changes, so does the price of the security. For example, if a trader buys a bond paying a fixed 5% interest payment and, immediately following this purchase, prevailing interest rates for similar instruments in the market rise to 8%, the 5% bond suddenly looks like a poor investment. If the trader tried to resell the 5% bond, other traders would demand a discount to accept a 5% rate when they can buy similar instruments paying 8%. This reasoning can explain why the 5% bond would gain in value if interest rates on similar instruments fell to 3%.

This example demonstrates why a fixed rate bond, or any other fixed rate instrument, is sensitive to interest rates. Notice the disclaimer about "similar instruments" in the last example. The interest rate that the fixed rate bond is sensitive to is always the rate being offered in the market on similar instruments. For example, a 10-year U.S. corporate bond will not be sensitive to changes in rates offered by 5-year Korean government bonds unless such changes affect rates of other 10-year U.S. corporate bonds. In the financial world, though, interest rates are highly correlated, making it crucial to track global flows and developments to effectively manage the interest rate risk. The degree to which a bond is sensitive to interest rate risk is known as duration, which is discussed later.

Finally, there are types of fixed income securities that do not face much interest rate risk. Such securities are known as floating rate bonds. These bonds, instead of paying a fixed cash flow, make coupon payments that are linked to some short-term interest rate that resets at a frequent interval. This way, as interest rates rise or fall the cash flows of the bond itself change to mirror the interest rate changes. These payments can be made for a period of time ranging from months to years. For example, a simple floating rate structure may make payments every three months indexed on the three-month London Interbank Offered Rate, a common short-term market rate we discuss in detail in Chapter 4. With a floating index, such a bond's interest rate risk is much lower than that of a fixed rate bond, but to be sure, it does have a small amount of risk associated with the three months between the payment dates as well as the rate risk, which stems from the choice of indexing rate. Such risks are generally minute, but during the short-term market stress of the recent credit crunch, these reset and indexing risks took on a vastly greater profile.

Credit Risk

In the pricing calculations discussed regarding bonds, there is an implicit assumption of timely coupon payments and repayment of principal. If this were not the case, the bond price could differ significantly from the simple calculation, especially if repayment of principal appears to be in doubt. Such risks are known as credit risks and stem from the issuer's possible inability to finance the issued debt. In such bonds, the pricing calculations become significantly more complex as probabilities need to be assigned to the bond payments in different scenarios. Note that even in the case of default—that is, if the issuer cannot repay the principal—the bond may have value since the assets of the issuer would be sold off to pay some recovery amount to the bond holders.

The fixed income instruments we consider in this book generally do not have any significant credit risk associated with them. The instruments discussed are mostly U.S. government credit risk, in either a direct or an indirect way, or are derivatives contracts with banks, which have a different source of credit risk associated with them. Credit risk can grow for even top-quality issuers; after all, Lehman Brothers debt was highly rated, until it was not. Even the U.S. government—which today is considered risk free from a credit risk standpoint—may not enjoy that status in the future. However, for an investor or trader attempting to value and trade government bonds, the credit risk of the U.S. government is not likely to have any meaningful impact on the price today. Credit risks are a dominant form of risk for fixed income markets, such as high-yield corporate debt issued by weaker corporate issuers, riskier emerging market debt, and subprime mortgage debt. Such markets are referred to, collectively and imprecisely, as credit markets. Even if the particular fixed income security being considered does not itself have credit risk, it is important to follow developments in the credit markets, as they are very sensitive to the economy and financial leverage. Perhaps the most glaring example of the importance of following these markets was the start of the credit crunch in 2007, which stemmed from cascading problems in the subprime mortgage markets.

Inflation Risk

Credit risk refers to the possibility of not receiving back principal or missing coupon payments due to the issuer's inability to pay. Inflation risk tends to affect bonds in a more subtle way by eroding the value of future cash flows. Even if an issuer's credit risk is almost negligible, such as the U.S. Treasury's, the constant coupon payments on bonds could lose money if prices rise. As an extreme example, a fixed $5 coupon payment is only half as valuable if prices double instantly. Inflation risk especially grows as a concern for longer-term bonds as more coupon payments, not to mention the principal, are at the mercy of rising prices. Some issuers, especially in the sovereign category, such as the U.S. government and other developed markets, do issue bonds whose valuations are linked to inflation and thus protect the buyer against erosion of cash flows in the future. For example, in U.S. Treasury Inflation-Protected Securities, the principal itself grows at the inflation rate, thus greatly reducing inflation risk for the buyer (see Chapter 3 for more details). However, the sizes of these inflation-linked markets are mostly dwarfed by "nominal" instruments where the fixed payments are not adjusted for inflation. In general, for inflation protection, investors tend to look outside fixed income to products such as commodities and equities.

Financing/Liquidity Risk

Financing and liquidity are related classes of risk that are easy to ignore during good times. In times of ample financing capacity and asset price appreciation, it is generally easy to borrow money to magnify ownership of a security and earn outsized returns if prices indeed keep going up (a concept known as leverage). However, if the tide turns and lenders themselves incur stress, they are likely to call back loans made to purchase other securities, which leads to a cascading effect of forced selling and declining asset prices. An example of this phenomenon is a prospective homeowner buying a house. If the house is worth $100,000, the homeowner may receive a loan for $80,000 and use $20,000 of her own money as a down payment. This way a relatively small amount of money ($20,000) controls an asset worth a fair bit more ($100,000). Suppose the mortgage loan is of a short tenor, such that the bank has to reauthorize the loan every month as it wishes—this is not common for a house loan but is common in more complex financial transactions. As long as the economy and general market conditions remain steady, there tends to be little problem with this leverage, but if funds become scarce and the bank lending money for the house faces losses, it may call back the home loan. In that case, the homeowner would need to pay back the $100,000 borrowed with interest. If the homeowner is forced to sell the house to pay back the loan, house prices will fall. Although I use a house in the example for the sake of simplicity, trillions of dollars' worth of securities are bought and sold in the market using loans with very short tenors such as overnight or one week. In financial markets, as with housing, the capacity to borrow, known generally as *liquidity*, is key to maintaining stable prices. Even with relatively solid fundamentals to begin with, a bond's value could decline considerably if there is a scarcity of borrowing capacity in the market or if financing markets themselves crumble under stress. Such problems in borrowing markets spread rapidly, as they did in 2008, and lead to wide differentials in prices of bonds based on ease of transaction. The lack of liquidity can also make seemingly uncorrelated assets move together as the need to raise funds leads to selling of assets across the financial markets, and can lead to seemingly sound assets dropping in value even if their fundamentals are strong. Managing liquidity risk is therefore key for a portfolio of securities, and tracking short-term funding markets closely is important in managing this risk.

Tax Risk

Taxation is an inevitable part of life. As tax rates change, they may make certain securities more or less valuable. For most fixed income securities, the interest payments are taxable at the income tax rate, and changes in the value of the security taxable at the capital gains rate. For two securities facing similar taxation, the tax risk differential between the two is not relevant. However, the municipal bond market does face differential taxation from the rest of the taxable universe. For municipal bonds, discussed in more detail in Chapter 3, the interest payments are tax-exempt from federal income tax. Given top federal income tax rates of around 35% to 40% today, this is a very valuable exemption. In general, tax risk is difficult to control for in most instruments, but the municipal bond market does offer tax-exempt instruments to at least mitigate some negative effects of taxation on returns.

Regulatory Risk

The term "regulatory risk" covers a large set of risks related to changing regulations and other possibly arbitrary government action that can have a negative impact on returns. Regulatory risk is almost by definition impossible to fully neutralize. However, certain precautions can be taken. Awareness of possible upcoming changes in regulation and their effects on the particular securities held in a portfolio is of great importance. Regulatory risk came to the forefront during the credit crunch of 2007 to 2008, with numerous events reflecting the sometimes arbitrary actions of the government during stress periods. For example, after months of denials and pronouncements about the safety of Freddie Mac and Fannie Mae, the agencies eventually were taken under government conservatorship (i.e., quasi-nationalization) with a wide range of outcomes for various agency securities holders. Senior debt holders came out in relatively good shape; owners of preferred stock, previously a fairly safe instrument in the context of the agencies, lost almost all value. Even owners of derivatives contracts on these corporations faced considerable uncertainty regarding payout, given the unusual outcomes.

Regulatory risk is an area many in the emerging markets space are well aware of and take in stride. The credit crisis of 2008 brought to the forefront the nature of such risks even in supposedly stable markets (the "developed markets"), where government action could be just as erratic and unpredictable as that of any emerging market. The uncertainty created by regulation caused doubts even in previously "safe" markets, leading to volatility and a new set of risks for investors in developed markets. Looking ahead, investors in all markets are likely to have a greater appreciation for the potential of regulatory risk to impact returns, whether in an emerging or a developed market.

DISCOUNTING

Understanding the cash flows and risks in bonds requires a quantitative framework to calculate a fair price for the bond. Luckily, this procedure is not too difficult, at least up to an approximation, and in general computers have largely removed the need for any manual calculation. The key focus in this section and subsequent sections describing calculations is to develop intuition for *why* a certain calculation works and what assumptions are behind the calculation. The concept of discounting is a central theme in arriving at the price of any financial instrument. The idea behind discounting is that money tomorrow is less valuable than money today. The premise here is simple: Discounting stems from the assumption that $1 can be invested today at a certain "safe" rate of return, therefore making that same dollar larger tomorrow. If you were offered $1 tomorrow instead of today, you forgo consumption today, making that $1 less valuable than the $1 today. Although the idea is simple, to understand pricing, we first need to understand discounting in a quantitative manner. Given the reasoning behind investing $1 at a safe rate of return, it is clear that interest rates are key to discounting.

Consider a situation where $1 is invested at an interest rate of 3% per year in a bank account. In one year, the $1 grows to $1 × (1 + 0.03) due to the interest payment. In the second year, the savings account has $1.03, which now receives another 3% of interest. Therefore, the money now grows to $1× (1 + 0.03) × (1 + 0.03) = $1 × (1 + 0.03)^2$. Instead of calculating actual values here, we leave it in the form shown to help with intuition. Continuing the logic, in the third year, the savings account pays another 3% interest on the money sitting in the account in the second year. Hence the money at the end of the third year is $1 × (1 + 0.03)^3$. The pattern here is evident with the 3% interest rate; to make it more general, suppose the interest payment is just r and again starts with $1. Then the account's total cash in different years is:

Year 1: $\$1 \times (1 + r)^1$
Year 2: $\$1 \times (1 + r)^2$
Year 3: $\$1 \times (1 + r)^3$
... Year n: $\$1 \times (1 + r)^n$

Therefore, $1 invested today at rate r becomes $(1 + r)^n$ in year n. Note that here the interest payment is made each year to the previous year's balance—this is an example of annual compounding, since the amount grows on a yearly basis. More common in the United States is semiannual compounding. In the semiannual compounding case, the example would be very similar except that half the interest would be paid every six months (i.e., $r/2$). The number of periods then would be $2 \times n$ for n years (every six months). Therefore, $1 with semiannual compounding would grow to $(1 + r/2)^{2n}$ over n years at an *annual* rate r. Although semiannual compounding is more common in U.S. fixed income markets, for now we shall discuss annual compounding, as it is more intuitive. Note, however, that the examples are easily modified for semiannual compounding.

Our example calculated that $1 today would grow to $(1 + r)^n$ in n years. We can now reverse the situation: Suppose, in n years, $1 will be given to you. We can now calculate the value of that $1 today. Suppose that value is X. Using the formula in the Year n, and replacing $1 with X, we know that X would grow to $X \times (1 + r)^n$ in n years. Then $X \times (1 + r)^n = 1 or

$$X = 1/(1 + r)^n \tag{2.1}$$

Equation 2.1 is the discounting formula. X is known as the discounted cash flow, and r is known as the discounting rate. To make the example concrete, consider our earlier example where the interest rate was 3% and $1 was given in 10 years. In that case, the value of that $1 today is $1/(1 + 0.03)^{10} = 0.744$. Therefore, $0.744 is the present value of $1 in 10 years *if interest rates are 3%*. Note that if instead of $1, an arbitrary C was given out in n years, our present value would be slightly modified to $C/(1 + r)^n$ instead of the $1 in the numerator. The reasoning is exactly the same as with $1. Note the dependence of present value on interest rates—if rates were 0%, for example, our reasoning behind $1 being more valuable tomorrow does not hold and the present value would equal the future value.

BOND PRICING

We have discussed the price of a fixed rate bond and how it is likely to change as interest rates moves. Although this is intuitive for a fixed rate bond because its attractiveness in the market will depend on relative interest rates, we need a more quantitative formulation to understand the link between a bond price and interest rates as well as to understand the risks in a bond trade. To understand how we arrive at the price of a bond, such as the Treasury bond mentioned earlier, we need to step back and consider a more basic sort of bond: a zero-coupon bond. A zero-coupon bond is a bond that pays no interest in the interim and instead pays a fixed amount at maturity. For the sake of simplicity, consider a zero-coupon bond that pays \$1 after 10 years. There are no payments in the interim—recall that this is our earlier discounting example. The price of the zero-coupon bond is just the present value of the final payment. In this case, for an interest rate r, the price of the zero-coupon bond would be $\$1/(1 + r)^{10}$; and for an arbitrary n years, it would be $\$1/(1 + r)^n$. For the specific case of a \$1 payment, the present value for n years of $\$1/(1 + r)^n$ is known as the discount factor for year n.

The zero-coupon bond forms the building block for the price of standard bonds with coupon payments. As with a zero-coupon bond, the price of a bond is the present value of its total cash flows. The notion of price being a discounted cash flow is an important one and is more general than just for bonds. To price a bond, we recast it in terms of an instrument we already know how to price: a zero-coupon bond. Consider a bond that pays \$2 each year and returns the principal of \$100 after 10 years. Although yearly payments are not as common in the United States (e.g., Treasuries are semiannual), annual payments serve to keep the examples simple. The cash flows are shown graphically in Figure 2.1.

Notice that in the 10th year, there is a \$102 payment, which is actually a combination of two different payments; the first is \$2 as the final interest payment and \$100 as the returned principal. Instead of considering this as one security, we can consider *each \$2 payment as a zero-coupon bond itself* and the final \$100 payment as another zero-coupon bond. This way a fixed rate bond paying interest at a regular interval can be thought of as a package of zero-coupon bonds. The price of the bond therefore is the sum of the prices of the zero-coupon bonds that form the package.

The price displayed in the market for a bond is generally the "clean price" whereas the true price at which actual money exchange happens is the "dirty price." The difference between these is accrued interest. Accrued interest is applicable when bonds are bought and sold between coupon periods. Figure 2.1 assumes a clean transaction with coupons presented in regular intervals, but if the bond is bought between coupon payment dates, the buyer owes the seller of the bond the *fraction of the coupon* up to that date. Without this adjustment, it would be disadvantageous for the seller to

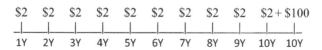

FIGURE 2.1 Simple View of the Cash Flows of a 10-Year Annual Coupon Bond

sell the bond before a coupon payment, which would make trading bonds very cumbersome.

With the deduction, we can now arrive at a formula for the price of a bond. The price of the zero-coupon bond paying $2 in the first year is $2/(1 + r)^1$. In year 2, similarly, the price of the zero-coupon bond paying $2 is $2/(1 + r)^2$. This process continues till year 10, where two payments are made, which are two zero-coupon bond prices: $2/(1 + r)^{10}$ and $100/(1 + r)^{10}$. Therefore, the price of the bond is the sum of the prices of the individual zero-coupon bonds:

$$\text{Price} = \$2/(1+r)^1 + \$2/(1+r)^2 + \cdots + \$2/(1+r)^{10} + \$100/(1+r)^{10}$$

where r = prevailing market interest rate (which will be discussed in detail later)

The formula here is less important than understanding the process by which we arrived at it. The formula here and many others discussed later can easily be looked up, and few of these computations need to be done by hand. However, intuition is not something that can be arrived at looking at just the formula; it requires breaking down the components of a bond. To generalize the formula for an arbitrary coupon rate c and maturity of n years:

$$P = c/(1+r)^1 + c/(1+r)^2 + \cdots + c/(1+r)^n + 100/(1+r)^n$$
$$= c \times [1/(1+r)^1 + 1/(1+r)^2 + \cdots + 1/(1+r)^n] + 100/(1+r)^n$$

With semiannual compounding, this formula is modified slightly to:

$$P = (c/2)/(1+r/2)^1 + (c/2)/(1+r/2)^2 + \cdots$$
$$+ (c/2)/(1+r/2)^{n\times2} + 100/(1+r/2)^{n\times2}$$
$$= (c/2) \times [1/(1+r/2)^1 + 1/(1+r/2)^2 + \cdots$$
$$+ 1/(1+r/2)^{n\times2}] + 100/(1+r/2)^{n\times2}$$

where c = annual coupon rate
 r = annual market interest rate

The semiannual nature of the compounding changes increases the number of terms to $2 \times n$, as each six-month period is considered a single period. The $c/2$ is the coupon payment every six months while $r/2$ takes the annual rate and converts it to a semiannual rate. The r here is also referred to as the yield to maturity or just yield for a standard bond. The yield of a bond can be thought of as the internal rate of return for a bond or as a constant interest rate that discounts the cash flows of the bond to equal its market price.

To see a numerical example of this formula, consider a 5-year bond with a price yield of 4% and coupon of 5%. Also, as with Treasury convention, assume that the bond is on a semiannual compounding schedule, which results in 10 compounding periods and half the interest rate for each period. Therefore, using the price calculation equation with semiannual compounding, we can calculate its price as:

$$P = (c/2) \times [1/(1 + r/2)^1 + 1/(1 + r/2)^2 + \cdots + 1/(1 + r/2)^{n \times 2}]$$
$$+ 100/(1 + r/2)^{n \times 2}$$
$$= 5/2 \times [1/(1 + 0.04/2)^1 + 1/(1 + 0.04/2)^2 + \cdots + 1/(1 + 0.04/2)^9$$
$$+ 1/(1 + 0.04/2)^{10}] + 100/(1 + 0.04/2)^{10}$$
$$= \$104.49$$

Although this simple example gives us the price, it is also very common to seek the reverse information. For example, suppose that in the market, our 10-year bond is trading at \$99 (per \$100). What is the yield? Here, we cannot just solve a simple algebraic equation, given the number of exponents involved, but using basic financial software, we can arrive at a yield to maturity for the bond. The price/yield calculations are extremely common nowadays, and manual calculation is rarely required. If we consider another case of this example, where the yield and coupon are identical at 5%, the price we will arrive at is \$100. Conversely, if we have a price of \$100 and a coupon of 5%, the yield we would arrive at would be 5% as well. This is no coincidence—in general, when coupon and yield are equal, the price of the bond is par. As price rises from here, say to \$102, the yield falls to 4.5%, while a drop in price, for example, to \$97, results in the yield rising to 5.7%. The price/yield equation also makes it clear that as the yield is in the denominator, an increase in the yield therefore would lower the price. Figure 2.2 shows the price/yield relationship for a sample 10-year bond at different price levels. In the market, bonds are generally quoted on a price basis, although dealers can quote on a yield basis as well.

In the Treasury market and other high-quality bond credit bond markets, yields are the standard way of comparing bonds. Although price is used to calculate final payments and other details, yield is the main parameter by which to analyze bonds. This is because, as we shall see later, the prices of bonds of different maturities change by greatly differing amounts in response to a change in interest rates of an equal magnitude. Since fixed income markets are concerned with interest rates, the varying price changes for equivalent interest rate changes make it difficult to compare

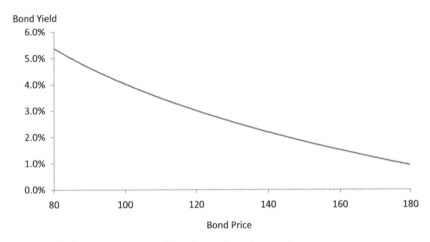

FIGURE 2.2 Price versus Yield Relationship of a Bond

a 2-year bond to a 10-year bond. The yield, or the internal rate of return of a bond, transforms the price into a measure that places bonds of different maturities on a level playing field. The yield is an imperfect measure but does eliminate some of the issues related to comparing prices of bonds. The inverse movement of yields with regard to price also alters terminology. A bullish market is characterized by falling yields; a bearish market refers to rising yields. Similarly, most participants refer to a decline in yields as a *rally* while a *selloff* is associated with rising yields. As with all colloquial terms, however, at times the meaning can be truly unclear.

YIELD CURVE

The yield to maturity of a bond is the fixed yield such that the sum of the discounted cash flows equals the price of the bond. For different maturity bonds, the yields to maturity will be different. Indeed, instead of discounting by a flat yield, each coupon can be discounted with a zero-coupon bond rate that applies to that maturity.

By placing bonds of different maturities on a level playing field, yields can help us see the state of the market at any given time. A simple way to do this is to chart yields of bonds of different maturities with maturity being the x-axis. Figure 2.3 displays such a graph for January 2, 2007, and for April 22, 2010 to show the variation in the shape over time. The idea behind Figure 2.3 is referred to as the yield curve, which more generally can be thought of as the relationship between yields and time to maturity.

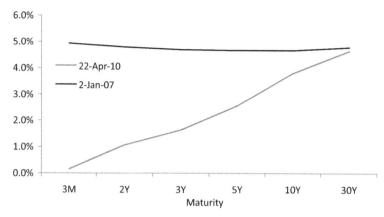

FIGURE 2.3 Two Different Yield Curve Shapes
Source: Board of Governors of the Federal Reserve.

Mathematically, the yield curve is the set of yields as a function of time; without using mathematical terms, the yield curve can be thought of as a "machine" that takes time to maturity as an input and outputs the yield for a bond of that maturity. The term "yield curve" can also be a source of confusion since the market uses the term "curve" as the *slope of yields* between two maturity points, that is, the difference in yields. These curves are referred to using the two points under consideration, such as 2s/10s curve for the difference between the 10-year and 2-year points. Yield curve trades are discussed specifically later in this chapter, but we will continue to use the general term "yield curve" when referring to the entire set of relationships between yields and time.

Why is the yield curve a useful concept? The yield curve can be thought of as the price of lending (borrowing) money over different points in time. For example, the yield curve in Figure 2.3 on April 22, 2010 has a steep upward slope, which means that investors are willing to lend money at short maturities for very little but will charge a much higher rate to lend money at fixed rates for longer periods of time. Explanations of the shape of the yield curve have tended to be bucketed in three broad categories: term premium, expectations, and segmentation. One reason for the upward slope for April 22, 2010 could be that investors are more comfortable lending out for shorter maturities, such as six months, but become increasingly risk-averse for longer periods of time, thus demanding higher yields. This extra yield stemming from risk aversion is known as term premium. Although it may be a contributing factor, term premium alone cannot explain the yield curve since, at times, the yield curve can be downward sloping. Instead, there are likely other factors at work, such as market expectations of yields, more formally known as the expectations hypothesis. Simply put, the hypothesis attempts to explain the yield curve as market expectations for interest rates in the future. Looking back at Figure 2.3, the steep upward slope in the yield curve on April 22, 2010, may indicate that investors are expecting rates to be higher in the future, which would lead to lending money at low rates for short maturities but at higher rates if the money is locked up for longer maturities. This interpretation of the yield curve can be important for judging the state of the economy and understanding how the yield curve itself may react to changing economic conditions, which we discuss in detail later. Finally, the segmentation hypothesis stipulates that certain investor classes prefer to invest in certain maturity ranges, and this segmentation produces the yields we see in the yield curve. Segmentation can be a factor in some parts of the yield curve, such as with pension funds buying longer-end assets to match their long-dated liabilities (e.g., pension payments in the future). However, segmentation is unlikely to be a satisfactory explanation of the yield curve overall—as rates markets have matured, the presence of investors such as hedge funds that are more nimble in their investments and can take advantage of mispricing across the curve makes segmentation unlikely as a major source of yield differences. In sum, the yield curve is likely a mix of market expectations as well as some risk aversion, while certain niche sectors may feel the effects of segmentation. We discuss more implications of the shape of the yield curve and trading the shape in Chapter 6.

DURATION

Since we are mostly discussing fixed income securities with little credit risk, interest rate risk comes to the forefront. To manage interest rate risk, we need detailed methods to measure it quantitatively. The varying sensitivities of prices of yields for different maturity bonds brings us to the concept of duration. The concept of duration often is confusing since various formulations are referred to as duration, such as Macaulay duration, modified duration, and dollar value of one basis point (DV01), alternatively basis point value (BPV). The starting point for duration is the Macaulay duration, which is generally the staple of most finance textbooks in school. The formula for Macaulay duration is:

$$D_{MC} = (1 \times (c/2)/(1 + r/2)^1 + 2 \times (c/2)/(1 + r/2)^2 + \cdots$$
$$+ t \times (c/2)/(1 + r/2)^{n \times 2} + 100 \times t/(1 + r/2)^{n \times 2})/\text{Bond Price}$$

The formula should appear relatively familiar—it is the price to yield formula presented earlier but with the cash flows multiplied by the time at which they occur. Macaulay duration is roughly the time it takes to recover half the cash flows of the security. This interpretation also brings us to another general rule: For the same maturity, a higher-coupon bond has a lower duration than a lower-coupon bond, since cash flows are recovered earlier. This may be confusing from the formula since an increase in c should also increase the duration, but remember that c and r are not independent; in general, as coupon rises, the bond's price rises, which lowers yield.

Needless to say, many new entrants into the fixed income world assume Macaulay duration is the same as the market's reference to the term "duration." However, the concept of Macaulay duration is not very useful in the context of trading and is rarely used. Instead, a more useful concept is modified duration, which is calculated as Macaulay duration divided by 1 + yield to maturity of the bond. Modified duration for our 10-year bond would be around 8.0. This means that for a 1–basis point (bp) move in the yield to maturity of the bond, the change in price would be $0.08 for a $100 priced bond. This interpretation is what makes modified duration a useful concept for investors—instead of cash flow recovery (few investors hold a long-term bond to full maturity), it focuses on change in profit/loss (P/L) for a change in rates. In our example, the $100 notional bond has a price change of $0.08 for a 1-bp change, but the $100 notional value can be scaled up and we can calculate the P/L impact on our full position for a 1-bp change in rates. For example, if we own $1 million notional of the bond, the change in value will be $800 for a 1-bp change in the interest rate (calculated as $0.08 × 10,000). Therefore, duration can be thought of as a measure of risk in the position, albeit just a first-order risk for small changes in rates. For a geometrical interpretation, we return to the price/yield graph, shown in Figure 2.2. However, now assume the figure also has tangent lines at various points of the curve representing the instantaneous rate of change in price for a change in yield. The slopes of these lines are exactly the duration concept. Mathematically inclined readers will see this as the first derivative of the price/yield function.

In the modified duration example, we assumed the bond's price was par ($100). However, this is generally not the case, and modified duration needs one more modification (fixed income concepts have many layers!). The concept of DV01 (or BPV) takes the modified duration and multiplies it by the dirty price of the bond (price + accrued interest). This product gives us the sensitivity of our position to a 1-bp change in the yield to maturity *for $1 million notional*. To clarify, assume the 10-year bond has a modified duration of 8.0 but a dirty price of $101. Then the DV01 of the bond is $808, which can be interpreted in this way: A $1 million position in the bond has positive \$808 profit if its yield to maturity declines 1 bp (and negative \$808 P/L if yield to maturity rises 1 bp). If we wanted the sensitivity for a different notional, say \$10 million, the risk in the position would be \$808 × 10 = \$8,080 per bp change in rates. The use of \$1 million may appear arbitrary, but one useful trick when working with bonds is to choose an arbitrary notional and use that as a base for calculations. In general, for the rest of this section, we use "duration" and "DV01" interchangeably as measures of risks to rates, but it should be understood that both terms stand for modified duration × price.

The discussion of duration as a risk parameter also points to a more general concept of using risk, rather than notional (the amount of the loan), as the primary comparison between fixed income securities. To see why, consider a 2-year bond with duration of 1.9 and the 10-year bond with duration of 8.0. Suppose rates rise 1 bp in parallel; that is, the 2-year and 10-year yields to maturity rise 1 bp. In this case, for \$100 notional of both bonds, the 2-year bond has an impact of \$0.019 and the 10-year bond has impact of \$0.08, nearly four times as large. If we consider notional amounts, we may believe that they have an equal position in these two securities when in fact the 10-year bond position is about four times as large. Using notional amounts tends to be an artifact of having prior experience in price-based markets, such as equities or commodities. For example, an equities trader may think of risk in terms of buying \$1 million worth of IBM stock. It is crucial to adjust one's mind-set in fixed income markets to think about risk rather than notional exposure, given the vastly different risk exposure of different maturity bonds. To be sure, as we will see later, duration is just a single number that expresses a very narrow definition of risk. For example, to compare the 2-year and 10-year bond positions, we assumed a 1-bp parallel move in rates (i.e., that a 1-bp move in 2-year and 10-year rates would occur). However, generally this is not likely; in different interest rate environments, 2-year rates may be more or less volatile than 10-year rates, leading to different likely moves in the two yields. The difference in rate movements across the yield curve would in turn affect our understanding of risk by adding further layers to our thought process.

Finally, another concept related to the use of duration is the conversion of an up-front cash flow to a running cash flow. In simple terms, this would be akin to winning a lottery of \$10 million and converting it to a yearly payment for 10 years. Due to discounting, the yearly payment is not \$1 million since the later payments are worth less in today's terms. The \$10 million up-front payment is referred to as being in "price terms" while the yearly payment is referred to as being in "yield terms." As a more market-relevant example, suppose an investment offers 20 bps up front (i.e., 0.2% of notional). This 20 bps is referred to in the bond market as being in price terms. Now suppose that another option is to receive the 20 bps over the course of 30 years. How much should the per-year cash flow be? Note that the per-year amount cannot be 20 bps/30 years = 0.7 bps, since that ignores the fact that the cash flows further out decrease in value due to discounting. Instead, the approximate, quick way to convert the cash flow into running terms is to divide by the duration of a 30-year bond at par. Such a 30-year bond would have duration near 15 years, so the running payment over 30 years would be 20 bps/15 years = 1.4 bps per year. This 1.4 bps per year payment is known to be in yield terms. Although the method is approximate, its simplicity makes it widely used to convert cash flows in numerous situations. We will see examples of this conversion throughout the book, starting with the "Carry" section. This method is also an example of concepts used as approximations on trading floors and among market participants that may not be present in textbooks but nonetheless make understanding conversations in rates markets easier for beginners.

CONVEXITY

The concept of duration can be thought of as a linear effect on P/L for changes in yields. As yields change, we can multiply the change in yield by the BPV, which then results in a profit or loss. This resembles the calculation of profit in numerous other markets, such as multiplying number of shares of stock and change in stock price to arrive at a profit/loss. In the bond case, then, the change in yield is equivalent to the change in the price of the stock, and BPV is analogous to the size of the position in the stock. However, the reality with bonds is more complicated due to the presence of convexity. Convexity can be thought of in a multitude of ways, but all rest on asymmetry. In the end, convexity is a concept meant to convey asymmetric benefit, or loss, when underlying conditions change. To make this idea clearer, we can elaborate on our equity analogy and modify the situation to illustrate convexity. Suppose you own 100 shares of XYZ stock at $50. However, unlike a regular share purchase, your broker allows you the following modification on your stock purchase:

1. For every $1 the stock price increases, your ownership will increase by 2 shares.
2. For every $1 the stock price decreases, your ownership will decrease by 2 shares.

Table 2.1 shows the profit/loss under various scenarios.

It is evident that the deal is in your favor. As the market moves in your favor, your exposure to the market grows, while a decline in market value

TABLE 2.1 Stock Convexity Example

Stock Price	# Shares	Profit/Loss
40	80	−1800
41	82	−1638
42	84	−1472
43	86	−1302
44	88	−1128
45	90	−950
46	92	−768
47	94	−582
48	96	−392
49	98	−198
50	100	0
51	102	202
52	104	408
53	106	618
54	108	832
55	110	1050
56	112	1272
57	114	1498
58	116	1728
59	118	1962
60	120	2200

reduces your exposure to the market. This phenomenon is referred to as positive convexity. The reverse situation can also exist, as we will see later; such a situation is known as negative convexity. The reader may be wondering why anyone would be willing to purchase an instrument with negative convexity where the owner faces increasing losses and declining gains. The short answer is that in markets, everything transacts at a certain price, and the owner of a negative convexity asset gets compensated for the disadvantage. The owner of a positive convexity asset, such as the client in the equity deal just discussed, has to pay a price for the privilege, and at times the price can be quite steep. We consider valuation of such asymmetric payoffs in Chapter 10.

This example shows the effect of convexity through changing exposure to the market. This is essentially how convexity manifests itself in a bond. In the last section, we discussed duration as a measure of a bond's exposure to interest rates. From the formula for modified duration (or Macaulay), it is evident that a change in interest rates changes duration itself. In particular, for a fixed rate bond with no embedded options, an increase in yields reduces duration, and a decrease in yields increases duration. Since duration represents our exposure to rates, this is very similar to our situation with the stock just mentioned. As yields fall and our

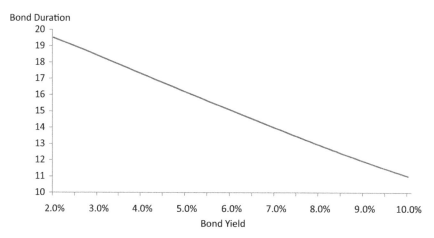

FIGURE 2.4 Relationship between Bond Duration and Yield

bond becomes more valuable, the increasing duration results in greater exposure to the market at an opportune time. As yields increase and the bond loses value, the duration reduction cuts exposure to the market. Figure 2.4 shows the duration of a 10-year bond under different yield shifts. Note that as with the price/yield graph, there is curvature here, too, pointing to a changing slope, or rate of change, as yields move. The slope of a tangent line at any given point on the curve in Figure 2.4 can be thought of as convexity. This is a similar concept to duration, which was the slope of the tangent line at any point on a price/yield graph. Table 2.2 shows the P/L for a 10-year Treasury bond under various yield change scenarios to reflect the effect of convexity (with some rounding of the numbers). Indeed, for a large decrease in yields, the profit is much larger than the loss in a commensurate increase in yields. Figure 2.5 shows the profit profile's curved nature, displaying asymmetry in the profit and loss.

The reasoning behind the presence of convexity in bonds stems from the nature of discounting. For any cash flow in the future, the value today is reduced to account for the prevailing interest rate. Suppose we consider a simplified example of a zero-coupon bond with one cash flow 10 years from now. Now consider an increase and decrease of ±100 bps in the yield of the bond. If interest rates decrease, the cash flow itself is being discounted at a lower rate, and it becomes more valuable today. If interest rates increase, however, the cash flow itself is less valuable on a present value basis. The nonlinear nature of compounding makes these situations asymmetric (i.e., the reduction in yields and the resulting rise in the value of cash flow outweigh the decline in value of the cash flow from an increase in yields). Since regular bonds are packages of zero-coupon cash flows (i.e., each of the coupons), the reasoning is similar.

TABLE 2.2	Profit/Loss Scenarios of a Bond	
Yield	**Price**	**P/L**
3.00%	120	19.7
3.10%	117	17.5
3.20%	115	15.4
3.30%	113	13.3
3.40%	111	11.2
3.50%	109	9.2
3.60%	107	7.3
3.70%	105	5.4
3.80%	104	3.6
3.90%	102	1.8
4.00%	100	0.0
4.10%	98	−1.7
4.20%	97	−3.4
4.30%	95	−5.0
4.40%	93	−6.6
4.50%	92	−8.2
4.60%	90	−9.7
4.70%	89	−11.2
4.80%	87	−12.7
4.90%	86	−14.1
5.00%	85	−15.5

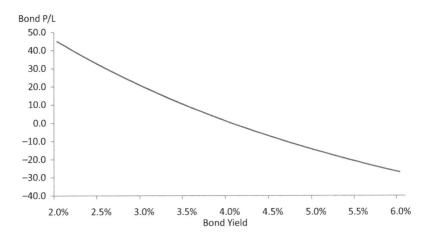

FIGURE 2.5 Profit/Loss of a Bond for Various Yield Levels

Another point to note from Table 2.2 is that only large yield moves display the effects of convexity. For small changes in yields such as ±1 bp and ±5 bps, the P/L is largely symmetric. However, the asymmetric nature of P/L manifests itself in larger yield changes, such as ± 50 bp. Hence, the advantage of convexity for the owner of a bond becomes more apparent in more volatile markets. In practice, for a simple Treasury bond, the effects of convexity are too small in day-to-day trading. However, the links among volatility, convexity, and asymmetry of payoffs are crucial to understand as we consider more complicated bond products and especially options.

For the mathematically inclined reader, duration and convexity combined represent the first two terms of the Taylor series describing price. The duration is the weight on the linear term while convexity is the weight on the squared term. Hence in equation form:

$$\Delta P = D \times \Delta y + \tfrac{1}{2} \times C \times (\Delta y)^2 + \ldots$$

where $\Delta P =$ change in price
$D =$ dollar duration
$C =$ dollar convexity
$\Delta y =$ change in yield

Higher-order terms become increasingly minute in their effects, although for more complex products, such as exotic options, they can be important to consider. The formula for convexity itself is

$$C = 1/[P \times (1 + y^2)] \times \sum_{t=1}^{\text{to } N} [C \times (t^2 + t)/(1 + y)^t]$$

The formula can offer insights, such as the nonstatic nature of convexity and its dependence on coupon and maturity, but its memorization is neither useful nor important. The formula is presented only for completeness' sake. Most financial software packages can display convexity of a bond in a matter of seconds. The important point here, and for the rest of the book, is to build intuition using whichever method the reader finds appealing.

Table 2.2 considered a single 10-year bond and its convexity effects. Convexity is not a static concept across different types of bonds and is affected by coupon and maturity. Instead of using the formula, we can rely on intuition about cash flows and discounting to understand convexity profiles for various bonds. As the maturity of a bond increases, the discounting effects increase, adding to the asymmetry stemming from compounding. In the case of coupons, a lower-coupon bond tends to have higher convexity than a higher-coupon bond. The reasoning here is similar to that for maturity: For a lower-coupon bond, a greater percentage of cash flows are farther in the future, thus amplifying the discounting effects.

REPO MARKETS

Many investors in bonds such as Treasuries do not actually pay the full notional amount to purchase the bonds. This is especially true of participants such as hedge funds. Such institutions generally will use a small amount of up-front cash and borrow a significantly larger amount to make the full purchase. This is known as leverage, and it serves to amplify gains as well as losses. To see this in a simple example, suppose a hedge fund wants to buy $100 worth of bonds but puts up only $10 of its own money. The remaining $90 is borrowed from a bank. Assume for now that no interest is charged on the borrowing. In this case, if the price of the bond increases by $2, the hedge fund still owes only $90 to the bank (since there is no interest) and gets the full $2 of gains. In percentage terms, the bond's price increased 2% (100 to 102) while the hedge fund's return increased by 20% (10 to 12). The factor of 10 here is no coincidence—it stems from the $100 being spent on the bond versus $10 of equity, leading to the term "10:1 leverage" for this situation (or occasionally 9:1, depending on convention). The leverage here allows the fund to reap outsized gains from a small amount of up-front money instead of having to raise a prohibitively large amount of money. However, leverage is a double-edged sword. If markets go against the fund, such as if the bond's price drops $2, the $90 is still owed in full, leading to a 20% decline in the fund's equity. For this reason, leverage is generally controlled and watched carefully by both the hedge fund and the bank lending the $90.

This example was based on two simplifying assumptions. The first was that the hedge fund could just reach out to a bank to borrow the funds. The second was that the loan was made at no interest. Given the multitude of investors of different sizes, credit ratings, and products out there as well as the massive volumes of transactions in fixed income markets daily, it would not be practical for investors to reach out to banks on a one-off basis for each purchase. To standardize this process, borrowers and lenders have access to the repo markets, which can be thought of simply as a market for short-term loans. The U.S. market in particular is noted for the size and depth of its repo markets, which in turn helps to create very liquid fixed income markets overall.

A detailed analysis of repo markets is beyond the scope of this book. However, it is crucial for rates market participants to understand the basic mechanisms of the repo market, as issues in this financing market can have reverberations throughout fixed income markets, including long-term securities. The full name for a repo transaction is a *repurchase agreement*, though almost all market participants use "repo" instead. The name gives clues as to how borrowing and lending function. In a repo trade, a lender, such as a bank or a mutual fund, will lend out cash with the agreement to receive it at a later date. The borrower of the cash, such as a hedge fund, will lend out bonds with the agreement to repurchase them later at a fixed price. The repurchase price agreed on the bonds will generally be higher (with exceptions), which is a form of interest compensation for the lender of the cash. Indeed, the difference in price, presented in annualized terms as an interest rate, is known as a repo rate, which can be thought of as the cost of financing a bond. The opposite of a repo transaction is a reverse repo. The reverse repo is the other side of the repo transaction; in the reverse repo, one of the parties in the trade lends out funds (i.e., sells cash) and then receives collateral, only to exchange those back at a later date. The side buying the bond (lending funds) will refer to the trade as a repo while the side selling the bond (receiving funds) will refer to the trade as a reverse repo. The repo counterparties are also not obligated to hold the collateral in place before the trade ends; a borrower of the collateral can go on and enter other repo trades, creating chains.

Another way to think about a repo transaction is that it is a collateralized loan. An easy way to understand a collateralized loan is to consider a simple loan of $100 between John and Jack. If John just lends $100 to Jack, this would be an uncollateralized loan, as there are no assets backing the $100. Instead, Jack can put up his watch as security for John to take in case Jack cannot repay the $100. Similarly, in a repo transaction, the borrower of funds puts up collateral in the form of Treasuries or other liquid assets for the lender to seize in case funds cannot be paid back. The secured nature of borrowing makes repo rates lower than comparable unsecured rates and allows far larger volumes to be transacted. The repo rate, otherwise known as the financing rate, will be an important rate when we consider net income from owning a bond in the "Carry" section.

To make these concepts clearer, consider a hedge fund XYZ that wants to trade the 10-year U.S. Treasury bond on a leveraged basis with bank ABC. In the repo market, hedge fund XYZ would lend $100 million worth of Treasuries and get $98 million of cash from bank ABC. The amount of cash is hypothetical here, but generally is lowered by an amount known as a haircut to shield the funds' lender from market volatility. At the end of the repo market transaction term, generally overnight, the transaction would be reversed, with the hedge fund paying a slightly higher amount of cash back as interest. For most Treasuries, the repo rate is near a standard rate known as the general collateral rate. The general collateral rate is the repo rate for a "standard" Treasury issue and represents a short-term risk-free rate.

Not all financing rates are at the general collateral rate, but financing rates in the market tend to be referenced as plus or minus the general collateral rate. For most fixed income bonds, such as Agencies, corporates, and mortgage-backed securities, the financing rate tends to be anywhere from a few basis points to a few percentage points higher than the general collateral rate. During the credit crunch, the stress in financing markets rapidly increased financing rates for assets perceived to be illiquid or risky, especially structured products. However, in the Treasury market, specific issues can trade well *below* the general collateral rate; these are known as special issues. An issue trade is special if there is a shortage of the collateral to borrow in the repo market. The shortage then results in a lower repo rate for the party lending the bond out and borrowing cash against it. This can happen if a large number of participants have gone short on the security and then need to cover it by borrowing the security in the open market. Even if there is not a large short interest, if there is scarcity of the Treasury issue due to flight to quality or concerns arise about lending the security, even on a secured basis, the shortage will lead to the repo rate falling well below general collateral rates. This tends to be the case with some on-the-run securities or cheapest-to-deliver securities in Treasury futures baskets (described in later chapters), especially if the original issue size of the security is small. Recently, as Treasury issuance has gone up, specialness has become less common.

Finally, the transactions just described assume that all the steps function perfectly. Repo transactions, however, have many moving parts, and specific rules exist to deal with failures. As mentioned, a party to repo trades borrowing collateral can then enter other repo trades where collateral is lent and subsequently borrowed again. If one of the parties fails to repurchase the security that was lent out, the counterparty would keep the securities and try to sell it to raise back funds. This is known as a repo fail. In isolated cases, repo fails are settled easily, as the collateralized nature of the borrowing protects the counterparties. However, in extremely volatile markets, a string of repo failures can lead to stress in the financing markets as participants pull back from the market altogether. Periods of such high levels of repo fails can make it tricky to trade Treasury bonds and can introduce distortionary effects generally not considered in normal, day-to-day trading.

BID OFFER

So far the price of a bond has been presented as a single number, but in reality the market has two numbers for any price: a number to buy the price and a number to sell at. Participants who provide prices for bonds such as Treasuries are known as dealers. For them to earn a profit, the price they buy the bonds at from investors should be lower than the price at which they sell the bonds to other investors. The price at which a dealer will buy is called the bid; the price at which a dealer will sell is called the offer. When prices are displayed, they are shown in a bid/offer format. In the Treasury space, prices are quoted in 32nds, as a XXX-YY, where XXX is the whole number of the fraction and YY is the numerator of the fraction over 32. For example a price of 112-10 is equal to 112 + 10/32 in decimals while a price of 112-10+ is equal to 112 + 10.5/32, with the plus sign referring to 1/2. Therefore, incorporating bid/offer, the price displayed may be 112-10/112-10+, meaning the dealer will purchase bonds at 112-10 and sell them at 112-10+, thus earning a 1/64 profit if he can match a buyer or seller. At times the market may trade only one way (i.e., with just buyers or sellers), in which case dealers try to manage their positions by holding onto the securities and adjusting prices rapidly to incorporate buying or selling pressure from the market. For benchmark Treasuries, given their liquidity, bid offer tends to be 0.5/32, but for less liquid Treasuries it can be higher; for less liquid fixed income products, the bid/offer can be substantially higher. Finally, at times bid/offer may be quoted in yield terms, where the direction is reversed. Therefore, a possible yield bid/offer can be 3.101%/3.100% since the dealer will buy at a *higher yield* and sell at a *lower yield* (recall that prices and yields are inverse).

CALCULATING PROFIT/LOSS OF A BOND

Calculating the P/L of a bond is simple enough if prices are used. The profit or loss on a bond position is just the change in the price of a bond multiplied by its notional. The P/L can be split into mark-to-market, which is pure price change, and carry, which is income from coupon cash flows. Since most of the market follows yields, the P/L can be approximated using yields by multiplying the duration with the change in yield. This approximation falls behind if yields move a large amount since it ignores the effects of convexity.

CARRY

Carry is a crucial concept to understand in the world of fixed income instruments. As with duration, the term "carry" often is used in an unclear manner, resulting in ambiguity even though the underlying concept is straightforward. Carry is the net income from owning an asset. Carry can be either positive or negative, depending on the asset. For example, the carry from owning a bar of gold is generally negative due to storage and security costs and lack of interest payments. Similarly, for equities, carry is the difference between any dividend income the stock provides and the cost of financing the stock on margin.

In the world of bonds, carry is the difference between the coupon and the financing cost of the position. Most of the time this difference has been positive since longer-term rates (i.e., the coupon) have tended to be higher than the short-term rates where the financing rate is benchmarked. This does not always have to be true; at times, short-term rates rise higher than longer-term rates, as occurred in parts of 2006 and 2007. We consider reasons for such a situation in Chapter 6.

To clarify, we consider the carry on a 5-year bond with coupon 4% and price $102. Suppose the modified duration calculated for this bond using the duration formula is 4.8 and that the financing rate is 1% per year. Also assume that we want the carry for a period of three months and that today is January 15, 2010. The bond pays semiannual coupons on December 15 and June 15 of each year. So:

Today: January 15, 2010
3 months later: April 15, 2010
Number of days: 90
Days between coupon dates: December 15, 2009 to June 15, 2010 = 182
  days
Coupon income in 3-month period: $4/2 \times 90/182 = 0.989$
Financing charge: $\$102 \times 0.01 \times 90/360 = 0.255$ (since entire bond
  price is financed; repo markets assume a 360-day year)
Carry: Coupon income – Financing charge = 0.734 = 23+/32 (23.5/32)
Carry (in bps of yield): Carry/Duration = 73.4 price bps/4.8 duration =
  15.3bps

Three points from this example are to be noted.

1. For the number of days, we used the actual number of days as we were considering a Treasury bond, which uses that particular convention. At times, in other bonds, such as corporates, a "month" is considered 30 days regardless of the actual number of days in the period.

2. The financing charge is calculated off the dollar price of the bond rather than $100. This enables the carry calculation to account for the fact that the entire price needs to be financed. The example also assumes no coupon payment between today and the desired forward date for the carry calculation for simplicity. In case there is a coupon payment date between today and the forward date, it is simpler to split the carry calculation between today and the coupon date and then from the coupon date until the forward date.

3. Finally, as explained in the "Duration" section, we can convert a price-based measure into a yield measure, which means in periodic payment terms rather than an up-front payment, by dividing the price-based measure by duration. Most often, the carry quoted in the market will be 15.3 bps per quarter.

This calculation uses a fixed financing charge, which is an implicit assumption of a constant financing rate for the duration of the carry period. In general, the repo markets trade in terms ranging from overnight to even a year, though liquidity is poor for over three months (and possibly less depending on the environment). Repo rates, or financing charges, that extend past overnight are called term repos and can be used to reduce the risk of large fluctuations in overnight financing rates. The term repo also allows an investor to lock in the carry for the period of the repo since in that case both the cash inflow (i.e., the coupon) and the cash outflow (financing charge) are fixed.

FORWARD RATES

The concept of carry is intertwined with forward rates. Simply put, the forward rate represents the yield of a bond that is purchased at a date in the future. In practice, a forward rate is denoted as $T_1 \times T_2$ rate, where T_1 is the date in the future when the bond is purchased and T_2 is the maturity of the bond. We can visualize the forward rate as shown in Figure 2.6.

How do we arrive at such a rate? We can arrive at a formulation for the forward rate using an example of a person A borrowing money from

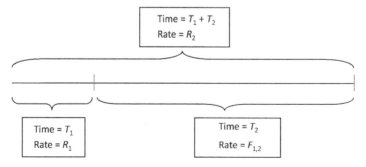

FIGURE 2.6 Forward Rate versus Term Lending Diagram

person B. For there to be no arbitrage (i.e., no free money), the investor has to be indifferent between these two scenarios:

1. Lend out money for period T_1, receive back principal, and then lend out for period T_2.
2. Lend out money for the period $T_1 + T_2$.

To be indifferent between the two, the total amount of money after earnings from interest are included should be equal between the two scenarios. Suppose that the interest rate for period T_1 is R_1 and the interest rate for period $T_1 + T_2$ is R_2. The rate we are interested in is the interest rate for period T_2 *starting at time T_1 that can be locked in today*. We can denote this as $F_{1,2}$. Consider the total cash flows in the two situations:

1. Lending out \$1 for T_1 results in interest of \$1 $\times$ $(1 + R_1)$ at the end of T_1, then lending out \$1 $\times$ $(1 + R_1)$ for the remainder T_2 period at the rate $F_{1,2}$, resulting in total cash flow of \$1 $\times$ $(1 + R_1)$ $\times$ $(1 + F_{1,2})$ at the end of $T_1 + T_2$.
2. In the second case, the \$1 is lent out for the entire $T_1 + T_2$ period at rate R_2, resulting in total cash flow of \$1 $\times$ $(1 + R_2)$.

For the lender to be indifferent between the two scenarios, both must result in equal cash flows. Therefore:

$$\$1 \times (1 + R_1)^{T1} \times (1 + F_{1,2})^{T2} = \$1 \times (1 + R_2)^{(T1 + T2)}$$

or

$$F_{1,2} = [(1 + R_2)^{(T1 + T2)}/(1 + R_1)^{T1}]^{(1/T2)} - 1 \qquad (2.2)$$

Why the need for indifference? If one of these scenarios was better, investors would prefer lending in that scenario until the rates adjusted to the point of indifference. For example, if $F_{1,2}$ was lower than the result in Equation 2.2, investors would migrate to lending money using scenario 2, which would in turn lower R_2 due to more investors willing to lend. If, however, $F_{1,2}$ was higher than the result in Equation 2.2, investors would migrate toward the more attractive proposition of lending at rate R_1 and rate $F_{1,2}$ until the rates aligned. This principle of finding the indifference point for buyers and sellers is central to the mathematics of finding prices for numerous securities. The formula given in Equation 2.2 can be a bit cumbersome for quick calculation and a reasonable approximation is $F_{1,2} = [(T_1 + T_2) \times R_2 - T_1 \times R_1]/T_2$, or in other words, the time-weighted difference in the rates divided by the time underlying the forward rate. This approximation is exactly true if rates are compounded continuously.

To see some of these concepts numerically, assume that a lender has the choice to lend for 5% over three years or for 3% over the first year and an unknown rate over the next two years. This unknown rate is referred to as the 1-year forward 2-year rate, which commonly is written as the $1Y \times 2Y$ forward rate (time to start $\times$ underlying time). Using the framework provided, we have:

$$1Y \times 2Y \text{ rate} = [(1 + 0.05)^3 / (1 + 0.03)^1]^{1/2} - 1 = 6.01\%$$

Using the simple approximation, we can estimate the $1Y \times 2Y$ forward rate as $(3 \times 5\% - 1 \times 3\%)/2 = 6\%$. Note the closeness between the two calculations. The second method has the benefit of giving a different intuition to forward rates, namely their link with the weighted difference of spot rates. Finally, one point to remember with these calculations is that the 5% and 3% have to be zero-coupon rates and not par rates; that is, yields of zero-coupon bonds rather than yields of coupon-paying par bonds. Using par rates can lead to large inaccuracies in forwards.

Forward rates can be thought of in a number of related, intuitive ways. In the framework just given, we arrived at forward rates as an indifference point between lending over the whole term versus lending twice, first over a shorter term and then over the forward term. We can arrive at forward rates using the indifference principle through another line of reasoning as well. Consider an investor who has the choice of buying a 3-year bond today or waiting one year and buying a 2-year bond then. Notice the similarity in the situation here and the lending one earlier. Suppose the bond gives some carry (i.e., net cash flow) to the investor for each year of holding it. In that case, to be indifferent between the 3-year and the forward 2-year bond, the difference in the prices of the two bonds has to be the carry over the one-year period. In particular, if the bond has positive net cash flow over the first year, the investor is *forgoing this cash flow* by buying a forward, so the price must be lowered to make it attractive compared to the full 3-year bond, where the investor does get the net income. The reader should go over this reasoning carefully; it forms the base of many carry calculations and can be a major source of confusion. It should also be clear that the price of the forward has to be adjusted by exactly the carry amount; if not, then it would be more attractive to either the 3-year bond or the forward 2-year bond and the interest rates would move until the indifference point was reached, as was the case in the lending example.

This reasoning with prices works with yields as well (just in reverse, since yields move opposite of price). Using the indifference reasoning, we can then calculate carry for owning a bond as forward yield minus spot yield. To make this concrete with an example, suppose we have two options:

1. Buy a 2-year bond with settle date January 31, 2010 expiring on January 31, 2012.
2. Buy the bond expiring January 31, 2012 on a forward basis on April 30, 2010 (assume no coupon payments occur between January 31, 2010, and April 30, 2010).

In these two choices, the second one assumes that the delivery of the bond will take place three months in the future. After the three-month period, both scenarios are equivalent since we are transacting in the same exact bond, just receiving it three months later in one scenario. Suppose the price of the bond bought on January 31, 2010 has a quoted yield of 1% and the yield of the same bond for delivery three months from now is 1.10%. It needs to be stressed again that the only difference between these two bonds is the first three-month period: The bond bought January 31, 2010 provides the investor with some net cash flows while buying the bond for delivery April 30, 2010 delivers no cash flows during this three-month period. Therefore, to keep the investor from being *indifferent* between purchasing the bond today (i.e., January 31, 2010) and in the future (i.e., April 30, 2010), the difference in forward and spot price has to be the carry from holding the bond. This carry will be identical to the carry calculated earlier using coupon income and netting out financing cost. In our example, therefore, the three-month carry on the 2-year bond is $1.10\% - 1.00\% = 0.10\% = 10$ bps. As mentioned, the bond market largely operates on yield terms, which makes it easier to compare valuations (and carry) across bonds of different maturities. To get the carry listed in price terms (in other words, dollars and cents), we can use the shortcut mentioned in the "Duration" section to convert between price and yield measures, which is multiplying or dividing by duration. In this case, we have the yield carry at 10 bps. Assuming the duration of a 2-year bond is 1.9, the price carry would be 10 bps $\times 1.9 = 19$ bps $= \$0.19$. Thus, duration is useful in verification and quick calculation when comparing a carry computation using the coupon income and financing rate costs.

The forward versus spot yield relation to carry points to some inherent assumptions about the *realization* of carry by an investor. Since carry is forward yield minus spot yield, monetizing full carry requires forward yields to converge to spot yields. In our example, the forward yield is 1.10% and the spot yield is 1.00%. If we buy the forward bond at 1.10% and wait for three months and its yield indeed converges to 1.00%, we fully earn that 10 bps in carry. This idea, however, requires that the spot yield stay the same—if the forward yield of 1.10% was an accurate predictor of where today's yield of 1.00% would drift to, then our 10 bps earned in carry would be lost due to a 10-bp loss on the bond's P/L (yield moved up from 1.00% to 1.10%). In general, forward rates are not good predictors of spot yields in the future, which makes carry trading attractive, but if rates become volatile, the steady gains from carry can also be easily overwhelmed. We discuss the considerations behind initiating trades for carry in Chapter 7.

ROLLDOWN/SLIDE

The concept of carry can be confusing in practice due to the different ways people use the word in day-to-day trading. The procedure just described is known as *pure carry*, as the number represents the net cash flows of owning the bond. However, ownership of a bond itself is not static; the bond ages over time because it has a fixed maturity. This aging effect in essence reduces the maturity and therefore duration of the bond over time. Consequently, the yield that applies to the bond changes over time if the yield curve is not flat. (Recall that the yield curve refers to the set of market bond yields across different maturity periods.) To make this clearer, suppose the yield curve today around the 10-year point resembles the following:

Maturity	Yield
11 years	5.20%
10 years	5.00%
9 years	4.80%

Our simplified yield curve has a 0.20%, or 20-bp, reduction for each year's reduction in maturity. Consider an investor who buys a 10-year bond today at a 5% yield. In a year's time, his bond will no longer be a 10-year bond but instead will be a 9-year bond. Since yields are not the same across maturities, it could be useful to estimate the benefit or loss from the aging effect. One simple way is *to assume that the yield curve will remain unchanged over the next year.* In that case, the 5% 10-year bond will age to a 9-year bond, and to stay in line with other 9-year bonds, the yield on this bond will drop to 4.80%. This would create 5% – 4.80% = 20 bps in P/L for the investor since yields have effectively declined over the passage of time. This 20-bp gain is known as rolldown or slide in the market. Note that the key assumption behind the concept of rolldown/slide is an assumption of a static yield curve. If the yield curve changed over the course of the year, the realized gain from rolldown could be very different from 20 bps; for example, if, in a year's time, 9-year bonds have a market yield of 5.20%, the investor instead loses 20 bps from the yield curve's movements.

The reader may be wondering about the assumption of an unchanged yield curve for the calculation of rolldown. Few investors have any realistic expectation of an unchanged yield curve over the course of a year, as in the above example. Furthermore, although carry can be locked in by the investor if the financing rate is fixed, in the case of rolldown, there is no such assurance; after all, the yield curve cannot be fixed for any period of time. Then what is the purpose of the rolldown calculation? Like carry, rolldown offers an estimate of the *breakeven* in a trade. The rolldown of a bond tells the investor how much the yield curve can move against her position before a negative P/L results. This is similar to the notion of the net income from pure carry, which indicates the yield change that can be absorbed before a loss. In our example, if the yield curve is unchanged, the investor has a P/L of 20 bps. Putting it another way, the yield on the bond can rise 20 bps before resulting in a loss *as long as the 9-year yield remains 20 bps below the 10-year yield*. Note that if we had stipulated that the pure carry on the bond was 20 bps in yield terms, the conclusion would have been quite similar. The link between the breakeven concept and slide/rolldown leads it to be considered along with carry. Indeed, in many cases, market participants use the term "carry" to refer to pure carry plus rolldown. We will continue to refer to carry as "pure carry" and denote carry plus rolldown when necessary. Finally, although the example uses one year as the rolldown period, the common periods for rolldown are one month and three months, which are more reflective of the usual holding periods for trades.

In the last section, the carry was shown to be the forward minus spot rate for an asset. For example, for a 10-year bond, we calculated the 3-month carry as the 3-month (3M) forward 9-year, 9-month rate (9Y9M) rate − 10-year (10Y) rate. The rolldown is calculated as the aging effect from the 10Y becoming a 9Y9M maturity bond over the course of three months. Mathematically, then, the rolldown is: 10Y rate − 9Y9M rate. Now we can combine the two expressions to arrive at a formula for carry plus rolldown:

$$3\text{M carry} + \text{rolldown} = (3\text{M forward 9Y9M rate} - 10\text{Y rate})$$
$$+ (10\text{Y rate} - 9\text{Y9M rate})$$
$$= (3\text{M forward 9Y9M rate} - 9\text{Y9M rate}) \quad (2.3)$$

Note that the 10Y rate is not even present in the expression to calculate the carry plus rolldown of a 10Y bond. The carry plus rolldown ends up being the forward rate with a final maturity of 10 years (i.e., 3M forward 9Y9M) less the aged 10Y rate after three months. To add to the already confusing situation regarding terminology, market participants frequently approximate the 3M carry plus rolldown as 3M forward 10Y rate minus 10Y rate because usually it is simpler to find a 10Y rate than an odd-maturity rate, such as 9Y9M. This approximation is reasonably accurate if the yield curve is flat (i.e., rates for different maturities are at similar levels) but can be misleading, especially for short-end rates, if the yield curve is very steep. The wide use of approximations and misleading terms can make carry a very confusing concept for newcomers to the interest rate world. Most of the confusion can be cleared up by understanding what terms are being used interchangeably and spotting likely approximations in calculations.

CURVES AND SPREADS

So far we have considered trades involving single bonds or, in market jargon, trades with a single leg. However, market participants frequently initiate trades with two legs or more as a way to trade the *relative* performance between two securities rather than the absolute performance of one security. At times, the view on the relative performance between, say, a 2-year bond and a 5-year bond may be clearer than the view on outright 5-year interest rates. Furthermore, multilegged trades at times can help reduce the volatility around taking certain market views. We consider the factors to watch for when initiating such trades in later chapters; this section introduces terminology and the basic setup of such trades. After all, sometimes understanding the basic nuts and bolts of a trade can go a long way in understanding the motivations behind it.

The simplest extension of a trade using a single security is to consider trades using two securities. When these two securities are in the same fixed income market, the trade is referred to as a *curve* trade, the reason for which will become clear shortly. Examples of curve trades would be buying a 10-year Treasury bond and selling a 2-year Treasury bond or selling a 5-year municipal bond and buying a 1-year municipal bond. The reason for the curve trade name refers back to our earlier discussion of the yield curve. Curve trades, such as buying a 10-year Treasury bond and selling a 2-year Treasury bond, attempt to take a view on the *slope* of the yield curve; in this case, we want the 10-year yield to come down (recall that lower yield = higher price = good for the buyer) and the 2-year yield to go higher (recall that higher yield = lower price = good for the seller). Therefore, in this case, we want the yield curve slope to go down (i.e., 10-year – 2-year rate). Note that we are only taking a simple view on slope—we have

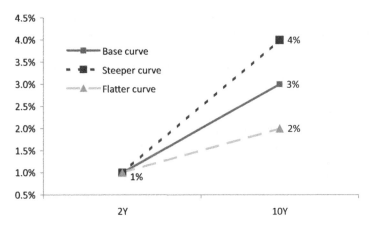

FIGURE 2.7 Different Yield Curve Slope Scenarios

not taken any view of the intermediate points, such as the 5-year Treasury bond, but only the slope between the 2-year and 10-year points. Although the reasoning is basic, it is important to have an intuitive feel for it. As trades become more complex, we can still deduce what yield curve shape we are aiming for using these building blocks.

Curve trades have a large amount of market jargon associated with them, which can make understanding even simple trades confusing at first. The trade used in the last example aimed for a reduction in the slope of the yield curve and is known as a curve flattener. The reverse trade, which would be to sell a 10-year Treasury and buy a 2-year Treasury, would be known as a curve steepener. In a flattener, we are aiming for 10-year yields to drop farther than 2-year yields; in a steepener, we are aiming for 10-year yields to go higher and 2-year yields to go lower, or, in other words, we want the slope of the curve to rise. In the market, these trades are referred to in short form as 2s/10s flatteners or 2s/10s steepeners. Figure 2.7 shows the basic idea behind these steepener and flattener trades. The general pattern here is that flatteners buy the longer-dated security and sell the shorter-dated security while steepeners do the reverse. One point to note is that both the flattening and the steepening could occur in a variety of ways. For example, in the flattener's case, both 2-year and 10-year yields could rise, but with 2-year yields rising a larger amount, thus still decreasing the slope. The price of bonds in both legs would decline, but the loss on the 10-year leg would be made up by the gain in the 2-year leg. A flattening in this case with yields rising is referred to as a bear flattening, since rising yields is a bearish move. We can also have bull flattening, where both the 10-year and the 2-year yields decline but the 10-year yield declines more than the 2-year yield, thus still reducing the slope. Here the gain in the 10-year leg outweighs the loss on the 2-year leg. The third possible case of both legs going separate ways—that is, 10-year yields declining and 2-year yields rising—is possible but uncommon as yields tend to have relatively high correlations. The steepening case has similar terms; if both 2-year and 10-year yields rise, and 10-year yields rise more than the 2-year yields, thus increasing the slope, the curve is said to bear steepen. The same steepening when yields are declining is referred to as bull steepening. These curve terms are useful for the reader to understand and know as they are used often in conversations among rates traders/researchers.

Curve trades take a view on differentials between yields of the same market. For differentials between markets, investors refer to such trades as *spread* trades. Spread trades involve buying an asset in one market and selling a similar asset in another market, hoping to take advantage of a change in the difference of the yields. Note the similarities with the curve trades just mentioned. One example of such a spread trade is buying the bond of a corporation (corporate bond) versus a similar maturity Treasury bond. When the difference in yields contracts—that is, the corporate bond yield declines relative to the Treasury bond yield—the spread is said to be narrowing, while the reverse case is called widening. Generally the market considers the lower-quality credit yield minus the higher quality credit yield, such as corporate bond yield minus Treasury bond yield. Therefore, spread narrowing is generally equated with the outperformance of the lower-quality asset in question. For example, in this case, the corporate bond yield would decline more than the yield on the Treasury bond, resulting in a lower spread. Spread widening presents the opposite situation. Finally, the narrowing/widening conventions given here are true most of the time, although as with most terms, the reader should not be surprised to discover occasional exceptions.

BUTTERFLY TRADES

The concept of curve trades can be extended further to three-legged or four-legged trades. Anything higher is very uncommon given transaction costs; indeed, even four-legged trades are not common outside the Eurodollar futures space or Treasuries, which have very low transaction costs. Butterfly trades involve buying (or selling) one maturity sector of the curve and selling (buying) two maturity sectors around it, one of greater maturity and one of lesser maturity. As with curve trades, the motivation here is to take advantage of changes in the relative performance of securities; unlike the curve case, which expressed a view on the slope,

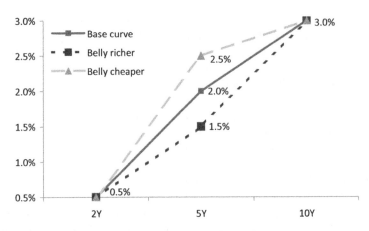

FIGURE 2.8 Different Yield Curve Curvature Scenarios

butterflies express a view on the *curvature* of the yield curve. To make this clear, we can consider the example of a common butterfly in the market: the 2s/5s/10s butterfly. The terminology means trading the 5-year Treasury versus the 2-year and 10-year Treasuries. The actual setup of such a trade, including the weights of the different legs, is discussed in detail in Chapter 8 on hedging risks, but the mechanics are not necessary to understand at the moment. The 5-year Treasury is referred to as the body or belly of the butterfly, and the 2-year and 10-year Treasury legs are referred to as the wings. Some market participants use terminology such as buying or selling the butterfly, but this is vague usage, and the meaning varies from market to market. More specifically, we refer to "selling the belly" of the butterfly or "belly-cheapening trade" in trades where we sell the 5-year Treasury and buy the 2-year and 10-year Treasuries. Conversely, "buying the belly" of the butterfly or initiating a "belly-richening trade" refers to buying the 5-year Treasury and selling the 2-year and 10-year Treasuries. Figure 2.8 shows the two situations for a stylized yield curve. The figure demonstrates the primary purpose of these trades, which is to trade the curvature of the yield curve. If we sell the 5-year and buy the 2-year and 10-year Treasuries, the aim is for a more "humped" shape of the yield curve. If we buy the 5-year and sell the 2-year and 10-year Treasuries, the aim is for a flatter structure.

SUMMARY

This chapter introduced a wide range of new concepts relating to bonds. The process of understanding bonds involves starting with the basic idea of the time value of money and discounting, which leads to the basic zero-coupon bond. At this point, all bonds can be understood as packages of zero-coupon bonds. For bonds with a fixed interest rate, changes in the market interest rate make them less or more attractive for investors, which exposes them to interest rate risk. Quantifying risks with concepts such as duration and convexity that measure a bond's sensitivity to interest rates is important for understanding and setting up appropriately sized trades. Beyond interest rate risk, other factors such as inflation and tax risks, as well as the income from owning the asset, need to be considered when deciding on a bond trade. Once a bond is understood as a single security, we can consider bonds across time to maturity, encompassed by the concept of the yield curve. Understanding the yield curve is important in constructing more advanced combinations of bond trades such as curve or butterfly trades, which allow a trader to express an opinion on the shape of the yield curve. The overview of the bond market given in this chapter will serve as an important reference point for the rest of the book when we discuss the thought process behind trading interest rate markets.

CHAPTER 3

Fixed Income Markets

The fixed income market forms one of the major asset classes for investors, along with equities, currencies, commodities, and others such as real estate. The term refers to debt markets that allow issuers to raise funds for a range of needs. This chapter provides an overview of different types of fixed income markets and their characteristics. Unlike equity markets, fixed income products generally do not offer a stake in the issuer, but instead allow the investor to lay claim to a stream of cash flows from the issuer. Fixed income markets are present globally, but the U.S. fixed income markets stand out in size and dominance. Over the years, the size of the U.S. fixed income market has increased rapidly because of increased issuance from traditional sectors such as government debt as well as the emergence of new areas such as asset-backed securities. Figure 3.1 shows the total size of the U.S. fixed income market; the aggregate amount outstanding has grown rapidly over the past decade, although this growth slowed with the 2008 credit crunch as more complex, securitized markets shrank.

The U.S. fixed income market has a number of subsectors that are separated by issuing entity. The major subsectors of the U.S. market we consider are the Treasury market; the Agency debt market; the mortgage-backed securities (MBS) market and, in particular, its high-grade component known as Agency MBS; the corporate market; and the municipal market. The Treasury market is debt issued by the U.S. government; the Agency debt market is debt issued by government agencies, such as Freddie Mac and Fannie Mae, to support the housing market; the MBS market is the collection of loans to homeowners to fund home ownership

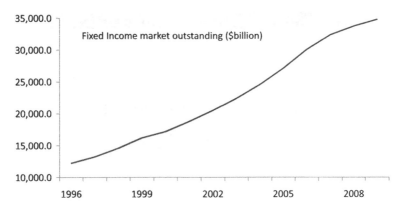

FIGURE 3.1   Total U.S. Fixed Income Market Outstanding Notional
Sources: Board of Governors of the Federal Reserve, Securities Industry and Financial
Markets Association.

(i.e., mortgages) with the Agency MBS subsector referring to government
agency guaranteed mortgages; the corporate market is debt of corporations; and the municipal market is the debt of cities, states, and other local
governments in the United States. Figure 3.2 shows the split of the fixed income market by aggregate size across these sectors in 2009. The mortgage,
Treasury, and corporate bond markets form the three largest components,
about 20% to 25% each; the remaining markets each form similar smaller
fractions, about 7% to 9% each. Generally, once debt is issued, it does not
stay with the same investor until repayment of principal. Instead, bonds
are bought and sold in bulk between investors in what is referred to as the
secondary market. As the size of the fixed income market has grown, so
has trading volume, as shown in Figure 3.3. In contrast to aggregate size,
the trading volume in the fixed income market is much more lopsided. The
Treasury market, for example, forms over half the trading volume of the
fixed income market. Combined with MBS, the two account for almost 90%
of fixed income market trading, as Figure 3.4 shows.

FEDERAL RESERVE

The Federal Reserve is an important institution that regulates the supply
of money in the economy and acts as a banker for the banking system
itself. To understand the Federal Reserve, it is important to start with
the basic structure of the banking system. Modern banks operate on the
principle of fractional reserve banking whereby most of the deposits they
collect from savers are lent out to borrowers of funds, such as businesses,

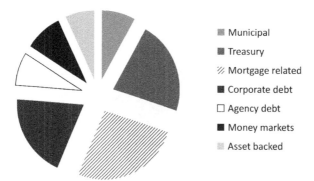

FIGURE 3.2 Fixed Income Market Outstanding for Different Market Sectors
Sources: Board of Governors of the Federal Reserve, Securities Industry and Financial Markets Association.

and the banks act as intermediaries. Since banks only hold a small fraction of deposits made at any given time, such a system revolves around the trust depositors have in the banking system to keep their deposits safe. If a large number of loans made by the banks are not repaid, banks will have difficulty honoring the deposits made by savers. Thus, if depositors feel that the banking system is under threat, they are likely to preempt possible losses and withdraw funds, even from banks that are otherwise healthy. This may cause a wholesale collapse of banks regardless of any individual bank's health. Such a cycle is not what the "free market" intended, but it took place in the United States at times in the nineteenth century and on

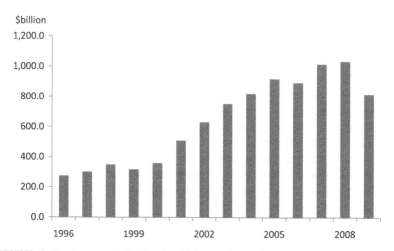

FIGURE 3.3 Average Daily Trading Volume of Fixed Income Markets

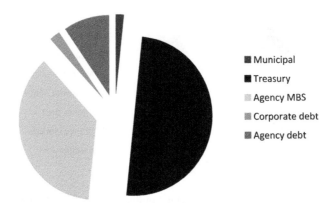

FIGURE 3.4 Split of Daily Trading Volume in Fixed Income Markets

a much larger scale during the depression in the early 1930s. In the United States, the nineteenth century was marked by numerous boom-and-bust cycles partly resulting from little supervision of the economy or banks by the government. A few years of explosive growth would accompany numerous ill-conceived loans made by banks and at times outright fraudulent activity, which would then unravel and lead to long periods of depression. To prevent such a domino collapse of banks, known as a bank run, deposits in many modern economies are insured by the government, but the risk of runs also requires a strict regulatory framework for banks.

To add a framework of regulation for banks and to cool down the wild swings of the economy, Congress approved setting up the Federal Reserve in 1913. The Federal Reserve was conceived as the banker of last resort for banks themselves and still retains that aspect today. Although its initial mandate was somewhat narrow, over time the Fed has grown to be one of the most important economic bodies in the world economy through its effect on interest rates and the supply of money and liquidity to reduce volatility in economic cycles. Given the Fed's considerable influence, any participant in the fixed income markets must follow it closely. The Fed's effect can be felt for both short- and long-term trades; a surprise comment by an influential Fed member in an interview can lead to considerable short-term rate volatility while a shift in Fed monetary policy over the course of months can fundamentally alter the shape of the yield curve. For an excellent discussion of the Fed, including many of its regulatory duties, see *The Federal Reserve System: Purposes and Functions* (2005), available at: www.federalreserve.gov/pf/pf.htm.

There is an inherent difference in projecting Fed action compared to other market phenomena because the Fed is essentially a board composed of a few individuals. The Federal Reserve System consists of the Board of Governors, which forms the central part of the system, and the presidents of 12 Federal Reserve banks sprinkled throughout the country. This structure provides a broad representation of different economic regions to enable better decision making. The Board conducts thorough analysis of the economy on a routine basis in the hopes of making more informed decisions. An important subcomponent of the Federal Reserve System is the Federal Open Market Committee (FOMC), which makes decisions regarding interest rates and open market operations, and conducts various market-relevant meetings. The FOMC is composed of the Board of Governors and four regional presidents on a rotational basis. The Fed is considered an independent body, given that its decisions do not need to be ratified by the president or any other member of the government. This discretion is not unlimited; the Fed is mandated to strive for full employment and price stability and is overseen by Congress. The Fed's structure is set up to allow for rapid decision making regarding the economy with less influence from short-term political trends. The Fed's mandate is easy to write but difficult to implement because of complex interactions between money supply, interest rates, and economic growth. Thus, the Fed has considerable discretion in its attempts to manage economic variables.

Although the Fed's mandate extends beyond monetary policy to bank regulation and consumer affairs, in this book we are concerned mostly with the monetary policy in particular due to its market relevance. The end goal of monetary policy is to manage the balance between economic growth and changes in prices (inflation). Chapter 6 discusses the Fed's interaction with economic forces and its influence on the interest rate markets. Here, we consider the underlying principles behind monetary policy and the set of tools the Fed uses to enact its chosen policies. Monetary policy is managed by directly or indirectly controlling the money supply. The term "money supply" here refers to the monetary aggregates known as M1, M2, and M3. M1 is cash and checking deposits. M2 includes M1 and other relatively safe accounts, such as money market deposits. M3 is even broader and includes various nonindividual accounts, such as institutional money market deposits and repurchase agreements. These underlying aggregates represent the supply side of the supply-demand interaction that determines interest rates. Money demand arises from the need for loans and credit by individuals and businesses.

To achieve its monetary policy aims, the Fed attempts to manage the market for banks to trade the depositary balances they hold at the Fed. The management of this market goes back to the idea of the Fed being a banker's banker. Unlike regular checking deposits, banks can trade their deposits at the Fed with each other. These balances trade at a clearing interest level known as the federal funds effective rate (or fed funds rate), which is determined by the supply and demand for such balances. The demand for balances stems from the need for banks to maintain certain levels of required funds at the Fed, known as required reserves, as well as other discretionary funds, collectively referred to as excess reserves. There are also contractual balances that banks use to manage large transfers of funds throughout the day. It is the excess reserves that can be traded by banks, depending on how attractive interest rates are in the federal funds markets, and can also leave excess reserves if banks need to use the funds to make loans to individuals and businesses. Before the credit crunch in 2007, the excess reserves earned no interest from the Fed. However, during the financial stress of 2007 and 2008, excess reserves grew to unprecedented levels, from less than $10 billion to nearly $1 trillion. This made it difficult for the Fed to manage the supply/demand balance for reserves. After congressional approval, the Fed was authorized to pay interest on excess reserves, which it could change in order to incentivize banks to keep excess reserves at the Fed instead of trading them in the market. The interest rate paid on excess reserves thus added another tool to the Fed's list of short-term rate controls.

On the other side of the demand for reserve balances is the supply of reserve balances. The supply of reserve balances comes from the Fed's securities portfolio, discount window lending, and other autonomous factors. The securities portfolio consists of debt securities the Fed buys and sells on either a short-term or long-term basis. Discount-window lending refers to the Fed lending funds to depositary institutions depending on their needs at a rate known as the discount rate. The discount window rate tends to be higher than the federal funds rate. In general, borrowing funds at the discount window can be a source of stigma for institutions; the market may take it as a sign that the institution is in trouble. The stigma tends to be more pronounced during periods of calm, but in times of financial market stress, institutions may approach the discount window in large numbers. Finally, autonomous factors are essentially outside the Fed's control and relate to various items ranging from Federal Reserve notes used by banks to order currency to the U.S. Treasury's account at the Fed. Autonomous factors will not be considered in great detail here as they are less relevant from a market standpoint.

As mentioned, the Fed manages the market for reserve balances to enact monetary policy. To manage a market, one can affect either the supply or the demand side. There are three basic actions the Fed can take:

1. Conduct open market operations (buying and selling securities).
2. Change a variety of short-term interest rates or targets (more details below).
3. Change the reserve ratio requirement.

Recall that interest rates are the clearing level for the supply and demand for money, so by altering interest rates, the Fed can control money supply. If the Fed raises interest rates, it is essentially curtailing money supply; reducing interest rates expands money supply. Money supply is generally curtailed by the Fed when there is a threat of rising inflation, while money supply is expanded if economic growth slows down. Since the mid-1990s, the Fed has set its monetary policy by setting a target for the effective Fed funds rate at policy meetings, which take place at six-week intervals. This target is known informally as the target rate in markets. Once the Fed has set a target, the bank can affect the supply of federal funds balances by buying or selling securities in the open market and altering its securities portfolio. These actions are referred to as open market operations. They are the most effective way for the Fed to ensure that the fed funds rate in the reserve balances market stays close to the target rate. Although the details of Fed activity can be intricate, the basic intuition is simple. When the Fed sells securities in the open market, it essentially credits securities to bank accounts, and money is transferred from these bank accounts to the Fed's account. When money enters the Fed account, it essentially leaves the money supply that is available to banks and the public. By selling securities, the Fed is reducing liquidity in the system and thus pressuring interest rates higher. The reverse logic applies when the Fed buys securities in the open market, which it does to lower the overnight rate toward the target. The securities bought and sold on a regular basis need to be liquid, so the common choice is Treasury securities. Based on the logic described here, the Fed could conduct open market operations by buying and selling any securities, but in general, its preferred securities are U.S. Treasuries. This is due to the unparalleled liquidity of U.S. Treasuries, which makes it easier to conduct large-scale buying and selling operations on a daily basis. Open market operations are conducted with certain large banks as designated counterparties, known as primary dealers.

Open market operations are not the only way to affect the reserve balance market. The Fed can also alter the reserve ratio requirement to directly affect the demand for reserve balances; however, this is a rather drastic action due to its large and immediate effect and it is rarely used as a policy tool. Another method is to change a range of interest rates. The target Fed funds rate, as mentioned, conveys the Fed's monetary policy signal to the markets. The Fed can also alter the discount window rate, but, as discussed, the discount window is used less frequently these days as a way for institutions to borrow funds. In general, the discount rate is set above the target Fed funds rate to discourage institutions from becoming dependent on funds from the Fed. Not surprisingly, then, the open market operation is the chief way for the Fed to ensure that the fed funds effective rate stays close to the target. As mentioned, during the financial crisis of 2008, the Fed began paying interest on excess reserves. The combination of financial stress and expanded liquidity during the credit crunch rapidly increased excess reserves in the Federal Reserve System. Since excess reserves were not earning interest and were flooding the system, it was difficult for the Fed to control the federal funds rate. By paying interest on reserves, the Fed can more easily control the federal funds rate and ensure that this rate tracks the Fed's target rate. As an example, if the target rate is 25 basis points (bps) and the excess reserve rate is 20 bps, the federal funds rate will not trade below 20 bps. If indeed the federal funds rate trades below 20 bps, banks can withdraw funds and leave the money in excess reserve balances to earn 20 bps, which therefore makes the interest on reserves rate a floor for the federal funds rate. Going forward, the interest rate paid on excess reserves is likely to be important for the Fed to manage the federal funds balance market. This is by no means unique for the U.S. Fed; many central banks around the world already use interest on reserves as an important policy tool to manage their reserve balance markets.

Once the federal funds rate approached zero due to rapid monetary policy easing, the Fed embarked on a range of new programs to offer funds to the market. These new programs included measures such as auctioning funds for banks and other institutions in need of liquidity for their assets. Apart from these temporary programs, the Fed also embarked on a program to buy a wide range of securities on a more permanent basis beyond the daily open market operations. The securities purchased were not just Treasuries but trillions of mortgage MBSs to help lower longer-term rates, especially in the housing market. Known as quantitative easing, this method had been tried by the Bank of Japan in the early 2000s. One way to think of quantitative easing is that it attempts to infuse funds into the financial beyond what a zero short-term rate can; its main aim is to increase the size of the Fed's balance sheet in order to lower longer-term rates. The hope of quantitative easing is that as longer-term interest rates decline, investors may be less willing to hold safer assets due to lower returns and invest more in riskier asset classes. This dynamic would raise asset values from housing to equity prices across the economy. However, the effectiveness of quantitative easing remains a matter of debate as investors with a bleak view of future economic prospects may be willing to keep money in safe assets even with low interest rates. The Fed's policies are likely to go through substantial changes over time as economic and political conditions shift, which underscores why anyone who follows the interest rate markets should understand and monitor the Fed closely.

TREASURIES

The Treasury bond market is one of the largest and most liquid financial products in the world. It represents the debt of the U.S. government, packaged into a neat set of standardized cash flows. The U.S. government has engaged in taking on debt since 1776, but the modern version of the market grew in importance especially in the late 1970s, as interest rates were freed from regulations and rising inflation made them increasingly volatile. The need to issue debt arises from mismatches in income from assets that an institution owns against the need to fund liabilities. For most governments around the world, tax receipts and expenditures do not align with each other, resulting in deficits due to cash flow timing, economic cycles, and other structural factors. If a deficit arises, the government can borrow money from investors in the market by issuing bonds in its home currency or by borrowing abroad in a foreign currency. The U.S. federal government is no different. It frequently issues bonds to borrow money in the Treasury market from investors ranging from individuals to foreign central banks. To fund the budget deficit, the net issuance of Treasury bonds—that is, issued notional of bonds less the maturing amount—should be equal to the budget deficit for the year. Given the sheer size of the U.S. economy and the size of the federal budget, the Treasury market is the largest and most liquid bond market in the world. Recently as deficits increased with the burden of wars, new social programs, and economic downturn, funding needs of the government increased sharply, leading to a flood of new supply of Treasuries.

The vast amount of debt issued by the U.S. government makes it necessary to have an organized process to connect the seller of the debt (government) with prospective buyers of the debt. The government issues two major classes of debt: public and intragovernment debt. Public debt, as the name implies, is the portion of the debt that is issued to the public; intragovernment debt constitutes a range of miscellaneous debt, such as special funds, revolving funds, and government trust funds issued as government account series. We will not be concerned much with intragovernment debt in this book, given that it is not particularly market relevant. Another split between the types of debt is marketable and nonmarketable. Marketable debt can be resold to other investors while nonmarketable debt is held to maturity. One of the most common examples of nonmarketable debt is savings bonds held by individuals that are not traded in the market. From a trading and market strategy standpoint, then, the most important segment of the U.S. government debt market is public, marketable debt. This section also forms the bulk of government obligations, and thus we focus on this debt for the remainder of the book. To keep the process of selling debt

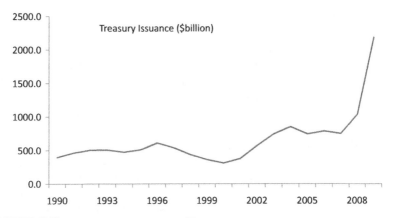

FIGURE 3.5 Treasury Issuance over Time
Sources: Board of Governors of the Federal Reserve, Securities Industry and Financial Markets Association.

efficient, the Treasury auctions each type of debt on a regular schedule to prevent unnecessarily large interest rate fluctuations. Since billions of dollars of interest need to be paid out each year for the borrowing, slight inefficiencies in the Treasury market auction process can lead to large losses for the government. Debt issuance itself also fluctuates over time, leading to a need to manage the market's expectations. Figure 3.5 shows Treasury issuance over the past decade. These auctions are an important factor in driving short-term yield cycles; thus, it is important to understand how they work.

Currently, the government sells four major types of securities: bills, notes, bonds, and Treasury Inflation-Protected Securities (TIPS). As described earlier, bills are securities with initial maturities up to 1 year, notes have maturities greater than 1 year and less than or equal to 10 years, bonds have maturities greater than 10 years, and TIPS have principal that varies with the inflation rate. Within each class are different standard maturities, which tend to fluctuate over time, given the government's borrowing needs. For example, the 7-year bond was reintroduced in 2009 after being discontinued in the early 1990s. Among the bills, the maturities auctioned are 4-week, 13-week, 26-week, and 52-week bills, with the first three auctioned weekly and the 52-week bill auctioned every 4 weeks. The Treasury also issues "cash management" bills for irregular financing needs. Due to their nature, these do not have a regular auction schedule. In the notes class, the Treasury currently auctions 2-year, 3-year, 5-year, 7-year, and 10-year notes. The 2-, 5-, and 7-year notes are issued near month-end while the 3-year, 10-year, and 30-year maturities are issued midmonth. Finally, in TIPS, the current maturities are 5, 10, and 30 years. They are auctioned two to four times a year with auction schedules currently in a state of flux. Not all auctions result in the issuance of a fresh security, but instead some auctions are "reopenings," which auction additional amounts of previously issued securities. This procedure is generally used for longer-maturity Treasuries. Currently, bills form about 20% of the amount outstanding of Treasury public, marketable debt; notes (2- to 10-year maturity) form about 60% of the debt; and bonds form about 10% of the total.

The Treasury auction process starts with an announcement of the auction. This announcement lists several attributes of the securities, such as auction amount, auction date, issue date, maturity date, and closing times. After the announcement, investors, especially individuals, can submit bids for securities at auction or make other arrangements to purchase securities at auction through broker-dealers or directly through the Treasury.

Next, the actual auction takes place. In the auction, an investor can place either a competitive or a noncompetitive bid. In a noncompetitive bid, the investor is a price taker and has no direct influence on the auction process. The noncompetitive bidder receives the yield on the desired security as determined at the auction. Currently, the limit for a noncompetitive bid is $5 million. Unlike the noncompetitive bidder, a competitive bidder is a direct participant in the auction process. The bidder submits the acceptable yield for the security being auctioned. To ensure fair auctions, no single bidder is allowed to bid for more than 35% of the auctioned amount. Once the auction's allotted time has passed—such as 1 PM for note and bond auctions—all valid noncompetitive bids are first allocated by the Treasury. After the noncompetitive bids are allocated, the competitive bids are allocated using a Dutch auction process. The bids are arranged in ascending order of submitted yield. For each submitted yield, there is also a quantity submitted, which represents the amount the bidder wanted. For the competitive bids, the Treasury then allocates the desired amounts starting from the lowest yield (i.e., highest price) submitted and moving onto higher yields (i.e., lower prices) until the total issue amount has been allocated. However, each bidder does not receive the yield submitted; instead, the highest accepted yield (i.e., lowest accept price) is allocated to all accepted bids. Primary dealers, counterparties in open market operations, are also required to participate in Treasury auctions to ensure a smooth process.

To the reader it may seem odd that the Treasury allocates all accepted bidders the highest yield, even if many of those bidders submitted lower yields at the auction. Would it not be more profitable for the Treasury to allocate securities at the level submitted by the bidder? There has been much debate about different types of auctions and their efficiencies over the years, and the answers are not as straightforward as they may seem.

In an auction where each bidder is allocated the price/yield he or she bids, there is always the risk of a winner's curse, where "winning" the auction may be the result of overpaying for the asset (in this case Treasury bonds). To counter this fear, bidders may actually underbid for the asset to make sure they do not end up winning an overvalued asset, which hurts the asset seller. However, if the bidders know that they will receive the lowest accepted price that fulfills the cumulative quantity being issued (i.e., highest accepted yield), the risk of a winner's curse is much lower and the participants are more likely to bid more aggressively for the asset. Although different countries choose different methods to auction debt, the Treasury's auction method seems to raise marginally higher revenue, although the evidence is not compelling on all comparisons (see Garbade and Ingber, 2005).

The standardization in bond form prevents the need for the government to negotiate a loan with each investor willing to lend money to it—the standardization using bonds creates a deeper, more liquid market. The Treasury bond market is currently over \$7 trillion in size, but this is likely to fluctuate as the government deficit changes. The interest rate offered by Treasuries for a given maturity forms the benchmark "risk-free" rate for that maturity. A freshly issued Treasury represents the benchmark rate for that particular maturity, but as it ages, it no longer represents the benchmark rate. For example, if a 10-year bond is issued, its yield is the 10-year Treasury rate, but if there is no 10-year auction for three months, the 10-year bond's yield represents a 9-year, 9-month (9Y9M) rate. To determine a benchmark rate such as the 10-year rate, a smooth curve can be fitted through yields of existing bonds (see Chapter 7). The same method can be used to determine a Treasury yield for nonstandard maturities where new issues are not auctioned, such as the 12-year rate. The Treasury does one such fitting and publishes "constant maturity Treasury rates" that represent a fixed maturity Treasury rate for a given date. Given the public nature of this data, we use the data set in working with Treasury data for the remainder of the book.

STRIPS

When pricing bonds, the starting point is the zero-coupon bond. Zero-coupon bonds offer no coupon cash flows and return the full principal at maturity. Although the structure is straightforward, the U.S. government does not directly issue zero-coupon bonds. However, these bonds can be created synthetically by separating the coupon cash flows from the principal cash flow. These synthetically created securities are known as Separate Trading of Registered Interest and Principal Securities, or STRIPS.

The zero-coupon bonds formed from the principal payments of Treasury bonds are known as principal STRIPS, or P-STRIPS for short. Each coupon payment can also be stripped out from a standard bond and becomes a separate zero-coupon bond itself. These zero-coupon bonds are known as coupon STRIPS, or C-STRIPS for short. C-STRIPS are fungible for the same maturity, but principal STRIPS are not.

STRIPS may be zero-coupon bonds, but using their yields to price Treasuries is not generally appropriate. This is because STRIPS have different liquidity profiles for different maturities, so their yields cannot be considered true zero-coupon yields for Treasuries. STRIPS yields can be traded versus corresponding Treasury bonds or versus other STRIPS by accounting for yield levels and the curve. The curve is a strong driver of the difference between STRIPS and whole bonds; a steepening in the par curve tends to steepen the zero curve by a greater amount. Care also needs to be taken when comparing STRIPS to whole bonds since there is a significant duration difference for the same maturity. In particular, the duration of a standard coupon bond tends to be lower than that of an equal maturity STRIPS issue. For a 30-year bond, for example, the duration is about 16, but for 30-year STRIPS, the duration is nearly 30.

Finally, STRIPS also have their own supply and demand dynamics. If a 30-year bond is stripped, for example, it adds to the supply of C-STRIPS all along the curve since it creates C-STRIPS for each six-month interval. Thus, modeling of C-STRIPS valuations even at the short end of the curve requires incorporating bond-stripping activity at the longer end of the curve. For longer-maturity P-STRIPS, a growing source of demand may be pension funds, as they seek longer-duration securities to match long-term liabilities.

TIPS

Like Treasuries, the TIPS market is also a market for government-issued debt, but with a twist. One of the biggest sources of risk for longer-term government bonds is inflation—as prices rise, the fixed coupon payments of Treasury bonds deteriorate in value. As with Treasuries, TIPS are guaranteed by the full faith of the U.S. government but add another layer of protection for the investor. In a plain Treasury bond, known as a nominal bond, the principal of the bond stays fixed for the life of the bond, at say $100. In contrast, the principal amount in a TIPS bond grows with inflation, which essentially removes the inflation risk from the final cash flow. The coupon rate on the TIPS issue stays fixed for the life of the bond, which leads to actual coupon payments varying over time. For example, if the coupon is

5% and the principal is $101 after accounting for inflation, the coupon payment for this coupon date is $2.525. As the principal changes, so will this payment amount, which makes TIPS different from usual Treasury bonds. The TIPS bond has a layer of protection against deflation (prices heading lower). The principal cannot go below the $100 at inception in case the inflation rate ends up being negative for the life of the bond. Although this is a minor risk for even short-term TIPS bonds because the inflation rate is rarely negative, at times, this floor on the principal has been of value (especially during 2008). The TIPS market began in the late 1990s and has grown steadily to be about 10% of the overall public debt market. The benchmark maturities have changed over the years, but currently the government issues 5-year, 10-year, and 30-year TIPS.

Since TIPS protect investors from inflation, they offer a lower yield than corresponding Treasury bonds. The yield on a TIPS bond can be thought of as a real yield—that is, the interest received after inflation is taken out. Since the yield on TIPS is lower, a certain amount of inflation needs to be realized to equate the return from a TIPS bond and a Treasury bond. TIPS are analyzed on a breakeven basis. The breakeven is defined as the inflation rate needed to equate the return on a TIPS bond and a Treasury bond. It is generally approximated as the difference between a Treasury bond's yield and a TIPS bond yield with similar maturities. For example, if the yield of a 5-year TIPS bond is 1% and the yield of a 5-year Treasury bond is 2.5%, the breakeven inflation rate needed to equate their yields is approximately $2.5\% - 1\% = 1.5\%$. The TIPS market is generally traded on a breakeven basis. When breakevens widen—that is, as Treasury yields rise relative to TIPS yield—TIPS outperform Treasuries; breakevens that narrow imply that TIPS are underperforming Treasuries. The breakeven can also be thought of as the market's expectation of inflation until the maturity of the TIPS bond. For example, a breakeven of 1.5% on a 5-year TIPS bond implies that the market expects a 1.5% inflation rate per year for the next five years.

Another possible source of confusion regarding TIPS is the inflation rate that they reference. There are a large number of ways to measure inflation; in fact, the government releases different types of inflation statistics. The TIPS principal grows using the monthly headline Consumer Price Index (CPI) number, which considers price changes on a wide basket of goods and services (described in more detail in Chapter 6). The headline CPI also includes the more volatile food and energy components, unlike the more widely followed core CPI measure for the bond markets, which excludes these volatile components. Given the relative volatility of the energy component compared to other prices, food and oil price movements can form a large part of the volatility in headline CPI itself. This leads to the unexpected outcome that oil prices are a major driver of TIPS breakevens.

MORTGAGES

As the Treasury market represents the debt of the U.S. government, the mortgage market represents U.S. household mortgage debt. In the United States, homeowners have a wide array of choices for mortgage debt, with terms of 30 years being the most common. Notwithstanding the variety of mortgage products, we discuss 30-year fixed rate mortgages in particular, as their aggregate size tends to have important effects on the interest rate markets. To create a deep, liquid market in homeowner mortgage debt, it would be impractical to trade single mortgage loans, which generally range from $100,000 to $1 million. Instead, the mortgage market embodies a broader concept known as securitization, whereby smaller loans are combined to form a larger security. Securitization began in the mid-1980s with residential mortgages but over time grew beyond its original roots to affect just about every fixed income market. Large pools of mortgages combined into a single security are known as mortgage-backed securities. Diverse arrays of securities, such as corporate debt and credit card debt, were combined and split into different tranches of risks. Figure 3.6 shows the increase of MBS debt up until 2007 and then a temporary decline due to market turmoil, followed by a modest rebound. Given the MBS market's importance, tracking MBS issuance is a key factor in determining fixed income supply pressures on the market.

Since every mortgage security is a pool of possibly hundreds of individual home loans, each such pool may have unique credit characteristics depending on the location, source of employment, and income of the

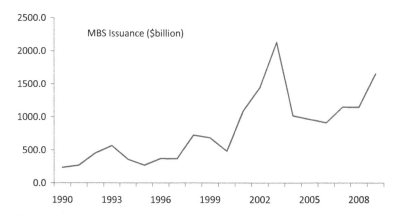

FIGURE 3.6 MBS Issuance over Time
Sources: Board of Governors of the Federal Reserve, Securities Industry and Financial Markets Association.

homeowners underlying that pool. Luckily there are some features of the mortgage market that help standardize the market. The first is the backing of the Freddie Mac or Fannie Mae government agencies, known as Agency MBS. These two government agencies are responsible for packaging and backing a large proportion of mortgage loans in the market. To qualify for a guarantee by either of these agencies, an individual mortgage loan has to conform to a range of standards, including currently being less than $417,000, although this can change depending on market circumstances and varies by location. Since the early 1990s and prior to the 2007 credit crisis, the two agencies operated with an *implicit* guarantee from the government—no actual guarantee was specified, but the market assumed that the government would step in if Freddie or Fannie faced trouble, given their role in the economy. We discuss the danger of such an implicit guarantee subsequently, but here the important point is that because of the agency guarantee, there is essentially no default risk for the MBS even if individual mortgages in the pool go into default. After the credit crunch, the government placed the agencies into conservatorship, which essentially took Agency MBS from an implicit guarantee by the government to an explicit one. Though the state of regulation remains in flux, any future changes are unlikely to change the support for Agency-backed mortgages, given their importance to the economy overall. We consider only fixed rate Agency-backed mortgages, which form the bulk of the market, in the rest of this section.

One of the unique characteristics of the mortgage market is that homeowners have a choice to refinance or prepay the debt at any time without penalty. Apart from more idiosyncratic factors, such as changing locations, the primary determinant in a homeowner's decision to prepay or refinance a mortgage into a new loan is interest rates, assuming the homeowner has a good credit rating. Note that the term *refinance* refers to prepaying an existing loan using funds from a new loan, almost always at a lower interest rate. Suppose a homeowner has a 30-year fixed rate 5% mortgage; that is, she pays 5% per year interest on the debt taken from the bank. If the market for similar mortgages in the market is also 5%, there is no economic incentive for the homeowner to get a new mortgage. However, if rates drop to, say, 3%, the homeowner can prepay the 5% mortgage and enter the 3% mortgage since that lowers her monthly payments. In contrast, if rates on comparable mortgages rise to 7%, the homeowner is happy to stay with the 5% mortgage; there is no obligation to switch. This asymmetry is known as an option and is discussed in Chapters 8 and 11. The salient point here is that if the homeowner benefits from the asymmetry, the investor in the mortgage is on the other side of the asymmetry. For simplicity, we focus on an investor in one particular mortgage loan rather than a large pool. In a standard bond, the investor knows exactly when coupons are paid and when the principal will arrive. In a mortgage bond, because the homeowner can prepay the existing loan (and possibly enter a new loan), the principal payment can arrive at any time. This creates a great deal of uncertainty regarding the maturity of the mortgage and its coupon payments; its *effective* maturity will vary depending on the chances of a prepayment. If other similar mortgages are at 5%, investors are indifferent between the homeowner's loan and other mortgages in the market. However, if rates on similar mortgages drop to 3%, the situation becomes more interesting. In a plain bond such as a Treasury, investors would be happy to have a 30-year bond paying 5% while comparable bonds are paying 3%. However, in a mortgage, homeowners can prepay the 5% mortgage and enter new 3% mortgages. Investors who were receiving a 5% coupon instead find themselves with cash on hand instead of a cash flow and have to reinvest it in new bonds at much lower rates. This way, even if interest rates fall, the price of the mortgage does not appreciate as much as it would in a standard bond. Indeed, as interest rates fall, the chances of the principal being prepaid increase rapidly and effectively make the mortgage a much shorter maturity structure than 30 years. If interest rates rise to 7%, however, investors face a full loss on the 5% mortgage as homeowners are unlikely to prepay in such an environment, and the mortgage will more closely resemble a 30-year security. To be sure, investors do not take on the negative asymmetry for free but charge a higher interest rate as compensation (discussed in Chapter 10).

The speed with which cash flows are expected to come back to investors is known as the prepayment speed. The prepayment speed can be expected to pick up as rates decline and to slow down as rates rise. Using the duration terminology from Chapter 2, the duration of a mortgage security declines when rates are declining (i.e., the prepayment speed is higher) and it increases when rates are rising (i.e., the prepayment speed is lower). This situation should be familiar from convexity, discussed earlier—an MBS has negative convexity, which will be important to remember when discussing managing rate risk. Prepayment speeds are incredibly complex to model due to the large number of factors that feed into deciding whether to refinance a home. Although interest rates are important in that decision, prepayment speeds are not uniform with interest rates. For example, if most homeowners in the market are paying 6% interest on their mortgages, then a decline of broad market interest rates from 6.5% to 5.5% will increase prepayments much more than a decline of rates from 8.5% to 7.5%. In another scenario, if interest rates have fallen to extremely low levels, prepayments may not be very sensitive to further rate movements. In short, equal magnitude changes in interest rates at different levels can cause very different prepayment speeds to manifest, making it important to understand the specific characteristics of the mortgage market in a given market environment rather than relying on general rules of thumb. Adding to the complexity of the problem, interest rates are not the only determining factor in prepayment speeds. During times of trouble in the banking system, as witnessed in 2008, the inability of many homeowners to pass credit checks and the general paralysis of the financial system led to very slow prepayments even with very low rates. Nevertheless, in most periods, rates are a major determinant of prepayments and for investors in mortgages, managing risks related to interest rates is key. We discuss more about offsetting MBS risk stemming from interest rates in Chapter 8. The importance of MBS for non-MBS investors arises from the effects on interest rate risk management by mortgage portfolio managers. The size of the mortgage universe causes mortgage bond investors to transact in large sizes across a range of fixed income markets, such as Treasuries, swaps, and options (see Chapters 5 and 10). Therefore, even for investors not directly involved in the mortgage market, understanding the risk management of mortgages is important for formulating views on a variety of fixed income products.

Finally, there is a variant on a standard mortgage, known as an Interest Only (IO), that is helpful in understanding a business that has a large impact on the rates markets. That business is the mortgage servicing industry. Mortgage servicers handle the logistics of paying the homeowners' monthly interest payment and principal to the investors in the securitization pool. The servicers charge a fee—generally on the order of 25 bps (0.25% of the payment)—to pass along the payment. Due to this fee and a few other charges, the interest paid by homeowners and the actual rate received by the investor differ. Notice that the servicer essentially has a cash flow resembling an annuity stream, which means a series of coupon payments with no principal at the end. This package of fees from coupon payments is collectively known as a mortgage servicing asset. The servicing asset resembles a traded product known as an IO security in the mortgage market. An IO is a security that is just the package of coupon payments of a mortgage bond without the principal at the end; a servicer's business is essentially an IO with a much smaller coupon than that of a mortgage bond. The IO also has a complementary Principal Only (PO) security, which is just the principal payment of the mortgage bond with no coupon payment. Notice that an IO plus a PO equals the full bond.

An IO—and by extension a mortgage servicing cash flow—has a few interesting properties. An IO is very sensitive to prepayments since there is no principal payment at the end. If a homeowner prepays a mortgage, there is no cash flow left over at the end that accelerates to today; instead the investor just loses any future cash flows from the security. Due to the negative impact of prepayments, an IO loses value if interest rates decline, because prepayments pick up. On the other hand, an IO gains value if interest rates rise, because prepayments fall. Given the opposite sensitivity to interest rates from a standard bond, the convention in the market ascribes a negative duration to an IO as opposed to the usual positive duration number for a Treasury or mortgage bond. Although the duration of the IO is negative, both IOs and mortgage bonds face negative convexity. This is because the reaction of IOs to prepayments is asymmetric. If the homeowner refinances in the event of lower interest rates, the investor suffers the full loss of cash flows. In contrast, if there are no prepayments in the event of higher interest rates, the upside is limited as the IO just resembles a fixed stream of payments. Thus, a decline in interest rates of a certain magnitude leads to larger losses than the gain if interest rates rise by an equal amount; in short, the investor faces negative convexity here as with a mortgage bond. Although any servicer takes only a small portion of each mortgage payment, the aggregate industry cash flows are in trillions. Due to the complex interest rate risks present in mortgage servicing assets, in recent years servicers have transitioned to using liquid interest rate products such as Treasuries, swaps, and options to manage their duration and convexity risks, in similar fashion to the mortgage portfolio managers discussed earlier (swaps are discussed in Chapters 5 and 10). As with mortgage portfolio managers, the large aggregate size of servicing assets means that risk management by servicers has effects on a wide range of interest rate products. Consequently, understanding day-to-day movement of the yield curve and changes in relative values between different market interest rates requires an understanding of servicing assets and their risk exposures (see Chapters 6, 8, and 9).

AGENCY DEBT

Freddie Mac and Fannie Mae were introduced in the last section as agencies that support the MBS market. These agencies not only guarantee mortgages but also hold an enormous portfolio of mortgage debt on their balance sheets. To fund these assets, the agencies issue debt into the broader market, known, not surprisingly, as Agency debt. The Agency debt market is $2.7 trillion currently and also includes debt from smaller government entities, such as the farm credit agency. The Agency debt market grew rapidly during the late 1990s and early 2000s, reaching over $1.2 trillion yearly issuance in the mid-2000s (see Figure 3.7). The agencies had a dual role, driven by both profit maximization and a social mission to provide support to the U.S. housing market. The dual mandate confounded the ability of an organization to operate efficiently as either a private corporation or a public one. For management, rampant growth was easy because the implicit guarantee from the government lowered interest rates for the agencies and allowed cheap funding for growth. The larger the agencies grew,

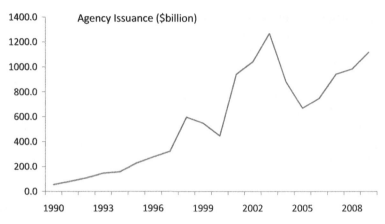

FIGURE 3.7   Agency Debt Issuance over Time

the easier it was for management to grow profits, even if this growth was driven by a cost of funding that did not reflect the true risks of the agencies' business. The dual mission led to massive growth in the agencies and led them to take on increasingly risky loans to increase profits and provide broader home ownership. When mortgage defaults soared in 2007 and 2008, not surprisingly, the agencies suffered enormous losses.

Prior to the 2007 credit crunch, the size and importance of the agencies led the market to assign an implicit guarantee to their credit. This was the *implicit* assumption that the U.S. government would support them in case of default, though the government had not explicitly said so. A true default by the agencies would lead to massive losses for investors worldwide, given that the debt is held even by foreign central banks. It also would lead to a sharp rise in mortgage rates for households. Until the credit crunch began in 2007, it seemed unlikely that the implicit guarantee would ever be tested. As a result, Agency debt tended to trade at only a slight discount to Treasuries to compensate for lower liquidity. As 2008 went on, it became increasingly clear that the agencies could not handle the large losses they were sustaining from defaults and their obligations to insure mortgages; the implicit guarantee theory came to a test. As expected, the U.S. government stepped in and took the agencies into conservatorship, making them essentially wards of the state and the guarantee essentially explicit. This has not reduced the importance of the agencies to the market—they still are responsible for guaranteeing trillions of dollars' worth of mortgages, and their balance sheets are in the hundreds of billions—but it does make their future dependent on political and regulatory considerations.

Unlike the Treasury market, the Agency debt market is composed of a wide variety of bonds ranging from plain bonds, known as *bullets*, to more complex structures, known as *callables*. Callables are essentially the same concept as the mortgage bonds described earlier, but instead of the homeowner, it is the agency that has the right, but not the obligation, to prepay the bond to the investor. This results in a similar asymmetry as with mortgage bonds, where the bonds gain less when rates go lower than they lose when rates go higher. For this asymmetry, investors earn a higher yield than on a comparable bullet. Unlike with mortgage bonds, the issuer cannot redeem Agency bonds at any time; instead, the redemption schedule is every six months. Furthermore, there is generally a noncall period when the issuer cannot redeem the bonds. An example structure would be a 3NC1 (3 noncall 1) bond, which is not callable for one year and then can be redeemed every six months after that up to the maturity date of three years. Agency debt has been a staple of the fixed income markets for years as a way for investors to earn extra yield. This is especially the case for buyers of callable debt, who give up the right of call to the issuer for the extra yield the debt offers. Compared to Treasuries, there is far more structural variety in the Agency market as investors can approach them in reverse inquiry, which involves asking the agencies themselves for a certain type of debt to be issued. If such a type of debt suits the agency, it can be issued for the investor to purchase. The heterogeneity may add variety, but it makes individual issues less liquid than the very standardized bonds of the Treasury market. Most of the liquidity in the Agency curve is present from the front end to the 10-year point with some debt issued in the 30-year space. Until 2007, the central banks considered the Agency market as a way to earn some extra yield over Treasury debt with the same implicit safety. This appetite has tended to fluctuate since the credit crunch, but as long as the credit risk is perceived to be that of the U.S. government, Agencies are likely to remain an important asset class for foreign central banks. As mentioned, the credit crunch brought forth serious doubts about the viability of the agency model, and the future of the agencies remains in doubt after their conservatorship. Nonetheless, due to the market's enormous size, Agency debt is unlikely to disappear for years to come.

CORPORATE BONDS

Debt issuers separate the different classes of fixed income debt. Treasury debt is issued by the government while mortgages are essentially issued by households. Another important class of issuers is corporations. Corporations are more commonly seen as issuers of equity, but they also issue debt to fund their activities. There are various pros and cons to issuing equity and debt, with equity offering investors a stake in the company but costing more for corporations to issue. With debt, a corporation gets a cheaper source of funding, and also receives a tax exemption for the interest payments. The drawback with debt is that coupon or principal payments cannot be delayed or canceled without triggering default. With equity, a corporation can suspend dividends at will without triggering bankruptcy.

The U.S. corporate bond market is one of the largest fixed income markets with about $7 trillion outstanding in debt currently, which is about 20% of the total fixed income debt outstanding. This amount of outstanding debt makes the corporate bond market important to keep track of, even for Treasury market investors. The corporate bond market is split between investment-grade and high-yield sectors. Rating agencies such as Standard & Poor's (S&P) and Moody's rate corporate bonds on their creditworthiness. The S&P scale, for example, rates bonds as AAA, AA, A, BBB, BB, B, all the way to CCC. Bonds rated above BBB– are known as investment grade; in other words, they are considered to be less likely to default. Due to their high credit rating and low risk of default, interest rate risk is important as with high-quality fixed-rate bonds in other markets. High-yield bonds are the higher credit risk bonds. For high-yield bonds, the bulk of the risk is the risk of default, rather than interest rate risk. Troubles in the high-yield market, such as sharp increases in defaults, can lead investors to rush toward Treasuries in a flight to safety. However, barring such events, it is the investment-grade corporate bond market that has much closer links to other low-credit-risk markets, such as Treasuries and mortgages. Figure 3.8

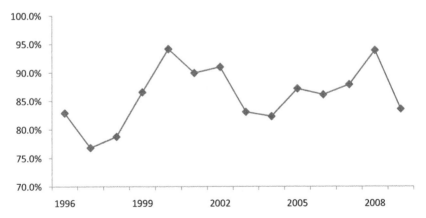

FIGURE 3.8 Percentage of Corporate Debt Issuance in Investment-Grade Category
Sources: Board of Governors of the Federal Reserve, Securities Industry and Financial Markets Association.

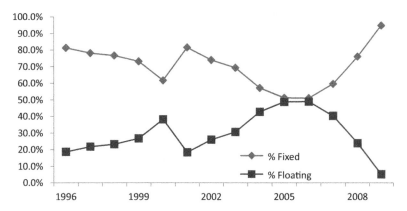

FIGURE 3.9 Percentage of Fixed Rate and Floating Rate Corporate Bond Issuance *Sources:* Board of Governors of the Federal Reserve, Securities Industry and Financial Markets Association.

highlights the importance of investment-grade securities, showing that they form the bulk of corporate bond issuance.

Corporate bond market issuance is an important factor for fixed income traders to watch. Corporations issue a variety of different types of debt, such as callable bonds and convertible, fixed-rate, and floating-rate debt. One important split for corporate bond issuance that is relevant for liquid market rate investors is the fixed rate versus floating rate split. Figure 3.9 shows the percentage of issuance in corporates between fixed rate and floating rate corporate debt. Much of the volatility in the percentage of floating versus fixed rate issuance stems from factors such as the steepness of the interest rate curve (i.e., floating rate versus fixed rate being paid out) and risk aversion toward issuing shorter-dated floating rate notes. Heavy fixed rate issuance of corporates can influence yields higher, either on a seasonal basis or as a broader trend of increasing fixed income issuance. We discuss the impact of fixed income supply on interest rate trends in Chapter 6. Floating rate issuance has a different type of impact on markets. It tends to be largely from banks, given the floating rate nature of the loans they make. Floating rate debt has little interest rate duration and therefore does not impact interest rate levels in the same way as fixed rate debt does. The corporate bond market is complex and dynamic, with numerous issuers of different credit quality and from different industries. For the purposes of this book, we look to factors in the corporate bond market, such as issuance patterns, which have a direct impact on the liquid interest rate markets. These effects on both yield levels and swap spreads are discussed in Chapters 6 and 9.

MUNICIPAL BONDS

Just as the U.S. government issues Treasury bonds to fund its expenditures, states, cities, and other local entities also issue debt known as municipal bonds (munis). Funds raised from issuing munis go toward paying for a large variety of expenditures ranging from schools and sewer systems to highways and airports. Given the vast scope of programs on a state and local level, munis form one of the largest markets in the U.S. fixed income space with a size close to $3 trillion. However, unlike the Treasury market, the municipal market involves the participation of thousands of different issuers with varying size, structure, credit quality, and regulations. This variety of issuers leads to many interesting possibilities for finding value but has the downside of leading to a more fragmented and less liquid market. Although large in aggregate, many issuers in the space have small amounts of bonds outstanding, which makes it difficult for institutions to trade large notional sizes. There are exceptions, such as the State of California, which issues large amounts of debt across the maturity spectrum.

To address the heterogeneous nature of the municipal bond space, these bonds are generally grouped into two broad categories: general obligation bonds (GOs) and revenue bonds. GOs are backed by the full taxation power of the issuer, which is generally a state or a city. If there is a funding shortage, the issuer in question can raise taxes on a local or state level to pay the coupon and principal of GO bonds on time. Revenue bonds, in contrast, are generally issued to fund specific projects, such as highways, sewer systems, airports, and museums. The proceeds of such bonds are directly tied to funds raised by the project through usage, such as from tolls for a highway bond. Given the lack of taxation power backing these bonds, revenue bonds tend to trade at higher yields (i.e., lower price) than comparable maturity GOs, although this may not be true in all cases given the large variety of issuers. There are also other types of bonds that do not necessarily fit into the GO/revenue bond mold. These include bonds issued to fund pension obligations of states and school district bonds that fund specific school districts but also can have the backing of the state from which they are issued. The maturity range for munis varies from short-term paper a few days in maturity to debt 30 years in maturity. Bonds issued with over 10 years in maturity tend to be callable after 5 to 10 years; that is, the issuer can redeem the bond at par after the noncall period (also see the earlier discussion for more details on callable bonds).

The muni market has a few unique characteristics that distinguish it from the rest of the fixed income market. Foremost is the tax-exempt nature of cash flows. For most financial instruments, any income received from owning the security is taxable at the income tax rate, and any gain from the sale of securities is taxable at the capital gains tax rate. The income tax rate (given the current path of legislation at the time of this writing) is expected to be 35% to 40% for top tax rate earners, while the capital gains tax rate is lower. Like other securities, munis are subject to capital gains taxes, but any interest income earned from owning a municipal bond is exempt from income taxes. The high marginal tax rate makes the cash flows from a muni more valuable than those of a taxable bond (informally known as taxables), such as a Treasury. This causes the muni yield to be lower than that of a comparable taxable bond.

Due to this difference in taxation, the municipal market tends to trade as a ratio to taxable yields such as Treasury yields rather than a spread (i.e., yield difference). One common way to compare municipal bond yields to taxable yields is to consider the ratio of a muni's yield to the Treasury rate for a similar maturity, known as the muni/Treasury ratio. As with the Treasury market, the muni market has its own yield curve, with munis of different maturities offering distinct rates of return, leading to a *muni/Treasury ratio curve*. When comparing a high-grade municipal bond and a U.S. Treasury bond, the muni/Treasury ratio should represent the market's expectation for the average tax rate over the period from today until bond maturity. This is because presumably if the city or state issuing the bond is of high credit rating, the main difference between the cash flows would be taxation, so if the tax rate was, say, 40%, the municipal yield should be 60% of the Treasury yield. This is generally the case for very short-term munis, barring market dislocations or seasonality. For example, if a 1-month Treasury issue was offering 2% and the income tax rate was 40%, an investor would be indifferent with the muni offering (60% × 2% = 1.2%). This logic breaks down near very low rates, as at that point the absolute difference is too small for many individual investors to allocate into munis. The ratio also breaks down during certain periods of the year, such as tax time in mid-April when individuals withdraw money from short-term money market funds to pay tax bills.

In practice, the short-term ratio tends to be near the current top tax rate on average, but this tends not to be the case for longer-end munis. Indeed, longer-end munis tend to trade at much higher ratios (i.e., cheaper) than most investors' expectations of tax rates. For example, 30-year munis may trade around 80% of 30-year Treasury bonds, which means that any tax rate higher than 20% over the next 30 years would lead to higher returns on the muni. Unfortunately, markets are never so straightforward, and the muni/Treasury ratio curve is a combination of risk factors present in all yield curves and some factors unique to the municipal bond market.

To understand the muni/Treasury ratio (or the ratio of the muni yield versus any taxable yield), consider the process of making a choice between buying a 30-year muni or a 30-year Treasury. The long maturity serves to magnify the differences between the markets, but the logic applies to varying degrees across the ratio curve. Both the municipal bond and the Treasury bond are exposed to interest rate risk and term premium. But the municipal bond incorporates three other risks.

1. Given the tax exemption of munis, there is uncertainty about the direction of tax rates. They may head lower, making munis less valuable. This is known as *tax risk*.

2. Munis have higher credit risk than U.S. Treasuries. The credit risk varies considerably, depending on the particular muni's characteristics, including its size, interest payment to debt ratio, and sensitivity to the economy. Even the highest-rated muni will incorporate a small premium in yield to account for the higher risk of default than a U.S. Treasury bond.

3. Individual munis are less liquid than U.S. Treasuries, given the heterogeneous nature of the market, resulting in investors demanding a higher yield on munis. This premium can grow to substantial amounts during times of stress when investors rush to own Treasuries and shun illiquid assets. Even during periods of little financial stress, the muni yield tends to have a premium to compensate the buyer for the higher difficulty of transaction than in the Treasury market.

The municipal market used to be a niche market dominated by individual investors looking for tax exemption, but over the years more institutional investors have entered the market. As the credit health of municipalities faces increasing uncertainty regarding reliance on property tax and increasing pension obligations, investor interest in municipals is likely to keep growing over the coming years.

SUMMARY

There are a variety of fixed income instruments, and there is no single "interest rate" for an economy. Bonds issued by different issuers display distinct market characteristics and carry a range of risks such as interest rate risk, prepayment risk, or tax risk. The overview provided here for each market is meant to introduce the reader to the possibility of a variety of trades to take views on all sorts of interest rates. Products in each market should be thought of as packages of their own unique sets of risks. Although each market discussed in this chapter is separate, there are strong connections between these markets, as their participants frequently transact across markets to manage risks or to earn higher returns. Thus, to formulate views on interest rates and spreads it is important to understand all markets within the fixed income space.

CHAPTER 4

Interest Rate Futures

C hapter 3 introduced bonds as the foundation product for the fixed income market. The bonds we considered are traded to be bought and sold immediately, in what is known as a spot transaction. However, this does not need to be the case. An agreement can be made to buy or sell a bond, or any other financial instrument, at a certain point in the future, known as a forward trade. For any tradable asset, the ability to trade the asset on a forward basis is one of the simplest modifications that can be made. This chapter considers the futures markets, which standardize the concept of forward products in order to enable more investors to participate and increase trading volume.

Trading a forward instrument entails buying or selling the underlying asset at a fixed date in the future at an initially agreed-on price. The buyer of a forward contract is obligated to receive the asset on the initially chosen forward date at the agreed-on price. Conversely, the seller is obligated to deliver the asset to the buyer. Since the price of the asset being delivered is fixed, the buyer of a forward contract benefits if the price of the asset rises while the seller benefits if the price declines. To make this concept concrete, consider the example of a farmer who plants corn in the spring and plans to sell it in the fall. The farmer could choose to avoid any transactions in the market at the moment and sell the corn at the prevailing price in the fall, but that would expose him to fluctuations in the price of corn in the meantime. The exposure of his future profits to the volatility of corn prices makes it difficult to decide how much to invest in his farm. However, if he chooses to sell a forward contract on corn with the forward date around the harvest period, he can deliver the corn at harvest time at the price agreed to today. Since the contract fixes this price for the farmer, it reduces his exposure to corn price volatility in the meantime. (See also Chapter 8 on hedging.)

BASICS OF FUTURES TRANSACTIONS

Futures markets started out as forward markets on agricultural goods and other "real" assets. These markets allowed farmers and other participants to buy and sell goods at a forward basis at a fixed price to reduce risk. By virtue of their standardization, futures exchanges provided a more liquid, transparent way to match buyers and sellers instead of individual pairings. The futures exchanges also provided a legal framework to allow buying and selling goods without the fear of counterparties engaging in foul play or defaulting on promised goods. As markets grew and the financial sector gained prominence, the need arose for financial futures, such as interest rate futures and futures related to equities. In particular, as interest rates became increasingly volatile in the late 1970s, financial futures proved to be very popular with investors to hedge interest rate risk. For example, a natural extension from the existing commodity futures was Treasury futures, where bonds were delivered instead of corn or wheat. Today, the underlying assets in futures markets cover an enormous range with most of the basic guiding principles of the early futures contracts still intact. Regardless of underlying product, the futures contract represents a binding agreement to buy/sell an asset at a forward date at a price agreed upon today.

An attractive feature of the futures markets is the ability for a buyer or seller to get large exposure to the market with little up-front cash. This stems from the margin concept, which accompanies all futures contracts such that neither party pays the actual quoted price of the asset. The simple way to think about margin is as buying without making the full payment for a product but instead borrowing part of the proceeds. Most houses are bought this way, for example, except there the term used is "mortgage." In the bond market, the repurchase agreement (repo) market functions as a way to allow buying bonds on margin. However, the futures markets have standardized margining principles. The exchange requires all investors to post funds at inception of the trade, known as initial margin. Next, it also requires investors to post additional amounts of money if the trade loses more money—the minimum amount required for this purpose is known as variation margin. These margin amounts vary by product and are posted on the exchange. Generally they are calculated based on the volatility of the product. The exchange calculates the profit or loss (P/L) of all trades on a daily basis using the futures contract closing prices; these calculations determine the additional amounts of margin required. Note that a favorable move in the market since inception would require no additional posting. This daily P/L calculation is known as *marking to market* and is another example of the standardization futures markets provide.

Futures contracts embody the forward concept with a few modifications. The term *futures* encompasses a concept very similar to forwards, but it tends to be specifically used in the context of a standardized, exchange-traded contract. The standardization, as mentioned, maintains consistency and helps create liquidity, as most transactions take place using contracts with commonly desired features. The exchange-traded aspect of futures introduces an entity known as the clearinghouse, which stands in between all trades to greatly reduce counterparty risk. Counterparty risk stems from the fact that for an investor, there is a possibility of default by the institution that the investor did the trade with. Since most trades in the financial space are done against large banks, one may consider this a minor risk, but the crisis of 2008 showed that ignoring counterparty risk could be perilous for investors. On the exchange, however, an investor does not face a direct counterparty; instead, the clearinghouse stands between trades. Therefore, the investor buys from the clearinghouse while the seller sells to the clearinghouse. In essence, the clearinghouse acts as a traffic cop for the market. To minimize the risk to the clearinghouse itself, the exchange takes precautions using the initial and variation margin postings described earlier. When a futures contract's delivery date arrives, the contract seller can make delivery of the promised goods to the buyer. In some contracts where delivery of actual goods is impractical, the buyer and seller cash-settle contracts; the party with a gain in the transaction receives a payment from the party with a loss. Examples of such assets include stock index futures or Eurodollar futures, where instead of making an actual delivery, the seller pays the buyer, or vice versa.

Another point to notice from our corn farmer example is that by transacting on a forward date, the buyer and seller do not have to incur the cost of holding the asset in the meantime (such as storage). On the other hand, if the underlying asset has positive cash flows, such as coupons from owning a bond, these are also not received in a futures transaction. For the buyer of a futures contract to be indifferent between owning a forward contract or the underlying asset, the price of this forward contract should be the current price of the asset minus the net cost of holding the asset between today and the forward date. Any deviation from this would allow either the buyer or the seller to transact in the underlying asset and forward contract simultaneously to earn risk-free profit. For example, if the forward price is higher than the asset price minus cost of holding the asset, an investor can sell the forward contract and buy the asset. After being held until the forward date, the asset can be delivered at a lower cost than the locked-in price of the forward.

In the U.S. fixed income space, there are two major futures contracts: Eurodollar futures and Treasury futures. Because these two contracts include some of the broader principles of fixed income futures across the globe, a thorough understanding of them is essential. Their basic features have been replicated for interest rate markets worldwide. Interest rate futures allow investors to take a variety of interest rate views internationally in a transparent manner. In the United States, both Eurodollar and Treasury futures are traded on the Chicago Mercantile Exchange (CME), which has grown to be one of the largest futures exchanges in the world. In the past, futures contracts were traded in futures pits with an open-outcry system, but as with many other futures markets, the pit market has moved to the electronic world. The principle of matching buyers and sellers remains the same, but electronic platforms are used due to their increased speed and efficiency. Futures markets have a rich history of peculiar conventions that survive until today. The first is the actual futures quotation, where the months of the year are referred to using the letters shown in Table 4.1. The four months in boldface—H, M, U, and Z—are especially crucial for fixed income futures, as most of these are on a quarterly schedule. The contracts also each have base symbols, such as ED for Eurodollar futures. These base symbols are shown in Table 4.2. To quote the symbol, then, the base symbol, month, and last digit of the year are combined. For example, the 10-year Treasury futures contract expiring in June 2010 (at which time bonds may need to be delivered or taken delivery of) would be quoted as TYM0. Next we consider three types of financial futures products in the

TABLE 4.1 CME Exchange Monthly Symbols

Symbol	Month
F	January
G	February
H	**March**
J	April
K	May
M	**June**
N	July
Q	August
U	**September**
V	October
X	November
Z	**December**

TABLE 4.2 CME Futures Codes

Base Symbol*	Contract
ED	Eurodollar futures
TU	2-year Treasury futures
FV	5-year Treasury futures
TY	10-year Treasury futures
US	30-year Treasury futures
WN	Ultra-long bond futures
FF	Fed funds futures

*Used by Bloomberg.

United States used to express rate views and manage risks by a large variety of institutions.

EURODOLLAR FUTURES

Eurodollar futures are cash-settled contracts that focus on short-term interest rates. In particular, the underlying asset on the contracts is Eurodollar time deposits, which are deposits of U.S. dollars held in offshore accounts. Such deposits grew in size rapidly after onerous U.S. tax laws in the 1960s led to a flight of dollars abroad. Since initially most of these dollars were held in Europe, they came to be known as Eurodollar bank deposits. Eurodollar futures are therefore instruments to take views on interest rates on these deposits at some point in the future. However, a futures contract on "deposits" could be a very ambiguous one since interest rates on deposits can vary widely depending on the bank, duration of the deposit, and size of the deposit. Therefore, as with all futures contracts, the exchange introduced standardizing features that were key to the success of Eurodollar contracts. To trade Eurodollar futures effectively, it is important to understand the details of these standardizing features.

- The Eurodollar futures contract has a notional of $1 million, which forms the standardized size of the underlying asset.
- The term of the deposits underlying the contract is three months.
- The standard rate assumed to be the reference rate for settling Eurodollar contracts, that is, determining P/L at expiry, is the three-month London Interbank Offered Rate (3M LIBOR). Details are discussed later in this chapter.
- The interest rate implied by a Eurodollar futures contract is assumed to be 100—the price of the contract.

- The contracts settle on a quarterly schedule in March, June, September, and December. Intermediate expiries known as serials occur in other months, but they are not very liquid. The quarterly contracts expire on the second London bank business day prior to the third Wednesday of the contract expiry month.
- A 0.01% change in the price of the Eurodollar contract generates a profit or loss of $25. Note that a 0.01% change in price is equivalent to a 0.01% change in interest rates, given that the interest rate underlying the Eurodollar contract is 100-price. A rise in interest rates reduces the price and therefore produces a loss for the buyer and a profit for a seller. Conversely, a drop in interest rates produces a profit for the buyer of the contract and a loss for the seller.

The list summarizes the main features of Eurodollar futures contracts. Next we go through some of the new terms and concepts introduced.

To understand Eurodollar futures, knowledge of the reference 3M LIBOR rate is critical. The 3M LIBOR rate is an unusual entity in the world of finance—it is one of the most important benchmarks in finance and determines the value of trillions of dollars of securities but is determined by a daily poll. The 3M LIBOR rate is supposed to represent the rate at which banks would lend each other unsecured loans for a three-month term. The market for such loans is known as the interbank market, and hence the "interbank" term in the LIBOR acronym. However, the interbank market is not very liquid. In order to get a daily estimate of LIBOR, a poll of 16 banks is conducted, asking them to give an estimate of the rate at which they could borrow from a similar institution in U.S. dollars. The member banks submit responses for lending to other institutions for a range of time periods ranging from overnight to one year (i.e., overnight loan rates to 1-year loan rates). The top four and the bottom four estimates are removed for each loan tenor to reduce the impact of extreme responses, and the remaining responses are averaged to arrive at the LIBOR rate for various maturities. These rates are released at 11 AM London time every trading day. LIBOR rates corresponding to other currencies are released as well, where these rates are for loans made in a currency other than U.S. dollars. One of the most commonly referenced rates is the 3M LIBOR rate, which forms the reference rate for Eurodollar futures contracts.

We mentioned earlier that Eurodollar futures are cash-settled. In this case, cash settlement is practical given that their underlying asset is relatively abstract and is not suitable for "delivery." Since it is a cash-settled contract, the seller gives or receives payments to the buyer in case of a loss or profit, respectively, at expiry. These payments are referenced against 3M LIBOR. To clarify, consider the example of a Eurodollar futures contract that expires in June 2011 and has a price of $97.00. Five points will help clarify the workings of the contract:

1. According to the fourth item in the last list, the rate underlying this contract (and others) is $100 - 97.00 = 3.00\%$.

2. The underlying deposit period is always three months. In this case, the Eurodollar contract is a futures contract on the three-month rate starting June 2011, that is, from June 2011 to September 2011.

3. The 3% rate is the rate that can be locked in by this futures contract for the three-month rate between June 2011 and September 2011.

4. If the underlying rate moves to 3.01%, the contract seller makes $25 per contract and the buyer loses $25. The case of the rate falling to 2.99% is the exact opposite.

5. Suppose that the 3M LIBOR rate ends up at 2.90% on the expiry date in June 2011. If the contract was purchased today, the locked-in rate was 3% for the three-month underlying period. Therefore, the seller pays the buyer $25 for every 0.01% that the settling rate was lower than the locked-in rate—that is, $(3 - 2.90) \times 100 \times 25 = \$250$ per contract. If the 3M LIBOR rate had settled higher than 3%, the buyer of the contract would instead pay the seller. Note that there is no delivery process and just the net payment is transferred.

This example illustrates an important point about Eurodollar futures—they are instruments to take views on 3M LIBOR at various forward dates since the P/L is referenced using this rate when the contracts actually expire. Although Eurodollar contracts are the standardized manner in which to take forward views on 3M LIBOR, investors can also use forward-rate agreements (FRAs) to take views on different LIBOR maturities. FRAs are traded directly against a bank and therefore lack the transparency and standardization that an exchange-traded product provides. The benefit of FRAs is that they can be customized to suit investor needs. Another difference between FRAs and Eurodollar contracts is that P/L is exchanged at the end of the forward period instead of daily margining as with an exchange.

The link of Eurodollar futures to 3M LIBOR is important since 3M LIBOR serves as reference rate for a variety of short-term loans ranging from floating rate mortgages to many types of consumer loans. 3M LIBOR is also closely linked to the fed funds target and, therefore, the Fed's monetary policy on a forward basis. This in turn allows investors to use Eurodollar futures to take views on the path of monetary policy and therefore the economy. For example, if it is June 2010 currently and an investor believes the Fed will be raising rates over the next year due to an uptick in inflation, one possible trade would be to sell the June 2011 Eurodollar contract to benefit from rising rates. Finally, since LIBOR represents the rate at which banks can borrow in the interbank market, it also has links to the health of the banking system—in times when banks are under stress, LIBOR rates can increase sharply.

The "fair value" of Eurodollar futures can be calculated in a similar fashion to other forward rates. As with any forward, the fair value for the forward rate is such that a borrower over two consecutive periods is indifferent versus borrowing across the combined period. Suppose R_1 is the spot LIBOR rate for the single period, R_2 is spot LIBOR for the short period, and F is the forward rate between the short and long period. In that case,

$$(1 + R_1 \times \text{Days}_1/360) = (1 + R_2 \times \text{Days}_2/360) \times (1 + F \times \text{Days}_{\text{fwd}}/360),$$

or

$$F = [(1 + R_1 \times \text{Days}_1/360)/(1 + R_2 \times \text{Days}_2/360) - 1] \times 360/\text{Days}_{\text{fwd}}$$

This forward rate is the fair value for the contract. For example, the six-month forward Eurodollar contract would have the single period as nine months (6M + 3M) and the second period as six months. The forward period in question is the Eurodollar rate, which is the six-month forward three-month rate. Given the liquidity and depth of the Eurodollar market, there are rarely sustained mispricings between spot-implied forwards and Eurodollar-implied forwards except in times of undue stress in the short-term markets.

CONVEXITY (OR FINANCING) BIAS

Although forward rates implied from FRA markets and Eurodollar futures contract rates tend to be nearly the same, the difference between the rates tends to grow for longer maturities. The growing difference is not a sign of mispricing that can be taken advantage of. Instead, it stems from convexity bias. Convexity bias, or financing bias, stems from the particular features of Eurodollar futures that separate them from standard bond instruments. In a bond, previously we discussed that the duration changes as yields move; in other words, the sensitivity of a bond to rates changes as rates themselves change. This phenomenon is called convexity, and it leads to asymmetric profits for the owner of the bond. For example, if interest rates decline 1%, the profit is greater in magnitude than the loss if interest rates increased also by 1%. This feature stems from the nature of discounting cash flows received in the future as a form of coupons, principal, or changes in the value of the bond itself. For Eurodollar futures contracts, there is no convexity in payoffs. The contract does not change its sensitivity to rates regardless of how rates move—the contract's value changes by $25 for a $0.01 move in the price (or equivalently, a 0.01% move in the rate). For the contract, the exchange credits or debits the P/L on a daily basis, so the investor can earn interest from the profits on any gains incurred, unlike the case for a bond or forward rate agreement. This creates an asymmetry for the short position betting on rates rising. For this side of the transaction, as interest rates rise, the positive P/L is credited to the futures account and earns a higher interest rate, since overall rates have increased. Conversely, for the long position in Eurodollars, positive P/L is incurred when interest rates fall, which results in less interest earned on the profits as rates are lower. To correct for this asymmetry against the long position, the Eurodollar rate is slightly higher (i.e., price lower) than the same rate for an equivalent forward rate agreement. This adjustment, known as the financing bias, depends on the volatility of interest rates and tends to be significant for Eurodollar contracts beyond two years or so. The financing bias can be calculated using financial software packages, and knowing its complex formula is rarely necessary for investors. The important thing is to be aware of the bias, which makes longer-dated Eurodollar futures and FRAs imperfect substitutes for risk management and pricing (see also Burghardt, 2003).

CREATING LONGER-DATED ASSETS USING EURODOLLAR FUTURES

We mentioned that Eurodollar futures reference the 3M LIBOR rate at various forward dates. However, Eurodollars do not need to be restricted to a three-month term. Eurodollar futures can be combined to form longer-dated assets, which allow investors to use them for risk management and taking views on longer-dated rates. The first step to doing this is to consider combining two consecutive Eurodollar contracts, such as June 2010 and September 2010. Such a combination turns a three-month rate into a six-month rate. This method can be extended by stringing consecutive Eurodollar contracts to create 1-year, 2-year, and longer assets. Such a chain of Eurodollar contracts is known as a strip of Eurodollars. An average of these rates weighted by the number of days corresponding to each individual contract is known as the strip rate. Using this method, longer-dated assets can be created or the risk of another longer-dated asset can be offset using Eurodollars. For example, for a 2-year bond, an offsetting trade may be to string together the first eight Eurodollar contracts. Groups of

Eurodollars in whole-number years are known as bundles; therefore, a 1-year bundle consists of the first four contracts and a 3-year bundle consists of the first twelve contracts. The starting point for the Eurodollar chains does not need to be the first contract. Groups of Eurodollars in the same calendar year are called packs, which are named after colors. The white pack is the group of the first four contracts. The red pack is the group of the four contracts starting after the first four contracts—it can be thought of as the 1-year forward 1-year rate (1-year rate because it is four contracts). Similarly, the green pack is the set of four contracts after that and can be thought of as the 2-year forward 1-year rate. Often, Eurodollar futures are used to manage and offset risks in longer-dated instruments such as bonds. An approximation many investors use is to just combine packs and bundles to match the maturity date of the bond (i.e., 3-year bundle for a 3-year bond). However, for a bond, the sensitivities to rates for cash flows nearby and further out are different due to discounting, whereas for Eurodollar contracts, this sensitivity is fixed at $25 per 1-bp move in rates. In present value terms, $25 movement per 1 bp means a different amount if it is for a Eurodollar contract one year from now or five years from now. Thus, for longer-dated Eurodollar strips, the contract amounts may not be equal for each three-month period, with the adjustment calculated by matching the *present value* of bond cash flows and Eurodollar contract sensitivities.

TREASURY FUTURES

Treasury futures are one of the largest futures markets in the world. As the name implies, Treasury futures allow the investor to buy or sell Treasury bonds at a given price on a forward date. Although the principle is simple, numerous features of Treasury bond futures can make them challenging products to master. Treasury futures are physically settled contracts, as mentioned, which obligates contract sellers to deliver actual Treasury bonds to buyers instead of a cash P/L. In the case of a Treasury futures contract, however, the bond to deliver is actually one of a basket of bonds—sellers can deliver any one of those bonds of their choosing. This choice has to be valued and not given away for free, adding a layer of complexity in Treasury futures contracts that is not present in cash-settled contracts such as Eurodollars. Why is there a need for a basket rather than a single bond to deliver? The reason stems from the fact that new bonds are constantly being issued in the market and bonds issued previously age, which limits the size of any one bond. This limitation could turn into a bottleneck if all sellers tried to deliver the same bond at the same time; to prevent disruptions in the Treasury bond market, the CME instead allows the seller a choice of bonds to deliver. As with Eurodollars, Treasury futures contracts exist on a quarterly basis: March, June, September, and December. The standard maturities for the contracts are the 2-year, 5-year, 10-year, and 30-year futures. Each contract is represented by its own symbol; the Bloomberg symbol is used most often (see Table 4.2). The 2-year is TU, 5-year is FV, 10-year is TY, and the 30-year is US. The codes for the specific contract months are the same as for Eurodollars: H, M, U, and Z. As an example, the 10-year Treasury futures contract expiring in June 2010 would be TYM0. Each contract has a basket of Treasury securities that are deliverable into the contract. For each contract, these securities satisfy certain conditions such as maturity ranges, described in Table 4.3. Any new securities issued that satisfy the criteria for a basket automatically enter it. In addition to these benchmark maturities, the CME introduced a 3-year Treasury futures contract, which remains fairly illiquid, and the ultra-long

TABLE 4.3 Treasury Futures Deliverable Basket Specifications as of 2010

Futures Contract	Deliverables Basket Criteria
2-year	U.S. Treasury notes with an original term to maturity of not more than 5 years and 3 months and a remaining term to maturity of not less than 1 year and 9 months from the first day of the delivery month and a remaining term to maturity of not more than 2 years from the last day of the delivery month
3-year	U.S. Treasury notes with an original maturity of not more than 5 years and 3 months and a remaining maturity of not less than 2 years and 9 months from the first day of the delivery month but not more than 3 years from the last day of the delivery month
5-year	U.S. Treasury notes with an original term to maturity of not more than 5 years and 3 months and a remaining term to maturity of not less than 4 years and 2 months as of the first day of the delivery month
10-year	U.S. Treasury notes with a remaining term to maturity of at least 6 years and 6 months but not more than 10 years from the first day of the delivery month
30-year*	U.S. Treasury bonds that, if callable, are not callable for at least 15 years from the first day of the delivery month or, if not callable, have a remaining term to maturity of at least 15 years from the first day of the delivery month
Ultra-long	U.S. Treasury bonds with remaining term to maturity of not less than 25 years from the first day of the futures contract delivery month

Note: Beginning with the March 2011 expiry, the deliverable grade for Treasury bond futures will be bonds with remaining maturity of at least 15 years, but less than 25 years, from the first day of the delivery month.
Source: CME Group.

bond contract. The ultra-long contract was introduced as a supplement to the 30-year contract with a deliverable basket composed of a subset of longer-maturity tenors in the 30-year basket. Starting with the March 2011 contract, however, the 30-year and the ultra-long basket will become mutually exclusive. The key point to take away from the table is that regardless of the name used to represent the contract, such as "10 year," the deliverable set of bonds has a range of maturities with the shortest maturity bond in the basket a fair bit shorter than the benchmark 10-year bond. This issue is more relevant for the 10-year and 30-year contracts as shorter maturity contracts have relatively narrow baskets. For the 30-year contract, the breadth of the basket extends all the way to 15-year bonds. This mismatch prompted the release of an ultra-long bond contract in early 2010 to have a basket that encompassed only the 25-year-plus maturity bonds in the 30-year contract basket. This was felt to be more representative of the long end of the Treasury curve.

Apart from the deliverables basket, the Treasury futures contract has other features to take note of. First, the contracts have a notional of $100,000 each, with the 2-year contract having a notional of $200,000. The contracts are quoted in price terms in increments of 32nds (known informally as *ticks*). An example of a price quote would be 110-16 for the 10-year contract, which would represent a price of $110 + $16/32 = $110.50 in decimals. Prices in 5-year and 10-year futures can also be quoted in $\frac{1}{2}$ ticks, shown as a + sign; that is: 110-16+ = $110 + $16.5/32. For the 2-year contract, even $\frac{1}{4}$ ticks are used. A full point (i.e., $1) change in price is worth $1,000 for 5-year, 10-year, and 30-year contracts and $2,000 for 2-year contracts. A tick, or 1/32nd, is then worth $31.25 in the 5-year, 10-year, and 30-year contracts and $62.50 in the 2-year contract. Although the notional and price increments are useful to know for determining contract sizes, they are in practice not very useful for the rates market. This is because unlike Eurodollar futures, the relationship between interest rates and prices for Treasury futures is not linear (i.e., the interest rate on Treasury futures is not equal to 100-price). Indeed, it is difficult to quantify a single "interest rate" for any contract, given the basket of bonds that form the deliverable set. For simplicity, however, we can consider the benchmark bond for each contract as its reference for yield changes (such as 2-year note hot run versus 2-year contract—note that the cheapest to deliver could also be used, but hot run is used here for simplicity). In this case, each contract has a different sensitivity to benchmark rates based on its duration (the calculation of which we discuss later). However, the concept is similar to bond duration, leading to vastly different price changes and, therefore, P/L impact for a 1-basis point (bp) change in the benchmark bond rate for the different contracts. As an example, consider taking a view on the spread between 5-year and 10-year rates using futures with both contract prices at $100.

Since both contracts have the same notional and same price, one may be tempted to buy or sell an equal number of contracts to initiate a curve trade. However, as with bonds, equal notional can result in mismatched exposure as the 5-year futures price changes with lower sensitivity than the 10-year futures price for equal changes in rates. This would leave the investor with P/L even if there was no change in the curve. To accurately position trades in futures, the metric needs to be risk exposure to rates, not notional. A rather extreme example of the concept would be trading Eurodollars versus 10-year Treasury futures. The Eurodollar futures contract changes $25 per 1-bp change in its yield while the 10-year futures contract may move closer to $80 per 1-bp change in the 10-year yield. However, based on notional, the Eurodollar contract is 10 times larger ($1 million notional versus $100,000). Setting up a notional matched trade in that case would result in a mismatched risk exposure, potentially leading to large losses.

The delivery process of a Treasury futures contract has some important details. Instead of a single day, the seller has a whole month to deliver the bonds. The first day eligible for delivery is the first business day of the delivery month. For example, the first eligible delivery date for any December 2010 futures contract for any maturity would be the first business day of December 2010. The last day varies by contract. For the 10-year, 30-year, and ultra-long contracts, the last eligible delivery date is the last business day of the delivery month. For the 2-year and 5-year contracts, the last eligible delivery date carries forward three business days into the next month to allow newly auctioned bonds at the end of the month to be eligible for the delivery basket. Thus, for TUZ0, for example, the last delivery date would be the third business day in January. For a seller who wishes to make delivery, the actual delivery process encompasses three days. The first day is the intention day, where the seller informs the exchange of the intention to deliver bonds for the contract and the exchange in turn finds a matching long position to take delivery. The second day is the notice date, when the seller informs the exchange of the actual Treasury security to be delivered and the invoice price is calculated. Finally, the delivery date is the last day of this process, when the actual bonds are delivered by the seller. Since the first date of delivery is the first business date of the delivery month, the first intention date is two business days before the delivery month and the first notice date is one business day before the delivery month.

The presence of a delivery basket introduces the need for a range of concepts not required in cash-settled contracts. The first such concept is the conversion factor. The conversion factor is a constant associated with *each* bond in the basket that converts the prices of the bonds to a 6% yield to maturity. The conversion factor for a bond does not change during a futures cycle. For example, the conversion factor of 4.5%

Feb-16 Treasury notes for the June 2007 Treasury futures contract would stay constant until the contract expired, but 4.5% Feb-16, which was also present in the September 2007 contract, would have a different, constant conversion factor for the September 2007 contract. The conversion factor places the bonds on a comparable yield of 6%.

To understand the need for a conversion factor, let's leave the world of Treasury bonds for a bit and consider a futures contract where the underlying asset is cars. In our example, assume that there are only two types of cars in the world: Chevrolets and Ferraris. The Ferraris cost $100 and Chevys cost $20 at all times. As with Treasury futures, the seller of the car futures contract has a delivery basket consisting of Chevys and Ferraris; that is, the seller of the contract can deliver either a Chevy or a Ferrari to the buyer at expiry. However, as the current contract is stated, since the Chevy is cheaper, the seller will always deliver a Chevy (not that the author has anything against Chevys). There is no upside to delivering a Ferrari. The problem with this scenario is that we have reduced our car futures contract to just a Chevy futures contract—at no point will a seller deliver a Ferrari, so the price of this contract will only track the price of a Chevy. This was not the original intention; the futures contract was supposed to represent a forward price of cars in general, not just Chevys. To address this issue we introduce a conversion factor as with Treasury futures. Here we assume the conversion factor of a Chevy is 5 and that of a Ferrari is 1. Now we stipulate that the buyer will pay the seller (price of car delivered) × (conversion factor). The situation changes considerably:

1. If the seller delivers a Chevy, the buyer will pay the seller (price of Chevy) × conversion factor = $20 × 5 = $100.

2. If the seller delivers a Ferrari, the buyer will pay the seller (price of Ferrari) × conversion factor = $100 × 1 = $100.

Given that the seller receives the same amount of money in either case, she is now indifferent between delivering a Chevy or Ferrari. This leaves the two cars on an equal footing and enables the futures contract to cover a wider range of cars. Of course, if the relative prices of Chevys and Ferraris change beyond the conversion factor, one of the cars may be more attractive to deliver for the seller. The most attractive car for the seller to deliver is precisely the *cheaper* car of the choices, which we will denote as the cheapest to deliver (CTD). We will return to determining the CTD bond for a Treasury futures contract shortly.

For the Treasury futures contract, the conversion factor serves to eliminate differences based solely on coupon. If the seller's decision was purely based on dollar price, then, as with the case of the cars, the seller would deliver just the lowest dollar price bond. The lowest dollar price bond will almost always be the bond with the lowest coupon. This would cause the Treasury futures contract to merely track the lowest coupon bonds, which is not the intention of the contract. As with the car contract, the conversion factors in the Treasury futures eliminate those differences that we do not want to be a factor between bonds—by placing bonds on a common 6% yield using conversion factors, coupon differences are no longer relevant. Once the conversion factor has been calculated for a bond, the futures invoice price for the bond can also be calculated. The futures invoice price can be calculated as futures price × conversion factor + accrued interest. The accrued interest is on the bond until the last delivery date. This invoice price tells the buyer how much to pay the seller *in case* the seller delivers this bond. Of course, if the seller chooses another bond, the invoice price will change. Calculating the conversion factor allows us to calculate the fair futures price of the contract. Each bond in the basket has a forward price until last delivery date, which can be calculated as the current price minus the carry until that date. If there was only one bond in the basket, the implied futures price is just the forward price of the bond, since at that point the contract gets distilled to just a future value of the single bond. With multiple bonds, the conversion factor is necessary, and the adjustment is the forward price divided by the conversion factor. If there is more than one bond in the basket, the "fair" futures price is the minimum of all the ratios of forward prices and their conversion factors. This is because, as discussed, the cheapest bond in the basket will be delivered into the contract, which means the futures price will track the bond with the lowest forward price, after adjusting for conversion factor.

Since the Treasury futures contract tracks a basket of bonds, the concept of a single yield is difficult to apply to the contract. However, most other fixed income instruments trade on a yield basis and trading Treasury futures along with them requires the calculation of a forward yield. The first step is to calculate a forward price for the CTD bond: This is the futures price multiplied by the conversion factor of the CTD bond with the accrued interest added. The use of the futures contract price to calculate the implied forward price of the CTD gives rise to the term *implied forward yield* of the futures contract. Once we have the forward price of the CTD bond, the forward yield can be calculated using the usual price/yield formula for a bond. Here, the forward start date is the first delivery date of the contract and the maturity date is the CTD bond's maturity.

The next concept after the invoice price is the implied repo rate, which will help us determine the CTD bond. The implied repo rate for a bond is the theoretical return from delivering the bond for a short futures position. The formula for implied repo rate is:

$$(\text{sales price} - \text{purchase price})/\text{purchase price} \times 360/\text{num days}$$

The 360/num days is an annualization factor. Given the implied repo rate, we can now determine which bond offers the seller the greatest return for delivery. Therefore, the bond with the highest implied repo rate is the CTD bond. The implied repo rate has another interpretation: It can be thought of as the synthetic financing rate of the bond in the futures contract, as opposed to the actual financing rate in the repo market. This synthetic financing rate interpretation is valid because the difference between the futures and bond price is the carry of the bond, as discussed earlier. The coupon income from the bond is known in advance for the bond, which leaves the financing rate the unknown here. The implied repo rate is the financing rate that balances the two sides—that is, it is the rate at which a long bond, short futures position is being financed. The interpretation of the highest implied repo rate as the CTD still makes sense—the short futures position will want to deliver the bond with highest implied financing rate.

The implied repo rate is one way to determine the attractiveness of a bond versus a futures contract. Another metric used to determine the relationship between bonds and futures is the basis. The basis, more fully known as the gross basis, is calculated as:

Cash price − futures price × conversion factor

The gross basis is essentially the difference between the cash price and the invoice price at delivery, which is the futures market's version of the forward versus spot differential. The basis is the most common way futures traders judge a bond's relative value versus futures, and the gross basis can actually be traded as a package. However, the gross basis encompasses a large amount of information, and breaking down its components is helpful.

The first component of the gross basis is the carry, since the basis is the difference between a futures price and a cash price. But carry is not the only component. The short futures position has an option to choose which bond to deliver from among the bonds in the basket. In the market, choices are not granted for free; in this case, the futures price is *lower* than it would be without these delivery options. (Since the short position has the delivery option, the futures price needs to be lower to compensate the long.) Now we can combine the two concepts:

Gross basis = carry + delivery option value

Since carry can be calculated easily, we can isolate delivery option value as gross basis minus carry, which is known as the basis net of carry (BNOC). The larger the BNOC, the richer the bond is versus futures (since the basis is cash futures − futures price × conversion factor). Thus, the contract seller will deliver the bond with the smallest BNOC. This preference gives us another way to find the CTD in addition to the implied repo rate: The CTD is the bond with the lowest BNOC. If the bond is the CTD, the BNOC informs us of the market's estimation of the delivery option value. Calculating the delivery option value requires some underlying concepts that are discussed in Chapter 10. Trading futures versus cash is a segment of the market in itself, known as basis trading. Trading the basis involves essentially trading the BNOC against the trader's own estimation of the delivery option value. We discuss basis trading in detail in Chapter 11. The BNOC also determines how attractive futures are as a risk management of cash bonds, which we discuss in detail in Chapter 8.

FED FUNDS FUTURES

Another segment of the fixed income futures markets is the fed funds futures markets. Like Eurodollar futures, fed funds futures are based on a short-term rate. However, there are three key differences:

1. The effective federal funds rate (abbreviated as the fed funds rate in the rest of the section) underlies the futures contract, unlike the Eurodollar futures contract, where the 3M LIBOR rate is the underlying rate. As with Eurodollar futures, the interest rate implied by the fed funds futures contract is 100-price. The fed funds rate is also known at times as the overnight index swap (OIS) rate.
2. Fed funds contracts are monthly instead of quarterly.
3. For the fed funds futures contract, the contract settles on the *average* daily effective fed funds rate for the month.

The fed funds rate is the rate at which banks trade excess reserves in the fed funds market (see Chapter 3). Excess reserves, as discussed earlier, are funds deposited at the Federal Reserve over and above required reserves. At times, an intermittent shortage or excess of funds may occur and can be traded by banks that are part of the Federal Reserve system. The effective fed funds rate is the daily rate at which excess reserves are traded. It is the rate that most closely tracks the fed funds target, and it is also the rate the Fed seeks to manage through open market operations. Three-month LIBOR, however, is the unsecured rate at which banks can lend or borrow from each other. The difference in the underlying nature of the rates makes the Federal Reserve rate a more "secure" one, making the fed funds rate trade lower than the 3M LIBOR rate. On average, the fed funds rate has tended to trade about 15 to 17 bps lower than the 3M LIBOR rate, but this rate has varied greatly. In particular, signs of trouble in the banking system or liquidity constraints are seen first, and most starkly, in these short-term rates. In particular, when a banking crisis takes hold, the 3M LIBOR rate tends to trade well above the fed funds rate since 3M LIBOR is the uncollateralized, unsecured lending rate.

Although the fed funds rate is a more direct reflection of Fed monetary policy, Eurodollar contracts with 3M LIBOR underlying are still much more commonly used as instruments to take views on short-term rates and Fed policy. This is because fed funds futures are the least liquid of the three types of futures mentioned in this chapter. The fed funds futures contracts have reasonable liquidity for the first six months or so, but it is difficult to trade them further out. Even traders who do not trade fed funds futures directly use them frequently to calculate the near-term implied probability of a Fed move. The basic way to calculate this can be best shown by an example. Suppose a Federal Reserve meeting is scheduled on January 31. Also let us assume that the current target rate is at 1%, and we need the chances of a 25-bp cut on January 31. If there is no meeting in February, then the February fed funds futures rate will settle at the average fed funds rate during February, which in turn will be linked to the target rate the Fed decides on January 31. Suppose the February futures rate is 0.80%. The chance of a 25-bp cut is calculated as:

$$(1\% - 0.80\%)/0.25\% = 80\%$$

The probability of a Fed cut to 0.75% on January 31 is therefore 80%, as implied by the market. Notice that the calculation was simplified because there was no meeting in February, leaving the February fed funds rate linked only to the January meeting rate. If we consider an artificial example where the Fed meeting is on January 31 and on February 15, then the January 31 probability is trickier. The February fed funds rate is still relevant, except now one fraction of the rate corresponds to the January 31 meeting, and the other fraction corresponds to the February 15 meeting. In particular, 15/28 of the rate corresponds to the January 31 meeting and 13/28 of the rate corresponds to the February 15 meeting. Therefore,

$$\text{February futures rate} = 15/28 \times \text{January 31 implied rate}$$
$$+ 13/28 \times \text{February 15 implied rate}$$

Here we have to make an assumption about looking for 25-bp cuts at the meetings, but essentially the procedure remains the same.

A note of caution is warranted on using fed funds futures to determine implied probability. In Chapter 2 on bonds, we discussed the breakdown of the yield curve in terms of both expectations and term premium. The same is true for any futures curve, including fed funds futures. Part of the fed funds futures rate is indeed expectations of Fed activity, but part of it is term premium. The term premium would make the fed funds rate higher than what is purely expected from Fed activity. To complicate matters further, there is another source of uncertainty with regard to using the fed funds futures to trade Fed activity. At times, the federal funds rate can trade at a spread to the Fed's target monetary policy rate due to technical factors in the excess reserves market. This was especially true in 2009, when an excess of funds from the agencies being lent out in the fed funds market kept the fed funds rate at 13 bps instead of the 25-bp target. The dislocation between the effective funds rate and the target rate arose from the fact that banks holding excess reserves at the Fed would get 25 bps as interest in reserves, but the agencies were not eligible to receive interest on reserves by law. When 25 bps were being paid in excess reserves, there was no incentive for banks to lend in the federal funds market below 25 bps. The excess cash at the agencies led them to lend out in the federal funds market at rates lower than the target, at around 13 bps rather than the 25-bp target. For fed funds futures, the probability of Fed activity was further muddled. The lesson here is that technical factors are always important to keep in mind before using futures to take views on the Fed.

The crisis of 2008 in particular brought the difference between fed funds futures and Eurodollar futures to the forefront. Banks' reluctance to lend unsecured funds due to credit fears or by their own desire to hoard liquidity led to a spike in 3M LIBOR. Because the fed funds rate is part of the Federal Reserve system and reflects the safety associated with the Fed, there was a flight away from lending unsecured in the LIBOR market, but there was no such flight from the fed funds market. To trade the spread between the fed funds rate and the 3M LIBOR rate, known colloquially as the LIBOR/OIS or LIBOR/funds spread, a trader could buy or sell fed funds futures and initiate the reverse trade with Eurodollar futures. However, fed funds futures contracts are monthly while Eurodollar futures are quarterly, which leads to three fed funds futures contracts versus one Eurodollar futures contract. This is an important point, especially in volatile times, when the difference between a one-month rate and a three-month rate can be very large in itself. We need to minimize risks that are not essential to the trade; in this case, such a risk is the difference between the fed funds rate and the 3M LIBOR rate, rather than the one-month/three-month spread risk.

The spread between the front Eurodollar contract and the first three fed funds futures rates reached an extreme level of nearly 200 bps in late 2008 after being on average 12 bps for years. Assuming markets are behaving normally and the spread is around 15 bps, the downside is perhaps 5 to 7 bps, but the upside could be considerable if there is a banking crisis.

Given the asymmetric nature of the spread, selling Eurodollar contracts and buying matched fed funds contracts offers a low downside way to position for a banking crisis.

FUTURES POSITIONING DATA

The U.S. futures markets are regulated by the Commodity Futures Trading Commission, and part of the regulatory framework requires exchanges to report on positions held by market participants on a weekly basis. In particular, for interest rate futures, at the time of this writing, positions are broken down into commercial and noncommercial accounts. Commercial accounts are supposed to represent accounts in the market for risk management purposes while noncommercial accounts represent those in the market for other purposes, such as speculation. The breakdown is not perfect; for example, a trader with a position in the basis involving buying Treasury bonds or notes and selling futures can arguably count as using futures for risk management or for speculation.

Though the breakdown is not perfect, as some institutions arguably are part of either grouping, the data does shed useful insight into market positioning as a whole. For example, watching noncommercial account positions across Treasury futures and Eurodollar futures can alert traders as to when markets are especially crowded. Since underlying cash Treasury position data is difficult to obtain, the futures contract positions can also indicate positioning in rates markets overall. A large contingent of longs or shorts can make it risky to add positions in the "popular" direction, as it is more susceptible than usual to disappointing news that may cause a rush to unwind. Figure 4.1 shows net long speculative positions (i.e., noncommercials) in the 2-year Treasury futures contract versus the 2-year Treasury yield on a concurrent basis. Although positioning data can offer useful clues, its importance is, at times, overvalued by both academics and market participants. Many times the positioning is merely a delayed reaction to market movement itself. For example, in the figure, as the 2-year yield increased sharply during summer 2009 (i.e., futures prices headed higher), speculative accounts increased their net longs chasing the market. It was only after the yields bottomed (i.e., prices peaked) that the short positions gave up and the trend turned. Notice that most of the positioning extremes coincide with yield peaks or troughs, rather than leading them, making it a mostly poor predictor. Although it is easy to decide in hindsight that a certain positioning extreme had been reached, at the pertinent time, positions and yields can trend for much longer than anyone expects. Indeed, it was difficult to deduce when the position was overcrowded during 2009

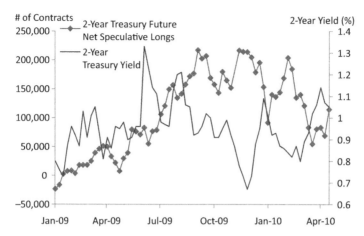

FIGURE 4.1   Net Speculative Longs in 2-Year Treasury Futures versus the 2-Year Treasury Yield
Sources: CFTC, Board of Governors of the Federal Reserve.

without the benefit of hindsight. An example of this is the first peak in net longs in September 2009, at which point it may have appeared that the trade was overcrowded. However, yields kept declining and net longs made yet another similar peak in November 2009 that actually turned out the bottom for yields at least until April 2010. In short, positioning data needs to be handled with care; nevertheless, it is an important factor to account for when deciding on trading positions to avoid entering extremely crowded trades.

SUMMARY

This chapter introduced the general idea behind futures products and the three main markets in the United States for trading interest rates. These products allow investors to take views on both short-term and long-run rates in the United States, and similar products exist for global fixed income markets. Each market has its own set of assumptions, and knowing these baseline features is key to effectively using these products to initiate trades.

CHAPTER 5

Interest Rate Swaps

T his chapter introduces another variation on the standard bond concept in the fixed income market: swaps. Swaps are one of the most ubiquitous financial derivatives around, encompassing markets as diverse as equities, commodities, and interest rates. In general, they are used to exchange one type of cash flow for another even if individual forms may differ across markets. For fixed income markets, swaps generalize the bond concept beyond a borrower and lender to interest payments of different types exchanged between any two parties. The most common swap in the rates space, referred to as a plain-vanilla swap, exchanges floating cash flows that vary based on the 3-month London Interbank Offered Rate (3M LIBOR) for fixed payments. One can imagine this as an exchange between parties: "You pay me 5 percent interest for the next two years, and I will pay you 3M LIBOR rate every three months for two years." The payer of the fixed rate may believe rates are about to rise; hence receiving floating makes sense. The receiver of the fixed rate may instead like the certainty of receiving fixed payments or may be confident that rates will not rise. The rates world was one of the earliest users of swaps, starting in the early 1980s to manage risks arising from floating rates. Over time, the use of swaps has expanded considerably to manage a wide range of risks and to speculate on interest rate movements. This chapter discusses the underlying principles in detail and considers numerous variations on the plain-vanilla structure that allow investors to express a variety of views on interest rates (also see Hull, 2006).

BASIC PRINCIPLES

The mechanics of a plain-vanilla interest rate swap are fairly straightforward and encompass five features:

1. The fixed leg of the swap is paid semiannually for the life of the swap. It is known as the swap rate for the maturity being considered.
2. The floating leg of the swap is linked to the 3M LIBOR rate. Each quarter, the 3M LIBOR rate is noted, and a floating payment is made at the end of the quarter based on it.
3. The present values (PVs) of the fixed and floating legs have to be equal at inception, or else one of the parties would not enter the swap. The swap rate for a certain maturity is the rate at which the fixed leg and floating legs have equal present value.
4. The swap is done against a dealer at a bank rather than on an exchange, making this an over-the-counter (OTC) product (more on this shortly).
5. The maturity of the swap can vary from the very short end to over 30 years.

These are the general characteristics of a plain-vanilla swap, but any can be changed with the consent of both parties. There are minor variations for swaps based on non-U.S. rates. Figure 5.1 shows the basic structure of a swap in visual form.

We encountered the floating leg of the swap in Chapter 4 as the underlying rate for the Eurodollar contract. Consider a single Eurodollar contract versus a swap with just one floating leg. The two assets have a very similar risk profile since they are both exposed to the 3M LIBOR risk. For Eurodollar futures, we also discussed stringing together multiple Eurodollar contracts to create a longer-dated asset, known as a strip. Now consider a strip of Eurodollars. In the case of the strip, the investor locks in the 3M LIBOR rates in the future. The investor is exposed to the 3M LIBOR rates at multiple points in the future—notice the similarity to the plain-vanilla swap. The similarity is not a coincidence. A plain-vanilla swap is a

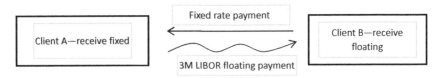

FIGURE 5.1 Basic Swap Diagram

generalization of the Eurodollar futures strip concept, creating a longer-dated fixed rate asset from a chain of smaller floating rate assets. Indeed, as with the strip rate, the fixed rate on an interest rate swap is a weighted average of forward 3M LIBOR rates. This interpretation implies that, when trading swaps, we are trading the market's average of forward short-term rates versus our own expectation of where the short-term interest rate cycle may end up. Another useful interpretation is to consider both legs as bonds themselves with the fixed leg as a fixed rate bond and the floating leg as a floating rate bond. The swap can then be seen as a transaction to exchange the returns of these two "bonds." Yet another way to think about a swap is to consider it as a fixed rate bond being financed at 3M LIBOR; that is, the repo rate for the hypothetical bond is 3M LIBOR. These concepts have theoretical nuances, but for day-to-day use they help build intuition and can help you grasp swap pricing.

How do we arrive at the fair value of the fixed rate for a swap? In the last list, point 3 mentioned that the fixed rate and floating rate sides should have equal present value *at inception*. Therefore, to determine the fixed rate, we need to consider the present values of both legs. For the floating rate leg, on a coupon payment date, the present value is par itself, that is, $100 for a $100 face "bond." To see why this is so, recall that the price of a fixed rate bond differs from par if interest rates move away from the fixed coupon it is paying. As interest rates rise, the fixed rate on a conventional bond becomes less attractive, leading the price lower, while lower market interest rates lead the price higher as the fixed coupon becomes more attractive. For a floating rate bond the coupon itself varies to exactly the market rate on coupon date. Therefore, on a coupon date, the floating rate bond is exactly equal in value to a fresh new fixed rate bond, which is at $100 or par. On a non–coupon date, the price needs to reflect the accrued interest up to that date. This adjustment would be necessary for a swap on a non–coupon payment date as well.

Now that we have the floating leg settled, we can calculate the fixed rate. For the fixed side of the swap, the present value is:

$$PV = (c/2)/(1+r_1/2)^1 + (c/2)/(1+r_2/2)^2 + \cdots + (c/2)/(1+r_n/2)^n$$
$$+ 100/(1+r_n/2)^n \qquad (5.1)$$

where c = fixed rate of the swap
r = zero-coupon discount rate for each fixed rate payment date

This formula should look familiar—it is the same as the bond pricing formula. The interest rates in the denominator here are the zero-coupon rates for the semiannual maturities, which we can arrive at through bootstrapping (explained in the next paragraph). This should be no surprise since the fixed leg resembles a bond with fixed coupon payments. The last term discounts a "principal" even though there is technically no principal exchange. The principal is included because we mentioned earlier that the floating leg has present value of par, but there are various alternative ways to arrive at a swap rate.

Once an on-market swap is initiated, the interest rate can vary and change the value of the swap. The cash flows are discounted at each maturity's zero rate, as described in Equation 5.1. To arrive at these zero rates, par rates from the market can be taken and reversed using bond pricing formulas; this process is known as bootstrapping. The intervals of the zero rates to calculate can be six months since that is generally the spacing between coupon payments. We can start with the shortest time frame rate, such as six months, and let that be the interest rate for that bond equal to the zero rate for that maturity. The 1-year discount rate can then be arrived at by solving for ZR_{1Y} in the next equation. For example,

$$(c/2)/(1 + ZR_{6M}/2) + (100 + c/2)/(1 + ZR_{1Y}/2)^2 = 100$$

where $ZR_{6M} = 6$-month zero rate
$ZR_{1Y} = 1$-year zero rate

Note that since c is the 1-year swap rate, the price of the bond is par (100), and we know ZR_{6M}, which then leads to ZR_{1Y}. Once ZR_{1Y} is known, we can calculate ZR_{18M} using the 18-month par rate. This way the entire set of zero rates and discount factors for different maturities can be calculated. These zero rates in turn can be used to discount cash flows and price a wide range of fixed income instruments. The discount factors can also be used to value existing swaps that are no longer new at par value. Discount curves can also be built using rates of instruments other than swaps, such as Treasuries, but swaps tend to have the most continuous curve and are not subject to idiosyncratic issue-specific risks. For example, Treasury bonds are not issued at equally spaced intervals, such as 10 years or 30 years, while the off-market rates can be influenced by varying financing rates and liquidity. Swap rates are not subject to these factors, which makes the discount curve smoother.

With the structure of valuation of both legs in hand, we can determine the swap rate. At inception, the present value of the floating leg is 100 and the fixed leg is Equation 5.1, leading to the equation:

$$100 = (c/2)/(1 + r_1/2)^1 + (c/2)/(1 + r_2/2)^2 + \cdots + (c/2)/(1 + r_n/2)^n$$
$$+ 100/(1 + r_n/2)^n \tag{5.2}$$

Equation 5.2 can be solved on a computer using relatively simple methods or even trial and error. The equation itself is a simple way to arrive at the swap rate, but it does not help us intuit what the swap rate actually is. Most of the time, as this book has stressed repeatedly, taking views on the market relies on having a firm understanding of the drivers and variable meanings rather than formulas for arriving at them.

To take a view that interest rates will rise, we would want to pay the fixed rate and hence receive floating. This way, if interest rates rise, we receive higher rates on the floating side and benefit from paying a fixed rate. Conversely, to take a view that interest rates will decline, we would receive fixed rates and pay floating. In market jargon, "receiving" or "going long" a swap refers to receiving fixed while "paying" or "going short" a swap refers to paying fixed. For the sake of safety, it is best to specify "receive fixed" or "pay fixed" when transacting. Once these views are taken, the profit or loss (P/L) on a swap requires the owner to calculate the PV of the fixed and floating legs using zero rates calculated from bootstrapping and take the difference. On inception day, this difference is zero; so any subsequent differences are P/L booked on the swap due to movements in interest rates and the resulting change in discount factors.

DURATION AND CONVEXITY

The concepts of duration and convexity for swaps resemble the calculation and logic for bonds. The fixed leg of the swap gains in value for a decrease in rates, which is very similar to the duration concept for a bond. The floating leg's duration is minimal since its PV stays at $100 for coupon payment dates. The duration of the floating leg is the time interval between payment dates, and so in the case of the common 3M LIBOR floating index, it is 0.25. Thus the duration of the swap is the duration of the fixed leg—0.25 in this case. The calculations are reversed if the investor is paying fixed; here the market convention is to call it "negative duration" as the swap benefits from rising rates rather than the usual falling rates. The dollar value of one basis point (DV01) defined for bonds in Chapter 2 is also applicable for swaps. For a swap at inception, DV01 is just the duration × 100 since the "price" of a swap initially is par. The convexity concept in swaps is also similar to that of bonds. Receiving a swap is akin to buying a bond. The discounting of the fixed payments creates positive convexity, as with buying a bond. The floating side has minimal convexity. Due to the symmetric nature of a swap, paying fixed in a swap has negative convexity.

Finally, duration can help approximate the P/L on a swap position. As with bonds, the approximate change in value of a swap is duration × yield change in fixed leg. If the yield declines, the P/L is positive for the receiver and negative for the payer. To improve on this approximation, the convexity correction can be added as well, which, as in the case of bonds, is:

$$\tfrac{1}{2} \times \text{convexity} \times (\text{change in yield})^2$$

The convexity correction is especially needed for days with large yield changes, where "large" is defined as the convexity adjustment being larger than the market bid/offer spread on the swap. The duration method and the convexity correction are both approximations for quick calculations. In general, if the cumulative P/L on a swap position is needed over a longer period of time, the swap position PV should be calculated on a daily basis and P/L should be calculated as the change in that PV. Although this method is more cumbersome, the small errors on a daily basis can add up to significant amounts in a cumulative P/L calculation.

USES OF SWAPS

Interest rate swaps are one of the most liquid financial products, mainly due to their wide range of uses among investors. Their flexibility, which partly stems from their OTC nature, allows them to be tailor made for investors seeking to offset interest rate risk and for speculators in the interest rate space. We highlight some of the uses of swaps here and discuss some of these uses in more detail in later chapters.

One of the original motivations behind swaps was to take advantage of pricing differences between floating rate and fixed rate instruments. To understand this, suppose a corporate bond issuer issues a 5-year floating rate bond at 3M LIBOR rate + 25 basis points (denoted as L + 25 in the market); that is, the rate paid each quarter is 3M LIBOR + 25 bps. Assume also that the 5-year swap rate is 4% and that the issuer wishes to convert the bond into a fixed rate bond so that it does not face the risk of interest rates rising. The issuer here is paying a floating rate to investors; to "cancel" this cash flow, the issuer would pay fixed and receive floating, thus changing the debt profile to a fixed rate payment. Figure 5.2 shows the canceling-out effect.

Notice that we added 25 bps to both the floating and the fixed legs of the swap to keep them evenly matched, which also allows the issuer to completely cancel out the floating rate payment, leaving only a fixed rate payment. The fixed rate payment ends up being the 5-year swap rate + 25 bps = 4% + 25 bps = 4.25%. The issuer has essentially converted the floating rate debt issue into a fixed rate debt issue and now does not need to

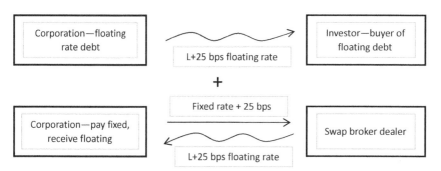

FIGURE 5.2 Debt Swap by Corporation

worry about the risk of rising interest payments on the debt. Such actions also help to keep the floating rate and fixed rate markets aligned.

Swaps link the fixed rate and floating rate markets for issuers, but this use of the product is not limited to just issuers. One of the most common trades in the interest rate space is to asset-swap bonds, which essentially converts them into floating rate instruments. To understand this, consider a bond investor who is receiving 4% fixed on a par bond but wishes to eliminate interest rate risk by converting the bond into a floating rate asset. Asset swapping is similar to what issuers do with swapping debt but is performed by investors. The bond buyer pays fixed in a swap of the same maturity and matches the coupon payments of the bond by adjusting both legs of the swap by an equal amount. Interest payments are canceled out by the pay-fixed swap position, which leaves the floating rate payment + (the swap fixed rate – bond yield). The latter difference is, not surprisingly, known as an asset swap spread. The example would be reversed if the investor was short the bond, in which case she would receive fixed in the swap, but the underlying mechanics would be very similar. Notice the similarities between this case and the previous example of the issuer converting the floating rate to the fixed rate. Finally, although the more rigorous way to asset-swap a bond is to match the coupons and cancel them out, many times investors initiate simpler trades of just matching maturities of the swap and bond. Specifically, investors would own a 5-year bond and pay fixed in a 5-year swap with no adjustments to the fixed and floating swap legs. The simple maturity match leaves a mismatch, as it does not entirely cancel the coupon payments—however, if the coupons are similar, this is rarely a major issue. These types of swaps, known as matched maturity swaps, are used extensively to swap Treasury bonds. For this case, the spread is known as a matched-maturity swap spread and can be considered almost an asset class of its own due to its unique drivers. We discuss Treasury matched-maturity spreads in detail in Chapter 9.

Swaps are used extensively to manage duration risks for large portfolios. This is partly because their OTC nature and lack of up-front notionals make them a convenient way to initiate large interest-rate trades. Another important reason is that swaps are not "issued," but instead created as a contract. They can be created for any maturity with equal effort; thus, unlike Treasuries, there do not need to be special benchmark points (although traders may occasionally refer to certain swap points as benchmarks, as they are widely tracked). This in turn allows swaps to offset risk for products with nonstandard maturities more effectively and is especially useful for products where durations change frequently, such as mortgages. For a bond portfolio, receiving in a swap increases the DV01 of the portfolio—that is, the sensitivity of the portfolio to interest rates—without taking up any up-front cash. Managers then have the flexibility to use funds to invest in other securities. For a manager wishing to cut the interest rate risk of a portfolio, paying fixed rates in a swap is negative duration and decreases the portfolio DV01. We discuss the use of swaps for managing interest rate risk further in Chapter 8.

These methods are instances of swaps being used to manage interest rate risk, but the structure of swaps also makes them ideal for speculating on interest rates. As mentioned, paying fixed on a swap benefits from an increase in rates, while receiving fixed on a swap benefits from a decrease in rates. The reader may be wondering why not to just take an interest rate view using Treasuries. While Treasuries are very liquid and are used widely to speculate on rates, swaps offer three benefits over Treasuries.

1. Swaps do not require any up-front notional, and unlike Treasuries, an investor does not need to transact in the repo markets to borrow or lend Treasuries to buy them on a levered basis. A swap comes with the 3M LIBOR funding in a packaged form.

2. A swap does not have the benchmark maturity constraints that Treasury bonds do, leading to a richer set of variables to take views on including spreads between rates.

3. Swaps for a given maturity do not face special financing issues or liquidity variations that can alter valuations.

One drawback to swaps is that they are transacted against banks rather than the U.S. government issuer, as in the case of Treasuries. Because of this, swaps have slightly greater risk than Treasuries. Most of the time, this risk factor is not pertinent because the differences in credit risk tend to be minor, but in crisis periods, when the health of banks is in question, the bank-credit risks embedded in swaps become important and need to be factored in before entering a trade.

COUNTERPARTY RISK

Unlike futures contracts, which have a clearinghouse between trades (discussed in Chapter 4), currently swaps are transacted directly against another firm, known as a counterparty. Markets that use a direct counterparty rather than a clearinghouse are known as OTC and a range of derivatives markets beyond interest rate swaps also fall under this category. Because they are derivative transactions, swaps are structured as an exchange of cash flows with no up-front notional amount exchanged. (Exceptions are considered later in this chapter.) As with futures contracts, there may be payments for initial and variation margin, but swaps do not have the standardized rules of an exchange. Their OTC nature means details such as margin requirements can be negotiated with the trade counterparty. Nonetheless, the contracts do share some common principles, known as ISDA (International Swap Dealer Association) specifications. OTC markets have both beneficial and risky aspects. They allow more flexibility in trading for investors than future contracts. Modifications to features can be easily introduced and a swap of any maturity is created equally easily. These features make swaps an efficient way to manage interest rate risk or to speculate on rates. The lack of a clearinghouse does have its downside, given that each party is exposed to the risk that the other may default on cash-flow payments. Mostly this default risk is not significant because the market is composed of institutions rather than individuals. However, the Lehman Brothers bankruptcy in late 2008 brought counterparty risk to the forefront with widespread disruptions to OTC markets from Lehman's default. Indeed, due to the opaque nature of one-on-one contract arrangements, it was difficult to assess the true scope of these counterparty risks, leading to fears of a domino of bankruptcies. As a result, the swaps market is evolving toward clearinghouse mechanisms already present in futures contracts to ensure greater transparency in the future. The addition of a clearinghouse to the swaps market is designed to reduce counterparty risk, but likely with some modifications designed to retain its flexibility. The hope is to add some benefits of futures exchanges without discarding all the positives of the current OTC system. Whether this balance will be achieved remains to be seen as the impact of changing regulations will be felt for years to come.

OTHER TYPES OF SWAPS

The interest rate swap introduced above is the standard variety. In general, the concept of a swap can be extended in numerous ways, especially given how easy swaps are to modify. There are a wide range of swaps across the interest rate space designed to package different forms of risk for investors. Instead of the specific details on the various swaps, the key points to focus on are the various types of risk exposure the swaps offer investors. The liquidity for these alternatives varies considerably and can drop sharply during generally illiquid periods in markets. We consider a few important alternatives next.

The first type of alternative swap we consider is the overnight index swap (OIS). These are fairly liquid in Europe, and in the United States their liquidity has improved more recently. The simplest way to think about an OIS is as a swap with the floating index altered to the overnight federal funds rate, the rate at which banks trade their excess reserves at the Federal Reserve (see Chapters 3 and 4). The other leg of the swap is fixed. As with any swap, the fixed rate here is again the rate that equates the PV of the fixed and floating legs. The floating payments can be structured to be monthly or quarterly based on the average fed funds rate for that period, since daily payments would be quite cumbersome. With less standard swaps like the OIS, the basic features can vary at times with the transaction and make it more difficult to deduce a "common" structure. In the fed funds swap, since the effective funds rate is an overnight rate, the floating payment is generally made on a quarterly average; the choice of various compounding methods depends on counterparty preference. Figure 5.3 shows a fed funds swap in visual form; notice the similarity with the LIBOR swap shown in Figure 5.1.

The second type of alternative structure is the cross-currency swap. As the name implies, cross-currency swaps are agreements where each side makes payments in different currencies. The payment types are very customizable. Both sides can be fixed legs, floating legs, or one of each with the two legs denominated in different currencies. Given the large size of the market, cross-currency swaps provide a liquid way for investors to manage currency risk. One feature that makes cross-currency swaps stand out is that notionals are exchanged at the beginning and exchanged back at the end of the swap. To make this concrete, suppose issuer A has issued 1-year debt in dollars at a 4% fixed rate and wants to convert his dollar liability into euro liability because of regulatory and valuation reasons. Issuer

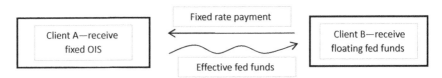

FIGURE 5.3 Fed Funds Swap

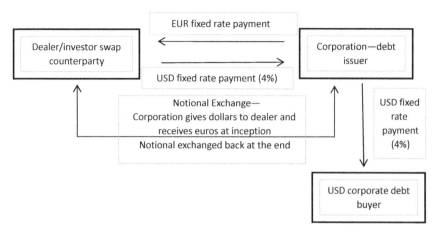

FIGURE 5.4 Graphical Depiction of a Cross-Currency Swap

A can then use a cross-currency swap to achieve this goal. Suppose bank B is willing to do such a swap. The cross-currency swap would resemble the diagram shown in Figure 5.4. Here, initially, the issuer pays the bank the dollar amount of the loan and receives this notional amount in Euros at the foreign exchange rate at inception of the transaction. Subsequently, the issuer receives dollar interest payments from the bank on the delivered notional amount and pays interest in euros for one year. At the end of the transaction, the notionals are reexchanged at the original exchange rate, which ensures that neither party is exposed to foreign exchange risk. With the issuer receiving interest payments in dollars, the issuer's payments on the initial dollar debt are canceled using the swap, leaving only the euro interest payments. The euro interest payment by the issuer resembles debt issuance in euro currency. In the example, both legs of the cross-currency swap are fixed legs, but there is total flexibility, as one or both of the legs can be floating. We return to the last case for cross-currency swaps shortly.

When both legs of a swap are floating, the swap is referred to as a basis swap. Basis swaps are ubiquitous throughout financial markets and have a great deal of variety even in the fixed income space. Just about any two floating rates can be combined into a basis swap, but liquidity is likely to be poor for customized transactions. However, some common forms are more widely traded; these are described next.

Fed Funds Basis Swap

A fed funds basis swap exchanges the two most commonly referred to floating rates in the U.S. market: the overnight effective fed funds rate and

FIGURE 5.5   LIBOR/Funds OIS Swap

3M LIBOR. Note that this swap should not be confused with the OIS swap introduced earlier, where there is only a single floating index, the effective funds rate versus a fixed rate. In contrast, the basis swap has two distinct floating indices. The payment conventions can vary, but for a quarterly payment interval, the fed funds rate can be averaged, as seen in other examples. The swap maturity can range from a few months to a few years and for any maturity. The fed funds rate, as mentioned earlier, tends to be lower than the 3M LIBOR rate. Therefore, exchanging fed funds for 3M LIBOR over a period of time with no adjustments is unlikely to result in equal present value for both legs. Notice that for all swaps, we keep referring back to the concept of equating present value at inception; if this were not the case, one of the parties would not consent to the swap. For the fed funds basis swap, then, the 3M LIBOR leg needs to be adjusted lower by a certain amount to equate the present values. This value is known as the *LIBOR/funds spread* for the maturity we are considering. The diagram in Figure 5.5 visually displays the workings of a fed funds basis swap.

The LIBOR/funds spread—or, for that matter, any basis swap spread—is the market's expectation of the average difference between the floating rate quantities being considered. The pricing and trading of this spread is driven by the market's expectations of the weighted average of each side of the swap over its lifetime. If the market expects funding stress to continue over the life of the swap, the 3M LIBOR leg will incorporate a greater spread over the fed funds leg to reflect the riskier/unsecured nature of LIBOR lending. Thus, fed funds swaps are a very direct way to position for higher (or lower) banking system stress. In "good" times, the spread can also have asymmetric payoffs. Three-month LIBOR tends to trade at least 8 to 10 bps over fed funds, given the lower credit characteristic of interbank lending. Therefore, if spreads are at historically low levels, investors can use long-maturity basis swaps to position for banking stress at a later date while having limited downside. Note that trading fed funds futures versus Eurodollar futures (discussed in Chapter 4) is an alternative way to position for banking crises. Using futures markets versus OTC-basis swap markets presents the usual trade-off between greater transparency in futures markets versus more customization in swaps markets. Furthermore, for longer tenors the fed funds futures market is not too liquid, leaving fed funds basis swaps as the only choice in that case.

Three-Month/Six-Month or One-Month/Three-Month Basis Swaps

Three-month/six-month (3M/6M) or one-month/three-month (1M/3M) basis swaps exchange one LIBOR tenor for another on a floating basis. Recall that each day, a range of LIBOR maturities is published by the British Bankers' Association starting from overnight up to 1-year LIBOR. The 3M/6M basis swap exchanges floating 3M LIBOR for floating 6M LIBOR while the 1M/3M basis swap exchanges 1M LIBOR floating for 3M LIBOR floating. As with the fed funds basis swaps, each of these will have some adjustment, which is generally applied to the 3M leg and is referred to as the 3M/6M basis or 1M/3M basis. Such swaps, although not very liquid, can present interesting opportunities to take views on bank lending fears, as in such situations banks are more likely to lend for shorter terms, or for taking views on a liquidity glut at the short end, which would force funds to extend out to longer maturities.

Cross-Currency Basis Swaps

We mentioned cross-currency swaps earlier; cross-currency basis swaps are the variant where both sides use a floating rate denominated in a different currency. One example of a cross-currency basis swap could be exchanging floating 3M LIBOR for floating 3-month Euribor (3M Euro Interbank Offered Rate; the European version of LIBOR used in euro swaps) for a year. In this swap, the two PVs should be equal when discounted on their own respective curves, but, at times, this is not enough. Specifically, if there is a shortage of one of the currencies, such as dollars, the notional exchange up front becomes a more difficult proposition. If dollars are in short supply, the party sending away dollars can demand a higher rate than the one implied purely by PV considerations, while the party receiving the dollars would be willing to accept a much lower interest rate on the foreign currency loaned out. The basis here is an example of how technical factors, when taken to extremes, can and do drive markets far from efficiency. During the 2008 crisis, as European banks were starved of dollar funding for the large amount of dollar-denominated assets they held, the cross-currency basis between euros and U.S. dollars increased sharply to account for handing over dollars in notional exchange.

Constant Maturity Basis Swaps

Constant maturity swaps (CMSs) also fall under the broader class of basis swaps. Here, one of the floating legs payments is referenced off 3M LIBOR every quarter as usual, but the other side is a swap rate referenced at some fixed interval. To clarify, consider a CMS swap with a 2-year maturity and having the 10-year swap rate as a floating, quarterly index. In this swap, the investor would pay the prevailing 3M LIBOR rate every quarter and would receive the *prevailing* 10-year swap rate every quarter for 2 years. In a regular fixed-floating swap, the 10-year rate is fixed based on the inception value but subsequently ages as the swap ages and ceases to be a "true" 10-year rate after the first day. In a CMS swap, the floating rate being referenced is always a current 10-year rate and there is no aging effect, which also helps explain the derivation of the term *constant maturity*. To equate the PV of the swaps on both sides, the 3M LIBOR rate is adjusted by a spread, known as a CMS spread, which can be one way to quote these swaps. Also, as with all basis swaps with a 3M LIBOR floating index on one side, a plain-vanilla swap can be overlaid to create one fixed leg. CMS swaps are not particularly liquid, although at times they can present interesting trading opportunities.

SIFMA/LIBOR Ratio Swaps and SIFMA Swaps

Securities Industry and Financial Markets Association (SIFMA)/LIBOR swaps are used in the municipal bond market as a way to manage risks between municipal (muni) and taxable bonds. As explained in Chapter 3, in the muni market, interest payments are tax-exempt; interest payments from other markets are taxable at the income tax rate (informally referred to as taxable yields). The SIFMA swap (formerly known as Bond Market Association[BMA]/LIBOR swap) has two floating components: The first is, as usual, 3M Libor, and the second is the SIFMA money market yield. SIFMA is computed weekly as an average of high-grade short-term muni market note yields. Since SIFMA represents a tax-exempt interest rate and, in the United States, top marginal tax rates are around 35% to 40% at the time of this writing, it tends to trade lower than 3M LIBOR. To equate the PV on both sides of the swap, the 3M LIBOR leg requires an adjustment. Instead of an additive spread, 3M LIBOR is multiplied by a ratio. This ratio is chosen to equate the PV of both legs in the swap, and it is how the SIFMA/LIBOR swap is quoted in the market. The ratio stays fixed for the life of the swap and can be thought of intuitively as the market's expectation for average top marginal tax rates over the tenor of the swap. The actual payments do vary since the 3M LIBOR and SIFMA legs are both floating. Figure 5.6 shows the swap in visual form.

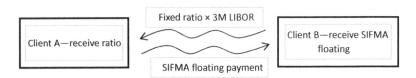

FIGURE 5.6 SIFMA/LIBOR Swap Graphical Depiction

As with other basis swaps, the SIFMA/LIBOR swap matures after a fixed time period, known as the tenor. If the investor is receiving the SIFMA leg and paying the 3M LIBOR leg, this is known as paying the ratio. Paying the SIFMA payments and receiving the 3M LIBOR payments is known as receiving the ratio. This convention may seem confusing, but it is designed to make ratios equivalent to the fixed leg in a plain-vanilla swap. If an investor is receiving ratios in a SIFMA/LIBOR swap, lower ratios imply that she is receiving a higher percentage of 3M LIBOR (as per the fixed ratio at inception) compared to the rest of the market. Conversely, paying ratios results in positive P/L if market ratios head higher, as now the investor is locked into paying a lower fixed ratio at inception than the market. This way, ratio conventions equate to the pay/receive fixed conventions for plain-vanilla swaps. The P/L on the basis swap stems from changes in the ratio in the market for the remaining maturity of the swap; as with other swaps, the payments on both sides of the swap need to be present valued using forward LIBOR rates and the ratio for each forward point.

If, instead of both floating legs, a fixed leg swap is desired to hedge municipal bond exposure, the SIFMA/LIBOR swap can be combined with a plain-vanilla LIBOR swap to arrive at the desired structure. Figure 5.7 shows this process of taking a certain notional of a SIFMA/LIBOR swap and combining it with a fixed-floating LIBOR swap to exactly cancel out the 3M LIBOR leg. The plain-vanilla LIBOR swap notional should be the ratio of the 3M LIBOR trading in the market; this ratio-adjusted notional ensures that the 3M LIBOR floating leg on the plain-vanilla swap cancels out the

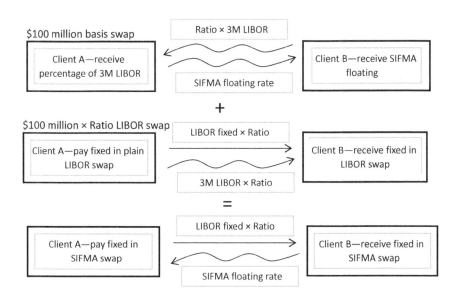

FIGURE 5.7 Converting a SIFMA/LIBOR Swap to a Fixed/Floating BMA Swap

payments of ratio × 3M LIBOR in the basis swap. As the diagram shows, this requires adjusting both legs of the LIBOR swap with the market ratio in the SIFMA/LIBOR swap market. This way, the 3M LIBOR legs drop out and a new swap, known as a SIFMA swap (or formerly a BMA swap) is left over, which has a fixed leg and *floating SIFMA* instead of floating 3M LIBOR. The diagram should also make it clear that the fixed rate on the SIFMA swap, known as the SIFMA rate, ends up being the ratio for the maturity × LIBOR swap rate for the maturity. This swap is supposed to be more closely linked to the tax-exempt market since the fixed rate here is the expected tax-exempt floating rate over the life of the swap in the same way that the fixed rate in a plain-vanilla swap is the expectation of floating 3M LIBOR over a forward basis. Unlike the SIFMA/LIBOR ratio swap, where both legs are floating, the fixed rate leg in the SIFMA swap adds tax-exempt yield risk to the package, not just the ratio between the two markets. Given the fixed rate exposure, the SIFMA swap can be used to offset interest rate exposure for municipal bonds under certain conditions. SIFMA swaps can also be used to convert fixed rate muni obligations to floating rate or vice versa, as with LIBOR swaps for corporate debt.

SIFMA/LIBOR ratio swaps of different maturities tend to have different ratios associated with them, which form a ratio curve akin to a yield curve. The short end of the ratio curve is driven first and foremost by the top marginal tax rate. Given a top tax rate of 40%, for example, the SIFMA rate *should* clear 60% of the 3M LIBOR rate. However, the actual rate can vary significantly from this baseline calculation for a few reasons, including seasonality, such as SIFMA rising in April just before taxes are due as individuals withdraw money from tax-exempt money market funds for tax bills. Similar effects take place around various corporate tax payment dates. Another reason for divergence can be changes in the basket of short-term municipal notes that are used to arrive at the SIFMA average.

Beyond the 1-year tenor, the ratio curve is mostly driven on a macro level by some of the same factors described for the muni yield curve, such as yield levels, the yield curve, and, most importantly, perceived future tax rates and uncertainty around these tax rates (although large variations in spot SIFMA can still have an impact). The ratio curve can differ from the cash muni/LIBOR ratio curve (i.e., muni bond yields/swap rate for a given maturity), which is essentially the municipal market's version of the swap spread. Some features of the SIFMA/LIBOR ratio swaps and their relation to muni bond market ratios are:

1. The SIFMA/LIBOR ratio swap and municipal bonds are linked to the extent that interest rate risk is the main driver of risk. If, instead, credit concerns overtake longer-term munis, a divergence occurs since the SIFMA swap has the risk of short-term SIFMA dislocations and the

risk of the bank counterparty with which the swap is transacted. On the other hand, the SIFMA swap will not be able to incorporate the risk of default from specific municipalities. If credit risk among municipal bonds rises, there can be divergence in their valuations.

2. If liquidity is very low, investors may penalize cash muni bonds by a greater amount since it can be difficult to buy or sell actual bonds, and it may be easier to transact in the ratio swap market.

3. Given the relatively higher quality of munis, if investors are desperate to raise funds during periods of stress, they can sell munis and other assets that hold their value.

4. SIFMA/LIBOR ratio swap valuations can face disconnects from the municipal cash curve due to hedging flows from issuers or investors.

Inflation Swaps

As SIFMA swaps are swap counterparts to the municipal market, inflation swaps are the swap counterparts to the Treasury Inflation-Protected Securities (TIPS) market. As with TIPS, inflation swaps provide protection against inflation risk. This protection is provided without the need to purchase actual issued TIPS bonds; instead, inflation swaps represent a contract between a dealer bank and the institution buying/selling the swap. Inflation swaps are far less liquid than plain-vanilla swaps, and currently few standardized terms are associated with them. That said, inflation swaps most commonly are zero-coupon swaps. The fixed leg of the swap assumes compounding the initial notional at a certain inflation rate while the floating leg of the swap is headline Consumer Price Index (CPI), as with the TIPS bond. The CPI on the floating leg is compounded at a fixed interval, and, at maturity, the residual cash flows between floating and fixed legs can be exchanged. For example, investors receiving CPI and paying fixed would wish for the inflation rate to outpace the fixed inflation rate they are paying. Conversely, traders paying CPI and receiving fixed would instead wish for inflation to decline. The CPI calculation terms are generally equated with TIPS to reduce confusion between the products, but the typical inflation swap structure does not have an embedded floor. This means that unlike with a TIPS bond, in inflation swaps, traders receiving CPI can incur negative P/L over the life of the swap if the inflation rate ends up being negative (see also Chapter 3 on TIPS). The risk of negative inflation over reasonably long tenors has been very low in the United States in the past, although that of course says nothing about the future. Finally, inflation swaps also give rise to trades between TIPS and maturity-matched inflation swaps, known as TIPS asset swaps. Given the relatively small size of the TIPS market, these asset swaps have been driven primarily by liquidity conditions; in particular, the 2008 credit crunch led to a sharp underperformance of TIPS versus inflation swaps as it was very difficult for dealers to hold TIPS in inventory for long periods of time, which led to selling at discounted prices. As conditions improved, the situation reversed, and TIPS asset swaps became an effective way to position for a normalization of liquidity in financial markets.

The swaps just discussed are some of the variety of products investors have to take views on the range of interest rates in the market. Most are either fixed rate swaps with varied floating indices or, in the case of basis swaps, two distinct floating indices. The pricing of each type of swap arises from present valuing of both sets of cash flows. In a basis swap, this may entail adding a spread to one of the floating legs; in a swap with a fixed rate, the fixed rate itself is solved for.

SUMMARY

This chapter introduced swaps for fixed income markets that allow investors to manipulate cash flows in a variety of ways to express views on interest rates or offset risks stemming from interest rate transactions. The plain-vanilla swap allows investors to take the side of a floating or fixed rate. A variety of other swaps allow investors to express views across interest rates, currencies, or tax rates. Regardless of variety, most fixed income swaps have similar underlying principles. Keeping these basic principles in mind enables the use of appropriate types of swaps to express a particular market view.

CHAPTER 6

Understanding Drivers of Interest Rates

S o far we have considered the mechanics of interest rate products such as Treasuries and swaps. Once we understand the mechanics of interest rates products, we can use them to take views on interest rates across maturities and markets. This chapter considers the thought process behind forming views on interest rates that can be implemented using the rate products discussed. Before we consider where interest rates may be headed, we must clarify what is meant by the term "interest rates." Instead of any particular maturity, we will consider the entire yield curve when trying to understand interest rate movements. By forming views on the yield curve, we consider both the level of rates and the shape of the curve as related concepts. Yield curve trades can be initiated in any fixed income market, such as swaps or Agency debt, but the starting point is to consider Treasuries as the baseline risk-free rate. Other rates can be considered as the combination of a Treasury rate and an additional spread to the Treasury rate. For example:

5-year swap yield = 5-year Treasury yield + (5-year swap yield

− 5-year Treasury yield).

The second part of the equation—5-year swap yield − 5-year Treasury yield—is referred to as a swap spread and can be thought of as an asset of its own with separate drivers. A view on fixed income markets other than Treasuries can then be formulated as the base Treasury interest rate view as well as the incremental spread view. For example, if both the interest rate view and spread view are compelling in the same direction, the spread product will be a better instrument to express the view in question. Here we consider the factors that drive the base Treasury yield curve itself. We consider some spreads, such as swap spreads, separately in later chapters.

SUPPLY AND DEMAND FOR BORROWING

Interest rates form the clearing level between the supply and demand of credit. As the forces of supply and demand change, so do interest rates to bring the credit markets back to equilibrium. To understand what may drive rates, we need to understand both sides of the demand/supply equation. Each side of the equation has its own motivations and risk factors for transacting at each rate. First we will consider the factors that affect long-term interest rate cycles on both the demand and supply sides.

For the demand side, the driving factors stem from the risks involved in owning the asset. As perceptions of these risks change, so does the valuation of the asset itself. This general principle will guide our thought process in forming views on rates. For a debt holder, the first major risk is a lack of savings to fund repayment of principal when the time to maturity arrives. For high-grade bonds, such as the U.S. government debt we consider here, the repayment risk is a minuscule one and generally not considered in valuations. For a Treasury bond holder, the major risk to the investment is the erosion of value of the coupon payments and the principal through price increases. The economic term for price increases is *inflation,* while price decreases are referred to as *deflation.* Since the coupon and principal stay fixed for fixed rate bonds, increasing prices of goods and services in the economy essentially lower the value of future cash flows (consider the value of $100 today versus its value 50 years ago). If inflation is high, bond holders will demand higher interest rates to compensate for the possible loss of value. If deflation takes hold, the value of the future cash flows actually increases, making the Treasury instrument more valuable. For the buyer of a fixed rate instrument, the current coupon payment is a small percentage of the total value of the bond—most of the risk in the bond is from the risk of erosion of value of the future cash flows. Therefore, it is the expectation of *future* inflation that is most relevant as a factor, rather than the current rate. Essentially, inflation expectations are a driver of the demand for debt.

What drives inflation expectations? There are a number of factors for an investor to consider when assessing the inflation risk in a government bond. The economic cycle is intimately linked to investor perceptions of inflation. The dynamic between the economic cycle and inflation expectations is complex and can be affected in numerous ways. The simple story goes like this: As economic growth heats up, firms increase production to meet increasing demand. As production increases, the utilization of existing capacity increases, leading to demands for wage increases as labor becomes scarce. Wage increases induce price increases of goods, which in turn lead to further wage increases, causing a chain reaction. Due to this chain reaction, consumers and workers expect prices to rise in the future, which increases *expectations* of inflation in the future. The level of current economic growth that may lead to inflation depends on a concept known as the potential growth rate of the economy. The potential growth rate of the economy is a vague idea encompassing education level, technological progress, and productivity. The higher the potential growth, the faster the economy can grow without triggering inflation. Another way to think about potential growth is that it is the capacity of the economy—the more investments in an economy toward education and technology, the higher the growth rates it can sustain. Since potential growth rate determines the balance between growth and inflation, it acts as a very-long-term fair value level for interest rates. However, the potential growth rate is not a useful quantity for trading, as it is largely a theoretical construct; instead it is meant to be a starting point for understanding long-term rate cycles.

Given that the potential growth rate of an economy is difficult to deduce, it is not surprising that current conditions are an important factor in forming future expectations. Indeed, if the current economic situation continues to experience high inflation, the expectation of rising prices in the future may become embedded in the economy as people demand higher wages and businesses charge higher prices. These embedded expectations can be self-fulfilling prophecies that are difficult to undo and can lead to runaway realized inflation. This was the dynamic that led to increasing inflation in the late 1970s in the United States. Subsequently, as inflation expectations rose, so did the rates demanded by bond investors to compensate for deterioration of their fixed rate payments. As Figure 6.1 shows, 10-year U.S. Treasury rates reached nearly 16% in the early 1980s in response to the high inflation rates at the time.

An important component in the link between economic growth and inflation is the increase in the utilization of capacity as the economy grows, leading to increasing wages and prices. Indeed, increasing economic growth tends to lead to rate increases as investors demand a higher rate for the higher chance of inflation in the future, while reduced economic growth periods such as recessions lead to lower rates. Figure 6.2 shows the Institute for Supply Management (ISM) index, which is a forward-looking indicator of the economy versus interest rates over the past two decades. As industrial production rises, so do interest rates as the demand for borrowing increases from firms and households and as buyers of debt demand higher fixed rates to protect against possible

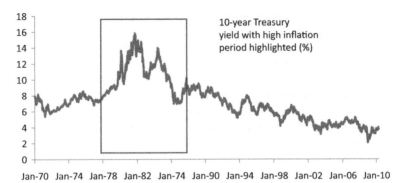

FIGURE 6.1   10-Year Treasury Yield over Time, including the High Inflation Period of the Early 1980s
Source: Board of Governors of the Federal Reserve.

inflation. However, not all episodes of economic growth necessarily lead to a cycle of increasing prices and wages, given that the level of capacity can be different for varying economic environments. Furthermore, an external influence such as the Federal Reserve can step in to slow down economic growth before the cycle of increasing wages and prices takes hold. We will discuss the influence of the Fed on the economy in subsequent sections. Over the long term, the potential growth of the economy itself can increase for a few reasons. For example, innovation can increase the capacity, and thus the potential growth rate of the economy. This was the case during the

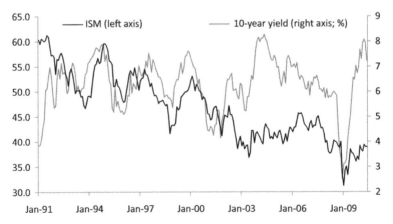

FIGURE 6.2   ISM Manufacturing Index and the 10-Year Treasury Yield
Source: Federal Reserve Bank of St. Louis.

technology boom in the 1990s as increasing productivity led to increases in potential growth of the economy. As potential growth increases, so does the ability of the economy to grow faster without leading to pressures of wage increases. This was one of many reasons increasing economic growth in the 1990s did not cause the same wage/price spirals as occurred in the 1970s. Technology may not be the only cause of increasing capacity in the economy without causing inflation. Another is an exogenous increase in the labor pool, which lowers the cost of labor and can prevent wage price increases. An indirect way this happened in the 1990s and 2000s was the rise of China and other emerging market (EM) nations, which provided an increased labor pool and again lowered the pressure of wages to rise in response to higher economic growth. In these cases, the introduction of new technology or an increased labor pool allowed the economy to grow at a higher rate without causing pressures for wage increases. However, not all cases are as optimistic. The reverse can also be true; even without economic growth, inflation pressures can build due to exogenous price shocks and a low potential growth rate. This situation, known as stagflation, was also present in the 1970s. At the time, even periods of low economic growth led to rising prices as costs of basic resources increased due to oil price increases. The link between economic growth and inflation expectations is close but can be present in numerous ways. Since the link between economic growth and inflation is tenuous, the reaction of interest rate markets to increasing growth can vary considerably.

The reverse dynamic can also play out with regard to economic growth and inflation. Declining economic growth, except in cases of stagflation, can lead to decreasing prices and wages. Such a dynamic is known as deflation and generally is seen in prolonged slumps, such as the Great Depression in the United States or in Japan since the 1990s. In such a situation, consumers hold off spending due to economic uncertainty and the prospect of lower prices later, while firms reduce production in response. These environments of low growth can sharply decrease required interest rates on fixed income instruments as declining prices increase the value of fixed payments in the future and expectations of future inflation recede. Indeed, as Figure 6.3 shows, Japanese government bond yields decreased and stayed low over the past two decades in response to such deflationary effects. In either case, economic growth has a close connection to inflation expectations and understanding the link between the two is an important first step for forming views on interest rates.

We discussed how cycles of increasing investment by firms to increase production and increasing consumption by individuals can lead to expectations of increasing prices. However, the other components of economic growth, such as government spending, can also cause increasing inflation expectations. The government sector has received more attention recently

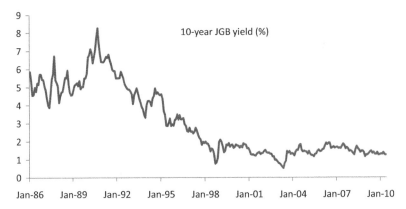

FIGURE 6.3 10-Year Japanese Government Bond Yield and Its Decline due to Deflation
Source: Bank of Japan.

as government expenditures rose in response to increasing demands for social welfare programs and for government intervention in economic downturns. The first group of spending increases comprises structural government spending mostly unrelated to the state of the economy; the second group of increases is cyclical, rising and falling due to the economy. Excessive government spending can overheat the economy just as excess production from firms can, and it can have other effects on the private sector. As government spending rises, the increasing amount of debt the government needs to take on also crowds out private sector debt, leading to interest rate increases. If government expenditures rise too rapidly, inflation expectations can rise among both consumers and producers, leading to a spiral of rising prices and interest rates. Such spirals have been seen historically, especially in the case of the Weimar Republic in Germany after World War I, when crushing war debts led to increasing the printing of money to pay the debts. As the supply of money increased in the economy, prices increased and inflation expectations kept rising, leading to inflation rates that reached stratospheric levels. Although this was an extreme case, excessive government spending can pressure economic growth higher and lead to increases in inflation.

The long-term demand for borrowing by various economic entities can be aggregated and generalized as the *leverage cycle*. The term *leverage* refers to the amount of debt versus assets of either an individual or the economy as an aggregate. The leverage cycle is punctuated by periods of rising aggregate borrowing followed by periods of decreasing borrowing. The drivers of the periods are cyclical components linked to the economy as well as structural factors and the mix of borrowing among entities such as households, corporations, or the government changes over time. The cyclical component of the leverage cycle is related to increased demand for loans as the economy improves and the reversal of this demand as the economy declines. This demand for loans arises both from households to increase consumption and from corporations for investment. Beyond cyclical fluctuations, a structural component to borrowing demand stems from desirability of leverage in an economy. In economies where credit is relatively accessible and there is a general level of stability, the demand for leverage will increase over time as households and firms become more comfortable with higher levels of debt to fund consumption and investment. Expansion of social programs or defense spending can lead the government to borrow more than tax receipts on a structural level. The growing demand to borrow more from different sectors of the economy is likely to pressure interest rates higher.

The leverage cycle has a strong effect on long-term interest rate cycles, but it is not as simple as increased borrowing leading to higher rates. Generally such processes are discontinuous; increasing amounts of leverage in an economy do not necessarily lead to steady increases in interest rates as a steady line. One example of this dynamic is the situation with smaller European economies, such as Greece, where government borrowing increased for years as interest rates headed lower due to beneficial effects from the European Union. As there were plenty of funds to borrow, there was no pressure higher on interest rates even as borrowing increased. However, the credit crisis starting in 2008 shook the foundations of finance and led investors to question all types of unsustainable borrowing, even by sovereign governments. As markets are founded on trust, this shaken trust led to a sudden restriction in the supply of funds, causing a sharp spike in borrowing rates for the Greek government. Although for years increasing leverage of the Greek government had little effect on its rates, the reversal was far more sudden. The lesson here is that large shifts in market systems are nearly impossible to predict. The important point to remember is that economies with large structural instabilities between borrowing and lending are susceptible to sudden reversals that can lead to sharp market reactions.

The demand for borrowing has to be balanced out by the supply for lending funds. The domestic supply for lending funds comes from the savings of individuals, corporations, and the government, if it runs a surplus. In the aggregate, this is referred to as the level of savings of an economy. The percentage of income saved is known as the savings rate. The savings rate is a very slow-moving variable and generally does not affect rates on a day-to-day basis. For individuals, generally savings increase during the middle years and begin depleting as their working years approach an end. Aggregated across the economy, and simplifying the matter considerably, we can assume that the level of savings in an economy will grow rapidly when it is composed of a higher proportion of younger people while economies with a larger proportion of elderly persons will witness a decline in the savings rate and perhaps even the level of savings as the rate heads lower than zero. More generally, demographics, which refer to the age characteristics of an economy, are an important determinant of the long-term savings rate in the economy. Over long cycles, the distribution of younger and older individuals does not stay fixed. In developed countries, over the past few decades the trend has been toward a greater proportion of older people. An enormous body of academic literature beyond the scope of this book has explored the reasons and implications of this aging population. Some of the possible factors that cause demographic change across societies include increasing wealth, constraints on having children in more urban settings, increasing numbers of women in the workforce, immigration, and higher life expectancy due to improved health care, among many others. In particular, as populations age, the level of savings shrinks, leaving fewer funds for investment in markets and the economy. Furthermore, fewer workers remain in the working age category relative to elderly persons who do not have excess funds to save in general. At the same time, given the structure of modern governments, as the proportion of elderly persons grows, the pressure to expand social programs to take care of them increases as well. Many social programs currently in place have become unsustainable as a shrinking workforce is paying for an increasing number of elderly persons. These programs are funded with tax receipts, which shrink relative to funding needs as the proportion of workers declines. Given their impact on the availability of savings and demand for borrowing, demographics are an increasingly important factor that will affect the level of savings and the long-term equilibrium of interest rates across the global economy.

Future expectations of economic growth and economic stability are also important determinants of the savings rate; economies that undergo severe slowdown or increasing uncertainty about future prospects tend to witness increases in the savings rate. The interest rate market can be thought of as an intermediary for savers and borrowers—as the level of savings decreases, the market clearing interest rate needs to rise. This analysis is simplified though, and numerous conditions can substantially alter the dynamics of the savings rate. One condition is the implicit assumption that the economy is closed—that is, savings from other economies cannot enter the domestic market. If the economy was not closed, an excess of savings from abroad could flow through and help lower rates. As international capital has become more mobile, savings have tended to flow toward assets in demand regardless of national boundaries. Countries offering a higher rate of return, especially adjusted for safety of capital and property rights, will attract more capital than other countries. A current example of this situation is the United States, where the savings rate declined for over two decades until 2007 and foreign capital substituted for the lack of domestic savings. In the U.S. case, the safety and liquidity of Treasuries attracts surplus savings from a wide range of emerging market countries that have high levels of savings.

The financial regulatory framework of an economy and the structure of its banking system also have an effect on the level of funds available for borrowing. Regulations that prevent inflow or outflow of capital can have a significant impact on domestic interest rates. If foreign inflows are prevented from entering the country, interest rates will tend to be higher than with an open economy; the reverse occurs if capital is held captive domestically. This is not much of a problem currently for U.S. markets, which are some of the most open in the world, but when trying to understand EM interest rate markets, capital flow regulations play a crucial role. After capital regulations, the structure of the banking system is also a key factor for determining system. Similar to interest rate and credit markets, banks are also an intermediary between savers and borrowers in an economy. Some economies, such as the United States, are more heavily reliant on market funding, while others, such as Japan, rely on banks to a greater extent. In either case, given their similar functions, banks interact a great deal with the interest rate markets to manage their interest rate risks and to earn yield on funds not being lent out. Consequently, banking regulations that affect their ability to make loans or force them into "safer" or more liquid assets will lead to more funds being invested in government debt. This is especially a concern in the United States and other developed countries in the aftermath of the credit crunch, when regulatory uncertainty with regard to risk assessments of banks tends to force excess funds into the Treasury market. Regulatory risk is likely to remain a key issue for years to come and one that investors even in "developed" markets will need to focus on. The structure of changing regulations will be an important driver of interest rates on a longer-term scale.

For the equilibrium level of interest rates, one has to consider the participants across all fixed income markets. This is because the supply and demand for funds is not segregated to particular markets—for example, if the Fed purchases all existing mortgages, banks will be forced to move some of their holdings to the Treasury market by buying in the secondary market. Consider, however, a situation where all the issuance in the fixed income space is in the corporate market. Also assume that total demand for fixed income is at $5 trillion but that corporates will issue $10 trillion. To digest this supply, some Treasury bonds will have to be sold and funds diverted to the corporate market. As the supply is too large to digest, yields will have to rise until they are attractive for investors.

Treasury yields will likely rise, as the selling of Treasuries to buy corporates will pressure yields higher, as will the need to compete with higher corporate bond yields. To be sure, corporate yields will likely rise more than Treasury yields; nonetheless, since the overall size of supply is much larger than aggregate demand, rates overall need to rise to clear the market. Thus, to understand interest rates, investors need to have a good handle on the supply/demand picture of both the Treasury market and the overall fixed income market.

Although these points are long-term factors affecting supply and demand for funds in an economy, for a horizon of months to a few years, the economic cycle has a strong effect on both sides of the supply/demand balance for funds as well. Any discussion of the interplay between the economic cycle and interest rates is incomplete without considering the role of the central bank. To regulate the swings in the economy stemming from the business cycle and the leverage cycle, the central bank controls short-term interest rates and has other tools, as discussed in Chapter 3. The central bank acts as the independent authority to control money supply in most modern economies; in the United States, this central bank is known as the Federal Reserve. The interplay between growth and inflation among consumers, producers, and the government is a driving factor behind interest rates. In most advanced economies, the presence of a central bank adds another entity in the interplay of economic growth and inflation. The central bank is meant to prevent rampant printing of money to fund government expenditures, which can lead to unchecked inflation. Beyond controlling money supply, the Federal Reserve acts as an external force to curtail volatility in the economic cycle and act as a lender of last resort in times of crisis. Although market economies allocate resources efficiently most of the time, at times they can encounter crises and periods of instability that can turn into vicious cycles. By intervening and providing support for financial markets, the Fed therefore serves an important purpose, and its actions have a major impact on all financial markets. To understand the interest rate cycles of the United States or other developed markets, we need to incorporate information from the economic cycle along with the likely reaction of the Federal Reserve to incoming economic data. The Fed's changes to short-term interest rates in response to the economic cycle affect the demand and supply for fixed income products across maturities, thus changing the level and shape of the yield curve.

The combination of economic data and related actions by the Fed creates cycles of interest rate movements that can last anywhere from a few months to a few years. The Fed directly controls the overnight rate in the United States, but its influence goes far beyond the short rate. This is because the short end of the yield curve is not independent of longer maturities. Short-term rates set the financing rates for longer-term assets;

for example, the short-term rate set by the Fed is close to the financing repo rate for Treasuries. This way, expectations of forward Fed activity lead to expectations of forward financing rates and thus affect longer-term Treasury yields. The link of the short rate to longer maturity rates is not an easily definable one, and it gets weaker as the interest rate maturity increases. For instance, the 2-year Treasury yield is generally much more closely linked to the Fed funds rate than the 10-year Treasury yield. These links from the short-term rate set by the Fed to longer-term rates are complex and change constantly. The link between the Fed's actions and longer rates becomes more difficult to determine, because longer rates are driven not only by the Fed's actions today but by future expectations of Fed activity, the economy, and inflation, all of which have considerable uncertainty. For example, if the Fed is raising rates currently to curtail economic growth, there is a strong likelihood of higher rates over the near term. The 2-year Treasury rate can be thought of as the market's expectations of the situation over the next two years, and thus there is a strong link between what the Fed is doing today and the 2-year rate. Over 10 years, the path of the economy is less clear. There is a chance that the Fed may overdo the rate increases and curtail economic growth in the future. If expectations of economic growth are curtailed in the future, the 10-year rate will not rise as rapidly as the shorter rates since lower economic growth results in lower rates, as discussed. If the Fed is sharply lowering rates, however, it increases expectations for growth in the future and thus prevents 10-year rates from declining as rapidly as the 2-year rate. Thus, the link between current Fed activity and changes in the 10-year rate is less clear.

There are many ways to understand the effect of the Fed on the yield curve. These effects act over the course of months to years as the Fed moves to temper the business cycle. Therefore, understanding the likely evolution of the Fed cycle and its effects on rates is important to forming a medium-term view on rates. These effects can be counterintuitive; for example, as described, just because the Fed raises rates does not mean the entire yield curve rises by the same magnitude. Indeed, some longer rates may even decline, depending on future expectations. One way to understand the effect of changes in the short rate is to first consider the relationship between the fed funds curve and the 2-year Treasury rate. Afterward, we can determine the evolution of the various Treasury curves, such as 2s/5s (i.e., 5-year rate − 2-year rate), 5s10s, and 10s30s, to understand the shape and level of the whole curve. In this way, the yield curve can be broken down into a combination of rate levels and slopes (i.e., 2-year rate + 2s/5s curve = 5-year rate, 5-year rate + 5s/10s curve = 10-year rate, etc.). To start with, the 2-year Treasury rate is closely linked to the current fed funds rate and to near-term expectations of changes in that rate. To retrieve these expectations from the market, it is common to use the rate

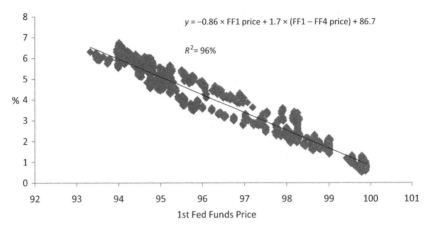

FIGURE 6.4 Relationship of the Two-Year Treasury Yield and the Short End of the Curve
Source: Bloomberg LP, CME Group.

curve from the fed funds futures market. Recall that the fed funds futures market settles on future realizations of the fed funds rate and the implied rate is 100-price. One common choice is the fourth fed funds futures rate minus the first fed funds futures rate. Given the six-week interval between meetings of the Federal Reserve, this difference is the expected change in the fed rate between the next month and six months out. Figure 6.4 shows the relationship between the 2-year Treasury rate and the first fed funds futures rate as well as the 1st/4th fed funds futures curve. Figure 6.5 shows

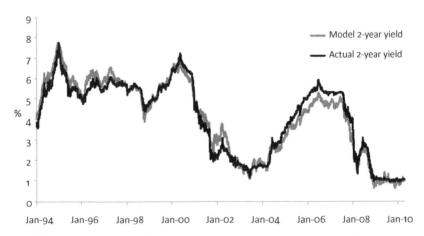

FIGURE 6.5 Model Yield from Figure 6.4 versus Actual Two-Year Yields
Source: Board of Governors of the Federal Reserve.

the linear model fit using the regression fit in Figure 6.4 versus the actual 2-year Treasury rate. The 2-year Treasury rate is the market's expectation of the Fed's activity over the next two years; thus it closely depends on near-term economic expectations. Once a view on the 2-year rate is established, the remainder of the yield curve can be constructed using additional slopes between rate pairs.

To understand the impact of Fed policy on the yield curve, it helps to separate Fed activity into regimes composed of step-by-step target rate policy decisions. Why does the Fed not just raise or lower the target rate all at once instead of in steps? One reason is that monetary policy tends to act in lags, and large one-time increases may have unpredictable effects on economic growth or inflation expectations in the future. Another reason is to avoid excessive volatility in markets as very large, sudden rate increases or decreases may create significant uncertainty regarding the direction of Fed policy. In general, Fed policy occupies one of three regimes:

1. Tightening, which refers to raising the target rate
2. On hold, which refers to no change in the target rate
3. Easing, which refers to lowering the target rate

In between these regimes are transition periods that tend to be more volatile due to higher uncertainty and can present different trading patterns than periods firmly in a single regime. We define a Fed regime as a series of consecutive similar decisions, such as tightening, which can understandably be a bit subjective. If there is a brief pause in easing or tightening, the regime will still be considered the same. Table 6.1 shows the regime dates

TABLE 6.1 Fed Regime Dates

	Start	End
Tightening	4-Feb-94	3-Jan-95
	30-Jun-99	15-May-00
	30-Jun-04	1-Jun-06
On Hold	2-Nov-92	1-Feb-94
	1-Apr-97	1-Sep-98
	2-Jul-03	31-May-04
	29-Jun-06	29-Jun-07
Easing	2-Jul-90	1-Oct-92
	3-Jan-01	1-Dec-01
	1-Nov-07	31-Dec-08

up to December 2008. Note that 2009 is not included here because zero interest rates at the front end and quantitative easing by the Fed during 2009
to 2010 altered the dynamics of the interest rate markets from the usual
responses to Fed regimes. For a discussion of quantitative easing, see the
Federal Reserve section later in this chapter.

To understand the evolution of different sections of the Treasury curve
during Fed regimes, we plot changes in the 2s/5s, 5s/10s, and 10s/30s curves
for quarterly sections of a Fed regime. We divide these sections in quar-
ters with each quarter representing 25% of a Fed regime and the average
changes in the yield curves taken across similar Fed regimes, such as easing, tightening, and on hold. The next three figures show the evolution of
segments of the yield curve across Fed regimes. The figures show average
changes in the 2s/5s, 5s/10s, and 10s/30s curves between fractions of easing,
tightening, and on-hold Fed cycles. Thus an x-axis value of 25% represents
one-quarter of the particular cycle, such as tightening, on hold, or easing.
The bar associated with this x-axis value represents the average change in
the particular curve between zero and one-quarter of the cycle. Similarly,
for the 50% x-axis value, the bar represents the change in the curve between
25% and 50% of the cycle. A negative value for the bar represents a flattening (i.e., negative change in the curve) while a positive value represents
steepening. These figures are meant to help determine the evolution of the
Treasury yield curve as the Fed proceeds through its monetary cycles. To
be sure, average changes can hide variations from cycle to cycle, and each
Fed cycle has unique factors that can cause the yield curve to move significantly differently from broader averages. Nonetheless, these figures can
serve as guidelines for thinking about the dynamics of the yield curve. An
important point to note is that magnitudes in these figures should be compared for the same curve across the cycle rather than across curves. This
is because front-end rates and curves, such as 2s/5s, tend to be much more
volatile than back-end curves, such as 10s/30s; thus the figures give more
information on the progressive changes in each curve as the cycle goes on.

Figure 6.6 depicts easing cycles. In easing cycles, front-end curves,
such as 2s/5s, steepen sharply as the Fed lowers front-end rates. The curve
continues to steepen during the first half of the cycle. Back-end rates
steepen initially but hold off again until later in the cycle as easing may increase longer-dated growth/inflation expectations. As the cycle progresses,
assuming easing lasts long enough, the intermediate rates begin to decline,
which steepens back-end curves, such as 10s/30s.

Figure 6.7 depicts tightening cycles. During tightening cycles, the yield
curve begins flattening from the front end with curves such as 2s/5s as the
Fed raises rates; the longer rates do not rise as fast. This is to be expected
as increasing rates by the Fed cut expectations of future economic growth.
The front end bears the brunt of rate increases. As the tightening cycle

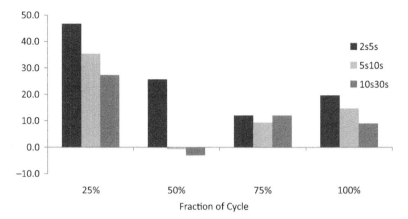

FIGURE 6.6   Change in Various Treasury Curves (bp) at Different Fractions of Fed Easing Cycles
Source: Board of Governors of the Federal Reserve.

progresses, curves across the yield curve flatten. The very back end stabilizes by the end of the tightening cycle as these rates hold off following through with the rate increases.

As the Fed stays on hold, initially curves show little movement, but as the cycle progresses, front-end curves flatten. As the cycle lasts, the back-end curves follow (see Figure 6.8). This tends to happen as the longer the Fed stays on hold, the more investors move out the maturity curve to try to earn higher yield, which progressively flattens the curve. The length of

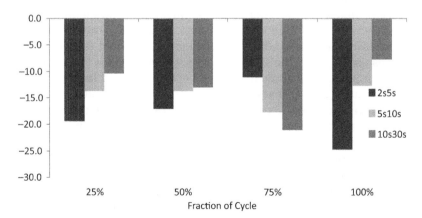

FIGURE 6.7   Change in Various Treasury Curves (bp) at Different Fractions of Fed Tightening Cycles
Source: Board of Governors of the Federal Reserve.

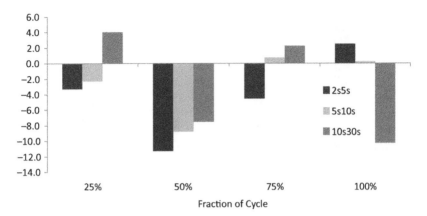

FIGURE 6.8 Change in Various Treasury Curves (bp) at Different Fractions of Fed On-Hold Cycles
Source: Board of Governors of the Federal Reserve.

the Fed on-hold period is critical to how the curve flattening progresses. Fed "on hold" represents a period where the Fed is *expected* to be on hold for the foreseeable future, since any expectations of tightening or easing would alter curve behavior. If the expectations of current economic conditions are anchored, it will make investors more comfortable about reaching out to longer maturities on the yield curve.

The interaction among the Fed, economic growth, and inflation helps formulate medium-term views on the Treasury yield curve, as described. The cycles of the economy and actions by the Fed in response affect all sources of fixed income demand and supply. They form the foundation of the rate cycle, but within this foundation, numerous demand and supply factors also affect the path of the yield curve. The Fed rate moves have the greatest impact at the short end of the curve since the Fed controls the overnight rate. As mentioned, the link between the Fed target and longer maturity rates (2 to 30 years) gets weaker as we move, adding volatility to the average curve reactions shown in Figures 6.6, 6.7, and 6.8. However, not all supply and demand for fixed income stems from the outlook for the Fed. Different participants in fixed income markets have either temporary or structural factors influencing their decisions beyond the influence of Fed monetary policy cycles. It is important to consider these motivations affecting both supply and demand for fixed income products to fully grasp movements in interest rates. These supply and demand factors, important for the whole yield curve, become increasingly important as the maturity of the debt increases, given the more tenuous link of these longer maturities to the Fed. We consider some of these factors next.

COMPONENTS OF FIXED INCOME SUPPLY AND DEMAND

Supply and demand of fixed income instruments stems from a range of issuers and investors. For a market such as Treasuries, there are idiosyncratic factors on both the supply and demand sides, such as the government's budget situation. However, the market clearing interest rate level depends on the aggregate supply and demand of fixed income instruments. For example, if we hold demand constant, just because Treasury supply is rising does not mean Treasury yields will necessarily rise if supply is declining in other fixed income markets (discussed in detail later in the chapter). This is the case because investors and their funds are not completely restricted to a single market. In the high-grade U.S. fixed income market, assets such as Treasuries and agency mortgage-backed securities (MBSs) are not perfect substitutes, but given that interest rate risk forms the bulk of risk in higher-grade assets, they can be considered close substitutes. If one of these markets is unbalanced from a demand or supply standpoint, funds would flow in or out of the market to take advantage of dislocations in pricing. Another way effects from one market spill over across the fixed income space is through hedging flows: If an investor buys a corporate bond, the dealer will be short the bond and tend to buy a liquid rate asset, generally Treasuries, to offset the interest rate exposure. To be sure, the dealer does not have to offset his risk in a different market, but often Treasuries or swaps offer a rapid, convenient way to manage rate risk. Thus, demand for any of these high-grade assets has the effect of pushing overall interest rates lower, although differing supply/demand dynamics in each market would determine their *relative* movements. The key point is that these markets are connected by secondary markets and that investors are not restricted to one asset; even if they were, dealers offsetting their risk are not. As with the demand side, a similar dynamic exists on the supply side, which we explore shortly. We consider different fixed income supply and demand sources in the next section.

TREASURY SUPPLY

In Chapter 3, we discussed the government's issuance of debt to fund gaps between expenditures and tax revenues. Given that the budget deficit drives net Treasury supply, it is crucial to understand the causes and likely path of the deficit to understand the supply side of the Treasury market. To think about the deficit, it is instructive to break it down into two components: cyclical deficits and structural deficits. Cyclical deficits arise

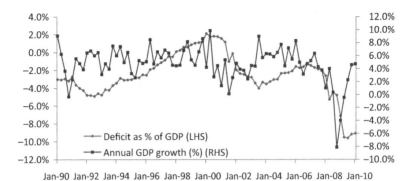

FIGURE 6.9 Federal Budget Deficit and Its Relationship to GDP Growth
Source: U.S. Bureau of Economic Analysis.

from the business cycle and tend to be highly correlated to gross domestic product (GDP) growth. These deficits arise from the fact that a slowdown in economic activity and the resulting decline in household and corporate incomes lowers the amount of taxes the government takes in. At the same time, expenditures on social insurance programs, such as unemployment insurance and one-time fiscal stimulus expenditures, rise. The combination of these factors leads to higher deficits during recession periods while boom periods tend to witness surplus government accounts. Figure 6.9 shows the budget deficit for the United States since January 1990 along with GDP growth. As shown, large GDP downturns have coincided especially with increased deficits. Although increases in cyclical deficits increase Treasury supply, this does not necessarily lead to increased yields due to conflicting effects from the coinciding economic slowdown.

Cyclical deficits tend to be easier to understand and model than structural deficits. The term "structural deficits" refers to excess spending by the government sector, regardless of the prevailing economic conditions. Another way to think of the structural deficit is as the gap that would exist if economic growth were zero. Structural deficits have grown across the developed world over the past 20 years, especially in parts of Europe and Japan. Before the 1900s, governments were a small portion of public lives and raised revenues through ad-hoc taxes on transactions, which were widespread but did not represent a deep source of revenue. Population and economic growth as a result of the industrial revolution, coupled with the introduction of income tax, resulted in governments having a deeper source of revenue to work with. The deep slump of the Great Depression around the world led governments to rapidly increase expenditures for public social safety nets, such as unemployment insurance and social security. These increases could be funded because the increasing population of workers combined with economic growth provided the government with a larger stream of income and other tax revenue. However, over time, as population growth and economic growth has inevitably slowed in the developed countries, such as the United States, Germany, and Japan, the funding sources for the social safety net have shrunk but the spending itself has grown. This difference in long-term spending and long-term tax revenue is known as a structural deficit. Although the specific reasons for increasing structural deficits vary by country, one common undercurrent has been aging populations in the developed world. As populations age, the social burden on governments has increased due to higher expenditure on healthcare, social security, and other social insurance programs. The size and scale of these programs vary widely, but most developed countries are likely to face higher costs regardless of economic cycles. In the United States, partly due to higher levels of immigration, the demographic shifts are taking place at a slower pace than in countries such as Japan and Italy. Nonetheless, the Congressional Budget Office (CBO) projects that the social security and Medicare programs are both headed to large deficits in a few decades as tax receipts are unlikely to keep up with rising costs. Beyond the federal government, state governments are likely to face their own burdens of providing defined benefit pension plans and healthcare as populations age. If states need federal help to shoulder these obligations, this could add to future federal government deficits. The structural deficit has to be understood not just in an economic context but in a political one as well. Any effort to cut long-term government structural obligations, as by increasing retirement ages for workers, runs into blockades by a political system unwilling to consider cuts to benefits. The rise in social funding programs has been coupled with difficulty in raising taxes to fund these programs due to lack of political consensus. The lack of political consensus stems in part from tax rates already being relatively high in the developed world; any significant increases can lead to detrimental effects on the motivation of workers or corporations. Understanding the intersection of economics and politics is important for the future direction of the structural deficit; if developed countries do not address these issues, the longer-term implications for interest rates could be significant.

Deficits add to the national debt of a country. As debt grows, so does the likelihood of default. To compare debt loads across countries, debt is divided by GDP since the ability to service a level of debt varies by the size of an economy. The debt/GDP ratio can be a rough indicator of the relative debt load of a country and therefore of its ability to repay the debt over the longer term. Furthermore, countries with very high debt/GDP ratios are also susceptible to increases in interest rates, which further increases the debt load, possibly leading to spirals of increasing debt. So it would appear that one should position for higher rates in countries with high debt/GDP ratios and lower rates in low debt/GDP ratios. Unfortunately, rate investing is not so straightforward. Although such a strategy may work in the long run, it is unlikely to be useful for day-to-day trading.

The debt/GDP ratio does not give the full picture of the ability of a country to repay its debts; instead, the diversity of the economy's production, ability to increase taxes, breadth of tax base, and a host of other factors determine a country's ability to repay its debt. Consequently, developed countries with a wide tax base and a large array of produced goods, which makes them less susceptible to volatility in isolated markets, are considered less of a credit risk than EM countries, even with higher debt/GDP ratios. Rising debt/GDP ratios can be sustained for extended periods if domestic or foreign pools of saving are willing to keep lending to the country in question. This is especially true if economic growth is low and loan demand is very low, leading savings to move to safe government debt markets due to a lack of alternatives. Such has been the case in Japan from the early 1990s, after the real estate bubble burst. However, this does not imply complacency about debt loads. Developed market debt/GDP ratios have been rising for the most part over the past 20 years, which again points to structural deficits. The larger debt/GDP ratios get, the greater the chance of a cycle of increasing interest rates leading to increasing debt servicing costs, which in turn lead to still higher debt. Although most developed countries currently may not be near such crisis levels, increasing structural deficits and growing debt levels pose a risk of higher interest rates over the coming decades. Indeed, the traditional distinction between "developed" and "developing" countries is less relevant these days as many supposedly developed countries have higher levels of debt/GDP than emerging market countries.

From an accounting standpoint, most countries, such as the United States, consider deficit funding only from a year-to-year cash inflow/outflow perspective. They make little attempt to value contingent liabilities. Contingent liabilities are those that are triggered under certain events but, prior to that event, require no cash outlay. A recent example of a contingent liability triggering would be the liabilities taken on by the U.S. government. Prior to the crisis, institutions such as Freddie Mac and Fannie Mae were partly independent corporations and partly required to fulfill various social mandates. The market considered these entities to be implicitly guaranteed by the government; it was widely accepted that if there was a failure in these companies, the government would step in to protect the debt holders, even if no such explicit agreement existed, due to the large size and importance of these entities to the housing market. For years, this guarantee remained implicit and was never accounted for in year-to-year government financing estimates. However, the onset of the crisis and subsequent stress on Freddie/Fannie balance sheets brought these entities near insolvency, requiring the government to take them into conservatorship. As the market had anticipated, most debt holders were left secure. It is widely accepted that the liabilities of these formerly "private" companies have become the government's liabilities. Given their massive size, the government's obligations have undergone a material increase. This case highlights the importance of assessing the likely impact of increased liabilities in the future from implicit and explicit guarantees.

Once the government has a need to fund the deficit, bonds need to be issued in the market to raise funds to plug the fiscal gap. Chapter 3 explained the basic process of auctioning bonds used by the U.S. Treasury. The size of Treasury issuance has an effect on the overall level of yields, but the allocation of this total size to different maturities can also have an effect on the overall shape of the yield curve. If demand remains constant, the government choosing to issue longer-term debt can cause longer maturities rates to rise faster, causing the yield curve to steepen. The choice of maturity of issuance is driven by the size of funding needed, liquidity in various parts of the curve, average maturity of the outstanding debt, and reducing the need for arbitrary issuance frequencies, which may destabilize the market. Funding needs that are rapid in nature, such as those in response to crises as in 2008, lead to a large spike in Treasury bill (T-bill) issuance, given the ability of the short-maturity sector to handle very large issue sizes.

Given the T-bill market's generally lower interest rate, why not issue the entire debt in that market? The answer to this question stems from the need by the Treasury, as with any other debt issuer, to avoid an overreliance on short-term debt, which can place undue stress on the market when the time comes to roll over the debt to raise new funding. For this reason, a healthy, liquid long-term debt market needs to be maintained that keeps the rolling of debt principal at moderate levels. Overreliance on a single point on the yield curve can lead to excess yield being paid to raise funds as investors would have trouble digesting the supply. A liquid yield curve with issuance spread out tends to result in lower yield levels as investors place extra value on liquidity, which presumably is beneficial to Treasury from an interest cost standpoint. During times of crisis when T-bill issuance spikes, the average maturity of debt tends to drop sharply; over time after any such disruption, Treasury likely will strive to increase the average maturity closer to the norm, which is around six or seven years.

OTHER SOURCES OF FIXED INCOME SUPPLY

Treasury supply is an important driver of yields, but investors need to think about overall fixed income supply when considering the likely trend in rates. To consider the total fixed income supply, the debt issuance volume needs to be weighted by the average duration of each market to account for different maturity debt in the market. For example, $100 billion issuances of 2-year notes and 10-year notes represent very different amounts of interest rate risk. The weighting of supply by the duration of a market is known as duration supply. For Treasury investors, it is just as important to track duration supply across fixed income as Treasury supply. Supply imbalances in one market can cause dislocations that can in turn lead to demand flowing over across fixed income markets, as discussed. For example, suppose that total demand for fixed income assets remains fixed but high-grade corporates have very low net issuance in a given year. In that case, a mutual fund manager looking to buy corporates will bid up the price of the bonds. As prices of corporate bonds get bid up, other investors may look to find other high-quality fixed income assets, especially since the issuance is low and corporates will be difficult to find. In that case, this money will flow into other high-grade fixed income markets, such as Treasuries. To be sure, the low supply of corporates will lead to corporate bonds outperforming Treasuries (i.e., a narrower spread between corporate and Treasuries), but if demand remains fixed, the overall yield levels across fixed income markets will be pressured lower. Secondary market flows chasing a smaller corporate market will spill over into other high-grade fixed income markets.

For this reason, considering just Treasury supply and demand dynamics to deduce Treasury yields can be deceptive. An example of this was evident starting in mid-2009 when Treasury yields began declining in spite of numerous dire predictions of rising yields due to rapidly growing Treasury supply. Even with record supply, Treasury yields did not shoot through the roof, but instead remained rangebound and even trended lower for various intervals in 2009. One reason for this divergence was that while Treasury supply was rising, net supply in other high-grade fixed income markets, such as asset-backed securities and Agencies, was falling rapidly as a lasting aftereffect of the credit crunch. This offsetting factor made the supply/demand imbalance far less dire than statistics of the Treasury market in isolation would have conveyed. Indeed, one example of secondary market substitution of demand was witnessed in the demand for fixed income securities by banks. When the available supply of assets, such as mortgages, had started shrinking, banks looking to invest their record levels of deposits began to dip into the Treasury market, something they had not done much in nearly two decades. The examples serve to emphasize the point that the supply/demand balances of Treasuries and other high-grade markets need to be considered for yields.

The most important sources of fixed income supply for a rates investor to watch for, from a supply standpoint, are the Treasury market, the high-grade corporate bond market, and the Agency MBS market. The municipal bond market and Agency debt market supplies tend to be smaller than these three and therefore have a smaller effect. The money markets have large volume of issuance, but the duration of the debt is very small; thus it tends to not add much duration supply to the market. For the corporate market, medium-term trends in issuance tend to be driven by the need for firms to expand their operations and capital expenditure plans. Though simple to summarize, the dynamics driving corporate supply are complex. Elevated levels of economic growth tend to lead to expansion in corporate spending and thus higher levels of corporate debt issuance. However, the relationship is not a straightforward one and depends closely on the overall corporate cash position. For example, if corporate margins are high and corporations have large reserves of cash, there is less need to issue corporate debt. If, however, the economy slows down sharply, increased risk aversion can lead firms to raise long-term debt in a hurry to bolster their cash reserves. Similarly, if firms have a large proportion of short-end debt that needs to be rolled frequently and markets become volatile, firms will tend to raise longer-term debt to prevent reliance on short-term debt. This dynamic was evident in early 2009, when the reopening of debt markets in the aftermath of the Lehman bankruptcy led firms to ramp up corporate debt issuance in case of another bout of risk aversion. Many firms overfunded their balance sheets as investors demanded more cash be held on the balance sheet to withstand economic volatility.

For Agency MBS issuance, a variety of factors are important, ranging from economic growth to credit availability. As home ownership rises, individuals need to take out new mortgages, increasing mortgage supply. Similarly, if credit is easily available, households will be eager to take on larger amounts of mortgage debt, perhaps to fund consumption. A full analysis of the mortgage market and its issuance patterns is beyond the scope of this book, but a rates investor needs to keep mortgage issuance forecasts in mind when trying to forecast medium-term trends of interest rates. Interest rates are an important driver of mortgage issuance. As interest rates decrease, homeowners in older mortgages with higher interest rates will wish to refinance into lower-rate mortgages. In the case of a refinancing, an older mortgage more "out of the money" (i.e., with a rate above current rates) is replaced with an "at-the-money" mortgage (i.e., with a rate near current rates). This replacement has an effect similar to issuing a new mortgage, albeit on a smaller scale; a mortgage near current rates has higher duration than one where the interest rate is higher from current rates. This is because a mortgage where the homeowner is paying higher interest than current rates is likely to get refinanced soon, making its effective maturity and duration shorter. On the other hand, a newly issued mortgage will resemble a longer-dated bond because it is less likely to get refinanced, unless interest rates decline further. As a fresh new mortgage adds duration to the market, so does a refinancing due to the increase in duration. Finally, a point to note is that we are concerned with fixed rate mortgage supply here. During the middle 2000s, there was an increase in the issuance of adjustable rate mortgages (ARMs), which are essentially floating rate instruments with far shorter durations than traditional 30-year fixed rate mortgages. The ARM issuance, though large, added much less to duration supply and was less important from the perspective of being a driver of intermediate maturity interest rates. After late 2007, when the mortgage market crisis started with subprime mortgages, credit availability shrank rapidly as banks pulled back from making risky mortgage loans. ARM issuance declined rapidly as well. Subsequent to the credit crunch, the mortgage market reverted back to mostly fixed rate issuances instead of more complex floating rate ones.

FIXED INCOME DEMAND

Fixed income supply does not exist in a vacuum and needs to be balanced by demand for fixed income products. U.S. fixed income market participants can be split into various groups of investors—such as foreign investors, households, mutual funds, the Fed, banks, and pension funds—each of which has a different motivation for investing in U.S. fixed income. As with supply, it is total fixed income demand that matters in determining the market clearing interest rate, similar to the reasoning about supply described earlier. The most widely used source of fixed income demand is the Fed quarterly flow of funds report.

Foreigner Holdings

Over the past decade, foreigners have grown to be increasingly important members of the U.S. fixed income market, especially Treasuries. In fact, the largest single block of holders of Treasuries is foreign accounts. As of late 2009, they held about 50% of the U.S. Treasury debt outstanding, and their share has grown steadily over the past 20 years. The large proportion of foreign debt ownership of Treasuries causes fear among the political class and the public, possibly because it is seen to be a less stable source of funding. This fear is especially strong with regard to foreign central banks that hold massive amounts of Treasuries and whose motives are not always economically driven, leading to concern about their decision-making process. Another source of concern about foreign holdings stems from their concentrated nature; China and Japan combined own a large majority of the foreign holdings, along with the nations of the Organization of Petroleum Exporting Countries (OPEC). The fear arising from the large proportion of foreign funding of U.S. debt tends to be overstated, but the underlying causes of the imbalance it represents for the world economy do point to worrisome issues.

To understand why foreigners hold such large amounts of Treasuries, one has to consider the nature of global trade in today's system. As an example, assume China manufactures and sells a shoe in the United States. For this shoe, the United States pays China in dollars. Although the individual firm selling the shoe may wish to convert the payment into domestic currency, the central bank of China in aggregate essentially reconverts and holds dollars. China is willing to hold U.S. dollars, due to the dollar's reserve currency status. The central bank has three major choices:

1. Leave all export earnings in domestic currency (renminbi).
2. Invest in "real" assets, such as commodities, including gold.
3. Invest in assets across various foreign currencies.

If China chooses option 1, the proceeds from selling the shoe will circulate in the domestic economy. The demand for Chinese exports then leads to a stronger Chinese currency relative to the dollar. Consequently, that same shoe will be more expensive in U.S. dollars next time China wants to sell. The result will be a decline in exports by China to the United States, leading to smaller surpluses in the future. Therefore, in this case, the self-stabilizing mechanisms of a free market cause the system to balance itself. However, from China's point of view, this has the undesirable consequence of lower exports. The Chinese economy is far more export driven than the U.S. economy, owing to the lack of domestic demand on a scale to match that of the United States. As internal consumption is lower, to maintain high growth rates, China has little choice but to push for a high level of exports. Therefore, out of this compulsion, China cannot convert its dollars into renminbi on a massive scale and therefore has to leave its stashed currency in dollars or other foreign currencies.

The second and third choices in the previous list are ways to avoid letting the domestic currency strengthen and thus weaken exports. Buying assets, either commodities or foreign currency assets, using export earnings prevents a surge in demand to convert to renminbi. However, China's export earnings are in the trillions of dollars, and it is impractical for more than a small percentage of these assets to buy commodities and real assets. Indeed, too much buying of real assets may increase their prices and hurt Chinese manufacturing. This leaves the third choice, which is to buy assets across a range of foreign currencies, which allows China to avoid converting dollars into renminbi and face pressure on exports from a rising exchange rate. By buying U.S. dollar assets, the central bank can even "peg" the domestic currency to within a certain range of values versus the dollar. Although other countries with large trade surpluses with the United States manage the currency in different ways, in almost all cases there is a similar attempt to keep the domestic currency weak in order to facilitate exports. Investing in assets across currencies inevitably leads China predominantly to U.S. assets, both because the United States is a major trading partner and because of the massive size and liquidity of U.S. asset markets compared to those of the rest of the world. In particular, for the vast sums of money needed to be invested by foreign central banks, Treasuries and other high-quality U.S. fixed income assets such as MBSs become a natural choice, given their liquidity and safety.

Although movements in the U.S. dollar exchange rate change the value of U.S. assets, the exchange rate does not tend to be a major factor behind foreign holdings of Treasuries. Given the dynamic of purchases described, it is not surprising that the trade deficit of the United States (i.e., exports less imports) is the major driver of foreign purchases. As the trade deficit rises, the U.S. is importing more goods and more export earnings need to be invested to keep exporter currencies weaker. Foreign purchases of Treasuries are also driven by flights to quality as with many other classes of investors. For example, foreign holdings of U.S. Treasuries in a year of crisis such as 2008 witnessed no sharp decrease or flight. This is especially striking given that the crisis began in the United States.

Given all this, fears of foreign accounts suddenly dumping Treasuries, at least in the current system of world trade, tend to be exaggerated. Nations that need exports to propel economic growth need to invest in U.S. assets as much as the U.S. needs foreign funding of its debt. A rapid change to this balance would be destabilizing and would not be in the interest of any trading parties, given the resulting drop in exports on one side and a sharp rise in interest rates in the United States. However, the system is in a state of disequilibrium today, as U.S. trade deficits are still very large and exporting nations have enormous reserves of foreign assets. The main vehicle for an adjustment toward a more balanced system would be an increase in domestic consumption in export-driven emerging market (EM) countries to make them less dependent on exports and more open to revaluation of their currencies. This process has been taking place over the past few years and is likely to continue over the coming decades barring major upheavals. EM consumer share of global consumption is rising steadily as living standards in those countries improve. Nonetheless, political pressure has risen from the United States and other developed countries on

EM countries to move toward stronger currencies as a way of fixing the trade imbalances. However, the shift toward domestic consumption in EM countries is likely to be a gradual one, which means that correcting the imbalances of debt and trade patterns will require time.

Unfortunately, the longer the imbalances continue, the more likely it is that large shocks will plague the system. What are some risks to the optimistic scenario of the system slowly working itself out and currencies gradually aligning?

- Social upheaval in EM countries could lead to a rapid realignment of the export-oriented nature of their economies. This would dramatically alter the foreign investment profile in U.S. assets such as Treasuries.
- Out-of-control inflation in the United States could require a reassessment by the foreign debt holders of U.S. dollar asset holdings, which would lose value rapidly in a high-inflation environment.
- Countries could engage in trade wars, erecting trade barriers to prevent imports and protect exports. In times of economic slowdown, the resentment in developed markets toward artificially weak currencies and other "unfair" trade practices in EM countries can lead to political action to prevent imports to the United States through nonmarket barriers such as quotas or tariffs. An escalation of trade wars could lead to global economic slowdown and financial market stress. For example, trade wars were extremely destructive in the 1930s and were a major cause for the deflation that plagued economies across the globe.

Such scenarios would cause major destabilization in the way Treasuries are held and valued, but they are not probable in the near term. Nonetheless, vigilance is needed by all parties to the global economic system to avoid vicious cycles that can destabilize a globalized world.

For interest rate markets, the dynamic of foreign investment into Treasuries is an important factor for yields. Although difficult to monitor on a high-frequency basis, a portion of foreign account holdings of U.S. assets are reported in the Fed custody holdings data. Foreign holdings of U.S. assets are important to monitor for any shifts in buying patterns in the aggregate or between asset classes. Investors need to be aware of any trends, either economic or political, that can change the current dynamic of world trade and affect interest rates in the United States.

Federal Reserve

Earlier we discussed the interaction of the Fed with the interest rate market. The Fed acts as an external agency that attempts to reduce volatility of economic cycles by changing interest rates and conducting open market operations. These open market operations are meant to keep the short-term interest rates near the target and involve buying and selling Treasuries in the open market. Such operations are not profit driven, which makes the Fed different from many other market participants. The interest rate implications of the Fed's monetary policy were discussed earlier, but it should be noted that occasionally the Fed becomes a large purchaser (or seller) of debt securities in order to conduct monetary policy.

Traditionally, the Fed owned about $700 billion in Treasuries in what is known as its System Open Market Account (SOMA) portfolio and tweaked the portfolio to reflect monetary policy changes and to manage portfolio runoffs. However, the situation changed drastically in 2008 and 2009. The onset of the credit crunch led the Fed to buy longer-term securities in order to lower interest rates across the curve after there was little capacity for short-term rates to go down. During 2008, this expansion was primarily led by a host of short-term programs to boost liquidity for the financial sector, such as term auction facility. To manage the rapid growth of these liquidity programs, the Fed reduced its Treasury holdings that year to neutralize some of the growth in other parts of the balance sheet. Treasury holdings fell from $740 billion at the beginning of 2008 to $475 billion at the end of the year. However, the Fed's actions were not bearish for Treasuries; instead, the overall growth in the balance sheet was the more important driver, along with the safe haven bid due to extreme volatility. The year 2009 was different for the Fed; it initiated a securities purchase program in March. As part of its quantitative easing effort, the Fed targeted buying of $1.250 trillion of MBSs, $300 billion of Treasuries, and $175 billion of Agencies (initially $200 billion) over the course of 2009. The purchase of Treasuries during 2009 brought their amount on the balance sheet close to the long-run average of $700 billion, although the Fed's balance sheet held far greater amounts of MBSs and Agency debt than in previous years. Indeed, the Fed balance sheet held over $1 trillion in mortgages by 2009. The Fed announced a second round of quantitative easing in the fall of 2010 to purchase more Treasuries in order to expand the balance sheet. Although the immediate effect of quantitative easing announcements has been to lower rates across the yield curve, there is much debate about its effectiveness in changing the course of the economy. Furthermore, there are risks of large-scale Fed balance-sheet expansion causing runaway inflation. The Fed has always been an important participant in interest rate markets even in its traditional role. As it attempts to implement policies such as quantitative easing and other new measures, the impact will be crucial for rates investors to assess.

Mutual Funds

Fixed income mutual funds have grown significantly in size over the past decade and their impact on markets ranging from Treasuries to MBSs has correspondingly increased. The mutual fund industry size is in the trillions and its Treasury ownership represents about 9% of the amount of marketable Treasuries. In addition to Treasuries, mutual funds are large buyers of corporate bonds. Although it appears that funds are a relatively small portion of the market, especially when compared to foreigners or the Fed, fund ownership is much more volatile and, on the margin, can have significant impact. This is especially true near heavy auction schedules of Treasuries where supply/demand flow balances are crucial and more responsive investors, such as mutual funds, can resolve temporary imbalances. To understand how funds may impact the market, we need to understand what drives their demand for Treasuries.

One characteristic of mutual funds that differentiates them from other categories is benchmarking. The term "benchmarking" refers to measuring returns on a relative scale rather than an absolute scale; for a mutual fund, most often the relevant statistic is under- or outperformance versus a benchmark index instead of judgment on a stand-alone return basis. For example, equity mutual funds may benchmark themselves against the Standard & Poor's 500 index—in this case they would be assessed by how much their investments outperform the index return. On the fixed income side, the Barclays aggregate indices (formerly known as Lehman aggregate) or its subindices are commonly used as benchmarks. A benchmark index such as the Barclays aggregate will represent the fixed income market by some choice of weighting, such as total outstanding amounts, for each subsector. Due to benchmarking, fund managers retain a "core" position in their portfolio that mimics the weighting of the asset classes present in the index they are benchmarked against. As the weightings of markets change in the reference index, so will a fund manager's demand level. Therefore, one takeaway from this fact is that the larger the weight of an asset class in an index, the more fund managers are compelled to buy it. Specifically, as the supply of a subsection of the market rises in comparison to other subsections, fund managers will be compelled to buy part of the supply. This dynamic was apparent during 2009 with the Treasury market, where fixed income fund managers had to increase exposure to Treasuries as their weight in the Barclays aggregate indices rose in response to higher supply.

Although fund managers tend to replicate the index they are benchmarked against, their replication is not exact; indeed, they have some discretion to be over- or underweight their benchmarks. This leads to movement of demand within the index as different asset classes are perceived to be rich or cheap. Fund ownership of Treasuries tends to track lagged aggregate corporate bond spreads, with fund managers moving into Treasuries in a flight to quality, especially when corporate spreads widen significantly. Finally, Treasury demand for fund managers is also influenced by the steepness of the curve (i.e., the difference between long-maturity Treasury yields and short-maturity ones). The larger this difference is, the more income can be made from owning longer-end Treasuries compared to keeping cash. Thus, the three factors described are important in understanding the asset allocation decisions of fund managers.

Banks

Banks are important players in the fixed income market in most countries, and the United States is no exception. Commercial banks are large holders of fixed income products, and their changing preferences for economic and regulatory reasons can be important structural drivers of interest rate levels. Commercial banks purchase securities from deposited funds that are not used to make commercial loans. Over longer time frames, the availability of alternative venues to hold cash for individuals and corporations can divert funding from deposits. This phenomenon took place during the 1990s and 2000s until 2007, as the proliferation of money market mutual funds and other alternative products diverted funds from bank deposits. Subsequent to the credit crunch, fear of the collapse of money market funds and the crisis in short-term markets led to a rush back into bank deposits. In most periods, deposits tend to be very slow moving, but the loan side can be much more volatile. One of the major driving factors of bank holdings of market securities is the demand for and willingness of banks to make commercial loans. The aggregate level of loan demand arises directly from economic growth and the need for businesses to expand. Economic slowdown can therefore cut demand for loans and leave more deposits to be invested in fixed income markets. Even if the aggregate level of loans stays fixed, there is competition from corporate debt issuance since bank loans are an alternate source of funding.

Mortgages are one of the largest classes of securities held by banks. This class includes both mortgages packaged as securities and those held as loans. Unlike the Freddie Mac/Fannie Mae agencies or hedge funds, banks do not tend to hedge their mortgage holdings and instead just hold to earn the yield. Banks tend not to keep a large portion of their holdings in Treasuries, which generally offer lower yield than other fixed income assets. Although the amount of Treasuries held by banks is low relative to mortgage holdings, it has grown in recent years. This shift offers a glimpse into the dynamics that drive bank holdings of different types of securities. After the credit crunch (2007–2008) abated, weak economic growth reduced loan demand and increased deposit growth, both of which increased funds for banks to invest in securities. Additionally, in the aftermath of the credit crunch, mortgage market supply and corporate bond market supply shrank in response to credit constraints for households and strong cash positions for corporates, leading their valuations to richen versus Treasuries. In response, banks diverted funds into Treasuries. In general banks will tend to shift allocation to markets that offer higher carry in comparison to the volatility of underlying securities. A similar shift into government securities by banks took place in Japan after the property bubble crash in the late 1980s. The dynamic in Japan was similar in some ways to that in the United States. On the bank side, there was little appetite to make loans due to overhang from bad property and real estate investments during the 1980s. In conjunction, businesses and households raised savings rates in the midst of economic uncertainty and reduced loan demand. This left banks with little choice but to shift bank funds into Japanese government bonds. Finally, regulations can also have an important effect on a bank's decision process regarding investment in securities. Generally there are complex rules regarding the amount of capital and liquid assets that banks are supposed to hold. As these rules change, banks have to buy certain types of securities regardless of economic considerations. For example, rule changes that force banks to hold more liquid assets to create safer balance sheets would also reduce loan disbursements and cause them to hold higher quantities of safer securities, such as Treasuries. Thus, for fixed income investors, both regulatory and economic changes for banks are important to follow; they can have a significant impact on demand for fixed income securities.

Pension Funds

Pension funds and retirement accounts hold a significant amount of fixed income securities, given the long-dated obligations for such accounts. For this segment of fixed income demand, a distinction must be made between defined *benefit* pension funds and defined *contribution* pension funds. Defined benefit pension funds are retirement plans where an employee is guaranteed a set pension and other benefits after retirement. Defined contribution funds are plans such as the 401(k), where employees contribute their own savings and are not guaranteed any benefits by the employer. Defined contribution accounts are mostly the norm now, while defined benefit plans are still present in some sectors of the economy, especially government jobs. Although defined contribution plans may be more common, they are also spread out among a large number of individuals, and their ownership of fixed income is generally through mutual funds, which were discussed earlier.

The large pension funds that manage defined benefit plans can have significant impact on fixed income markets overall, especially for long-maturity securities. This is because by pooling assets, pension funds greatly increase their presence in the market compared to individual accounts. In general, a pension fund's aim is to ensure that the assets it invests in grow rapidly enough to pay for the benefits the fund promises in the future. Because the benefits promised by the pension funds are far in the future, most of the assets a pension fund owns need to be long-dated in nature.

The liabilities of a pension fund—the promised future cash flows—currently are benchmarked off AA-rated corporate bond yields. This benchmark rate is used to discount future obligations to calculate the present value of liabilities. In years past, pension funds had a large portion of their asset exposure in equities (sometimes over 70%) in an attempt to bridge gaps between asset values and growing liabilities arising from aging populations and other demographic shifts. The value of these liability cash flows grows even larger in present value terms as interest rates fall. Therefore, environments with steep equity and interest rate declines are especially painful for pension funds. These situations are encountered in recessions and periods of financial stress when investors abandon equities and the Fed lowers rates sharply to counter the economic slowdown. The gaps between asset and liability values have grown large in recent years because of optimistic assumptions of stock market gains that were not realized given large equity market declines in 2000 and 2008. Given the problems associated with owning equity assets for pension funds and for regulatory reasons, there is a trend to move toward matching asset and liability profiles more closely. To accomplish this, pension funds have been increasing the fixed income portion of their assets, given that the future promises of fixed cash flows resemble the profile of fixed income assets.

The result of this asset liability matching trend has been an increased demand for longer-dated fixed income assets such as 20- to 30-year corporate bonds. The supply of corporate bonds is limited at the long end and they venture across asset classes for longer-dated assets such as Treasury bonds and STRIPS. Funds have even ventured into the swaps space for synthetic, derivative-based exposure to long-dated fixed income markets (explained in more detail in Chapter 5). Although pension fund allocation shifts do not have a day-to-day effect on yields, the cumulative increase in demand for long-end fixed income assets for asset liability matching is a significant factor in understanding the behavior of long-term interest rates. Pension fund regulations, and in particular accounting rule changes, are important for investors to watch, as these regulations may impact pension funds' approach toward asset liability matching.

Households

The household sector of the Fed's flow of funds incorporates not just individual households but also nonprofit firms and even hedge funds. Thus, its changes in composition can be a bit difficult to decipher, but nonetheless the sector does offer clues as to what smaller investors are doing. Household ownership of Treasuries makes up about 10% of holdings as of 2010 and mostly takes the form of small positions in marketable debt and savings bonds. The household group can be at times a catch-all, but here we focus on true households in particular. Although households on aggregate hold a large amount of Treasuries, they are a relatively stable group of holders and generally are not major factors driving incremental demand. Over the longer term, household ownership of Treasuries has declined as the savings rate has declined. Households do not contribute to incremental demand most of the time, but their ownership share can be volatile during crisis times. During periods of steep declines in equity markets, their purchases of Treasuries and other high-quality fixed income assets rise sharply in a rush to safety. Furthermore, stock market recovery does not imply a rapid flight out of Treasuries; instead, the ownership share of households has tended to stay high after risk-aversion periods.

Another factor to watch with regard to households buying Treasuries is the savings rate. Although it is notoriously difficult to measure accurately, even rough measures pointed to a decline in savings rates in the United States over the past 20 years until the credit crunch. This was driven mainly by rational considerations: As volatility in markets and incomes declined coupled with easier access to leverage and credit, individuals scaled down savings and increased consumption in response. One possible outcome of the massive shocks that U.S. households went through during the credit crunch in 2007 and 2008 may be a higher savings rate than prior to the crisis; indeed, the savings rate has climbed sharply since 2007 and now stands around 6% to 8%. If higher savings rates are sustained, households will represent a greater source of Treasury demand than the market was accustomed to during the 1990s and early 2000s.

SHORT-TERM YIELD DRIVERS

The structural factors driving supply and demand of fixed income products as well as the Fed monetary policy cycles just described act over longer periods of time and serve as a backdrop for positioning for trades. However, over shorter time scales of a few days or a few weeks, numerous short-term factors can sometimes exacerbate or contradict the longer-term trends. For investors who buy and hold bonds until maturity, such short-term trading factors are largely irrelevant. However, for most institutional accounts, the need for routine performance evaluation or mark-to-market pressures mean that short-term swings can easily force an exit from a position that may be sound on a longer-term basis. For example, a hedge fund may own a bond for fundamental reasons but if the value of the bond decreases over the near term, the hedge fund may be forced to sell to avoid sustained daily mark-to-market losses. Sometimes, sharp losses in the value of some assets may force institutional investors to unwind unrelated, profitable trades to raise funds. Trading interest rates requires a solid understanding of not just the big structural factors but also the short-term factors that can cause large fluctuations. Here we consider some important factors that affect Treasury yields on a short-term basis. Some of the important short-range drivers of yields include:

- Economic data and Fed events
- Flight to quality
- Debt auctions
- Mortgage hedging flows
- Corporate issuance
- Exotics hedging flows (mostly long end)
- Seasonality

Economic Data and Fed Events

Economic data is crucial for any financial market to follow, but for a macroeconomic-driven space like rates, it is a significant day-to-day driver. The details of each piece of economic data are key to deducing broader trends in the economy. To understand these underlying trends, adjustments for unrelated or confounding effects such as seasonality, weather, calculation changes, or temporary government policy need to be accounted for. Given the importance of economic data in day-to-day rate movements, it is necessary to understand how the data is calculated as well as its shortcomings. The United States has one of the richest economic data sets of the world economies. The model of a "perfect" data series would be one that is frequent, stable, and forward-looking, but in general no single series can qualify for all three. Instead, to build a more complete picture of the economy, numerous signals from a range of data sources need to be included. Since we are trying to infer trends in economic growth, it helps to start with the components of GDP. GDP represents the production of goods and services in an economy and is the sum of consumption, investment, government spending, and net exports, or GDP $= C + I + G + NX$. This is the "spending side" of GDP. It can also be arrived at by adding up production by firms of goods and services. Unfortunately, although GDP data is released periodically in the United States, it tends to be a backward-looking measure of growth that has already happened. It also can be subject to significant revisions, due to the complexity of collecting the data. Instead, it is more useful for a bond investor to consider forward-looking data. We consider some data sources that form the components of GDP that may be more frequent, stable, or forward-looking than actual GDP data. Another important point regarding data releases is that the actual release is less relevant than its *difference from what was expected*. For most major releases, economists are surveyed, and their expectations of the data release are averaged. Although imperfect, these expectations serve as a benchmark for what is "priced in" to the current level of yields. Any major deviations in the actual release can be especially important. Economic data largely falls into a few major categories covering employment, manufacturing, inflation, housing, consumption, and other sentiment- or survey-based indicators. We present an overview of important economic releases that are necessary for day-to-day rates trading. For a discussion of U.S. economic data releases, also see Carnes and Slifer (1991).

The employment category pertains to data releases that provide a glimpse into the state of the labor market. Although generally a backward-looking indicator, for the interest rate space, the employment picture is crucial in determining the slack built up in the system. *Slack* here refers to the capacity that firms have to expand production without resorting to wage increases due to scarce labor, which can in turn raise prices throughout the economy. An environment where the unemployment rate is very low is at risk of becoming inflationary, which can cause bonds to lose value as future cash flows become less valuable. Employment data stems from two distinct sources: household and establishment surveys. Household surveys directly question households and ask about their employment. Individuals with jobs are counted as "employed," but if they are without a job and currently looking for one, they are counted as part of the labor force. The nature of household surveys can cause inaccuracies, as members of some households may be reluctant to give accurate answers to employment questions for various reasons, such as illegal residential status. Establishment surveys attempt to get the employment picture from another angle—they survey businesses instead of households. Establishment surveys collect data on a range of aspects relating to employment, such as average hourly earnings and hours worked. The two types of surveys also differ in the way they count the labor force; in household surveys, a person holding multiple jobs is counted once while in establishment surveys, multiple jobs would be counted.

The three employment releases that are tracked closely are the monthly nonfarm payrolls report, the monthly unemployment report, and weekly jobless claims. The monthly nonfarm payrolls report is an establishment survey; it surveys firms about job gains and losses. The payrolls report is released on the first Friday of each month and is one of the most important barometers of the labor market. Fed activity is very sensitive to the state of the labor markets and this makes payrolls a crucial data release to watch. Payrolls data is very difficult to forecast, frequently resulting in large errors versus expectations. Variation of the data from expectations can be major short-term market driver. Other data released at the same time as payrolls are average weekly hours and earnings. These releases give a more complete picture of the labor market. For example, even if the main hiring number is flat, an increase in hours worked indicates an improvement in the labor market as firms are making greater use of existing employees. Hourly earnings can also be useful in determining the path of worker income, which in turn affects consumption.

The second widely watched employment measure, released in conjunction with the monthly payrolls report by the Bureau of Labor Statistics, is the actual unemployment rate. This rate counts the number of people currently out of a job and actively looking for a job out of the total labor pool. The unemployment rate is an example of a household survey, where individuals answer survey questions to denote their status in the labor market. One caveat with the unemployment rate is that it counts only those actively looking for work as part of the labor force. Persons unemployed for a sustained period of time and too discouraged to look for work are excluded from the survey, which at times can cause the main data release to be misleading. Another employment data release of note is the weekly jobless claims number. Released every Thursday morning, this number represents applications for unemployment insurance. Although the data can be volatile due to one-time effects, such as weather and strikes, the benefit of the jobless claims release is its weekly frequency (most other data is released much less often). Shifts in the trend of the jobless claims number can be especially important as they offer a glimpse into the direction of payrolls and the unemployment rate.

Although employment is a key metric for the Federal Reserve's monetary policy cycle shifts, it can be a lagging indicator for the broader economy. For longer-term rates that depend on Fed policy over the course of the next few years, marked shifts in the growth picture can foreshadow higher interest rates in the future, even if lagging measures, such as payrolls and the unemployment rate, have not stabilized. For firms, especially in the manufacturing industry, layoffs tend to occur as the economic picture gets increasingly cloudy and recession sets in. As the economy troughs and the outlook for the future brightens somewhat, firms first try to increase output from existing workers, since hiring new workers entails fixed costs of its own. As employee productivity rises, beyond a certain point the existing employees can no longer produce enough, assuming demand continues to grow, and eventual increases in hiring result. This dynamic is especially pronounced in manufacturing industries. Although manufacturing is a smaller part of the U.S. economy than it was in the past, its sensitivity to the economic cycle makes it a valuable and closely tracked barometer for the entire economy. The manufacturing data releases of significance are the Institute for Supply Management (ISM) manufacturing survey, industrial production data, and regional surveys.

The ISM manufacturing survey is released on the first business day of each month. It is an index calculated from a survey of manufacturing firms on six topics: production, orders, employment, prices, inventories, and vendor performance. These subindices are then weighted and added together to arrive at the overall ISM index. The overall index is designed such that 50 marks a neutral point, while index levels below 50 indicate overall contraction of the manufacturing industry and levels over 50 indicate expansion. The ISM manufacturing survey is one of the most forward-looking economic data releases as it captures changes in manufacturing sentiment that tend to occur long before actual growth or contraction takes place. Of course, sentiment can be fickle and the ISM can give false signals, but its focus on the limited set of manufacturing managers makes the ISM less prone to wild swings. Figure 6.2 showed links, albeit volatile ones, between ISM and Treasuries. The ISM manufacturing survey acts as a better leading indicator of an upturn or downturn in the economy than employment data. Beyond the overall index, the components can provide extra information about the state of manufacturing. For example, the new orders component of the ISM can be especially useful as a forward-looking indicator of industrial growth. Another indicator tracked by some market participants is the ratio of new orders to inventory ratio since a buildup of inventories is less promising than new orders. The ISM can be also estimated using regional survey data, which are released in installments during the month. Other than estimating the ISM, regional surveys can give a glimpse into the breadth of a downturn or recovery from a geographical perspective. A data release related to the ISM is the ISM nonmanufacturing survey, which covers the nonmanufacturing sector of the United States. Although the nonmanufacturing sector, such as services, is a much larger fraction of the economy than manufacturing, the manufacturing survey is more widely followed as it is more sensitive to the forward-looking picture of the economy.

The ISM manufacturing survey and the regional surveys are just that: surveys. Some data releases also provide a forward-looking picture of industrial production. Durable goods orders represent spending on goods that are supposed to last awhile, such as airplanes, washing machines, and dishwashers. Durable goods orders allow firms to scale up actual production; if durable goods orders are strong, firms will have more confidence to expand capacity. However, durable goods orders are also extremely volatile and subject to revision; for instance, a single order for a jumbo jet can move the number a significant amount. Some of these issues can be fixed by excluding defense spending and transportation and by smoothing the data. In general, durable goods order trends start well ahead of the actual GDP data trends, sometimes by a year. Data such as surveys and orders all contribute to the attempt to get a picture of industrial production before it turns. The actual growth in industrial production (IP) in the United States is released monthly. IP essentially measures the change in the quantity of production in the economy. The IP measure is by definition a look-back measure; it measures production that has already happened rather than looking forward. To the extent that IP takes a sharp turn, the information is useful for the market, but overall surveys such as ISM tend to have more forward-looking value than the IP number itself. Another related economic data measure released in conjunction with IP is capacity utilization. Capacity utilization measures the maximum sustainable capacity of firms in the economy, assuming they maintain a normal level of labor and capital inputs. Capacity utilization is a key measure to watch for signs of overheating or excess slack in the economy. For example, a capacity utilization measure of about 90% would imply risks of a cycle of increasing wages and prices whereas capacity utilization below 70% can be a sign of deflation. Capacity utilization is just one of various measures to gauge the risks of inflation in the economy; we discuss more of these measures next.

Inflation is the third category of data releases we consider. Inflation is a crucial economic variable to track for financial markets in general and interest rate markets in particular. For an investor in a long-term Treasury bond, inflation is one of the most significant risk factors as it erodes the value of fixed cash flows. Inflation data releases are examined closely for signs of overheating in the economy and, in recent years, for deflationary threats. The two main inflation data releases are the Consumer Price Index (CPI) and Producer Price Index (PPI). Simply put, the CPI considers a fixed weighted basket of consumer goods and calculates the price change in that basket. Essentially CPI is measuring the cost of living of a basket of goods in a given year. The PPI is similar but considers inflation from the perspective of inputs to producers. Both indices also are split further into a "headline" release and a "core" release. The headline number is the actual CPI release using the full basket, whereas the core release excludes food and energy items from the basket. The reasoning behind excluding food and energy is that these series are much more volatile and can hide the true trend in prices, especially over shorter time intervals. For example, if higher energy prices did have lasting effects, their price increases would begin to be reflected in all the output goods and thus show up in the core number. The core measure of CPI (and PPI) has become increasingly important as the economy has become more energy efficient and services oriented, both of which reduce the impact of energy price swings. To be sure, sharp rises in energy prices during periods of economic growth cannot be ignored, especially if fossil fuels decline in availability. Currently for the fixed income market, the core CPI continues to be the dominant inflation measure to determine the effects of monetary policy on the growth/inflation balance. The one exception to this is the Treasury Inflation-Protected Securities (TIPS) market, where, as discussed in Chapter 3, the principal is linked to the headline CPI, making oil a strong driver of TIPS valuations.

The PCE (personal consumption expenditure) is another way to measure inflation. Unlike the CPI-type indices, which use constant dollars, the core PCE measures inflation by using chained dollars. The term "chained dollars" refers to adjusting the weighting of the basket used to calculate inflation on a yearly basis. The measure uses averages of weights over consecutive years that roll forward over time, thus giving the name "chained dollars." In contrast, CPI uses constant weighting in its basket and is more a measure of cost of living than inflation over time. As with CPI, PCE has a core component that excludes the more volatile components of food and energy. The core PCE gained importance because the Fed uses it as one of its measures when measuring inflation. The Fed stated in 2000 that it was moving toward using PCE-type chained dollars methods instead of CPI, since chained dollars account for shifting baskets of goods in a more effective way and tend to be more stable than CPI. Nonetheless, CPI and PCE tend to be closely correlated, and any surprise in either index is likely to cause volatility.

The industrial production and inflation data provides a picture of broad economic trends. Various groups of economic data provide information about specific, important parts of the economy. One such group is housing data. The housing data to be discussed is released by the Census Bureau, a division of the U.S. Department of Commerce. The housing market is one of the most crucial sectors of the economy in the United States. The construction of new houses employs a large number of workers, and the secondary effects of purchasing new materials and other household goods result in further effects on the broader economy. A robust housing sector can also lead to wealth effects as rising home prices make homeowners feel wealthier, leading to higher consumption, while a falling housing price environment can lead to the reverse effect. The starting point for housing data is data on building permits and housing starts. Building permits, as the name implies, provide information on the number of permits given for new houses and tends to lead housing starts by one month. Housing starts count new units; a single-family home adds one unit while a multifamily unit adds the number of units in that apartment complex. As expected, the multifamily housing starts can be volatile if large new complexes are built. Furthermore, the weather can be another factor adding to volatility in the data set, as inclement weather can delay starts. Nevertheless, any sustained trends in housing starts and building permits can be useful leading indicators for the direction of the economy.

Housing starts indicate likely house-building activity in the economy. New home sales give a view of housing transactions. In addition to sales data, data on new home sales gives information on median prices, volume of houses for sale, and the inventory of housing in the market waiting to get sold. Similar to new home sales, there is also an existing home sales release. Data from home sales can be valuable in mapping the state of the housing market, including the amount of excess capacity from the inventory data and whether sellers are disposing of houses in distress. However, new home sales data can be volatile as well, and some amount of smoothing is generally needed to deduce a trend. Construction spending data is related to housing data. Construction spending represents a significant portion of the economy and has numerous spillover effects, from employment to related spending. It is separated into residential and nonresidential as well as spending by state and local governments, such as infrastructure. Construction spending data can at times be a useful indicator of an economic turning point.

One of the largest components of GDP in the United States is consumption (GDP $= C + I + G + NX$). A range of data is provided to give a glimpse of consumption. One of the most important indicators for consumption is the retail sales release around the middle of the month. The retail sales number represents the percentage change in the dollar volume of spending on goods in the economy. Given that consumption is about 70% of the economic growth in the United States, retail sales offer an important glimpse into the direction of the economy. The Commerce Department releases the retail sales number and in general, the number is split between durable and nondurable goods. Durable goods comprise longer-lasting expenditures, such as automobiles and building materials; nondurables represent day-to-day spending, such as on food. Autos form a large portion of durable goods spending. Consequently, the market also watches the "retail sales ex autos" number to remove any special effects from the autos sector. The retail sales number therefore offers a glimpse into the consumption section of GDP, but just on the goods side. For example, retail sales data does not incorporate medical or legal spending or other services. Furthermore, the dollar value spending number released is not inflation adjusted, although this is generally not a big issue, given lower inflation in recent decades. Retail sales represent only end user sales, not wholesale transactions, and can be forecasted from chain store sales data from individual retailers. Finally, as with all numbers, retail sales are seasonal with strong effects due to the holidays or inclement weather. Generally the expected retail sales number is supposed to incorporate seasonality.

Beyond the daily stream of economic data, a key set of events to watch for is Fed-speak—speeches, formal releases, and other communications by members of the FOMC or the Fed governors that discuss monetary policy and its direction. The Fed is not just a long-term backdrop, but is crucial for interest rate market participants to follow over the short term. Interest traders are constantly searching for news or developments that may give hints about the Fed's next move, which generally has a strong effect on the entire yield curve. The economic data releases just described are an indirect way to decipher the Fed's near-term policy moves by assessing the growth/inflation balance picture of the economy. For example, if core CPI rises substantially higher than a "comfortable" 1.5% to 2%, it is likely to increase the chances of interest rate hikes. More directly, Fed events provide a glimpse into the Fed's thoughts on where the economic cycle is heading. The main Fed event is the Federal Open Market Committee (FOMC) meeting that takes place every six weeks. At the meetings, FOMC members decide their next action on interest rates and release a statement outlining their view of the economy. Detailed minutes are released a few weeks after each meeting with specific discussions regarding the economy; these are known as the Fed minutes. The FOMC meeting tends to create volatility for the yield curve, especially if the market perceives there has been a change in the future path of the target rate. Figure 6.10 shows the one-day change in the 10-year Treasury rate and 2s/10s curve around FOMC meeting dates between 2007 and 2010, an interval when the market had a great deal of uncertainty about the Fed's future action. The standard deviation of 10-year yield changes was 12 basis points (bps) on these meeting dates compared to 7.4 bps for overall daily changes during the same period. For the curve, the standard deviation of the one-day changes was 8 bps compared to 5 bps for overall daily changes. These volatility numbers point to the market-moving importance of Fed meetings on the interest rate markets. During times of extreme financial stress, the Fed may meet in an "intermeeting" if it feels the six-week interval is too long to take action. Such meetings are rare but add considerable volatility to the market

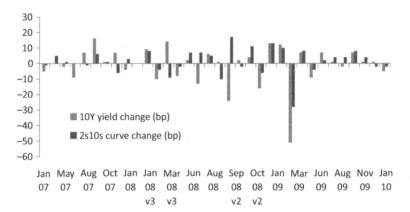

FIGURE 6.10 Change in the 10-Year Treasury Yield and the 2s/10s Curve around FOMC Meeting Dates
Source: Board of Governors of the Federal Reserve.

when they do occur. Beyond the (mostly) regular Fed meetings, Fed board members may speak to Congress or at other events and provide clues as to the Fed's stance on monetary policy. Traders are always watchful for any references to growth or inflation worries or any other references to future rate hikes or decreases. For example, if a few Fed board members feel that the current level of inflation is worrisome, yields are likely to rise. At times, a speech may be on an unrelated and non-market-relevant topic; nonetheless, the market may look for hints related to monetary policy. At other times, such as during the testimony of Fed chairman Humphrey Hawkins to Congress, the questions can be far more direct. Over the years, Fed-speak has changed character as the style of the FOMC has evolved. During the Greenspan years, Chairman Greenspan's influence on committee decisions was outsized and deciphering his words was key to figuring out possible changes in Fed thoughts about the economy. After Greenspan, under Ben Bernanke, the Fed has moved toward a more even balance among senior committee members. Deciphering Fed-speak increasingly requires understanding the importance of different members in Fed meetings.

Flight to Quality

An important, if unpredictable, short-term factor for Treasury yields is a flight to quality. Although economic cycles have their ups and downs, financial systems can encounter shocks that suddenly increase the risk premium in most assets. The market goes through phases of being comfortable with risk followed by bouts of risk aversion that lead to profit taking on winning trades and a flight back to safe assets. A variety of assets can be touted as "safe," such as certain currencies and gold, but Treasuries by far remain the product of choice. This is not necessarily because Treasuries are safer than gold, but more because of their liquidity. Given the ease with which money can flow in and out of Treasuries, they attract funds during stress times while investors try to avoid losses in more exposed risk markets. These swings in psychology can be very difficult to anticipate, but for Treasury yields, a negative shift in sentiment can cause yields to trade much lower than fair value estimates of Treasury yields relative to supply and demand and Fed policy. An episode of risk aversion may lower expectations of future economic growth, but the rush to Treasuries tends to be much more rapid than any reassessment of economic growth. Instead, the rush for safety and liquidity tends to be an overreaction and fades rapidly. It is exceedingly difficult to estimate "fair value" of yields in such a stress situation, as part of the yield premium is driven by weak economic prospects and part by excess funds flooding into safe assets.

Market risk aversion has effects not just on the level of yields but also on the shape of the yield curve. As funds flee from riskier assets, the sectors at the front end receive the greatest amount of flows, given their easy access for liquidity purposes. This situation was starkly evident in the T-bill market in late 2008, where shorter-end bills traded at negative yields. Across the yield curve, then, there tends to be a steepening effect. Longer-end rates tend to decline as well, but the extent of the decline is determined by the severity of the crisis; for more severe crises, the expectation of prolonged weak economic growth can cause longer-end rates to head successively lower after the front end does not have any lower to go. For example, the Long-Term Capital Management crisis caused a decline of 149 bps for 2-year rates and 96 bps for 10-year rates between the end of July and the end of October 1998. In the credit crunch, the severity of this crisis led 2-year rates to all-time lows. Ten-year rates then followed on a lagged basis as prospects of economic growth stayed gloomy until March 2009. As the economy showed signs of improvement, both rates headed higher, but this time, the 10-year rate led the charge. As discussed earlier, 10-year rates are linked to longer-term economic prospects; 2-year rates are far more linked to near-term Fed monetary policy, which was expected to stay on hold for 2010.

Risk aversion tends to be characterized by a flight to Treasuries and generally does not discriminate much among the different buyers of fixed income. Indeed, risk aversion affects market participants across asset classes such as equities. Flights of quality mostly arise from factors affecting the whole financial system, making it difficult to deduce the magnitude or length of their effect.

Debt Auctions

We discussed the importance of fixed income supply trends as drivers of interest rates. On a shorter-term basis, Treasury auctions are important cyclical events for the Treasury market. The Treasury releases its auction schedule for bonds well in advance. Increasing overall supply of Treasuries can pressure yields higher over the course of a few years, but here we are more concerned with the short-term effects of the auctions themselves. The auctions can have a stronger effect in times of heavy supply as dealers struggle more to take down supply and hold inventory amid a constant stream of new issuances. To deduce the near-term direction of yields in times of heavy supply, one must keep the auction schedule in mind. At times, a bullish or bearish view on a sector of the Treasury yield curve pays off more by careful entry and exit around auctions. For example, a 5-year auction tends to cheapen the 5-year sector against neighboring ones that are not facing an auction, such as 3-year and 10-year sectors. To trade such relative value, we would use a 3s/5s/10s butterfly, which would involve selling 5-year bonds and buying 3-year and 10-year bonds. Nothing in markets is constant, however. For trades such as these auction cycles, it seems obvious that the sector-facing issuance would cheapen, which caused many trading accounts to take advantage of the pattern in 2009, for example. Although the cycles were consistent for a large part of the year, over time, the profit on the trade began to disappear. As with any other principle, rather than taking them at face value, it is key to backtest any claims that market participants make.

Treasury auctions are not the only types of supply that can affect the Treasury market. The corporate bond market tends to have periods of heavy supply, partly due to seasonal factors related to corporate funding needs. When a corporation is about to issue a large amount of debt, during the period between the announcement and actual issuance, the corporation is exposed to rates rising and therefore needs to sell Treasuries/pay swaps to offset this risk. (If rates rise, the sale on Treasuries or paying in swaps offsets the loss on the debt issuance.) Such activity, known as rate locking, can temporarily lead to a rise in rates, which is generally reversed after the issuance is complete. Of course, if issuance is of a sustained nature, the supply hitting the market can lead to a more significant rise in rates, as described earlier in the section on fixed income supply. The increase in rates from temporary bouts of issuance tends to reverse itself; nonetheless, it is important to track the corporate issuance calendar for any unusual increases in activity.

Mortgage Hedging Flows

Treasury auctions and FOMC dates are mostly regularly scheduled, but other effects are less predictable. One such important effect stems from the mortgage market. In Chapter 3, we discussed the homeowner's ability to refinance the mortgage if interest rates decline. This option makes the interest rate risk of a mortgage bond shift more rapidly than that of a conventional bond. Declining rates reduce the duration of a mortgage bond; increasing rates increase its duration. We discuss the process of hedging mortgages in more detail in Chapter 8, but, essentially, as rates head lower and mortgage durations shrink, a mortgage bond owner needs to buy more Treasuries or receive more swaps to maintain the same duration risk. As rates head higher, the reverse situation takes place. Mortgage durations increase and mortgage bond owners need to sell Treasuries or pay swaps to maintain the same duration risk. These effects lead to cycles where increasing rates lead to more mortgage participants selling Treasuries or paying fixed in swaps and causing even higher rates. On the other hand, decreasing rates lead to mortgage participants buying Treasuries or receiving in swaps, resulting in even lower rates. Although mortgage market effects are present day to day and make it important to track aggregate mortgage durations and convexities frequently, the effects are not uniform. At certain interest rate levels, there may be more pent-up need to hedge mortgages than at other levels, making the process discontinuous. If rates have remained low for an extended period of time, the issuance of new mortgages may add more supply to the market due to refinancings, and any subsequent rise in rates can induce significant mortgage hedging through selling Treasuries. Furthermore, mortgage hedging has effects on the entire yield curve shape, not just any single point. Mortgage hedgers do not use a single maturity point for swaps, but instead vary their choice of maturity for duration-matching purposes or other considerations such as relative value and carry. For example, if rates decline sharply and mortgage durations decline with them, mortgage hedgers may shift from using longer-maturity securities such as in the 10-year sector to a shorter maturity sector such as the 3-year. The hedging then would have effects not just on the level of rates but also the shape of the curve due to the switch to buying in shorter maturity sectors (i.e., it would steepen the curve). Figure 6.11 shows the 10-year Treasury rate and 2s/10s Treasury curve during one such episode in the summer of 2003. Interest rates hit rock-bottom levels in June 2003, causing mortgage durations to decline as well. As the economic picture improved during the summer and rates began to rise, the mortgage hedging brought along significant increases in rates through the feedback loop mentioned earlier. The sharp steepening of the curve shows that the mortgage hedging effect was focused in the 5- to 10-year rate

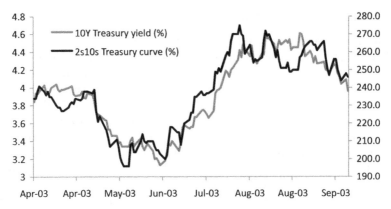

FIGURE 6.11   10-Year Treasury Yield and the 2s/10s Treasury Curve during the 2003 Mortgage Duration Extension Period
Source: Board of Governors of the Federal Reserve.

sector of the curve rather than at the front end. A similar process took place in June 2008 when, even as the unemployment picture looked bleak, rates rose sharply due partly to positioning and partly to mortgage hedging. Frequently, outsiders ascribe increased volatility in the rates market to rapid reassessment of the economy; in reality, the volatility may be exacerbated by mortgage hedging. Another point to note with mortgage hedging is its effects on the swap versus Treasury market. In general, mortgage participants hedge using swaps more frequently than Treasuries. Thus, even as mortgage hedging affects rates, it has an even greater effect on the *spread* between Treasuries and swaps, known as swap spreads. We discuss swap spreads in more detail in Chapter 9.

Exotics Hedging Flows

Another effect on the rates market due to hedging activity is at the long end of the curve from hedging of exotics. The term "exotics" refers to securities with nonstandard payoffs that generally are not widely traded. However, at times, certain types of exotics notes are issued in large enough size that hedging of their risk by dealers can affect the rates market as well. In general, these effects are felt most at the longer end of the curve since most exotics notes tend to be long-maturity notes. Furthermore, lower liquidity at the long end of the yield curve means trades have a larger effect on rates than in the intermediate maturity sector. At any given time, different types of exotic securities may be popular in the market. Since these types tend to vary considerably, it is difficult to generalize their effect on the rates market. As with mortgages, the bulk of exotics hedging is done in the swaps market. Although interest rate levels at the long end are affected, the effect is felt even more on swap spreads (swap yields – Treasury yields). We discuss exotics hedging and its effect on the swap spreads in more detail in Chapter 9.

Seasonality

The final factor to consider as a short-term driver of yields is seasonality. Seasonality is an important factor to keep in mind when making short-term trading decisions, but it must be considered with care. Seasonal patterns can arise in the market in various ways. They tend to occur due to some structural facet of the market that may be difficult to arbitrage. Figure 6.12 shows the change in the 10-year Treasury yield averaged by month since 1990. It is apparent that April tends to see the largest increase in 10-year yields while August and September tend to see decreases. It is important to note that the average change in these months is on the order of 10 to 20 bps while the standard deviation of yield changes across these months is on the order of 20 to 30 bps. The average level compared to the standard deviation indicates some level of statistical significance for the months of April, August, and September, though the standard deviation also indicates substantial variability around the average change. The other months are not very significant. These are changes across a large number of years and ignore the Fed cycle and economic growth. One source of cyclical patterns arises from quarter-end and month-end behavior by institutions, which tend to rebalance positions based on the performance across asset classes. For example, poor performance in equities during a quarter may lead

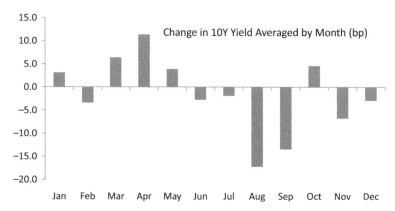

FIGURE 6.12 Seasonality of the 10-Year Treasury Yield
Source: Board of Governors of the Federal Reserve.

cross–asset class investors to rebalance into equities and out of bonds at quarter-end, which tends to be the usual rebalancing time. Another example tends to be bond fund managers rebalancing at month-end to match index components and duration. As new bonds are issued in the market, the composition of broad fixed income indices changes, and the issuance of new bonds can increase the duration of the index, leading managers to buy more bonds in the market at month-end. Yet another cyclical effect takes place with redemptions of bonds in the market. February and August tend to be months of heavy issuance with quarterly 10- and 30-year bond issuance along with the other maturities. As bonds mature, the principal repayments, known as redemptions, add cash back to the market. These principal payments are generally reinvested in the Treasury market and can, on the margin, act as a bullish factor for bonds. All these effects add to the cyclical behavior of Treasuries, but their importance must be understood in context. Given the standard deviation highlighted earlier around seasonal effects, they should not form the primary reason for a view on rates. Instead, they can be important in substantiating an already existing view of lower or higher yields. The starting point for views on interest rates is to assess the combination of broader medium-term trends in Fed policy and the economic cycle as well as shorter-term hedging flows, auction-related cycles, and other factors discussed in this chapter. Once these factors have been accounted for, seasonality can be an important factor to bolster one's view or, at times, to wait before entering a trade if seasonal factors do not line up with the main view.

SUMMARY

Numerous factors can affect rates. These factors are constantly in a state of flux with different factors increasing or receding in importance as the economic winds shift. Beyond the factors mentioned in this chapter, new factors are sure to emerge over time to affect interest rates. To deal with the dynamic nature of interest rate markets, it is important to approach them logically, taking into account drivers whose horizons range from decades to days. With rate markets, it is important to know the major drivers on long and short time scales; it is just as important to be on the lookout for new factors that may arise from time to time.

CHAPTER 7

Carry and Relative Value Trades

I n Chapter 6 we considered the process of taking views on where interest rates or curves may be headed. For such trades, the aim is to take a
view on the level and shape of the yield curve. In certain regimes, such
as when the Fed is firmly on hold, rates and curves may be rangebound for
long periods of time. This chapter considers trades ideal for such environments: carry trades and relative value trades. It may seem at first glance
that trading involves mostly taking directional bets on interest rates. However, carry trades and relative value trades are important classes of trades
where the main motivation is not to take an outright view on the market.
Instead, the aim is to initiate trades that either generate net income from
holding interest rate securities or take advantage of dislocations in markets. Carry and relative value trades have distinct methods to earn profits,
but have many similar underlying principles. They are essential concepts to
understand not just to profit from rangebound markets but also to express
views on interest rate markets more effectively in any environment.

CARRY TRADES

The chief aim of a carry trade is to earn income from holding an asset.
Chapter 2's introduction to bonds showed that carry is calculated as the
coupon income of a bond less the financing cost. The term "carry trade" is
more general than just the carry from buying a bond, but at their core, carry
trades tend to optimize net income from holding the trade. To consider

how carry interacts with price change in profit or loss (P/L), we can recall that the P/L of an asset equals net income from holding asset (carry) plus price change in asset. The price change in the asset is also referred to as the mark-to-market (MTM) P/L. Two points become clear from this simple equation.

1. The ideal carry trade will try to benefit from a large term in the first term of the equation, which is net income from holding the asset.
2. The threat to P/L from the carry trade is from negative MTM P/L that offsets gains from the asset's net income.

The second point is very important, and has key implications for when carry trades work. For example, we mentioned that carry trades work best during periods when the Federal Reserve has interest rates anchored at the shorter maturities, or when market volatility is low. We can see why that is the case from our P/L equation. For carry trades to be attractive, small changes in price (or yields) are desirable. In such cases, the volatility of P/L will be low (since net income from holding the asset does not fluctuate much), leading to high risk-adjusted P/L. If the MTM P/L of the trade is in the carry trade's favor, such profits are surely beneficial but generally are not the main reason to initiate a carry trade. Indeed, if MTM gains are reversed rapidly, the trade will seem poor on a risk-adjusted basis.

When judging a trade, the P/L to volatility (or risk) ratio is the more relevant metric; it is the statistical equivalent of demonstrating that the P/L was not just luck. Therefore, when we initiate a trade whose primary motivation is carry, we want trades with as little price (or yield) movement as possible. The aim is to just sit on the trade and earn the income. Given that we want trades with as little volatility as possible, we can use that aim to compare different carry trades and to quantitatively judge the attractiveness of any given one. A simple metric is the ratio of carry to volatility (also called the carry-to-risk ratio). Since a carry trade's aim is to have P/L equal carry, carry-to-risk ratio is the analogous concept here. As with the risk-adjusted P/L concept, the risk component is ambiguous. We can use a long-term standard deviation of yield changes for fixed income instruments, as with risk-adjusted P/L. In this case, the "change" period for yields or prices tends to be the same as the period over which carry is being measured, such as three months. As with risk-adjusted P/L, at times it might be more instructive to consider a short lookback period for standard deviation (i.e., sample size), if recent times have been very different from the past.

Finally, before presenting an example, it is important to note that carry trades may involve no actual income inflow. This is true when carry trades are constructed using futures or forward starting trades, where there is no actual inflow of coupon income. As discussed in Chapter 2, in addition to carry, instruments with fixed maturity dates, such as bonds, have rolldown. *Rolldown* is the change in the price or yield of the asset as it ages. For carry trades involving bonds, it is common to incorporate carry + rolldown when judging the trade, including when taking the ratio of "carry" to volatility. Therefore, going forward, *carry-to-risk ratio* will refer to the ratio of carry + rolldown to volatility of yield changes for bonds. For futures or forwards, there is no pure carry in the sense of cash flows. Instead, the entire "carry" is the rolldown. How does this relate to our simple P/L calculation? In the case of forward starting trades or futures, the P/L on the asset will be the price (or yield) change in the asset, but part of the price change will be just from the aging of the asset toward a spot trade. Note that the motivation behind the carry trade remains exactly the same: We want the asset to age and present us with a gain from the price change, and ideally there would be minimal price changes stemming from other factors. There is one subtle difference between pure carry and rolldown: Pure carry can be fixed for a certain time period using a term repo rate, whereas there is no such mechanism to lock in rolldown. From a trading standpoint, though, this distinction is less important than it may appear at first glance. For thinking about either carry or rolldown, the aim is still to control volatility in the trade to take advantage of profits from a steady stream of P/L from the asset.

CARRY TRADE SETUP AND EVALUATION

Although we mentioned that the chief aim of carry trades is to benefit from net income or rolldown rather than taking a view on markets, many carry trades are exposed to broad movements in rates, particularly, simple carry trades that mostly involve the purchase of a bond or futures contract to take advantage of expected carry and rolldown. When the curve is upward sloping—that is, when longer-term rates are higher than shorter-term rates—buying a Treasury bond or receiving in a swap is positive carry, since the financing cost is referenced off the very short end while the yield of the instrument is a higher, longer rate. A simple example of such a trade was buying the 2-year Treasury bond in late 2009. Given the Fed's target rate near zero and the 2-year yield near 0.9%, the steep curve provided investors with a large amount of carry and rolldown. However, the outright nature of the trade exposed the investor to the risk that 2-year yields would rise sharply. To quantify, the carry and rolldown combined over a 3-month (3M) period on the trade was about 20 basis points (bps) every quarter (calculated as 3M forward 2Y yield − 2Y yield approximately; see Chapter 2 for more details). This meant that a 20-bp rise in yields could wipe out all carry gains in a quarter. The standard deviation of daily yield changes of the 2-year yield was 5.3 bps/day in the second half of 2009, or 84 bps on an annualized basis. This is calculated as $5.3 \times \sqrt{251} = 5.3 \times 15.84 = 84$ bps (also see Chapter 2 for more details). The 3M carry can itself be annualized; 20 bps every three months is equivalent to 80 bps every year. Annualizing both carry and volatility allows for easy comparison between the two. Although carry is a motivation for the trade, that does not exclude directional considerations. For example, the odds of benefiting from carry would be increased if the 2-year Treasury was bought at a cheaper level near the upper end of its local range, say 1.10%, rather than at the lower end of its range near 0.70%. Additionally, investors buying it had to believe that the Fed was going to be firmly on hold, which would cap any increase in 2-year yield rises and keep volatility low. A trade such as this is an example of a directional trade where carry from the asset is a fundamental factor for initiating the trade.

The 2-year Treasury is one of many such examples of a carry trade. For investors looking for carry, the Eurodollar futures market is a common one to trade. Carry trades in a futures contract such as Eurodollars attempt to exploit rolldown rather than pure income carry, but the aim of the trade is the same nonetheless. As explained in Chapter 4, Eurodollar futures rolldown is simply the yield on the contract being considered minus the yield on the 3-month aged contract. This simple calculation makes Eurodollar futures an effective way to demonstrate the idea behind hedged carry trades. Table 7.1 shows the Eurodollar futures contract table as of August 2010 and the carry for each contract next to it, which is calculated as the simple difference between successive contracts. At first glance, we may want to buy the December 2011 (EDZ1; see Chapter 4 for symbol conventions) as an outright carry trade. This would be similar to the 2-year Treasury example and earns about 20 bps in rolldown every three months. There are other maturities with similar levels of carry, such as EDM2 and EDZ2 (June and December 2012). To optimally compare between the trades, the carry should be controlled for by the level of volatility since the more volatile the trade, the less attractive is the carry. Often the annualized carry-to-volatility ratio is used for a quick comparison between different carry trades. Table 7.1 shows these annualized ratios, which are calculated by multiplying the carry by 4 (3M carry) and annualizing the daily volatility by multiplying by 15.84. Alternatively, the volatility of three-month changes in the contract yield could be used. For investors in these markets, comparing carry-to-volatility ratios of

TABLE 7.1 Eurodollar Contract Carry Table

Contract	Rate (%)	Rolldown (bp)	Daily Volatility* (bp)	Annualized Ratio[†]
EDU0	0.37			
EDZ0	0.42	5.0	3.9	0.32
EDH1	0.50	7.5	4.2	0.45
EDM1	0.60	10.5	4.9	0.54
EDU1	0.75	14.5	5.6	0.66
EDZ1	0.94	19.5	6.1	0.80
EDH2	1.12	18.0	6.6	0.69
EDM2	1.31	18.5	6.9	0.67
EDU2	1.48	17.5	7.2	0.62
EDZ2	1.67	18.5	7.3	0.64
EDH3	1.83	16.5	7.5	0.56
EDM3	2.02	19.0	7.6	0.63
EDU3	2.20	18.0	7.6	0.59
EDZ3	2.39	19.0	7.7	0.62

*Standard deviation of daily changes in the Eurodollar rate over past six months.
[†]Calculated as annualized rolldown ($\times$ 4) divided by annualized volatility ($\times$ 15.84).
Source: Bloomberg LP.

instruments across fixed income products should be a key factor for trade selection.

Carry trades do not have to be done as outright trades. Indeed, outright trades can have significant volatility and at times erase all the carry embedded in them from negative MTM P/L. To mitigate the volatility, more complex combinations of instruments can be considered, which maintain a high level of carry but lower the volatility due to offsetting risks. Some examples include curve trades and butterfly trades across Eurodollar, Treasury, and swap markets. Comparing a large variety of trades makes the carry-to-volatility ratio even more important. Often a curve trade or a butterfly trade would appear to have lower outright carry than the outright trade, but it may also have lower volatility and can be more attractive as a trade. One example is a weighted curve trade. Consider the EDM1/EDZ2 curve from the Eurodollar contract table above. The simple 1:1 curve trade generally needs to be weighted since EDM1 can have different volatility from EDZ2, which can cause the curve to be directional with underlying interest rates. To weight these trades, a regression tends to be the simplest method. Figure 7.1 regresses daily changes for six months between EDZ2 daily changes against daily changes in the EDM1 rate. The beta of this regression is the sensitivity of EDZ2 to EDM1; it means EDZ2 moves 0.94 times as much as EDM1. Thus, to remove the difference in volatility between the curves, the weighted curve trade would have a 0.94:1 weighting,

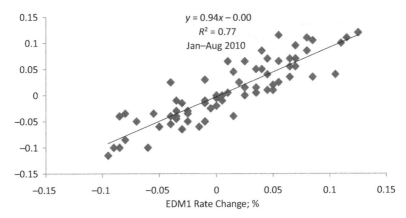

FIGURE 7.1 EDZ2 Changes (%) Regressed versus EDM1 Changes during Early 2010
Source: Bloomberg LP.

which means sell 0.94 risk weight on EDM1 and buy 1 risk weight on EDZ2. Note that 0.94 risk weight implies that the dollar value of one basis point (DV01) weight on EDM1 is 94% of the DV01 weight on EDZ2. For Eurodollar contracts, the DV01 weight is equal to the weighting in contracts, since the DV01 is equal at $25 for both (i.e., for every 100 EDZ2 contracts we buy, we sell 94 EDM1 contracts). The weighted curve's daily volatility, calculated as the standard deviation of daily changes in EDZ2 $-$ 0.94 $\times$ EDM1, is only 2.7 bps/day, which is much lower than the 4.9 bps/day volatility of EDM1 and 7.3 bps/day volatility of EDZ1. The carry on this weighted trade is 1 $\times$ carry on EDZ2 $-$ 0.94 $\times$ carry on EDM1, or 1 $\times$ 18.5 $-$ 0.94 $\times$ 10.5 $=$ 8.6 bps. Here, the annualized carry-to-volatility ratio is 0.82 (8.6 $\times$ 4/(2.7 $\times$ 15.84)), which is higher than the ratio of each of the outright carry trades. Therefore, weighted trades such as this curve trade offer more efficient ways to earn carry.

PITFALLS OF THE CARRY TRADE

Carry is an inherently attractive concept for investors, but the dangers of the carry trade deserve their own section. A positive carry trade starts investors off on the trade with an advantage, since the trade needs a certain threshold of adverse price movement before investors actually start losing money on the trade. However, this apparent cushion can be misleading and may result in adverse consequences if investors become complacent. As mentioned, carry trades work best in low-volatility environments where mark-to-market P/L is unlikely to impact the steady income from carry.

However, a single investor is not an isolated entity. As markets settle into comfortable ranges, other investors discover the same attractive carry trades with high carry and low volatility. This leads to a slow buildup of positions into the market's favorite carry trades. The longer the calm times continue, the more investors jump on the carry bandwagon. Although this narrative is somewhat simplified, the essence of this argument plays with disturbing regularity in markets. The tendency of investors to herd into similar trades likely arises from the search for returns in rangebound markets that do not offer many opportunities to profit from directional movements. Furthermore, rangebound markets make an increasingly large number of carry trades attractive as historical volatility measures begin to look increasingly muted. However, the cycle cannot continue forever; at some point, the market's favorite carry trades become saturated. At that point, a small spark from perhaps an unfavorable piece of news or a hedger compelled to initiate the opposite trade in the market can provide just the impetus needed to scare carry traders. As successive waves of carry traders escape, the previously attractive carry trade suffers MTM losses with other investors doing the opposite trade to unwind their positions. As these losses grow, even more investors holding the trade are forced to unwind the trade. The vicious cycle only stops once a large number of investors in the crowded trade have abandoned it; in the meantime, the volatility of the trade has increased sharply, making its carry-to-volatility ratio look poor in comparison to prior calculations.

An example of the dynamic of crowding into popular carry trades was evident in the rates markets in early to mid-2009 with the front-end carry trade. In January 2009, the Fed lowered its target rate to near zero and the rate was expected to remain there for an extended period of time due to structural weaknesses in the economy. This expectation of a firmly anchored front end led to long positions in the 2-year Treasury (and related trades) as a market-favored carry trade. It is easy to see why, since an investor could buy the 2-year Treasury yielding near 1% and fund it at near zero in the financing markets. As long as there were no large changes in Fed expectations, the trade was an effective carry trade. Figure 7.2 plots the net long positions in the 2-year Treasury futures contract and 2-year yields in early 2009. We use the Treasury futures position data rather than that of cash bonds since position data is easily retrievable for futures from the exchanges from the CFTC. Positioning tends to be similar in the cash and futures space, as many investors use these markets interchangeably to take views on interest rates. The figure is instructive regarding the dangers of carry trades. As the 2-year yield was rangebound between February and May, the long positions at the front end continued to build up. Note that as long as the 2-year yield remained in its range, the carry trade remained profitable; investors just bought the bond and earned the coupon income

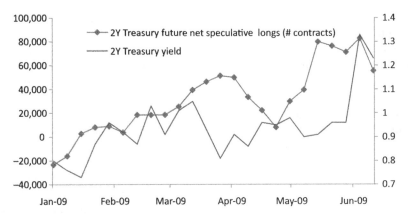

FIGURE 7.2 Net Speculative Long Positions in 2-Year Treasury Futures Contracts Chasing the 2-Year Treasury Yield
Sources: CFTC, Board of Governors of the Federal Reserve.

after funding the bond at near zero. However, the favorable dynamic broke down in late May/early June. At that time, some doubts arose about the Fed's timeline of increasing rates as faint optimism returned about the health of the economy. At the same time, there was a buildup of mortgage hedging needs because rates had remained low for a long time, leaving mortgage hedgers susceptible to increases in duration. Indeed, as 2-year yields drifted higher in late May, the floodgates opened in early June and the 2-year yield broke its ranges from the last few months. This increase led to escalating losses on those long 2-year Treasury carry trades. As the losses became too large, more investors sold their positions. The vicious cycle finally ended as 2-year yields got near 1.50%; at that point, it seemed that most of the carry-driven long positions were flushed out. With the benefit of hindsight, an investor then could have bought the 2-year Treasury at 1.50% to take advantage of its decline back to 1% over the next few weeks, but during such violent trade unwind episodes, it is difficult to judge when the large positions are done unwinding. After all, the exchanges release position data only weekly, and during such episodes, a week can encompass a great deal of volatility. The sharp increase in 2-year rates soon reversed course as incoming economic data convinced the market that the Fed would remain on hold near zero. In the meantime numerous carry traders had suffered large losses.

The 2-year Treasury example does not mean that carry trading should be abandoned. The key point to remember for carry trading is that the risk measure we are using is almost always a backward-looking measure. Calm, low-volatility markets can turn violent rapidly, and complacent investors can lose months' worth of carry gains in a matter of days. For the carry investor, it is important to understand the risk in a trade beyond just recent standard deviation. Low-volatility regimes that make some carry trades look attractive can suddenly turn into high-volatility regimes, making the same carry trades appear unattractive. Although standard carry-to-volatility ratios form a great starting point for the hunt for trades, constant vigilance around positioning is required. For example, if a trade becomes very popular and is touted as an obvious one, there is a high likelihood that too many investors are already involved, making it susceptible to rapid exits. Finally, it can also be useful to calculate carry to volatility using volatility from some high-risk past regimes to get a better sense of the downside in the trade.

Two clues can be used to better judge how crowded a trade is. Position data needs to be tracked very closely across markets where it is available. For U.S. markets, the futures exchanges release positioning data on a weekly basis. This data can be tracked to get a sense of a rapid buildup in certain trades (see Chapter 4). Also at times, the same global financial flows that rush into attractive U.S. trades are also funding other carry trades, such as currency pairs with countries where the interest rate differentials are large. An example would be Australia versus Japan in 2009. Australian yields were closer to 5% versus near 0% in Japan. Therefore, buying the Australian Dollar and earning Australian yield versus the low Japanese Yen yield was an attractive carry trade. As financial flows from similar sources went hunting for carry across the globe, seemingly unrelated trades from a range of markets were closely tracking the Australian Dollar/Japanese Yen currency pair. To be sure, this was a temporary phenomenon since different environments spawn interest in different popular trades. However, when correlations between these seemingly unrelated trades increase rapidly, it is a sign of the same global flows chasing the same carry trades. Large unwinds in other big carry trades can be a warning signal.

Crowded trades tend to display muted moves with regard to favorable news or favorable movements in other markets but oversize moves in the face of negative news. This asymmetry is difficult to quantify but by watching markets closely, over time a trader can become aware of changes in the behavior of different market sectors. An example of such asymmetry can be a long Treasury position where weaker-than-expected economic data fails to drive yields much lower but stronger-than-expected economic data leads to a large rise in yields. This will tend to happen because there are already too many long positions in the market and there is little appetite to add more on the back of favorable news; unfavorable news, however, leads investors to the exits. Although it may seem obvious, often such signs are more subtle but can be helpful in judging how long to hold carry trades and, one hopes, exit out of them before others try to.

CARRY-EFFICIENT
DIRECTIONAL TRADES

So far we have considered trades where carry is the prime goal. At times such trades also have incidental exposure to the markets, such as the long 2-year Treasury position discussed earlier. Here carry is the main motivator, and any exposure to yields is secondary. We also discussed hedging more complicated trades to take advantage of pure carry rather than having exposure to the market. At times, however, a trader can have a certain view in mind but trades initiated to take advantage of the view could have negative carry. In such situations, the term "carry-efficient trades" refers to trades that are correlated with a particular trade, but with reduced negative carry.

It is difficult to generalize carry-efficient trades as they take numerous forms in different environments. An example may help to clarify the concept. Earlier we discussed the long 2-year Treasury as a carry trade in 2009. The mirror image trade that positioned for higher front-end rates suffered from steep negative carry. Thus, for a trader, a short 2-year Treasury position was a risky one as the position lost about 20 bps every quarter without the market even moving. This negative carry made the trade a steep uphill climb; the trader needed the rise in 2-year yields to take place rapidly to earn a profit. However, in general, it is difficult to time the moment when investors in a crowded trade would head to the exits. The longer the wait for such an event to take place, the more difficult it is to make profits for the position. Carry-efficient trades are those that are highly correlated to the 2-year Treasury in this case but face less negative carry than the short 2-year Treasury position.

In general, there can be numerous carry-efficient trades. An important criterion to judge such trades—other than lower negative carry—is the correlation with our market view. One example of a trade that was correlated to the 2-year rate in 2009 but with less negative carry was a weighted 2s/5s flattener. To take apart the jargon, this trade would involve selling the 2-year Treasury but buying 30% risk weight on the 5-year Treasury. Figure 7.3 shows that this trade is indeed correlated to the 2-year Treasury yield. As the regression shows, this trade has a 0.6 beta to the 2-year yield and therefore has only 60% of the risk. To compare carry between two trades, we need to ensure that the trades have equivalent risk weights; therefore, we need to scale down the negative carry in the outright 2-year Treasury position by 60%. Generally, for any view on rates that has negative carry for holding the position, trades can be found that reduce the negative carry of the position but are still highly correlated to the original view.

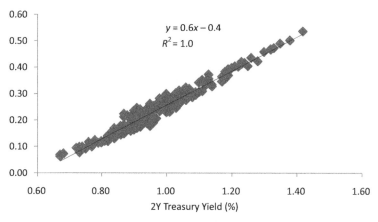

FIGURE 7.3 30% Weight on 5-Year Treasury Yield − 2-Year Treasury Yield (%) Regressed against the 2-Year Treasury Yield
Source: Board of Governors of the Federal Reserve.

RELATIVE VALUE TRADES

Relative value trades are those where the investor intends to exploit market relationships that have become dislocated. Relative value trades ideally are placed without taking outright views on the markets. The relative value of a trade versus similar instruments is an important factor in understanding a trade. The goal is to find a relationship between two or more market variables that is away from its long-run average and points to a "cheap" and a "rich" instrument. Relative value trading entails taking a view that this relationship will revert back to the average. Pure relative value trades should be based on trades that show few sustained trends and instead resemble a white noise series that is at an extreme level. To clarify with an example, suppose bond A trades at a 5% yield and bond B trades at a 4.50% yield in the market. The spread between the bonds is 0.50%, or 50 bps. Assume that this spread is unusual and that, on average, the spread trades at 20 bps. This means that bond A tends to trade only 20 bps higher in yield than bond B on average rather than the current 50 bps spread. A trader can buy bond A or sell bond B outright since bond A yields appear too high and bond B yields appear too low. However, such trades have a large exposure to overall interest rates and may make or lose money regardless of the relative value differences between these two bonds. A more specific trade to take advantage of the dislocation is to buy bond A *and* sell bond B to position for the yield difference to narrow. Note that such a trade is protected against any general rise in interest rates since if both bond A and bond B yields rise by an equal amount the P/L on bond B offsets the P/L on bond A. However, if bond A yields *decline more* than bond B yields, thus narrowing the difference between the two bonds, the trade makes money (since we bought bond A and sold bond B, and a decline in yields makes money for the buyer). The situation is reversed if bond A yields rise more than bond B yields, further widening the spread between the two. The reader should make sure to understand why the trade makes or loses money only if the spread between the bond yields changes rather than if overall levels of interest rates change.

In the example trade just given, the trader positioned for a reversion of the 50-bp spread toward its long-run average of 20 bps and in that case would net a profit of 30 bps. There are some points to note about the expected reversion to 20 bps. First, the reversion from 50 bps to 20 bps is more compelling if the spread has lower volatility. For example, if the spread has volatility of 100 bps, the 30 bps difference between the current level and long-run average level is not particularly unusual. On the other hand, if the volatility of the yield spread is 5 bps, the 30 bps difference seems truly unusual. In short, the ratio of the current discrepancy to the volatility of the underlying trade is important to keep in mind when judging the attractiveness of relative value trades. Second, a relative value trade has a greater chance of reverting back to the long-run average if the trade is not caught up in a strong trend. Market variables with a strong trend up or down may not revert to any particular level for long periods of time. Such situations can occur if the fundamental drivers of the trade undergo a structural change, essentially altering the long-run average level itself. For example, in our bond A versus bond B example, if bond A's credit rating was downgraded sharply, the 20-bp long-run average difference between the two yields is unlikely to be meaningful, and the spread may keep widening well past 50 bps. For a trader positioned from a relative value standpoint, such a fundamental change would be a signal to get out. Finally, at first glance, carry trades and relative value trades seem very distinct, but they are actually driven by similar motivations. As with carry trades, the prime environment for relative value trades is a low-volatility, rangebound market. Dislocations of different sectors in such markets are unlikely to grow too large, and such environments tend to encourage other investors to take advantage of dislocations to keep them in line. Not surprisingly, from a monetary policy standpoint, Fed on-hold regimes tend to be most effective for relative value trades overall, but all regimes are likely to have local relative value dislocations that can be exploited at times.

Given similar underlying motivations for carry trades and relative value trades, similar pitfalls for both exist as well. In particular, in low-volatility markets, certain relative value trades can have a large consensus behind them, leading to overcrowding. If the trade is crowded, a rapid exit by investors may only cause the dislocation to get worse. If dislocated relationships do not revert back to the mean for long periods of time, the trader needs to reassess the premise behind the relative value trade itself. This is especially true of relationships that have been dislocated for a long period and are failing to revert back to their average. If the reversion to the mean fails for a long period of time, it may indicate that the underlying fundamentals behind the trade itself have changed. This in turn can change the long-run average of the trade itself, eliminating any expectation of a reversion to the original target average level.

SETTING UP RELATIVE VALUE TRADES

Trades with little broad market exposure are referred to as pure relative value and these are the ones we will consider here. A relative value trade typically will have two or more instruments traded in opposite directions. Setting up relative value trades entails weighting the different instruments of the trade in such a way that there is minimal exposure to the broader market. This is set up by ensuring that the weights reflect the relative volatility and sensitivity of each instrument. Regression analysis is a useful tool for weighting relative value trades since it is an effective way to determine market variable exposures (using the regression betas). To understand these factors, we focus on a common example of a relative value trade from the Treasury market. The important point here is the thought process behind selection of the relative value trade, calculating appropriate weights for the legs, and backtesting the relative value strategies.

The relative value trade we focus on is between the 5-year Treasury and the 2-year and 10-year Treasuries. This is a common trade in the Treasury market and involves buying or selling 5-year Treasuries against the opposite transaction with both 2-year and 10-year legs. Chapter 2 described such a trade as a butterfly trade. The 2-year and 10-year legs are the "wings" while the 5-year leg is the body. To make the example clearer, we choose a time period where the 5-year Treasury was dislocated versus the wings. In general, selecting relative value trades with other products or maturities involves identifying the dislocation described in the 2s/5s/10s example below. To start with, consider the 50:50 weighted trade (i.e., 50% weight on each of the wings): 5-year Treasury yield $-$ 0.5 $\times$ 2-year Treasury yield $-$ 0.5 $\times$ 10-year Treasury yield. This trade can be thought of as the difference between the body of the butterfly and the average of the wings. Figure 7.4 shows the 50:50 butterfly. This spread may be partly driven by other factors, such as the level of the yield of the body (i.e., 5-year yield). If only the

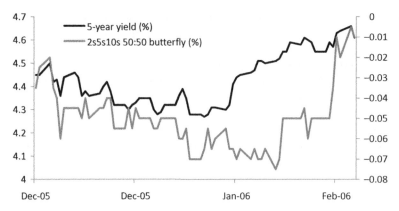

FIGURE 7.4 2s5s10s Butterfly (50:50 Weight) against the 5-Year Treasury Yield
Source: Board of Governors of the Federal Reserve.

50:50 trade is done, these hidden factors may drive the butterfly rather than just relative value considerations. Since this is a trade with three securities, we look for two factors to explain it. In the end, it may be the case that only one factor is the main driver, but we start with two factors here. The first choice is the 5-year yield shown in Figure 7.4. Many market participants in the rates world have a preference for 50:50 butterflies as they seem more intuitive; but in fact various hidden factors can drive such trades. Even if these factors are accepted as necessary risk factors when doing a 50:50 trade, the magnitude of their effects can vary. Finally, suppose the 50:50 butterfly was highly correlated to the 5-year yield. In that case, a trader is paying three times the transaction cost for a much simpler trade that likely will present similar P/L; after all, just because it is a butterfly, it does not make it a less risky trade.

To truly take a view on the relative value of the 5-year sector versus the wings, we must remove the effect of just the 5-year yield changing or the 2s/10s curve changing (i.e., 10-year yield − 2-year Treasury yield). Once these effects are removed, the trade is driven purely by the relative performance of the 5-year sector versus the 2-year and 10-year sectors, rather than movements in yields or the slope of the curve. To do this, we require a multiple regression using both variables (using only one variable separately will mask any cross-relationship between the yield level and the curve). Furthermore, using a multiple regression allows us to isolate the partial betas after controlling for the other variable's effects. The multiple regression equation shows that $(5Y - 0.5 \times 2Y - 0.5 \times 10Y) = beta1 \times (5Y \ yield) + beta2 \times (10Y \ yield - 2Y \ yield) + intercept + residual$. Figures 7.5 and 7.6 show the partial regressions of the 50:50 weighted butterfly against the body yield and the curves between the wings (2s10s).

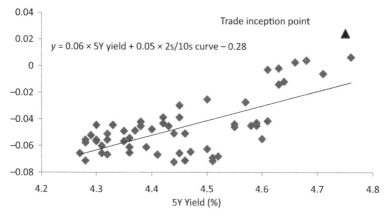

FIGURE 7.5 2s5s10s Treasury Yield Butterfly (%) Regressed against the 5-Year Yield after Adjusting for the 2s/10s Curve
Source: Board of Governors of the Federal Reserve.

The residual is above the regression line, which means the 5-year yield is too high relative to the 2- and 10-year yields; in other words, it is trading too cheap (higher yield = lower price). The relationship with the 5-year yield is stronger than that with the 2s10s curve, but this relationship can change over time. Both are included here for completeness' sake. In particular, beta1 = 0.06 and beta2 = 0.05. Beta1 = 0.06 implies for every 1-bp change in the 5-year yield, the butterfly changes by 6 bps, while beta2 = 0.05 implies for every 1-bp change in the 2s/10s curve, the 50:50 butterfly

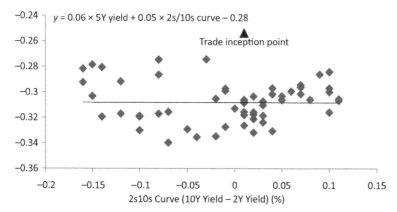

FIGURE 7.6 2s5s10s Treasury Yield Butterfly (%) Regressed against the 2s/10s Curve after Adjusting for the 5-Year Yield
Source: Board of Governors of the Federal Reserve.

changes by 5 bps. The regressions show that the last point—that is, "today's point"—is far from the regression line, which denotes the fair value of the butterfly for various levels of the yield and the curve. The goal of the trade is to position for the dislocated current point to revert back to its fair value regression line. Instead of the 50:50 trade, the dislocated trade to initiate is the one weighted to remove the curve and level effects; this process is known as making the butterfly curve and level neutral. Geometrically, the purpose of curve and level-neutral weighting is to trade the regression line and not just the average of the 50:50 weighted trade, which will hopefully increase the chances of a reversion back to fair value. The regression shown in this example is meant to show conceptually the 50:50 butterfly's dependence on the level of yields and the curve. A quicker way to find curve- and level-neutral weights is to regress the 5-year Treasury yield directly against 2-year and 10-year Treasury yields over the same time period. The two methods give the same results since we are dealing with linear quantities. If we rearrange the previous equation, we arrive at:

$$(1 - \text{beta1}) \times 5\text{Y} - (0.5 + \text{beta2}) \times 2\text{Y} - (0.5 - \text{beta2}) \times 10\text{Y}$$

$$= \text{intercept} + \text{error}$$

or

$$5\text{Y} - (0.5 + \text{beta2})/(1 - \text{beta1}) \times 2\text{Y} - (0.5 - \text{beta2})/(1 - \text{beta1}) \times 10\text{Y}$$

$$= \text{intercept} + \text{error}$$

Substitution of 0.06 for beta1 and 0.05 for beta2 leads to $5\text{Y} - 0.60 \times 2\text{Y} - 0.48 \times 10\text{Y} = \text{intercept} + \text{error}$. Here we want a weighted combination of 5-year, 2-year, and 10-year rates to revert back to its long-run average and have reduced it to trading the residual of the regression, which is a white noise series. Also note the divergence from 50:50 weights. Indeed, the weighted spread shows that equally weighting both the 2-year and the 10-year sectors leads to being too long on the 2-year leg (–0.60 versus –0.5 in equal weighting) and too short on the 10-year leg (–0.48 versus –0.5 in equal weighting). The reason why equally weighting the wings rarely works well is that there is an implicit assumption that the sectors have equal volatility, which, given their different drivers, is unlikely to be the case. As a simple example, if the Fed is firmly on hold, the 2-year sector is likely to be far less volatile than the 10-year sector, and weighting these two equally can cause the 10-year sector to have too much weight in the butterfly. The weights on the butterfly here are 0.60 and 0.48; however, when trading, actual notionals need to be calculated as traders will not trade based on risk weights. In the Eurodollar curve example in the "Carry Trade Setup and Evaluation" section, the Eurodollar legs have equal DV01, which results in the contract weighting and DV01 weighting being equal. However, for Treasuries, DV01s vary considerably, which makes notional weighting and DV01 weighting very different.

A common mistake made by investors becoming familiar with markets is to treat the weights on a trade as notional weights. Unless the weights are stated that way, this is rarely the case. In general, the weights refer to DV01 weightings across the trade; notional weights can be derived subsequently. For our Treasury trade, suppose the 2-year leg has $190/bp DV01, the 5-year trade has $450/bp, and the 10-year leg has $850/bp. The notional weights (i.e., how many dollars of notional on each leg) can be derived in this way:

1. The 5-year leg has weight 1. So we can assume it has the base notional, $100 million in this case. The DV01 on the 5-year leg then is 100 × $450/bp = $45,000/bp. This base can be any amount that we wish to risk on the trade in notional terms.
2. The 2-year leg has risk weight 0.60. This means that it needs 60% of the $45,000/bp DV01 weight in the 2-year leg = $27,000/bp. For each $1 million of notional, the 2-year leg has DV01 of $190/bp. Therefore, the notional on the 2-year leg is $142 million ($27,000/$190).
3. The 10-year leg has risk weight 0.48. This means that it needs 48% of the $45,000/bp DV01 weight in the 10-year leg = $21,600/bp. Per $1 million of notional, the 10-year leg has DV01 of $850/bp. Therefore, the notional on the 10-year leg is $25 million ($21,600/850).

This methodology converts the risk weights that are calculated from a regression to notional weights. The aim should be to think of trades in terms of their risk weights, as notional weights are not as informative, since different maturity bond prices move by their duration-weighted amounts. The notional weights are merely the last step before executing a trade.

Once the trade has been set up, the aim is for the curve-and-level-neutral weighted trade to revert back to its long-run average. Figure 7.7 shows the weighted spread up to the point in time of the Treasury multiple regressions in the example and then subsequent to initiating the trade. Given the choice of our example, the spread reverts back to the mean, with the trade making about 7 bps in profit. The example represents an ideal case where the weighted spread reverts rather soon after trade initiation. However, even in this example, if the trade was initiated a week earlier, the weighted spread would have continued to become more dislocated, resulting in large initial losses. In general, although a relative value trade may seem attractive on a regression basis, the regression is just a first step. Indeed, much can go wrong in such trades. For those taking frequent

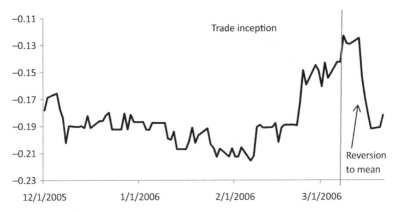

FIGURE 7.7 Weighted 2s5s10s Butterfly (%) Trade Inception at an Extreme Level
Source: Board of Governors of the Federal Reserve.

views on the rates market, knowing what can go wrong is just as essential as knowing how to identify and set up such trades.

The last example focused on cleanly removing the effects of the interest rate levels or the slope of the curve when warranted and arriving at a "pure" relative value trade. Unfortunately, the market is rarely as well-ordered. In particular, any time an empirical method is used to arrive at a trade, we should be wary of shifts in assumptions as new data comes in. Relative value trades can be quite susceptible to shifts in the betas of the regressions if market conditions change. This is why such trades work best when markets are stable, such as in Fed on-hold regimes, and why they should be avoided when market volatility picks up due to dislocations or transition phases. For instance, if the betas in the 2s/5s/10s trade shown above change, the weighted spread is no longer weighted as intended and is no longer representative of the residual; in fact, as the curve and level-neutral betas change, the trade can become significantly exposed to the level or slope of the curve. Figure 7.8 shows a weighted 2s5s10s butterfly initiated in July 2007 and held until year-end 2007. The initial weights of the 2s5s10s butterfly with a 47% weight on the 2-year leg and 71% weight on the 10-year leg were chosen from a 3-month regression, as in the earlier examples from 2006. However, unlike the relative stability of 2006, fall 2007 was a tumultuous period with the credit crunch starting and the Fed making a rapid transition from being on-hold to easing. Instead of reverting back to a fair value, the 2s/5s/10s weighted butterfly trended for months as the fair value, and the true curve and level-neutral betas shifted. This was partly because as the Fed went into easing mode, the volatility of the short end increased sharply while the volatility of intermediate maturity

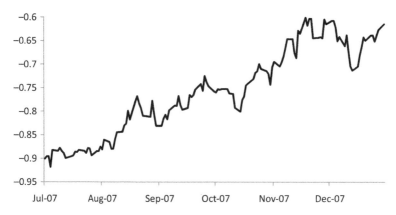

FIGURE 7.8   Weighted 2s5s10s Butterfly (%) Not Mean Reverting as the Underlying Market Regime Changes
Source: Board of Governors of the Federal Reserve.

yields decreased in comparison, changing the betas over time. Indeed, if a trader had initiated the 2s5s10s trade in July 2007 with fixed weights, it would have trended higher for months without any reversion to the original mean. If the weights of the relative value trade were not updated, such a trade could lose money for a sustained period of time. For this reason, relative value trades are especially susceptible to changing regimes, such as a Fed transitioning from easing to on hold or on hold to tightening. Generally such trades should be avoided in transition periods, until it is clear that one particular stable regime has set in. Constant vigilance is required against changing relationships between the securities used in a relative value trade.

Finally, at times, a trader may like a butterfly's curve exposure or its level exposure. To this end, the butterfly can be made just level neutral by regressing only against the 5-year yield or just curve neutral by regressing only against the 10-year − 2-year rate spread, the 2s/10s curve. Such trades can be quite profitable if the relative value and the resulting risk exposure—that is, the curve or the level—both move in the trader's favor.

TREASURY BOND RELATIVE VALUE—PAR CURVE

Treasury market bond yields do not form a smooth yield curve, but instead yields can vary for a range of issue-specific reasons. Bonds can trade at varying valuations depending on individual factors, such as the issue-specific repo rate, age of the bond, and market flows that may dislocate it from nearby bonds. For example, due to liquidity, an old 10-year bond (a 30-year bond aged for 20 years) will trade in a distinct manner from a 10-year bond that has been freshly issued. To come up with relative value trades, then, one can scan each bond of the Treasury market and compare it to nearby bonds on a current and historical basis to discern if it is dislocated. However, this method can be intensive and inelegant.

To determine Treasury bond relative value in a more systematic way, we need a fair value yield curve for the Treasury market. Once we have such a curve, we can calculate a bond's "mispricing" as the difference between a bond's yield and the fair value yield corresponding to the same maturity. This method has its drawbacks in oversimplification but is a valid starting point for identifying bonds that appear dislocated. How do we calculate a fair value yield curve? Since we are calculating a yield curve, we need to define a concept of the fair value yield for a given maturity. This fair yield is known as the par yield, the yield of a theoretical bond with the given maturity trading at par. The idea is to fit a smooth yield curve using the yields of actual bonds in the market as anchors. Numerous fitting techniques are possible; we present the underlying idea behind curve fitting next.

One of the simplest techniques used in fitting a yield curve is to calculate a set of model prices for the bonds in the market and to minimize the sum of squared errors of actual prices versus model prices. To calculate model prices, the price of a bond can be written as the sum of the zero-coupon bond prices that form the package of the whole bond (see Chapter 2). Recall that these zero-coupon bonds are the individual coupons and principals that form the coupon bond, and their prices depend on the yield of each maturity. Therefore, we can start with a model set of zero-coupon rates. From these model rates we can infer the prices of each bond in the market. By iterating repeatedly, we can arrive at a yield curve that minimizes the error between prices from the model curve and actual prices from the market. The idea behind most par curve fitting techniques is similar to this: A price or yield is arrived at using some model variable that is relevant in pricing a bond, then errors are minimized versus the model output and the real value in the market. This "model" value is the yield of a zero-coupon bond of a given maturity and the price derived from it (i.e., the discount factor is used to calculate the price of a model bond, and price errors are minimized). Generally, when calculating the par yield curve, certain types of bonds, such as hot runs, Treasury Inflation-Protected Securities (TIPS), Separate Trading of Registered Interest and Principal Securities (STRIPS), and other securities that tend to have distinct trading patterns, are excluded so as not to bias the fair yield curve in a certain direction. For example, hot runs tend to trade rich compared to nearby bonds due to extra liquidity.

Once a par curve is calculated, it can be used to find relative value trades. First, for each bond, we calculate the difference between the bond's yield and the model yield, which is the yield residual. The yield residual indicates the dislocation of the bond against the fair value curve, similar to the residual of a regression. A negative yield residual implies that the bond is rich compared to nearby bonds (i.e., bond yield < fair yield), while a positive yield error indicates that the bond is cheap compared to nearby bonds. However, certain bonds, such as hot runs, will tend to trade below the yield curve in yield due to higher liquidity as described. Therefore, the yield error of a hot-run bond will tend to be negative, but this does not mean the hot run is rich and should be sold; its yield error tends to trade negative all the time. To better use the yield curve to discover relative value, we need to generate a history of yield residuals as well. The yield residual of a bond then needs to be compared to the history of the bond's yield residual to distinguish between positive and negative yield errors. For example, if a bond's yield residual on average trades at –6 bps and currently is at –2 bps, the bond is trading 4 bps cheaper (i.e., bond yield is 4 bps higher than average) relative to nearby bonds. Therefore, a par curve is an essential construct to smooth out idiosyncrasies of individual bonds and to determine relative value in the Treasury bond market.

OTHER TREASURY RELATIVE VALUE TRADES

The standard Treasury relative value trades involve buying one set of bonds and selling another. The aim is to take advantage of likely convergence between rich bonds and cheap bonds. Beyond this general principle, there are specific types of trades in the Treasury market with driving factors that deserve further attention. These types of trades highlight the need to consider all factors driving the relative relationship between securities, not just the plain yield difference. Two such relative value trades we consider here are STRIPS versus bonds and coupon switches.

STRIPS were introduced in Chapter 3 as zero-coupon bonds in the Treasury market. Although yields of zero-coupon bonds and coupon bonds have mathematically established relationships, such relationships do not hold in the market due to other differences between STRIPS and coupon bonds. For one thing, different STRIPS have varying levels of liquidity, which can cause valuations to trade away from an equal duration coupon bond. Recall that for the same maturity, a zero-coupon bond has greater duration than the corresponding coupon bond. Thus it is important to consider equal duration pairs and not equal maturity pairs. The coupon bond can also have idiosyncratic differences, such as financing rates driving its valuation relative to the STRIP issue. In the STRIPS market itself, there are differences between coupon STRIPS and principal STRIPS. Coupon STRIPS are fungible and principal STRIPS are not fungible (i.e., unique). All these factors cause differences among the issues. There are also supply-related differences between STRIPS and actual bonds. For example, for a coupon STRIPS (C-STRIPS) issue, any stripping of a longer-end bond creates new C-STRIPS across the entire curve and therefore adds to the supply of C-STRIPS issue across the curve. This can cheapen C-STRIPS valuations above and beyond the mathematical yield formulas.

Coupon switches are another relative value trade where mathematical formulas tend to not hold. The term "coupon switches" refers to trading higher-coupon bonds for low-coupon bonds in the Treasury market. These coupon switches must be weighted by the duration of the two bonds since coupon differences can lead to large duration differences. The concept of yield should account for coupon differences, since the coupons are discounted by the same yield curve for both bonds. However, as with STRIPS versus bonds, differentials between yields of different coupon bonds stem not just from the mathematical formula for yield but also, crucially, from liquidity. It is not as much the coupon that is the issue here but the fact that high-coupon bonds are currently older, aged bonds from earlier when interest rates were much higher. For example, 30-year bonds issued in the 1980s have coupons in the 8% range and have aged down to the 7- to 10-year range. These bonds are far less liquid than freshly issued 7- to 10-year bonds and therefore tend to trade cheaper than newly issued bonds. The differences between high-coupon bonds and corresponding low-coupon pairs tend to be relatively small in normal times, but when illiquidity comes back, these spreads can widen sharply. During the credit crunch, some of these spreads widened to over 50 bps. Trading the relative value between these high- and low-coupon bonds requires understanding where liquidity may be headed. Shorting higher-coupon bonds and buying low-coupon bonds when the spread is narrow can provide an asymmetric payoff to set up trades in good times that benefit in times of illiquidity with less downside.

SUMMARY

This chapter introduced new classes of trades in the rates space that attempt to earn carry or exploit relative value opportunities. These trades are ideal for low-volatility environments where taking directional views adds little value. However, with carry and relative value trades, it is key to realize that they tend to earn small, steady profits. If markets experience volatility or go through rapid transitions of regimes, the same trades can suffer large drawdowns. Low-volatility regimes can make investors complacent, as the carry or mispricing in a trade may increasingly look large in comparison. Thus it is crucial to look for signs of regime shifts and avoid crowded carry or relative value trades.

CHAPTER 8

Hedging Risks in Interest Rate Products

C hapters 6 and 7 discussed different techniques investors use to profit in the rates market, either from taking outright views on the yield curve or through carry and relative value trades. These methods pertain to taking advantage of a view on interest rates, relating to either specific trends or rangebound conditions. This chapter considers hedging, which focuses on controlling different risks that arise in any trade. The term *hedging* refers to transacting in an offsetting manner relative to the current holdings of an investor in order to reduce a particular risk to the transaction. Recall from Chapter 2 that a single bond has a package of risks embedded in it, such as interest rate risk and taxation risk. With more complex trades, the range of embedded risks increases and more sophisticated methods of hedging are required. The goal of hedging in general is to reduce exposure of a risk in the market; in this chapter, we will focus on interest rate risk given that it is a dominant risk for a wide variety of fixed income instruments. Often, investors view speculation and hedging as separate—speculators are supposed to have a view on rates and trade based on that view, while hedgers are supposed to be involved purely for risk offsetting purposes. However, such a view can be misleading. Hedging is essential to understand not just for investors looking to offset risks but also for traders expressing views in the market. Traders also need to be on the lookout for hidden risks even after hedges have been put on to avoid unexpected losses. Indeed, the line between speculation and hedging is a very thin one; often the key to speculating more intelligently is to try to hedge unwanted risks in order to take views in a more specific way.

PRINCIPLES OF HEDGING

The example of a corn farmer can clarify some concepts about hedging. Suppose the farmer grows corn on his farm and is scheduled to harvest the corn in three months. At this point, the farmer is "long" corn—that is, he benefits if the price of corn goes higher. However, his risk in this position is high. If corn prices in the market drop, he is fully exposed to such drops and could face substantial losses if corn prices are lower by harvest time. This exposure calls for hedging at least some of his risk to corn prices. To hedge the risk, the farmer can make an agreement now to sell corn at a fixed price at harvest time. This is referred to as selling forward. Now, when harvest time arrives, the farmer is less concerned about corn prices since he has an agreement to make a sale at a fixed price, regardless of the prevailing market price at the time. Of course, the farmer still may be exposed to differences in location or quantity of his corn versus the corn the futures exchange trades against. As is always the case with hedging, some risks are always present, no matter how closely hedged a trade appears.

Although our example uses corn, the same principles apply to a manager owning bonds. In the case of bonds, there is no fixed harvest schedule, but bonds are exposed to interest rate risk on daily basis. In particular, if rates rise due to improving economic conditions or due to an uptick in inflation expectations, the holder of bonds is faced with losses. In the case of bonds, some readers may wonder why the manager cannot just sell the holdings if she is concerned about the risks in the position. Indeed, unlike corn growing in a field, the bond owner does not wait for a position to grow but has the choice to unwind her position at any point. Selling the position is always an option but can be a suboptimal one in many cases. If a trader has a small position in a liquid security, such as a benchmark Treasury bond, then buying or selling it rapidly can be relatively easy. However, large positions in most securities are tough to sell or buy quickly due to transaction costs and logistical difficulties. This is especially true if other market participants suspect large amounts of selling or buying may arrive that can drive prices to disadvantageous levels. In illiquid markets, which consist of securities that are difficult to buy or sell, even small trades can be difficult to maneuver. Beyond these constraints, sometimes the investor may just expect market volatility to be a temporary phenomenon. In this case, hedges can smooth profit or loss (P/L) volatility without needing to make expensive sales of the asset. An example of this situation would be a corporate bond where the company fundamentals are strong but the bond faces the risk of higher rates over the next few months due to concerns about monetary policy tightening. Additionally, the corporate bond may be illiquid and incur large transaction costs. In this case, corporate bond managers likely are better off holding the bond and hedging the interest rate risk over the near term.

In other cases, a particular bond may be attractive to hold due to some risks embedded in it, but other embedded risks may need to be hedged. For example, an investor may own fixed-rate municipal bonds, which are exposed to both tax risk and interest rate risk. Fixed rate municipal bonds benefit when tax rates rise as their tax exemption becomes more valuable, but also lose value if interest rates rise given their fixed coupon. An investor may believe tax rates are on their way up, but may be worried about interest rates rising or not have a strong view on interest rates. Therefore, instead of selling the municipal bonds to protect from rising rates, it may be advisable to hedge the municipal bonds using swaps or Treasuries to offset rate risk. Then, the bond retains its favorable tax exposure without the unfavorable interest rate risk. As these examples show, effective hedging gives investors the flexibility to manage risks in a more efficient manner than just purely buying or selling the assets they own.

Another important point with regard to hedging is the potential for "lost" gain if the scenario of concern does not come to fruition. To go back to our corn farmer example, if the price of corn ends up increasing by harvest time, an unhedged farmer would reap these gains, but a farmer who sold corn forward at a fixed price would miss out on any increases beyond the fixed price. Due to the potential lost gains and possible transactions in derivative markets, some risk managers may be wary of hedging. Losses on a hedge are to be expected if the asset itself is profitable. The point of a hedge is not to add extra profits but to lower volatility and hopefully increase the Sharpe ratio of trades. For managers involved in markets to offset risks, they must keep in mind the risk-reducing aim of hedging. Many unrealized losses can occur if hedges are unrelated to the risks facing the manager.

The corn farmer example is deceptively simple. It ignores many nuances that arise when choosing a hedge and in calculating the amount of exposure to hedge. In particular, most trades can be thought of as a bundle of risks, some of which may be hedged by instruments in other markets whereas others cannot be offset by available instruments. In the case of our corn farmer, perhaps the type of corn he grows is different from what he is required to deliver into the futures exchange. In that case, while he can hedge against decreases in the overall price of corn, as mentioned, he is exposed to the difference between prices of *varieties* of corn, which generally cannot be hedged easily. The fixed income version of this example would be a bond fund manager owning an off-the-run 7-year Treasury bond (such as a 9.25% Nov-16 bond, maturing in November 2016) and hedging its interest rate risk by selling a more liquid 7-year Treasury bond (such as 3.25% Nov-16). In this case, as with the corn farmer, the fund manager has hedged baseline exposure to interest rates; that is, if the yield of both these bonds rises one for one, the manager's P/L will be unaffected as negative P/L from the 9.25% Nov-16 will be offset by gains from the more liquid issue. This is, of course, assuming that the correct amount of hedge was placed, which will be discussed later. However, in this case, the fund manager is exposed to changes in valuations of 9.25% Nov-16 *versus* 3.25% Nov-16 due to issue-specific factors, such as liquidity or financing. To make an analogy with our corn farmer, the type of "corn" of our bond fund manager differs from the "corn" widely used in the market.

Essentially, hedging converts an outright risk, such as exposure to broad rate movements, into exposure to differentials (known as a basis or a spread, depending on the situation) between the product being hedged and the hedge instrument. It is essential to remember that a hedge rarely creates a risk-free trade—instead, the hedge is intended to convert a more volatile risk into a less volatile one. Of course, hedging is useful only to the extent that the outright exposure being hedged is far more volatile than the basis or spread exposure that results. For example, hedging a bond such as 9.25% Nov-16 with Treasury futures reduces the outright interest rate exposure as the prices of these two instruments are likely to move in a similar fashion, but subsequently the investor is exposed to the *difference*, or basis, between the futures contract price and the bond price (see also Chapter 4). Another example of this concept is hedging the 9.25% Nov-16 Treasury bond with a swap of the same maturity instead of with Treasury futures. Here again, the interest rates are likely to move in a similar fashion. Paying in the swap versus owning the Treasury bond offsets a great deal of the interest rate risk but does expose the investor to changes in the difference in yields between the two instruments, also known as the swap spread (i.e., yield of 9.25% Nov-16 Treasury – yield on Nov-16 swap). In each of these cases, the hedge is worth initiating only if the volatility of having an outright exposure in the Treasury bond is far greater than the resulting basis versus futures or spread versus the swap. If the volatility of the spread is too high, then the Treasury futures hedge or the swap hedge is of little use. In general, the outright rate exposure is much more volatile than the spread, making the hedge worth the effort.

With less liquid products, such as municipal bonds (debts of cities and states, where the interest income is tax-exempt), few products exist to effectively hedge risks specific to the municipal (muni) market. Suppose a manager holds bonds issued by New York City (NYC). Such a security is subject to risks from general interest rate movements; risks specific to the municipal market, such as tax law changes; and finally risks stemming from changes in the financial situation of the city itself. A fund manager can hedge exposure to general interest rate risk by transacting in liquid instruments, such as Treasury futures. Less liquid products exist to hedge some of the muni-specific risks, such as ratio swaps (see Chapter 5). However, hedging risks specific to the credit risks stemming from NYC is generally not possible, and managers have to be cognizant of their exposure to the city's credit risk at any given time. That said, as discussed earlier, a manager may have bought NYC bonds precisely because she is bullish on the city's prospects, in which case hedging allows her to isolate that risk and reduce exposure to external factors, such as general interest rate moves on which she may not have a strong view.

The discussion so far is meant to show the central role hedging should play in any portfolio manager's decision-making process. Rather than being just a sideshow, hedging allows the offsetting of unwanted risks while keeping risks on which the manager may have a strong view. At times, the unwanted risks may be all the risks in a position—the investor may want to be neutral on all levels. Additionally, hedging can also allow a more subtle approach to investing. By isolating specific risks, trades are likely to respond more effectively when the underlying fundamental views driving the trade do indeed occur, while unrelated factors are less likely to cause unexpected losses.

We now discuss more details related to unbundling risks embedded in bonds through hedging. To provide a logical framework for isolating risks in any fixed income instrument, let us consider a generic corporate bond with a fixed coupon. Analysis for other fixed income securities is similar, although some specific credit risks differ across asset classes. The corporate bond's three risks are:

1. *Interest rate risk.* This is general interest rate risk, which moves along with macroeconomic factors and expectations of central bank policy.

2. *Market-specific risk.* This category encompasses risks to corporate bonds as a whole. These may arise from an increase in risk perception toward corporate bonds in general or due to other supply/demand dynamics relating to the market under consideration.

3. *Issue-specific credit risk.* This risk relates specifically to the issuer of the security. For a corporate bond, issue-specific credit risk relates to the performance of the issuing company; for a municipal bond, the corresponding risk rests with the city or state issuer of the bond.

In general, decisions about purchasing specific securities should be based on the risks that one is willing to take. For example, the main reason for buying a specific corporate bond should generally be the issue-specific risk, with as much of the interest-rate and market-specific risks as possible hedged out. An investor wishing to take corporate credit risk in general, but not any specific issuer, would ideally buy a basket of corporate bonds or gain exposure to a corporate bond index. The combination of market-specific and issue-specific risks is called spread risk. This terminology is clear if one considers the hedging of a corporate bond with a Treasury bond in mathematical terms: A buyer of a corporate bond with yield Y% who hedges with a Treasury bond of yield X% is taking a view that $(Y - X)$% will decrease; that is, the yield on the corporate bond will fall more than the Treasury yield (remember that yields falling = price rising = asset outperforming). The yield difference $Y - X$ is referred to as a spread of the bond over Treasuries, and hence the term *spread risk*. Swaps have a similar rationale, and when necessary, a distinction is made between taking a view on spread to swaps or spread to Treasury for a given bond. Hedging a corporate bond with Treasury or swaps therefore changes the risk profile from overall interest rate level to taking a spread risk.

Finally, Treasuries and swaps in particular are generally equated with pure interest rate risk in the previous list, with Treasuries being the cash version and swaps being the derivatives version. Treasuries and swaps are used on a wide scale to take views on overall level rates in the economy and to hedge the interest rate risk of other fixed income securities. In particular, to hedge the rate risk embedded in any fixed rate bond instrument, an investor would sell Treasuries or pay in swaps; as discussed previously, a short position in Treasuries or a pay position in swaps gains in value as rates rise, which offsets the loss in value from a rate rise for the fixed rate instrument being hedged. Issue-specific risks can at times arise in Treasuries, generally stemming from upcoming supply in nearby sectors or in relation to scarcity of the issue in repo markets. For the most part, however, these risks are dwarfed by overall rate sensitivity for outright positions. For swaps, as discussed previously, there are few issue-specific risks for specific maturities, but swap markets can dislocate in periods of heightened risk aversion because the counterparty in a swap is a bank—if banking system health is in question, swaps can dislocate from other interest rate instruments.

CHOICES OF INSTRUMENTS FOR HEDGING

The previous section discussed the package of risks in fixed income instruments and the benefits stemming from hedging unwanted risks and taking more specific forms of risks in investments. Once a decision to hedge has been made, in many cases multiple instruments can provide a way to hedge the risk in question. This is especially the case regarding interest rate risk. Given that interest rate risk is a component of any fixed interest rate instrument, interest rate risk is prevalent across fixed income markets and needs to be managed carefully. To hedge interest rate risk, there are four major choices for investors:

1. *Treasury securities.* These are actual Treasury notes and bonds. To hedge using Treasuries, the investor needs to short the security using the repurchase agreement (repo) markets.

2. *Treasury futures.* These are futures markets on Treasury securities. As discussed in Chapter 4, these futures are present for 2-year, 5-year, 10-year, and long-end sectors. However, the futures markets are quite liquid and are easy to transact, and no repo market transaction is necessary to go short.

3. *Eurodollar futures.* These are some of the most liquid futures markets in the world. Although the futures themselves are 3-month rates, as we discussed in Chapter 4, longer-dated assets can be created by chaining together futures contracts of successive quarterly periods. This makes Eurodollar futures ideal for hedging shorter-duration exposure, especially less than three years. Furthermore, by altering notionals of individual components of a Eurodollar strip, irregular cash flows can also be hedged.

4. *Swaps.* Swaps can be thought of as an extended version of Eurodollar futures. Swaps are extremely liquid and flexible instruments with just about any maturity date transactable with relative ease. Other forms of customization are also fairly easy, and swap terms can be modified to match less regular cash flows. Their liquidity and ability to track interest rate risk in a wide range of instruments have made swaps one of the most widely used instruments to hedge interest rate risk. One disadvantage of swaps compared to the previous instruments is that swaps are transacted versus a bank, which exposes an investor to counterparty risk. In normally functioning markets, this is generally not a major issue, but the 2008 credit crisis brought it to the forefront (more on this below).

Thus there are a number of products to hedge rate risk, but how does an investor pick which instrument to use? First, we lump the choices into two broader categories: swaps and Treasuries. Treasury bonds and Treasury futures have very similar characteristics from an overall hedging standpoint, as do swaps and Eurodollars. We delve into the differences between these pairs later, but for simplicity's sake, we first consider the broader choice of Treasury versus swap markets as hedge vehicles.

Generally, the first condition in choosing a hedge is ensuring that price changes of the hedge instrument are closely linked to price changes of the asset being hedged in most scenarios. The link between price changes will in turn ensure that any losses encountered on the asset being held are likely to be offset by similar profits on the hedge instrument. Any deviation between price changes on the hedge and the asset being hedged is known as tracking error. To ensure a low tracking error between an asset and its hedge, changes in prices (or yields) of the two instruments should have high correlation. High correlation is a subjective measure and depends on the markets being considered. Nonetheless, for an investor it is crucial to make sure a given hedge's likely tracking error is within the threshold for his/her risk tolerance. Recall that the interest rate hedges are used to hedge overall rate risk only; generally they are not used to hedge any spread risk. For most instruments, in normal market conditions, the tracking of interest rate risk in an instrument versus the Treasury or swap markets is similar. Of course, if the instrument being hedged is subject to a great deal of volatility in its *spread* over Treasuries or swaps, neither instrument will prove very valuable in hedging since, as discussed, Treasuries or swaps hedge interest rate risk, not spread risk. An intuitive way to think about high spread volatility is that the asset and a possible hedge move independently of each other; in other words, if Y is the yield of the asset being hedged and X is the yield of the hedge, Y − X being very volatile implies that Y and X have little correlation with each other. This lack of correlation will result in high tracking error and makes X an unsuitable hedge. For example, during 2008 for various markets including mortgage-backed securities (MBSs), the volatility of the spread of mortgage yields over Treasuries was exceedingly high. In such a situation, hedging the mortgage bond with a Treasury bond reduced little risk since mortgage rates and Treasury rates were moving with little correlation to each other.

For interest rate risk, we mentioned that in "normal" market conditions, swaps and Treasuries perform a similar job from a tracking error standpoint. However, this statement breaks down when market conditions are not normal and especially if there is a flight from risk into the safety of Treasuries. Although one may consider these to be rare events, the 2000s have taught us that the biggest P/L swings for a portfolio can occur during periods of stress. Hedges, which tend to work in normal times but run the risk of failing massively in stress periods, may defeat the purpose of hedging to begin with. During stress periods, swap hedges tend to track other higher-risk fixed income instruments better than Treasuries and are likely to do a better job in hedging.

Why do Treasuries perform poorly as hedges in stress situations? In times of crisis, investors flee from risky assets and generally buy the most liquid and safe assets available. For this, the top candidate would be U.S. Treasuries. The size of the bond market combined with the faith in the

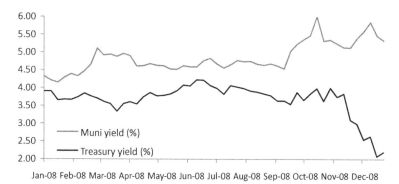

FIGURE 8.1 Failure of Hedges: Muni Yields and Treasury Yields during the Crisis
Source: Board of Governors of the Federal Reserve.

market about the United States' ability to repay its obligations leads investors to bid up Treasury prices at the expense of most other assets. If investors hedge using swaps or Treasuries, they benefit if the hedge *underperforms*, since they will have sold the hedge asset to offset the long exposure in the market. Given this need for underperformance of a hedge, it is easy to see why Treasuries make poor hedge choices during stress times. The rush into Treasuries in flight-to-quality events leads them to richen, and in extreme situations, investors can lose money on the position and the hedge. Figure 8.1 shows a stark example of this in 2008, when municipal bond yields continued rising amid financing stress conditions (i.e., prices kept falling) but Treasury yields dropped sharply. Imagine an investor owning municipal bonds and selling Treasury bonds to hedge the interest rate risk—the municipal bonds lose money as municipal yields rise, but the Treasury hedges also lose money as their yields fall (remember, we *sell* Treasuries to hedge). The municipal market in 2008 merely highlighted the risk of hedging with Treasuries in a rather extreme manner, but Treasury hedges face this risk in flight-to-quality events. In general, given that a hedge is needed most during times of crisis, Treasuries generally should not be used as core hedges for riskier asset classes. However, Treasury hedges certainly have their place in any bond portfolio, as tactically switching between swaps and Treasuries over shorter time intervals can enhance returns, which we discuss later.

The general rally in Treasury assets during crisis periods tends to increase longer-term tracking errors of Treasury hedges versus higher-risk fixed income assets. However, swaps and many other credit assets tend to underperform during stress periods, given that they are transacted against other banks and therefore face bank credit risk rather than U.S.

government risk. The relative performance of swaps, as we discussed in Chapter 5, is determined by the swap spread. If swap spreads are widening, swaps are underperforming and therefore are superior *hedges*; narrowing swap spreads present the opposite situation. During stress periods, swap spreads widen as investors flee to the safety of Treasuries. However, there are two conflicting drivers of swap spreads during such periods:

1. *Credit concerns.* Stress periods tend to increase concerns about the health of banks. Since swap counterparties are banks, swap spreads widen as investors demand a higher penalty for swap spreads versus Treasuries.

2. *Mortgage hedging.* The fall in overall Treasury rates during stress periods leads mortgage hedgers to increase duration in response, leading the hedgers to receive swaps. This puts narrowing pressure on swaps.

A more detailed description of the above two forces is given in Chapter 9 on swap spreads. In general, the response of swap spreads to crisis periods is determined by the interaction of credit concerns and mortgage hedging. The initial knee-jerk reaction is indeed widening spreads, which leads swap hedges to outperform versus Treasury hedges. However, financial stress periods require rapid response and agility on the part of bond portfolio managers. This is because if Treasury yields fall sharply enough, the "normal" response from the mortgage market will be to narrow swap spreads, as described in the point above on mortgage hedging. This can result in the widening of the spread to be a fleeting event and the relative advantages of swaps in hedging being fairly short-lived. This was the case during various shorter-lived crisis events in the 2000s, such as the February 2007 subprime debt market scare. However, during more sustained crisis events such as 2008, swap spreads widened sharply and stayed that way as credit concerns far outweighed any receiving pressure from mortgage hedgers.

So far, we have discussed tracking error in the context of swaps versus Treasuries. However, within each of these markets, tracking error can be further reduced via matching duration. The principle here is simple: The hedge's maturity/duration profile should be as similar to the profile of the asset being hedged in question as possible. For example, a 5-year corporate bond should, all else being equal, be hedged with a 5-year swap or 5-year Treasury since different parts of the yield curve are driven by distinct factors and can even have different classes of buyers. Although this idea may seem simple at first glance, there are occasions when deviating from the closest maturity/duration hedge can increase returns even while having a minimal impact on tracking error. Such opportunities arise frequently and point to the benefits of an opportunistic approach to hedging at least part of the portfolio.

Tracking error is the primary metric when deciding on a hedge, especially when markets encounter volatility. However, there are long stretches in markets where relative calm rules. During such periods, there is little difference in tracking error between the broader liquid market interest rate hedges (Treasuries or swaps). In such low-volatility periods, Treasury and swap markets offer similar protection against interest rate risk across fixed income bonds. This brings us to our second criterion for picking hedging choice: relative value. It is important for managers to closely track trends in the liquid rates markets and tactically switch at least part of their hedges between Treasury and swap markets on some relatively frequent basis. The relative value factors that drive the choice between swaps and Treasury hedges are the same as those that drive swap spreads. As discussed, swap spread widening implies an underperformance of swaps; swaps are the ideal hedge in periods of widening spreads. Periods of narrowing swap spreads imply an outperformance of swaps versus Treasuries, making Treasuries the ideal hedge. Some factors that drive swap spreads are Treasury supply, Fed activity, MBS hedging flows, and the bank credit situation. For example, if a sustained period of improvement in bank health is expected, swap spreads are biased narrower. The narrowing is even more notable in periods where the central bank rapidly increases liquidity in the system to improve bank liquidity; such a scenario was on display after the Lehman Brothers bankruptcy when the Fed introduced new programs to boost liquidity. From late October 2008 to early 2009, 2-year swap spreads narrowed an astounding 100 basis points (bps), from about 165 bps to about 65 bps. In a period of such sharp swap spread narrowing, a swap hedge would have been suboptimal compared to Treasury hedges, given the outperformance of swap yields. The example of relative value between Treasuries and swaps to select hedges can be generalized to any situation where multiple hedge instruments can be selected. It is important to not sacrifice tracking error between hedge instruments, but relative value can serve as a secondary guide in hedge selection.

Finally, our third criterion for deciding between hedges is carry. At times, there can be substantial differences in carry (carry + slide) between different parts of the Treasury or swaps curve. However, the tracking error for deviating between nearby maturities is generally not that large. Consequently, a significant carry pickup for such a switch should be used as a welcome opportunity to increase hedge performance. The carry difference can arise not just from maturity differences but also from products themselves. At times, different hedge products may offer varying levels of carry, which can make one of the hedges more attractive. Note that if a long position is being hedged, the carry comparison for a hedge needs to be considered on a short position. An example of optimizing carry would be hedging an MBS position with the choice of 5-year or 3-year swaps. In very steep curve environments, such as late 2009, the 3-month slide for a short position the 5-year swap was –10 bps while the 3-month slide for the 3-year swap was –16 bps. Hence, the difference between the two was 6 bps, which translates into an extra $168,000 of loss per $100 million notional of a 3-year maturity position (assuming approximately $280/bp of dollar value of one basis point [DV01] on a 3-year swap per million notional). The tracking error for switching between such close maturities is generally not significant, especially in low-volatility periods, making it important to track carry and slide across the curve for opportunities.

So far, we have discussed choices between the broader Treasury and swap markets. Within these broader market classes, there is additional choice between closely related instruments such as Treasury futures or Eurodollar futures. First, we consider Treasury futures versus Treasury bonds from a hedging standpoint. Treasury futures are one of the most commonly used hedges for the fixed income world, due to their simplicity of use and the benefits conferred on them by trading on the exchange. From a simplicity standpoint, as discussed in Chapter 4, Treasury futures transactions need no interaction with repo markets to borrow or lend bonds. Furthermore, buying and selling are completely symmetrical in the market, making shorting Treasury futures one of the quickest ways for an investor to initiate a hedge. Given that futures trade on an exchange, there is little counterparty risk and very standardized collateral requirements, which simplifies the transaction process further. However, at times, the price of such standardization and simplicity is higher tracking error with respect to hedging due to a smaller range in the instruments available. In particular, the liquid Treasury futures contracts are 2-year, 5-year, 10-year, and long end, which consists of traditional bond futures contracts and newly introduced ultra-long futures contracts. Furthermore, each of these futures tracks a basket of securities, which further muddles the duration-matching concept introduced earlier. For example, the 10-year contract actually tracks a basket of 7- to 10-year Treasuries. In lower yield environments, it mostly tracks the 7-year bond, while in higher yield environments it will track closer to a 10-year bond. During low yield environments, an investor hedging a 10-year security with 10-year futures contracts, and failing to account for the maturity difference in the hedge, would be exposed to swings in differences in the 7-year and 10-year Treasury maturities. Investors hedging long-end securities with bond futures contracts face a similar problem, as these mostly track 15-year bonds. To address this problem, the exchange has introduced an ultra-long contract covering only the 25- to 30-year sector of the Treasury curve in its basket, but the problem of maturity mismatch remains. Unlike with the swaps market, the exchange-traded nature of the Treasury futures market makes it impossible to change terms or to customize cash flows to better match certain assets. Regardless of these issues, however, the depth of the market and its simplicity make Treasury futures contracts a prime choice for investors for hedging, especially for standard fixed income products near benchmark maturities.

Beyond the tracking error issues just discussed, relative value is the major determinant in choosing between Treasury futures and Treasury bond markets. The basket nature of Treasury futures contracts along with the embedded optionality they confer leads to periods of large relative value discrepancies between the futures and cash markets. As discussed in Chapter 4, Treasury futures are compared to their bond market counterparts using the basis net of carry (BNOC). In periods when this number is large, the implication is that Treasury futures are trading cheap to bonds; when the BNOC is very small, Treasury futures may be trading rich. To fully assess the richness/cheapness of futures, one would have to value the embedded optionality in the contracts and compare it to the BNOC to determine whether the market is over- or underpricing the optionality. In the absence of such a valuation model, richness/cheapness can be estimated using the current BNOC value compared to the value of other regimes of similar yield levels, curve steepness, and volatility levels. If Treasury futures are trading cheap, they are unlikely to be attractive hedges versus Treasury bonds, since, as mentioned, a hedge for a long position in an asset needs to *underperform* (i.e., cheapen further). In general, Treasury futures add value as hedges if they are trading rich to cash bonds and therefore present an opportunity to collect the expected reversion to the mean. More details on the nature of the futures basis are given in Chapter 11.

Treasury futures make especially good hedges in environments where a rise in yields, coupled with a steeper curve, is expected. In such environments, the chance of a cheapest-to-deliver (CTD) bond switch to a higher-duration bond is likely. The increasing duration in the rising yield environment tends to cause futures to underperform a greater amount than their bond counterparts. This can be thought of in another way: In a futures contract, the short position—that is, the hedger—has the option to deliver a different bond, and in periods when yields are rising and the curve is steepening, this option is more likely to be exercised (i.e., CTD is more likely to switch), making the short's position more valuable. At this time the bond position has positive convexity, whereby the bond begins to relatively outperform in a yield rise as its duration decreases.

Finally, the 2008 crisis offered an interesting glimpse into a situation where Treasury futures were used as hedges regardless of tracking error or relative value concerns. The main drivers here were balance-sheet constraints and counterparty risk fears, which characterized many other phenomena seen in financial markets that year. The turmoil in markets produced many dislocations in Treasury futures markets leading to interesting hedging opportunities (see Chapter 11 for more details). One of these was a lack of alternative vehicles to hedge interest rate risk, leading to a rush of investors hedging their exposure to other asset classes using Treasury futures. This led to a sharp cheapening of 10-year futures (i.e., a rapid rise in BNOC), and futures in the intermediate-maturity sectors remained cheap for a sustained period of time. In such an environment, the usual guidelines of relative value were thrown out of the window, reminding us that markets are apt to make us rethink all rules of thumb at some point. As hedges, 10-year futures seemed optimal due to their low cost, leading them to keep cheapening well beyond what was considered normal as large numbers of investors sold them to hedge interest rate risk on other fixed income products that could not be traded easily due to the turmoil, and the cheapening only stopped once investors' risk-taking appetite recovered somewhat.

Finally, we come to Eurodollar futures, which are futures contracts of a much shorter duration than the other instruments discussed here. Nevertheless, by using strips of Eurodollars, longer-dated assets can be synthetically created, as described earlier. However, the strip limit is five years, and in practice it generally is no more than three years due to liquidity constraints in very long-dated Eurodollar contracts. This means Eurodollar futures are best used for hedging assets with three years or less in maturity. Eurodollars can be considered the atomic-level breakdown of swaps, and so relative value considerations that lead to swaps generally proscribe Eurodollars as well at the shorter end. Therefore, an expectation of wider short-end swap spreads can make either swaps or Eurodollar hedges optimal to use, rather than Treasuries. Between swaps and Eurodollars, though, relative value is rarely a consideration as the markets are very well arbitraged by dealers. Investors wishing to keep the transparency and ease of transaction that an exchange provides tend to prefer Eurodollar hedges; those who need hedges with longer maturities and/or a high level of customization tend to use swaps. Eurodollar futures are also preferred hedges for shorter-term floating rate instruments where cash flows may be irregular or exposed to frequent floating rate reset risk. The atomic-level cash flow hedging provided by Eurodollar futures makes them a preferred hedge in such cases.

CALCULATING HEDGE RATIOS

So far we have discussed the fundamental reasons for hedging and the criteria to use in deciding which product to choose for the optimal hedge.

Whichever hedge is chosen, the next step is to calculate the amount of the hedge to trade. This is important since the use of too large or too small a hedge amount can leave the investor with unwanted exposure to the market and lead to higher-than-expected volatility in P/L.

We initially consider the case of hedging with a Treasury bond, as the other choices are modest modifications to the general principles presented here. The main principle in hedging interest rate risk is to match the exposure of the asset and hedge security to interest rates. Recall that in Chapter 2 we introduced the concept of duration and the closely related DV01 (modified duration × price) as the P/L sensitivity to a move in interest rates for a unit amount of notional. The basic process of calculating hedge ratios—that is, the amount of notional of the hedge per unit notional of the original asset—is to equate DV01s for the total asset position and the hedge position.

An example will help clarify. Suppose we own a corporate bond of XYZ corp. with a maturity of 5 years and duration of 4.5. The duration can be calculated using various financial software packages or Microsoft Excel. Let us also assume this bond is trading at a price of $99 (per $100 face value) and that we own $50 million notional of the bond. The four-step process to calculating the hedge ratio is:

1. Calculate the sensitivity to interest rate moves for the bond we wish to hedge. This is the total DV01 of our position. For each $1 million notional, the DV01 of the corporate bond is duration × price = 4.5 × $99 = $445.50 per bp. The $445.50 tells us that if the yield on the corporate move rises by 1 bp (1/100 of 1%), the loss on the bond is $445.50 for *each $1 million notional*. Therefore, for $50 million, this bond's sensitivity is $445.50 × 50 = $22,275.00 per bp. This number sums up this bond's interest rate sensitivity in dollars and cents. If we only want to retain the risk specific to XYZ Corp. rather than overall interest rates, we should offset the $22,275.00 sensitivity to market interest rates.

2. Select a hedge instrument. Given that our corporate bond is five years in maturity we can select a 5-year Treasury note as the hedge. The 5-year Treasury note's exact maturity date is likely to be different from that of the corporate bond, since each bond ages after being issued, but for Treasury hedges, we generally select the nearest available benchmark security for liquidity reasons.

3. Calculate the hedge instrument's sensitivity to rates. Assume that the 5-year Treasury bond has duration of 4.6 (again, this can be determined from software depending on exact maturity and coupon rate) and the price is currently $101. Here the DV01 per $1 million notional is

$4.6 \times \$101 = \$464.6$ per bp. Therefore, our selected hedge moves $464.60 per bp move in its yield for each *$1 million notional.*

4. Calculate the hedge ratio. We know that the corporate bond's aggregate position P/L is impacted by $22,275.00 per bp move in its yield. The hedge in turn moves $464.40 per bp move in its yield. Therefore, to offset the $22,275.00 sensitivity of the corporate bond, we need $22,275.00/$464.40 = $48 million notional (rounded) of the Treasury bond. Note that the notional of the Treasury bond is not the same $50 million as that of the corporate bond. A notional matched hedge would have led to selling too much of the Treasury bond and left the investor exposed to declining rates. In general, notional matching may have an intuitive appeal but can lead to very large errors in hedging, especially when derivatives are used.

This example demonstrates the risk-offsetting purpose of the Treasury hedge. Assume that the Treasury yield and the corporate bond yield rise 1 bp. In this case, the move in rates has been one of a general nature, rather than related to any specific corporate bond reason, since the spread between the two is still unchanged. The 1 bp increase in the corporate bond yield leads to a negative P/L of $1 \times \$22,275 = \$22,275$. The Treasury bond witnesses a profit since we took on a short position for the hedge. The Treasury bond's sensitivity to its yield for a 1 bp rise is $464.50, and thus for $50 million notional, it is $464.50 \times \$50 = \$22,275$ per bp. This is no coincidence, of course, given that we chose the Treasury notional precisely to equate the Treasury position DV01 to the corporate bonds. For the 1-bp rise in the Treasury bond, the positive P/L therefore is $22,275, which exactly offsets the negative P/L on the corporate bond. Therefore, the net P/L for an equal rise in yields in the Treasury and corporate markets is zero.

Taking this example one step further, let's now assume that the yield on the corporate bond rises by 1 bp again, but this time the Treasury yield is unchanged. Consequently, the spread (or difference) of the corporate bond to Treasuries has gone up 1 bp. This underperformance in the corporate bond could be due to a range of issuer- or market-specific factors, such as a disappointing earnings report. Recall that the Treasury hedge is meant to hedge risks from overall interest rate movement in the economy, not the market- or issue-specific risks; in fact, we likely purchased the corporate bond in the first place to take a view on these risks. Returning to the assumption, the 1-bp rise in the corporate bond once again causes us to lose $22,275, but the unchanged Treasury yield leaves us at zero profit on the Treasury bond. Therefore, our net position loses $22,275 as the spread between the corporate and Treasury market widened (in other words, increased) by 1 bp. If the spread had contracted 1 bp, we would have gained

$22,275 due to our hedged corporate bond position. The example therefore demonstrates the unbundling risk principle we discussed. Here, by hedging the overall rate risk, we are taking a specific spread risk related to the corporate market and avoiding a macroeconomic interest rate view. If we had left the corporate bond unhedged, its P/L would be affected by all interest rate moves, regardless of their origin, instead of being affected just by spread moves.

The last example used a Treasury bond as a hedge. Now we consider the other derivative market hedges, such as swaps, Eurodollar futures, and Treasury futures. The main principle of equating dollar sensitivity to interest rates across the asset and the hedge is true across markets and instruments. However, one of the chief mistakes of those new to interest rate derivatives is to use the notionals of the contracts to hedge, such as using the fact that the Eurodollar contract has $1 million notional or that the 10-year Treasury futures contract has $100,000 notional. This can be disastrous; in general, for derivative contracts in fixed income, notional or market value is not a relevant concept in risk management. This is due to the levered nature of Eurodollar contracts and swaps. The key point to focus on is their sensitivity to interest rates. For example, the Eurodollar contract has $1 million notional, but it is *not* 10 times more risky than the 10-year Treasury futures contract with $100,000 notional; instead, one 10-year futures contract is much more sensitive to interest rates than one Eurodollar contract. A risk manager focused on notional or market value could end with a rather painful position that looks "hedged" but is in fact massively exposed to interest rate moves. The process of calculating interest rate sensitivity varies significantly across instruments. The differences from the basic example above that stem from using swap, Eurodollar, or Treasury futures hedges are shown next, with details about risk measurement presented in their respective chapters.

Hedging with Swaps

The procedure to calculate hedge ratios when hedging with swaps is nearly identical to that of calculating hedge ratios with Treasury bonds. As discussed in Chapter 5, an intuitive way to think about a swap is as a par bond financed at the three-month London Interbank Offered Rate (3M LIBOR). Given the close links between swaps and bonds, the duration and DV01 calculation procedure is very similar. In the case of swaps, if an investor pays in a swap at the current market rate, the DV01 is calculated as duration × 100 since swaps start out at a price of par. Most frequently, the swap maturity is matched exactly to that of the asset being hedged, given the swap market's flexibility. There tends to be no extra payment stemming from this maturity matching. The rest of the hedging procedure is the same as described for the Treasury case.

Hedging with Eurodollar Futures

For Eurodollar futures, the hedge amount is generally expressed in number of contracts rather than as a notional amount. For example, sizes would be quoted as 10 Eurodollar contracts instead of quoting $10 million notional of Eurodollars. This is because transaction on the exchange is conducted in number of standardized contracts. To hedge a 5-year bond, the most accurate method to hedge would be to create a 5-year strip of Eurodollars. The exact amount of each Eurodollar contract in the strip can be calculated using a financial program, such as on a Bloomberg Finance L.P. terminal. Often, the strip amounts are nearly equal throughout most of the Eurodollar strip, so investors prefer the simplicity of bundles (see Chapter 4). Since bundles are equally weighted amounts of Eurodollars out to a certain number of years, we could use a 5-year bundle in this case for a 5-year corporate bond. For Eurodollars, the DV01 calculation is simple: It is just $25 for each contract used. Therefore, for a year's worth of Eurodollars, the sensitivity is $100 (per pack) per 1-bp move in the yield, assuming that yields change by the same amount across the curve. Taking this one step further, for a 5-year bundle, the sensitivity is $500 per bp. Recall that this is close to the $464.50 we calculated for the Treasury bond, but Eurodollars have a larger sensitivity because the contract sensitivity is fixed by the exchange and not discounted for longer-dated contracts. Once we know the sensitivity of $500 per bundle, we can calculate the number of bundles to sell by dividing $22,275 by $500. This equates to 44.55 bundles, but since fractional orders cannot be given, the number would be rounded to 45. For cases where we wish to mix and match Eurodollar contracts in different maturities, the rate sensitivity is equally straightforward to calculate; it is the total number of contracts used × 25.

Hedging with Treasury Futures

As with Eurodollars, the calculation for Treasury futures hedges entails a number of contracts rather than a notional amount. However, in contrast to Eurodollar futures, the sensitivity to rates for Treasury futures is not a fixed value, but instead is a far more involved process. As discussed in further detail in Chapter 11 in the section on Treasury futures, the DV01 of a Treasury futures contract can be estimated by taking the CTD DV01 and dividing by its conversion factor. This rule of thumb has the benefit of convenience, but has the drawback of implicitly assuming a constant CTD for the futures contract. In reality, even without a CTD switch, as interest rate moves, the likelihood of different bonds being CTD changes, which in turn changes the DV01 of the contract depending on the durations of the likely candidates. For this reason, using the rule-of-thumb DV01 (i.e., CTD DV01/factor) is generally fraught with errors and can leave an investor unhedged in precisely those volatile times when a hedge is needed most. The option-adjusted hedge ratio is more accurate as it accounts for the probability of a switch, but has the downside of requiring a model of the switch option embedded in the contract. If a CTD switch option model is lacking, an approximate DV01 can also be determined empirically using regressions of Treasury futures prices against Treasury bond yields. The beta of such a regression will approximate the sensitivity we are looking for (also see Chapter 11 for more details). Another complicating factor in the Treasury futures hedge is the fact that Treasury futures track a different maturity from what the contract refers to due to the deliverable basket (i.e., 10-year futures tend to track a 7-year bond). We must use an empirical adjustment between different yield curve maturities if a 10-year asset is being hedged with a 10-year futures contract to minimize the risk of dislocations between 7-year and 10-year Treasuries (discussed in the next section). For this chapter, assume that the DV01 is known. Chapter 11 presents the calculations after we discuss Treasury futures in more detail.

YIELD BETAS

We have discussed the case of hedging one bond using another bond by equating their DV01s. Suppose we unimaginatively call one of the bonds "bond A," and we want to hedge it using "bond B." Say bond A's DV01 is $200/bp and that bond B's DV01 is $1,000/bp. Recall that the DV01 of a bond is expressed as the dollar impact on the value of the bond *per basis point move in its yield*. In our example, we equated the DV01 of the asset we are holding to the asset being used for the hedge. This process seemed to be logical but it incorporates a subtle assumption: By equating the DV01s, we are assuming that 1-bp move in one of the assets coincides with a 1-bp move in the hedge asset. To clarify, let's return to our bond A/bond B example. Bond A's P/L is $200 per bp move in bond A's yield. Bond B's P/L is $1,000 per bp move in bond B's yield. We would sell $20 million of bond B for every $100 million of bond A we own to equate their DV01s, given the DV01 ratio. In this case, if bond A yields rise 1 bp and bond B's yield rises 1 bp, bond A loses $20,000 (due to $100 million notional) but bond B recovers that loss with a profit of $20,000 given its total exposure. However, in the real world, yields rarely move in sync. More realistically, it may be the case that bond A's yield moves only 80% of bond B's yield *on average*. In this case, a 1-bp move in bond B yields would correspond to only a 0.8-bp move in bond A yields. Therefore, a 1-bp move in bond B would create $20,000 of P/L; in bond A, the P/L would only be $20,000 × 0.8 = $16,000 for the $100 million notional, assuming a 0.8-bp move in bond A. Therefore, the appropriate hedge ratio would need only 80% of the "pure" hedge ratio on bond B, that is, $20 million × 0.8 = $16 million. It can be verified that if the bond A yields change 80% of the change in bond B yields, $16 million is the appropriate hedge ratio.

In formulaic terms, our simple hedge amount on the hedge bond B can be calculated as

$$DV01_{bond\ A}/DV01_{bond\ B} \times (\text{notional of bond A})$$

The 80% ratio is known as a yield beta, the reason for which will become clear shortly. When the yield beta is not 1, it means the security we own and the hedge security do not move 1:1 even after adjusting for different durations of the two securities. A yield beta describes how much the asset we are holding moves relative to the hedge asset. Then, if we define yield beta in the above example as the change in bond A's yield for a 1-bp change in bond B's yield, the formula for the amount of bond B to hedge bond A with is:

$$DV01_{bond\ A}/DV01_{bond\ B} \times (\text{notional of bond A}) \times \text{yield beta}$$

How do we arrive at the yield beta in practice? The name "yield beta" stems from its calculation using regression, where the quantity we want is the slope of the regression equation (known as beta) between the security we hold against the hedge security. Generally a regression of daily or weekly changes between the securities is used, rather than outright levels as regressions on changes tend to be more stable. As an example, consider hedging a 5-year swap with a 5-year Treasury bond. We will encounter such trades in Chapter 9. In general, a 1-bp move in the 5-year swap does not lead to a 1-bp move in the 5-year swap yield. Figure 8.2 shows a regression between 5-year swap and Treasury yields since 2003. As the figure shows, the 5-year swap yield has tended to change 7% more than the 5-year Treasury yield. Therefore, a trader wishing to initiate the spread trade, or hedge the 5-year swap with a 5-year Treasury bond, needs a yield beta of 1.07 in the hedge ratio. If the 5-year Treasury has a DV01 of $450/bp, the 5-year swap has a DV01 of $440/bp per million notional, and the trader wishes $100 million notional on the 5-year swap, the Treasury hedge notional is:

$$\$440/\$450 \times \$100 \text{ million} \times \text{yield beta} = \$104.62 \text{ million}$$

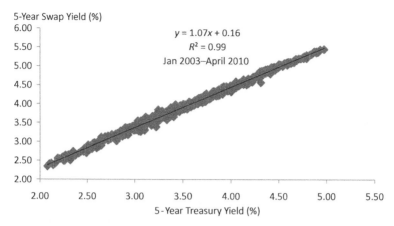

FIGURE 8.2 Five-Year Swap Yield Regressed against Five-Year Treasury Yields
Source: Board of Governors of the Federal Reserve.

Therefore, the Treasury leg needs $104.62 million notional for a hedged trade. The yield beta is also a good check against using uncorrelated assets. During the credit crunch, the dislocations in the markets made hedging very difficult. The muni versus Treasury yield shown in Figure 8.1 is just one example out of many. One reason for the difficulty in hedging risk across markets during the crisis was that long-standing yield betas broke down. Figure 8.3 shows the same regression of daily changes in 5-year

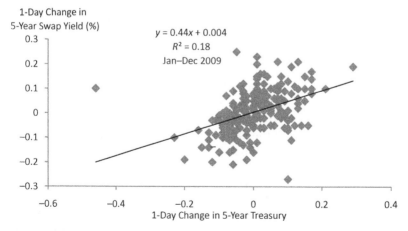

FIGURE 8.3 Change in Five-Year Swap Yield Regressed against Change in Five-Year Treasury Yield during 2009
Source: Board of Governors of the Federal Reserve.

Treasury yields and 5-year swap yields between January 2, 2009, and September 30, 2009. Here the yield beta has gone to near zero, as there is little correlation between the two. Initiating a 5-year Treasury trade as a hedge to a swap trade would be futile as it would provide little risk offset.

CONVEXITY HEDGING

So far, the hedges we have discussed assume that the duration, or DV01 of the asset and its hedge, remains constant. However, as discussed in Chapter 2, fixed income instruments have convexity, whereby a bond's duration itself changes in response to interest rate changes. *Convexity hedging* is a term broadly, and sometimes vaguely, used in the market referring to offsetting risk from the changing duration of bonds. The hedging examples so far described in this chapter offset the first-order price change in the bond for a change in interest rates. If interest rates change by a very large amount, the price change can be greater than is implied by just the duration—in such situations, a modification to the basic hedge notional is needed to account for the increasing or decreasing duration. However, for plain-vanilla bonds such as Treasuries, the convexity is generally not significant enough to require frequent rebalancing of hedge ratios. This is because interest rate changes over short time frames are rarely large enough to make a significant impact on the hedge ratios.

Convexity does become very important for bonds with more complex cash flows where the issuer can choose to redeem or prepay the bond at will. Such a choice by the issuer causes the duration to change by far greater sensitivity to interest rates than with a plain Treasury bond; as underlying interest rates move and prepaying the bond becomes more or less attractive, the effective maturity of the bond changes. For example, if an issuer can redeem a bond from the buyer at $100 and the price is currently $99, the bond is unlikely to be redeemed any time soon. However, if interest rates drop and the price reaches $101, suddenly the bond can be redeemed very soon and its effective maturity (and thus, duration) has been cut to near 0. The presence of the issuer's option to prepay the bond makes the duration far more sensitive to interest rates than with a plain bond, resulting in much greater convexity. For such bonds, the standard calculations shown in this chapter so far assuming a fixed DV01 are not appropriate and a more dynamic approach is needed.

The most important example of a bond where the issuer has the option to prepay at will is the fixed-rate MBS sector. Here we focus the thought process behind hedging mortgage bonds, which form one of the largest segments of U.S. fixed income markets. Mortgage bonds were introduced in Chapter 3 as securities where the issuer, the homeowner, has the choice to prepay the bond at any time. The hedging of mortgage bonds gives insight into general principles of convexity hedging for a wide range of instruments with nonstandard cash flows. Due to the enormous size of the mortgage market, mortgage hedging activity by large entities in the fixed income market can have significant impacts on broader interest rate markets. Thus, by understanding mortgage hedging, we can also recognize how the hedging activity may affect broader interest rate market trades, such as swap spreads (discussed in Chapter 9).

A mortgage bond can be thought of as a collection of a large number and variety of individual mortgage loans to purchase homes. Although each home loan may be small compared to the sizes of transactions in the rates markets, the collection of such loans into large mortgage bonds creates one of the largest fixed income markets in the world. In addition to size, the mortgage market can also be bewildering in its complexity (see Chapter 3 for more details). Here we attempt to distill some important aspects of mortgages and especially how their interest rate risk is managed, as this has important implications for the liquid interest rate markets such as Treasuries and swaps.

The main feature that separates a mortgage bond from its plain-vanilla swap and Treasury cousins is the embedded optionality of the homeowner to refinance and prepay the mortgage. In the United States, in a *fixed rate mortgage*, a homeowner has the option to prepay or refinance a mortgage into a new one at any point in the mortgage's life. The choice to refinance may take place for a host of reasons, including moving to a new area due to change in jobs. However, one of the chief factors behind prepayments is interest rates. If rates decline and allow the homeowner to reduce his/her monthly payments, the homeowner is likely to prepay the existing mortgage and enter into a new mortgage at the lower rate, which is known as refinancing. For the mortgage bond owner, the refinancing results in the principal being returned immediately, precisely at a disadvantageous time when other interest rates are lower. Of course, if rates rise, since the mortgage is fixed rate, there is no need for the homeowner to take any action and the mortgage bond investor takes the losses from rising rates, as with any bond.

Since the homeowner owns the option to refinance, the investor in a mortgage bond is short the same option. In the United States, many mortgages are fixed rate and most of these fixed rate mortgages have a 30-year term. Thus, the homeowner can stay with the same fixed rate for 30 years. The situation is then asymmetric against the owner of a mortgage bond. If rates rise, the value of the mortgage bond providing a fixed rate falls. In such an environment, there is no relief from homeowners as they will not refinance the mortgage and return principal on this bond. If rates decline, the mortgage bond *should* gain in value as its fixed rate becomes more attractive, but the gains are limited as it becomes more likely that homeowners will just prepay the mortgage. In simpler terms, say we lend $100 to a friend at a 10% interest rate. If interest rates for similar loans spike to 25%, the friend happily keeps the borrowed money and keeps paying 10%. However, if interest rates for similar loans fall to 5%, you are only momentarily happy at getting 10%; soon our friend returns the $100 principal and we can only relend the money at 5%! This asymmetry that the mortgage bond owner takes on does not come for free; instead the rate charged to the homeowner is higher than it would be without the option. We can think of this premium as compensation for the bondholder for the asymmetric risk.

As this discussion shows, the value of a mortgage bond is very sensitive to changing interest rates. For a portfolio of mortgages, hedging this interest rate exposure is necessary to avoid excessive volatility in the value of the portfolio, which can overwhelm any gains from interest income. The actual estimation of a mortgage bond's duration and its changes as rates move is a complex problem requiring the modeling of probabilities of prepayment by the homeowner. Such probabilities are modeled as dependent not just on rates but on a multitude of variables characterizing different sets of homeowners. A description of a prepayment model is beyond the scope of this book, but various financial software programs can calculate mortgage duration. For our purposes, the important aspect of mortgage hedging is its effects on rates. Hedging a mortgage bond, however, can be far more complex than hedging a Treasury bond where the DV01 does not move all that much, at least in smaller rate moves. To understand duration movements in mortgages, consider again a homeowner with a mortgage and an investor owning the bond. Suppose the mortgage initially has a 30-year term, as is common in the United States, and a fixed rate of 5%, which the homeowner pays to the mortgage holder. If rates rise, the mortgage is unlikely to be prepaid or refinanced into a new mortgage by the homeowner, which extends the "expected life" of the mortgage toward 30 years. To restate more rigorously, the duration of this mortgage increases. At an extremely high level of rates, the duration of this mortgage bond would approach the duration of a 30-year plain-vanilla bond, such as a 30-year Treasury. If interest rates decline sharply, however, say to 1%, the homeowner has an incentive to refinance very soon. The expected life of this mortgage bond will have shrunk rapidly in this case, so the duration is much shorter. The duration here could be just the duration of a 1-year bond or even less. The rate moves we have considered are on the extreme end, but, in general, the duration of a mortgage bond goes through swings due to interest rate moves. In past interest rate regimes, most of the movement has occurred between

2- and 7-year duration. The movement in duration, of course, means the DV01, which is modified duration × price, varies as well.

For a mortgage portfolio manager, movements in the DV01 of the portfolio can cause significant P/L volatility and vary risk exposure in different interest rate environments. To control this risk, the portfolio manager can attempt to maintain a stable DV01 for the portfolio. Consider the example of a manager with a portfolio of similar mortgages with current DV01 of $5,000/bp move in swap rates. Suppose that the manager prefers to use 5-year swaps to hedge his portfolio for tracking error and transaction cost reasons. Now assume that rates decline and the DV01 of the portfolio declines to $2,000/bp. Now the portfolio is far less sensitive to rates, which is what cuts the upside of the P/L. To maintain a $5,000/bp exposure, the manager would have to add $3,000/bp exposure using his preferred hedge security—that is, a 5-year swap. To add the $3,000/bp, the manager would *receive fixed* in the swap. The notional for this would be the number of millions of the swap needed to equate to $3,000/bp DV01, which we calculated earlier. If rates rise and the DV01 increases to $9,000/bp as the expected life of the mortgage rises, the manager needs to *reduce* DV01 by $4,000/bp. This time, DV01 is reduced by paying fixed in a swap. Paying fixed in swap is the mirror image of receiving and is assigned a negative duration since this position benefits from rates *rising*, in contrast to the receiving position, which benefits from a *decline* in rates (see also Chapter 5). As discussed earlier, any position in the rates world that benefits from yields declining is assigned a positive duration, and any position benefiting from increasing yields is assigned a negative duration. To reduce DV01 by $4,000/bp, the manager would pay in a 5-year swap in a notional amount that aggregates to $4,000/bp in DV01. Now, a 1-bp increase in rates causes a $9,000 loss on the mortgage given its DV01, but causes a $4,000 gain in the swap since the manager paid on the swap, leaving a net $5,000 exposure to interest rates as desired.

Note that the procedure here is similar to the hedging methodology described earlier in the chapter with plain bonds. The difference with mortgages is that the changes in durations due to rate movements require *dynamic* hedging rather than keeping a static hedge ratio. Due to the size of the mortgage market, dynamic hedging by receiving or paying in swaps to increase or decrease DV01 as rates move has a feedback effect on the level of interest rates itself. As rates increase, paying fixed in swaps by mortgage hedgers puts further upward pressure on rates; when rates decrease, receiving fixed in swaps puts further decreasing pressure on rates. Thus, mortgage hedging is an important factor to understand to trade interest rate markets beyond just the mortgage bonds. The effects from the hedging activity are not just constrained to a single maturity on the yield curve. The manager in this example used only a 5-year swap to modify the DV01 of the portfolio. Mortgage portfolio managers do not stick to a single maturity point given the complexities of mortgage bonds. Given the uncertainty of cash flows with a mortgage, a mix of swap maturities is generally preferred to prevent overexposure to a single point on the yield curve in case durations change rapidly. As durations change with interest rates, the mortgage bond itself tracks different parts of the yield curve. For example, if the duration of the bond is eight, the bond is closer to a 10-year maturity swap, but if the duration shrinks to near five, the bond is closer to a 5-year maturity swap. Therefore, as durations change, the closest maturity swap for the portfolio itself changes and mortgage hedgers respond by changing the mix of swaps used for hedging. If interest rates start rising, the rise in durations may prompt mortgage hedgers to change the hedge mix to pay in longer-maturity swaps. The paying in swaps increases yield levels, but also causes the yield curve to steepen, as hedgers increase their pay fixed positions in longer-maturity swaps versus shorter maturity (longer-maturity yields rising more than shorter-maturity). Since mortgage hedgers tend to prefer swaps due to convenience and refined maturity points, their hedging activity also impacts valuations of swaps versus Treasuries, which affects swap spreads (discussed in detail in Chapter 9). Finally, mortgage hedging can also have effects on the interest rate options market because an alternative to dynamic hedging with swaps is to use options on swaps. We cover options and convexity hedging using options in Chapter 11. These hedging activities also vary considerably in their time horizons and magnitude and require constant monitoring on the part of investors. In short, mortgage hedging dynamics are key for U.S. interest rate market participants to understand.

The mortgage convexity hedging concept comes up once again in regard to hedging mortgage servicing assets. Servicing assets can be thought of as interest-only mortgages (IOs, introduced in Chapter 3) that gain value as interest rates rise and lose value as interest rates decline. Unlike a mortgage bond, the servicing asset gains in value with increasing rates and thus has a negative duration. However, similar to mortgages, servicing assets also have negative convexity, with the investor facing the asymmetry of payoffs due to rate movements. The magnitude of profit for the investor when rates increase is smaller than the magnitude of loss when rates decline by a commensurate amount. As interest rates decrease, the duration of the asset gets more negative. To maintain a stable duration in this case, servicers would have to receive in swaps as rates decline (i.e., add to duration) to add back the decrease in duration. As interest rates increase, the duration of the asset gets less negative. As rates rise, servicers enter to pay more in swaps to add back negative duration. Note that the actual level of stable duration the servicer wishes to maintain for the portfolio is largely irrelevant for our purposes. Instead, the important point is the dynamic of paying in swaps as rates are rising and receiving in swaps as rates are declining, which leads to feedback effects on the rates market. The mortgage-servicing industry's large size and increased presence in the market to manage interest rate risk makes it important to understand its hedging needs. These hedging needs translate into large quantities of transactions in swaps and Treasuries and affect a range of interest rate market trades such as interest rate level, yield curve shape, and swap spreads. Over the past few years, the need to manage interest rate exposure has led servicers to enter the rates market more frequently. One way to predict their hedging activity is to model the aggregate servicing industry as a large IO and attempt to anticipate their hedging activity by expected changes in duration or convexity of the aggregate portfolio. However, care needs to be taken to not deduce too much from aggregate calculations as servicer hedging flows can be discontinuous. As with hedging activity of mortgage bonds, understanding mortgage servicer risks under different market conditions is a key factor in understanding the yield curve and spreads.

SUMMARY

The ideas described above point to the complexity of controlling risks in the rate markets. This complexity stems from a variety of sources, from the embedded risks in products being hedged to the products available to hedge these risks. An interest rate market participant may be involved in the market purely to hedge interest rate exposure with no intention of directly profiting from market movements, or may be a pure speculator attempting to profit from yield curve movements. The concepts underlying the process of selecting which risks to hedge and choosing the optimal products to hedge are essential to both hedgers and traders if they are to intelligently control risks.

CHAPTER 9

Trading Swap Spreads

C hapter 8 introduced the concept of hedging, whereby similar products can be traded in opposite directions to offset risks. As mentioned, hedging will not eliminate all risks in such transactions; instead, it leaves the investor with exposure to the difference in valuation of the product being hedged and the hedge instrument. Trading or hedging Treasury bonds versus swaps is so commonly done that it has a special designation: a *swap spread* trade. Whether viewed as a speculative trade or a hedge, a swap spread essentially takes a view on the difference in interest rates between the swap market and the Treasury bond market. Although a difference between two rates, the swap spread can be thought of as a separate trading entity of its own to express views. This chapter discusses the fundamental principles of the trade and the large variety of factors that may drive such trades. Swap spread trades allow investors to take views on a range of concepts, ranging from the path of federal budget deficit to mortgage market activity.

HOW SWAP SPREADS WORK

Before we begin on details, a clarification on market convention is needed. The difference between any two rates in fixed income is known as a spread, with spreads such as corporate spreads (corporate yield – swap yield) and mortgage spreads (mortgage yield – swap yield). As with corporates or mortgage-backed securities, one can look at Treasury spreads to swaps—that is, Treasury yield minus swap yield. Given the liquidity and the widely followed nature of this spread, it is generally just referred to as a swap spread and is mostly quoted as swap yield minus Treasury yield, since the Treasury yield *mostly* trades below the swap yield.

Before exploring the factors driving swap spreads, we first need to understand how to set up such a trade. To start with, we first need a reference Treasury bond, since swap rates can be found for any bond in question, given their continuous curve (see Chapter 5 on swaps). Suppose we pick a Treasury bond such as 2.375% Oct-14, that is, the 2.375% coupon bond maturing in October 31, 2014. The second component of the swap spread is the actual swap. Most commonly, we choose a swap also maturing on October 31, 2014. Suppose the yield on the bond is 2.36% and the swap yield is 2.76%. In this case, the swap spread is 0.4%, or 40 basis points (bps), with bps being the most common unit of quotation. To take a view on the spread, we buy one of the legs and sell the other. Recall that in the context of a swap, to buy is the same as to receive, while to sell is the same as to pay the fixed leg. Whether we buy or sell the Treasury leg (and vice versa for the swap leg) depends on whether we believe the spread is going to narrow or widen. A widening swap spread means the swap spread just described goes from 40 bp to, say, 45 bp. This implies that the swap yield rises a larger amount than the Treasury yield since the swap spread trade is swap yield – Treasury yield. Therefore:

1. Widening swap spread = the swap yield rises more than the Treasury yield (or, falls less than the Treasury yield) = swap underperforms Treasury (remember, yield up = price down).

2. Similarly, narrowing swap spread = swap yield falls more than Treasury yield (or rises less) = swap outperforms Treasury.

Therefore, if we believe the swap market will underperform the Treasury market, we initiate wideners (aim for the 40 bp to rise). To position for a widener, we would pay in the swap and buy the Treasury bond. For the opposite view, we initiate narrowers (aim for 40 bp to fall) by receiving in the swap and selling the Treasury bond.

In this example, we picked a specific Treasury bond and found the swap spread for it; in general, it would be cumbersome to keep track of actual bond issues when tracking generic swap spreads. For that reason, the market tends to look at quantities such as a 2-year swap spread, 5-year swap spread, and other maturity points corresponding to benchmark points on the Treasury curve. These generic quantities are just like the specific bond spread example we considered, with the difference being that they use the current on-the-run Treasury issue in that maturity as their reference, which rolls after each auction. As an example, the 5-year swap spread in mid-January 2010 would have referred to the on-the-run 5-year Treasury at that point, which was the 2.625% Dec-14, but the same 5-year spread would have referred to the 2.375% Oct-14 in mid-November 2009. In each of these cases, the swap used has had the same maturity as the Treasury bond; these are known as matched-maturity swap spreads and are the most widely watched types of spreads. Sometimes market participants also follow spreads known as headline spreads, where the spread would be a 5-year swap yield minus 5-year Treasury bond. In mid-January 2010, for example, the 5-year headline spread would be a January 15, 2015 (i.e., five years from quote day) swap yield − 2.625 Dec-2014 Treasury bond yield (maturing on December 31, 2014), instead of using a December 31, 2014 swap. The difference between matched-maturity and headline spreads arises because the 5-year Treasury bond is not exactly a 5-year security whereas a 5-year swap exactly matches a five-year date. This difference may seem minute, but in steep curve environments, the difference can be noticeable. Nonetheless, broad historical trends in swap spreads are captured in a similar fashion by both headline and matched-maturity spreads. In this chapter, the term *swap spread* will refer to matched-maturity spreads and we will specify headline spreads if referring to those. To show matched-maturity swap spreads historically, this chapter uses the difference between constant-maturity Treasury rates and the equal-maturity swap rate as published by the Federal Reserve (also see Chapter 4). Figure 9.1 shows the 2-year swap spread and 10-year swap spread over the past 10 years; the swap spread tends to vary greatly over time and indeed shows strong trends, the reasons for which are discussed later.

We now know which entities a swap spread refers to. To finalize a trade, we would have to calculate what notionals to use on the swap and

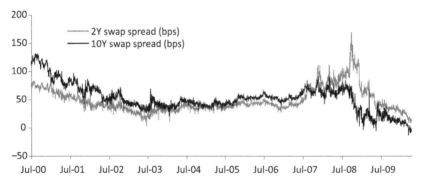

FIGURE 9.1 2-Year and 10-Year Swap Spreads over Time
Source: Board of Governors of the Federal Reserve.

bond. To do so, we return to our 2.375% Oct-14 matched-maturity spread example. The two keys to initiating a swap spread trade are:

1. Match the swap's maturity to the maturity of the bond.
2. Equalize the dollar value of one basis point (DV01) of the Treasury and swap components.

Each of these points is meant to mitigate unwanted risk. The first point reduces the risk that arises from using different maturities and the resulting exposure to the yield curve. The second point is meant to reduce exposure to yield movements. If the DV01s of the Treasury and swap legs are equal, then if the Treasury and swap yields move an equal amount, and therefore leave no change in the spread, there is no gain or loss from the spread. As an example, suppose we buy $1 million of the Treasury and sell $1 million of the matched-maturity swap, with the swap spread at 40 bps. Also suppose the Treasury leg DV01 is $450 and the swap leg DV01 is $400. Now, the net exposure is $50/bp in the trade. If the Treasury yield and swap yield both move up by 1 bp, our spread trade value moves $50 (up or down depending on whether we bought or sold the Treasury leg). However, since both moved up by 1 bp, our spread has not changed. Given that we want to just trade the difference in yields and not be exposed to yields moving in a pure spread trade, matching DV01 instead of notionals is necessary to isolate the *spread risk*.

Given these two principles, we can now set up a swap spread trade. Going back to our example of 2.375% Oct-14, suppose we want to initiate a $50 million position in its swap spread and that our view is of a *narrowing* (i.e., Treasury underperforms). Note that we make assumptions about DV01s for the bonds and swaps used in the example here and for the rest of the chapter. The DV01s are assumed to be calculated either using the formulas listed in Chapter 2 for bonds and similar ones for swaps, or more commonly, using software. Suppose the DV01 per $1 million of notional for the Treasury bond is $475. The four steps to setting up the trade are outlined next.

1. Total DV01 of the Treasury position is $475/bp for $1 million notional × $50 million = $23,750.
2. The matched-maturity swap here is a swap with maturity October 31, 2014 (the Oct-14 bond maturity).
3. Find the DV01 of the swap. We assume it is $450/bp for $1 million notional.

TABLE 9.1 Swap Spread Trade Profit/Loss in Different Yield Shift Scenarios

Treasury Yield Changes (1)	Swap Yield Change (2)	Swap Spread Change (3): (2) − (1)	Treasury P/L (4): DV01 × (1)	Swap P/L (5): DV01 × (2)	Swap Spread Net P/L (5) + (4)
5.0	5.0	0.0	118,750	−118,750	0
8.0	**5.0**	**−3.0**	**190,000**	**−118,750**	**71,250**
5.0	8.0	3.0	118,750	−190,000	−71,250
−5.0	−5.0	0.0	−118,750	118,750	0
−8.0	−5.0	3.0	−190,000	118,750	−71,250
−5.0	**−8.0**	**−3.0**	**−118,750**	**190,000**	**71,250**

4. Equate the swap DV01 to the Treasury DV01. Our notional required is $23,750/$450 = $52.8 million of the swap.

To set up a narrowing swap spread trade, we would sell $50 million of the 2.375% Oct-14 and buy $52.8 million notional of the swap. The notionals are not the same as the DV01 of Treasuries, and swaps are generally not the same due to different coupons. To see that the trade is indeed going to take a spread-narrowing view, we consider different scenarios of yield moves in the Treasury and swap markets in Table 9.1.

As the table shows, the spread trade makes a profit in situations when the swap spread narrows; that is, the Treasury yield rises more or declines less than the swap yield (shown in bold). Note that the opposite scenario leads to loss while an equal change in yield in both markets leaves us with an unchanged spread and, as expected, a net zero P/L.

In these examples, we equated the maturity of the swap to that of the Treasury bond. However, we left the coupons untouched, leaving a mismatch in cash flows. Another version of the swap spread trade takes the Treasury price and equates it to par, with the residual cash flow being spread out over the life of the trade. For example, if the Treasury bond is trading at $103, the initial swap spread trade is initiated assuming a price of $100 of the Treasury, with the $3 being divided through the maturity of the trade. This is known as a par/par asset swap and is not commonly used in Treasury swap-spread trading, given the small differences between coupons of Treasuries and swaps. However, it is useful in the context of wide coupon differences, as with corporate bonds versus swaps or with very old high-coupon Treasury bonds. In general, as mentioned, we will stay with matched-maturity swap spreads since, in the context of Treasuries, the analysis would be very similar.

WHY TRADE SWAP SPREADS?

Now that we have set up a swap spread trade, we come to the important question of *why* investors should trade swap spreads. Given their liquidity, swap spreads provide an efficient way to take a wide range of views on the driving factors of swap spreads, which are discussed in subsequent paragraphs. Furthermore, many times, swap spreads offer a cheaper or more carry-efficient way to take views that would be too expensive using just outright rates. To understand these motivations, we explain the drivers of swap spreads, which will lead us to understanding the motivations of initiating narrowing or widening trades. First we consider fundamental factors that tend to be important most of the time as well as some technical factors that arise at particular times.

The swap spread encompasses the relative value between the Treasury and swap markets. Therefore, drivers of swap spreads are economic and financial factors that affect these two markets in a dissimilar manner. Consider the varying nature of these two markets: As we saw in their respective introductory chapters, Treasuries are the debt of the U.S. government while swaps are conducted against a bank/broker dealer. This fact brings us to the first difference between the swaps and Treasury market: In the swap market, investors are exposed to the risk of their counterparty bank failing to make payment; in the Treasury market, investors are exposed to the risk of the U.S. government failing to make payments. Therefore, the swap spread is exposed to a weakening of the banking system, in which case swap yields would rise much more rapidly than the Treasury yields, leading to wider swap spreads. The widening arises from investors demanding higher yields for swaps to compensate for banking system fears. The Treasury market's debt would not cheapen due to such concerns since the market is backed by the U.S. government. Indeed, Treasury yields would likely decline amidst a banking crisis as investor funds would flee to Treasury debt looking for safety. In general, bank credit has not been a day-to-day trading factor for swap spreads as banks in the United States have not had frequent crises, but some of the greatest moves in swap spreads have been driven by bank credit issues. The Long-Term Capital Management hedge fund bankruptcy led to swap spread widening out of fear for the financial system. In more spectacular fashion, the severity of the credit crunch starting in 2007 led to swap spreads widening to all-time highs. The bankruptcy of Lehman Brothers and stress in other institutions, such as Merrill Lynch and Bear Stearns, led to widespread fear of financial system collapse and sharply increased counterparty credit concerns. When such crisis events are imminent, shorter-maturity swap spreads bear the brunt of the widening. For example, during the Lehman

Brothers bankruptcy around September 2008, 2-year spreads had widened to over 150 bps, much above the 30 bps that had been their stable level for years prior. Therefore, trading swap spreads requires vigilance of bank credit concerns. Indicators such as large changes in bank equity prices or credit default swap contracts on bank debt are key to track for any signs of increased risk aversion.

The bank health driver for spreads listed tends to extend to corporate or emerging market credit overall. If corporates or emerging markets are facing trouble, one would expect banks to suffer losses, as banks make loans to these entities. For this reason, even general flights to quality, where investors rush to the safety of Treasuries, tend to lead to wider swap spreads as a reaction. Such flights to quality lead investors to Treasury debt, making Treasury yields head lower. The decline in Treasury yield will likely prompt lower swap yields, but by a smaller magnitude. However, investors need to be careful in using swap spreads to trade flight to quality; the general decline in yields around such events can trigger other factors, such as mortgage hedging, which we discuss later. Declining rate environments may lead hedgers to receive in swaps, actually putting narrowing pressure on swap spreads and making the swap spread reaction to the flight to quality murky. This is generally true in more isolated and contained scare events when swap spread widening tends to be short-lived. In the type of banking stress seen in 2007 to 2008 or the systemic fears about Long-Term Capital Management in 1998, technical factors such as mortgage hedging were largely overwhelmed.

The difference between the Treasury and swap markets also stems from the nature of supply in the two markets. Treasuries are bonds issued to fund U.S. public debt and government expenditures as they arise. Swaps, however, are derivative contracts that can be created and are not issued by an institution to fund any obligations. Therefore, the swap spread is exposed to supply dynamics from the U.S. Treasury side. If the U.S. government has to issue a large amount of Treasury bonds, the supply of Treasuries rises, which will likely cause Treasury yields to rise (i.e., Treasury prices fall) faster than swap yields. One proxy for the Treasury supply is the budget deficit—the budget deficit is the second significant factor in the direction of swap spreads. There are a few things to note here with regard to the budget deficit and Treasury supply. The budget deficit is generally a slow-moving factor, because government funding needs do not tend to change rapidly. An exception to this situation occurs in times of crisis when large funding obligations arise to stabilize the economy. In such times, though, the counterparty credit factor and the general flight to safer Treasuries tends to outweigh supply-related factors. Although not a short-term factor, the effect of supply can be significant over time, especially if it is expected to be persistent. In general, for forecasting spreads, expected

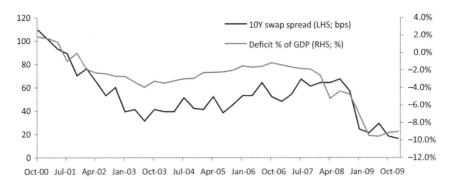

FIGURE 9.2 Link between Swap Spreads and the Budget Deficit
Sources: Board of Governors of the Federal Reserve, U.S. Bureau of Economic
Analysis.

future deficits are of greater importance than the current deficit unless
rapid changes in near-term deficit projections are expected. The dynamics of the deficit also lead to another general observation: Supply-related
issues tend to affect intermediate-maturity swap spreads, such as 5- to 10-
year maturities, more than the very short maturities. An example of the
effect of supply was seen in the early 2000s, when the future deficit projections looked quite rosy as the government was running large surpluses.
These large surpluses led to an expectation of low Treasury supply over
the next few years, causing swap spreads to widen consistently as Treasuries outperformed. Swap spreads and their interaction with the government deficit played a major role in the aftermath of the 2008 credit crunch.
Figure 9.2 shows the link over long time periods between the federal budget deficit and the 10-year swap spread.

The budget deficit as a driving factor allows investors the ability to
use swap spreads to express views on long-term federal budget deficits
for the U.S. government. However, trying to isolate just one driving factor can be difficult, since myriad factors in markets affect swap spreads
in conflicting ways. As mentioned, a rush into Treasuries for safety and
bank credit concerns can overwhelm even in the midst of increases in government spending to avert a crisis. Consequently, swap spreads tend to
widen regardless of increasing Treasury supply. Indeed, a cyclical budget
deficit, which is driven by a slowdown in the economy that causes tax receipts to fall along with the business cycle, generally is not reflected as
strongly in a swap spread. This type of deficit is expected to reverse itself
once the economy picks up and tax receipts pick up. A structural deficit,
however, which the market perceives to have long-term effects beyond the
current economic cycle (perhaps from rising medical or welfare costs),

can increase Treasury issuance well beyond the business cycle and have a multiyear narrowing effect on swap spreads. Although the effect of structural deficits may be slow to materialize, swap spreads tend to be a much more effective way of taking a view on the government's fiscal situation than just selling Treasury bonds outright. The idea of "selling Treasuries because the government is issuing too much debt" is generally an effective one because Treasury yields are affected not just by government issuance but the supply of leverage across the economy (see Chapter 6 for more details). Due to this link with debt issuance across the entire economy, not to mention numerous other factors that can drive outright rate levels, shorting plain Treasuries to express a view on just the federal deficit is rarely fruitful. However, swap spreads isolate the Treasury market's supply dynamics to a far greater extent, since the offsetting swap yield removes much of the outright interest rate level risk. Although swap spreads are also driven by many other factors, they are more useful in isolating the U.S. government issuance path than outright Treasuries. Finally, the relationship between swap spreads and government budget is not just a U.S. phenomenon; it is an important factor for any spread between swaps and government debt. Trading swaps versus government debt can allow investors to take more specific views on fiscal situations across a range of countries.

Although the deficit tends to be a slow-moving factor, at times Treasury supply can also have a short-term tactical impact. This is especially true if the amount of supply is so large that the market has trouble digesting it all at once. In 2009, for example, Treasury supply increased sharply with the government auctioning over $100 billion per month in bonds. As auctions approached, swap spreads tended to narrow as Treasuries underperformed due to the upcoming supply. However, as auctions passed, most of this underperformance was reversed, making the auctions attractive tactical events around which investors could trade swap spreads.

Another major fundamental factor for swap spreads is liquidity, with periods of increasing liquidity generally witnessing narrower swap spreads. The concept of liquidity can be tough to grasp at first because it is not easily measurable as a number; instead, it can be best described as "availability of money." In times of high liquidity, adding leverage to trades by borrowing funds tends to be relatively easy; also, times of high liquidity tend to drive investors in search of higher-yielding instruments, as more money needs to be put to work (i.e., invested in markets). Finally, a trend of increasing risk tolerance is also a hallmark of increasing liquidity. Such an environment tends to lead to narrower spreads as investors prefer higher-yielding instruments, such as swaps, relative to safer Treasury yields. If liquidity is plentiful, financial conditions are stable and by receiving in a swap instead of a Treasury, an investor can earn extra bps of return for little additional volatility. The increased need to receive in swaps lowers swap yields relative to Treasury yields, thus narrowing the swap spread. For example, in the credit boom years of 2005 to 2007, swap spreads traded at extremely narrow levels, with 2-year swap spreads averaging 40 bps. The liquidity effects are even stronger in periods when the Federal Reserve is loosening monetary policy rapidly and adding to the money supply, which can have a substantial narrowing effect. This was witnessed during the recovery from the credit crunch in 2009. Although increasing liquidity narrows swap spreads, how do we account for it quantitatively? Given that ambiguous nature of liquidity, we can use a proxy, such as the fed funds target rate less the inflation rate, to stand in for liquidity. This quantity is known as the real funds rate, with *real* referring to the difference of a nominal rate and inflation. When the real funds rate is very low, the Federal Reserve target rate is indicating easy monetary policy, which entails higher liquidity. Note that this factor is not always reliable; at times, the very loose policy could be reflecting a rapidly weakening financial system, which would actually entail wider spreads. However, over time, if high levels of liquidity are maintained, swap spreads tend to eventually narrow in response.

An important factor for swap spreads in recent years (and that is likely to gain further prominence) is demand for long-end fixed income products from pension funds. Defined benefit pension funds promise certain benefits to workers upon retirement and therefore need to grow current assets over time to meet obligations in the future. These future liabilities leave pension funds with exposure to long-dated streams of income, leading their liabilities to resemble long-dated bonds. Previously these pension funds had large exposure to equity markets in an attempt to grow these assets at a rapid pace. This turned out to be a suboptimal method because equity prices went through very large swings and ended with little return during the 2000s. Apart from historical disappointments, there are also more fundamental issues with having equities on the asset side when the liability resembles long-dated fixed income products. Due to discounting effects, as interest rates decline, the value of these liabilities rises. On the asset side, equities can be a very poor offset for the long-dated fixed income exposure, since environments with rapidly declining interest rates coincide with a sharp slowdown in the economy—in such a situation the value of equities on the asset side declines, but the value of liabilities increases from discounting. In response to these issues, and due to prodding from regulators, pension funds have been moving toward matching assets and liabilities; we discussed the effects of this on their long-end fixed income demand in Chapter 6. However, the fact that pension funds have moved toward long-dated fixed income exposure also has had implications for swap spreads, in particular 30-year swap spreads. Swaps provide a simple and relatively liquid way to gain exposure to the long-end fixed income market; unlike the Treasury market, there are no auctioned amounts at intervals.

For the large position sizes pension funds seek, the swap market tends to be the preferred way to gain exposure. Pension funds for long-end fixed income in part led to 30-year swap spreads trading at negative levels during 2008 and continuing to do so into late 2010. This was the first time a swap spread turned negative in the U.S. markets (i.e., the government yield was higher than a swap yield). This is not necessarily a poor reflection on government credit versus bank credit over the next 30 years; it is more a reflection of structural demand for long-end fixed income assets as demographics change. The changes in pension funds and their investing are likely to take decades to fully manifest themselves, but the size of pension funds makes them an important subset for investors to follow closely, especially for the long end of the interest rate curve.

The factors discussed so far are fundamental or structural in nature and tend to be important when trying to understand longer-term trends in swap spreads. However, for day-to-day movements, a variety of shorter-term factors related to flows from various market participants play a crucial role. Even if longer-term trends are obvious, investors ignore these shorter-term factors at their own peril: Any trend can have massive reversals that force even the most steadfast investors to abandon their positions.

Three major technical factors affect swap spreads: mortgage hedging, corporate issuance hedging, and exotics hedging. As can be seen from these factors, hedging activity plays a very important role in swap spreads, mainly because to a certain extent, hedgers have less choice over when they transact due to exposure to wider market conditions. Traders who understand these factors are therefore in a better position to anticipate swap spread movements on an intraweek or intramonth basis.

Mortgage hedging is one of the dominant drivers of swap spreads. Although of a short-term nature, the effects of sustained mortgage hedging activity can last for months. We discussed the nature of hedging mortgages in detail in Chapter 8. To summarize, a U.S. homeowner who takes out a 30-year mortgage has the option to prepay the mortgage at any time, which makes the mortgage bond's expected life (and duration) variable. As rates rise, the expected duration of the mortgage increases as it is less likely that someone will refinance their mortgage, given that they would have to take on a new mortgage at a worse rate. The investor has to offset this increase in duration by engaging in a trade that lowers duration, such as paying in swaps or selling Treasuries, both transactions that have negative duration. The reverse is true if rates are declining; in such a case, the duration of the mortgage will drop as refinancing becomes more likely. This situation leads the mortgage investor to receive in swaps or buy Treasuries. In the United States, most of the hedging by mortgage participants is done using swaps, due to some of the advantages listed in Chapter 5. This preference for swaps over Treasuries leads to mortgage hedging activity affecting the swap market to a greater extent than the Treasury market and consequently leading to an impact on swap spreads. Therefore, when interest rates are rising, mortgage hedgers pay in swaps to cut duration, which tends to widen swap spreads. Conversely, when interest rates are falling, mortgage hedgers receive in swaps to increase duration, which tends to have a narrowing effect on swap spreads. Consequently mortgage hedgers are also the main reason why swap spreads tend to be directional with yield levels; that is, they widen when interest rates increase and narrow when interest rates decline.

The largest mortgage hedgers tend to be the Freddie Mac and Fannie Mae government agencies, which owned well over $1 trillion in mortgages at the time of this writing. To hedge this massive collection of mortgages, the two agencies transact in huge swap notionals. To understand swap spreads, it is crucial to track these agencies. In particular, after the credit crunch, the status of Agency portfolio size and composition was politically uncertain, which could over time change the way mortgage hedging impacts swap spreads. Another subset of the mortgage world that has taken increasing importance for swap spreads is the mortgage servicing community. We discussed the hedging needs of mortgage hedgers and servicers in Chapter 8. As interest rates change, the duration and convexity of mortgage hedgers such as agencies and servicers change as well. To trade swap spreads, it is crucial to have a sense of these risk exposures to the market for different classes of mortgage hedgers if yields change. To be sure, neither class of hedgers hedges at each market increment in a predictable manner; instead, at times, they will leave themselves unhedged, which can lead to a buildup of a need to pay or receive and cause discontinuous moves in spreads. Understanding when large mortgage hedgers and servicers are exposed to the market and are likely to face large paying or receiving needs in the swaps market can help traders better set up for swap spread movements.

Although mortgage hedging activity is a nearly daily factor for the interest rate market, at times it can become so intense as to drive yields substantially higher and spreads substantially wider (or, less commonly, lower and narrower). Such events are known in the market as duration extension events, since a large-scale extension of durations in mortgages ends up dominating other factors we have already discussed. These episodes can last over a month in some cases, although they are mostly short-lived. One of the most compelling examples of such an event took place in the summer of 2003, when yields reached multidecade lows. The drop in rates led to a boom in refinancing, which is shown in Figure 9.3 on the mortgage refinance index. As homeowners refinanced their existing mortgages into new ones, these new mortgages were unlikely to be refinanced any time soon given the very low rates; this in turn led to a flood of new,

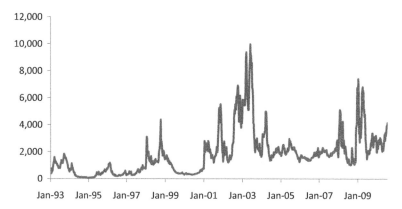

FIGURE 9.3 Mortgage Refinancing Index
Sources: Bloomberg LP, Mortgage Bankers Association.

long-duration instruments into the market. As the pressure to hedge these mortgages built up, the "dam" broke in the summer of 2003, and 10-year swap yields rose sharply. The effect on swap spreads was stark as well: 10-year swap spreads widened over 40 bps that summer, given the mortgage hedging flows. This risk of a buildup in mortgage duration hedging after a period of low rates is important to monitor; following refinancing volumes can be a useful way to anticipate large increases in mortgage. June 2009 witnessed a similar mortgage-driven swap spread widening after rates reached near-all-time lows.

The second factor with short-term impact on spreads is corporate issuance hedging. In general, banks are one of the largest issuers of debt in the corporate bond market. Furthermore, banks tend to prefer floating rate liabilities. If they issue debt in the fixed rate market, recall that swaps can be used to convert the debt into floating rate debt. If a bank issues fixed rate debt, it is essentially paying a fixed rate; to convert to floating, it can receive fixed in a swap and pay floating. The coupons on the fixed legs can be arranged to cancel out, leaving the corporation paying floating plus or minus a spread with the details shown in Chapter 5. Given that the bank would receive fixed in swaps, a large amount of financial fixed rate corporate issuance tends to cause narrowing pressure on swap spreads. However, this effect tends to be temporary, as the initial fixed rate receiving is absorbed by the market and then almost always reversed in a few days. Nonetheless, the issuance calendar is important to keep in mind when initiating swap spread trades; issuance can offer opportunities to set up trades at more favorable levels. Furthermore, larger-than-usual corporate issuance tends to occur in certain months, such as September and January. Indeed, swap spreads show a pattern of narrowing after Labor Day and in the first couple of weeks of January (which is also due to increased risk-taking appetite when the new year starts).

The effects of these factors on the market are generally predictable, even if the magnitudes are uncertain. The next factor, exotics hedging, is far more difficult to generalize. The term *exotics hedging* refers to the offsetting of risks incurred by banks selling nonstandard products, which are called exotic securities on Wall Street. Most exotic securities are sold in quantities that are too insignificant to affect swap spreads. However, at times, certain products gain in popularity to such an extent that they become drivers of swap spreads. Furthermore, almost all exotics hedging effects are seen in long-end spreads, such as 30-year swap spreads, since the relative illiquidity of the long end leads them to react more than spreads in the intermediate sector for similarly sized hedging activity.

The nature of exotics hedging makes it very difficult to generalize since at any given time, different products gain and lose popularity. However, to understand swap spreads, especially in the 10- to 30-year sectors, it is key to understand the products that are relevant at any given time, and especially their risk exposures to the market, which drives hedging activity from dealers. While we cannot anticipate future products, it is instructive to understand some that have been drivers over the past few years and to isolate the risk factors that lead to the impact on swap spread markets. The first such products we discuss are power reverse dual currency (PRDC) notes, which were sold in large size starting in the mid-2000s, mostly to an Asian client base that was looking for yield enhancement. PRDCs, in essence, had coupons pegged to the U.S. dollar/Japanese yen currency exchange rate (USD/JPY) level, where if the yen depreciated in value the coupon payment increased and vice versa. In short, the dealer's risk was similar to owning Japanese yen against the U.S. dollar since as the JPY appreciated, the coupon payments the dealer had to make were reduced. These notes tended to be of long maturity—in some cases 10 years and above—leaving the dealer with currency exposure at various points forward in time. Although exposure to the nearby coupons could be hedged in the foreign exchange (FX) market, the very-long-dated exposure to a currency is difficult to hedge directly in the FX market. Instead, long-dated FX exposure can be replicated via current FX exposure and interest rate exposure until the forward date; this concept is similar to the forward rate decomposition into spot + carry we analyzed earlier. In the FX case, the "carry" is actually the difference between two interest rates, here the U.S. dollar and the Japanese yen. As USD/JPY declined, especially toward certain trigger levels if the notes had embedded options, the dealer would need to buy larger amounts of forward USD/JPY. To do so, the dealer would buy USD/JPY spot and receive in long-dated U.S. swaps and pay in long-dated

JPY swaps. The receiving in long rates in turn led to narrowing 30-year swap spreads when USD/JPY declined or as the JPY appreciated vis-à-vis the U.S. dollar.

This example of PRDC notes has been greatly simplified. The true risk profile of these notes is fairly complex. Furthermore, our example is stylized; in general, different notes have distinct features including trigger levels and other embedded options, resulting in a large variation of hedging needs. Also, dealers know that if their hedging activity is too predictable, rates and FX traders will be waiting to take advantage of it, which would lead to losses for dealers. Partly to avoid being too predictable, exotics hedging flows tend to appear in chunks, and the source can be difficult to decipher; many times, exotics hedging may even be used to explain why swap spreads moved, just because other reasons do not seem apparent. The PRDC example, however, does point to the fact that markets are increasingly interconnected. Seemingly unrelated moves, such as large drops in USD/JPY, can have repercussions in markets as distant as U.S. 30-year swap spreads. The key point here is not the specifics of the PRDC notes, which are likely to be replaced by new sets of popular notes depending on the levels of interest rates offered; instead, the point to remember is that rates investors must be aware of popular exotics structures and must assess their possible effects. Hedging flows from such notes can allow investors to capture attractive entry points for different swap spread views.

Earlier we discussed some of the general factors that drive spreads. This is not an exhaustive list—such a list is not possible as new factors are likely to emerge over the coming years. The credit crunch provided examples of the emergence of unexpected factors, where overall illiquidity can lead to large effects on spreads even from previously insignificant factors. One such link that appeared was between equities and long-end swap spreads. Although in "normal" times such a link is essentially nonexistent, the steep declines in equity markets led to new sets of problems for insurance companies. Insurance companies had sold a wide range of variable annuity notes with the general idea of offering investors a return from some basket of risky assets, such as equities, and at the same time guaranteeing a minimum return, such as 4%. These notes tended to be of a long-term nature, which in turn exposed the insurance companies to declines in the value of the equities that the notes tracked. Although the exact mechanisms of these products were complex, essentially if the value of these equities fell, the insurance companies would have to pay out a floor of 4% from their own earnings rather than relying on equity earnings. Thus, falling equity values created increasing exposure to long-end rates for the companies; they would have to rely on these long-end interest rate instrument payments to honor the floor. To offset this risk, as equity markets fell, insurance companies bought long-end fixed income, mostly by receiving fixed in swaps. As equity markets stabilized, this need to receive in long-end swaps abated, as did the correlation between the equity markets and long-end fixed income. Nonetheless, fixed income buying by insurance companies kept reasserting itself during sharp equity drops throughout 2008. The surprising and fleeting correlation of swap spreads with equities is just one of many examples of the complexity of swap spreads. Although this complexity makes swap spreads a difficult product to understand, it also adds to the richness of views investors can take using trades in this space.

DIRECTIONALITY OF SWAP SPREADS TO YIELDS

In the mortgage hedging example, we noted that mortgage hedging is one of the main factors that leads to swap spreads being positively directional with yields *for the most part*. Note that by the term *positively directional*, we mean that spreads widen as swap yields rise and spreads narrow as swap yields fall. The magnitude of this directionality has been 7% on average over the long term; that is, spreads widen 7 bps for a 100-bp move higher in swap yields (see Figure 8.2 in Chapter 8). This directionality, of course, varies quite a bit; in mortgage duration extension periods, it can reach upward of 20%. The link between swap spreads and yields can also be reversed; in periods of flight to quality, investors rush to the safety of Treasury yields, leading to lower Treasury (and swap) yields. However, as discussed, such periods witness swap yields declining at a slower pace than Treasury yields, leading to *wider swap spreads*. Consequently, in such cases, lower yields coincide with wider swap spreads, which is not the "normal" reaction. In most periods not characterized by stress in markets, the positive directionality reasserts itself.

The directionality of swap spreads can either be kept by the trader as a favorable aspect or hedged out. If the trader decides to only have a pure spread view, where the impact of yield movements should be limited, such a trade can be constructed where the risk weighting on the swap leg or Treasury leg is modified away from being equally weighted between the two. Note that this "weighted swap spread" is not what generally will be shown on screens or discussed by market participants, since those matched-maturity spreads are 1:1 risk weights. Another way of making the same point is that the common matched-maturity spread is tracked as swap yield – Treasury yield, while a weighted spread is tracked as swap yield × weight – Treasury yield. The setup for such a trade is shown in Chapter 8.

At times, however, the positive directionality of swap spreads with yields can be a beneficial aspect of the trade. It presents interesting opportunities to position for rising or falling yields, especially when doing the same trade in the interest rate market would be too expensive from a carry standpoint. For example, in early 2004, rates were at extremely low levels and there was anticipation of a Federal Reserve tightening, which would lead to rates rising over time. A basic trade for an investor looking to position for higher rates would have been to pay fixed in a 10-year swap. However, such a strategy had much negative carry, given the steep curve, so it was an expensive proposition. Another way to position for higher rates would be to initiate a 10-year spread widener if investors believed that the 10-year spread would widen with higher rates, given the normal, mortgage hedging–driven relationship between the two. The spread widener trade had far less onerous carry, since in a swap spread trade, we are simultaneously entering a long Treasury and paying a swap combination. Indeed, by mid-year 2004, 10-year spreads widened along with rising 10-year swap rates, pointing to an interesting use of spreads to take interest rate views in a more carry-efficient manner.

FUTURES ASSET SWAPS

A variant on the typical swap spread we have just discussed is the futures asset swap spread. As the name implies, this trade involves buying or selling a futures contract, in particular a Treasury futures contract, versus the swap instead of a Treasury bond. The asset swap spreads discussed earlier can be done versus any Treasury bond available, but in the case of Treasury futures contract, the choice of maturity points is limited by the liquid contracts available, which are currently 2-year, 5-year, 10-year, 30-year, and ultra-long contracts.

The Treasury futures asset swap concept is very similar to the Treasury bond swap spread discussed earlier, with some differences stemming from the setup of the trade. As mentioned in Chapter 4, Treasury futures can be thought of as forward contracts on Treasury bonds. Therefore, to take the maturity-matching concept one step further, the swap component of the Treasury futures contract needs to be a forward swap as well. The next six points describe the setup of a Treasury futures asset swap where the investor wishes to initiate a spread widener in the 10-year space using 1,000 contracts.

1. Buy 1,000 10-year Treasury futures contracts expiring in March 2010. Assume the DV01 of each contract is $79/contract calculated using

either a delivery option model or empirical method as described in Chapter 11.

2. Total DV01 of the futures position = 1000 × $79/contract = $79,000.

3. Last delivery date = March 31, 2010. This is the forward start date of the swap.

4. Cheapest-to-deliver (CTD) bond: 4.875% Aug-16. Maturity of CTD bond = August 15, 2016. This bond will be the maturity date of the swap.

5. Forward swap = 3/31/2010 × 8/15/2016 (i.e., it starts on March 31, 2010 and lasts till August 15, 2016). Assume DV01 of swap calculated using software package per $1 million notional = $625/million.

6. Forward swap notional = $79,000/$625 = $126.4 million.

As these points show, the basic concept remains the same, but in the futures asset swap case, we replace the bond with a futures contract and match the swap using the contract's last delivery date and CTD maturity date. One point to note is that if the CTD bond is changing rapidly, it may be difficult to set up the futures asset swap correctly, given that the swap maturity relies on a fixed CTD. In such cases, it may be best to do the swap spread trade using actual bonds.

Since Treasury futures trade in price terms, it may be difficult to figure out what yield swap spread we entered or exited the trade at. In the case of bonds, it was simple: We subtracted the Treasury yield from the swap yield. In the case of futures, we use the implied forward yield of the CTD, the details of which are presented in Chapter 4. Once we have the implied forward yield, we can calculate our swap spread by a similar difference: forward swap yield – implied forward yield of the futures CTD bond. By converting the futures spread into a yield, it becomes easier to estimate the trade P/L on a day-to-day basis.

Finally, the reader may be wondering why a futures asset swap is necessary. In general, the advantage of the futures asset swap is that it keeps the swap spread trade in derivatives space. This way, investors do not have to transact in the repo markets and take on Treasury bonds, which can be balance-sheet intensive. The use of futures contracts may also result in more relative value benefit for the swap spread trade if the contract is mispriced with respect to bonds. For example, if investors wish to add on a spread widener and the futures contract is trading cheap to bonds, buying the futures contract can be advantageous versus buying a cash bond for the trade. Of course, one disadvantage that arises is that the futures contract does not represent the maturity stated in the contract but instead tracks a CTD bond. This can result in performance of the 10-year futures asset swap trade, for example, being different from that of the 10-year screen swap spread trade.

SPREAD CURVE TRADES

In the interest rates section we saw that trading the spread between two interest rates (i.e., curve trades) is another commonly chosen strategy by investors. The same is true with swap spreads. In general, trading two swap spreads, with one being a widener and one being a narrower, is known as a *swap spread curve trade* (or at times a spread of spreads trade). The language is also imported from interest rate curve trading: A spread curve steepener attempts to benefit from a widening in a longer-dated spread relative to a shorter-dated spread, while a flattener aims for the opposite.

To clarify, consider an interest rate curve where the 2-year swap spread is 40 bps and the 10-year swap spread is 60 bps. In this case, the spread curve is 20 bps (60 bps – 40 bps). If we initiate a spread curve steepener, we initiate a widener in 10-year spreads and a narrower in 2-year spreads; now, if the spread curve increases to, say, 25 bps, we benefit by 5 bps. Conversely, for a flattener, we would initiate a narrower in 10-year spreads and a widener in 2-year spreads.

Spread curve trades can be cumbersome to set up since they have four legs (two for each spread trade). The principle in setting these up is a hybrid of the principles we have seen in setting up spread trades and those for setting up curve trades in interest rate space: equating DV01s. Suppose we want to set up the 2-year/10-year spread curve steepener trade just mentioned. Assume that we aim to have $100 million notional exposure to the 2-year bond leg:

1. Sell $100 million of the 2-year bond, since we want a narrower in the 2-year space. Assume the DV01 is $190/million for the 2-year bond. Therefore, total DV01 for 2-year bond is $19,000. Since the aim was to have $100 million exposure to the 2-year bond leg, the $19,000 DV01 will form the base for the rest of the calculations and all other notionals will be chosen to equate DV01s to this base amount.

2. Assume DV01 of maturity-matched swap is $185/million. Then the swap notional is $19,000/$185 = $102.7 million to receive fixed (see earlier text for the setup of a swap spread trade).

3. Now assume the 10-year bond has a DV01 of $770/million. We want the 10-year spread position to have the same DV01 as the 2-year spread trade, which is $19,000. So 10-year bond notional = $19,000/$770 = $24.7 million to buy.

4. Assume a matched-maturity swap to a 10-year bond has a DV01 of $760/million. Then this also needs to have $19,000 DV01, or notional of $19,000/$760 = $25 million to pay fixed.

Our spread curve steepener trade is a narrower in 2-year maturity and widener in 10-year maturity, which entails selling $100 million notional of a 2-year Treasury bond, receiving in $102.7 million maturity-matched 2-year swap, in addition, buying $24.7 million notional of a 10-year bond and paying in $25 million of a maturity-matched 10-year swap. The buying/selling and receiving/paying can be difficult to keep track of, but it is easier if one thinks of the trade as two separate entities: one narrower, where (as with all spread narrowers) the bond is sold and the fixed coupon is received on the swap, and one widener, where the bond is always bought and fixed leg on the swap is paid. Note that a spread curve can alternatively be thought of as a Treasury curve steepener/flattener hedged with the opposite curve trade done in the swap market.

The spread curve trade is a fairly involved one to set up. The reader may be wondering what benefit this complexity offers. Spread curve trades can allow an investor to take very specific views that are hedged against not just broad rate moves but also broad swap spread moves. We listed factors that affect swap spreads and mentioned that in different maturity sectors, the magnitude of their effects is different. For example, bank credit concerns tend to manifest themselves most strongly in the 2-year space while mortgage hedging tends to get reflected more in the 5- to 10-year space. Suppose we have a view that mortgage hedgers are likely to stay quiet over the coming month but that one of the larger banks may have trouble refinancing some of its debt. In this case, a 2-year spread widener may first come to mind, but at times an outright widener is exposed to other risks, given the numerous factors that drive it. It may be better to isolate the bank credit view using a 2-year/5-year spread curve flattener, which is a widener in 2-year offset via a narrower in 5-year spreads. This trade is exposed to relative differences between the 2-year and 5-year space, but if another factor drives all spreads wider or narrower, the trade is hedged.

Spread curve trades can also be useful when trying to isolate sector-specific factors in Treasuries. Suppose we know that an auction is coming up in the 30-year sector in a week. We also realize by looking at the data that dealers are already holding too much inventory and may have trouble handling the large size of Treasury bonds auctioned. This is likely to cheapen the 30-year sector versus another sector not facing issuance, such as the 20-year sector. The first reaction may be to sell 30-year Treasuries. However, as discussed in Chapter 8, the exact view of the trader can greatly improve the effectiveness of a trade and hedge out unnecessary risks. Doing this will generally improve the Sharpe ratio (return/volatility) of a trade, even if the absolute return is lower. By selling 30-year Treasuries outright, the investor is exposed to literally hundreds of factors that could come into play and may make all Treasury yields go lower. At best, we can only say that the auction will likely make the 30-year sector underperform *versus the rest of the curve*, but if there is a flight to quality into Treasuries, yields would likely rally all over the curve. Given this factor, the next choice may be to sell 30-year Treasuries and buy 20-year Treasuries—in other words, put on a curve steepener (see Chapter 3 for the terminology). This is more specific but is still exposed to the overall shape of the Treasury curve. In particular, a Fed statement that makes tightening more imminent, as discussed in Chapter 6, may flatten the curve sharply and overwhelm the supply factor. Here, a spread curve trade may isolate the supply factor in the best way. By initiating a spread curve flattener—that is, a spread widener in 20-year space and a spread narrower in 30-year space—we are aiming for a cheapening of 30-year bonds versus 20-year bonds. Furthermore, a spread curve trade is not as exposed to a yield curve trade because it is a Treasury curve trade hedged with a swap curve trade (buy 20-year bond/sell 30-year bond, but also pay 20-year swap and receive 30-year swap). Since each leg is a spread trade, it is also less exposed to the overall level of interest rates. Although one can never fully isolate the trade to be exposed only to the Treasury auction, with a spread curve trade, we have cut down the number of factors that could influence our P/L.

SUMMARY

This chapter discussed trading swaps spreads and the factors that drive the differential between the Treasury bond and swap markets. Although relatively easy to conceptualize once the basic concepts of bonds and swaps are understood, it should be clear that swap spreads are not just the difference between two rates. Instead, they encompass a large number of sometimes-conflicting factors that can be difficult to express with just a Treasury or swap instrument. The importance of these factors also varies along the maturity curve of swap spreads, which adds another layer of both risk and opportunity for the swap spread trader.

CHAPTER 10

Interest Rate Options and Trading Volatility

Options are an important class of products in most financial markets, and fixed income is no exception. An understanding of options allows a trader to use a wider set of tools to express views on the underlying rates and opens up the opportunity to trade volatility, which can provide uncorrelated returns to a rates-trading portfolio. This chapter provides a basic introduction to options, especially in the rates world, and to the concepts underlying trading volatility. Many readers are likely familiar with the basic feature of options: They provide the buyer with the right, but not the obligation, to purchase or sell an asset. The right to purchase an asset is called a call option, while the right to sell the asset is called a put option. The price at which the right can be exercised is called the strike, and the option purchaser tends to have an expiration date to exercise the right. The position of the price versus the strike is known generally as the *moneyness*. If the strike is equal to the current underlying price, the option is said to be at the money. If the strike is at an unfavorable level compared to the current level (i.e., the option would not be exercised currently), the option is said to be out of the money; the reverse case is called in the money. The amount of value in the option due to the strike difference is known as the intrinsic value, which can be thought of as the profit if the option was exercised immediately. The option's price on any day prior to exercise day is generally more than its intrinsic value (referred to as the time value). Time value is a measure of the value of the option holder's choice to exercise the option at a later date. The exercise conventions can also vary: An American option can be exercised at any time while a European option can be exercised only at expiry date. There are a wide

FIGURE 10.1   Payoff Profile from Buying a Call and a Put Option

range of combinations of these two extremes, such as Bermudans, which can be exercised on a given set of dates, such as every six months.

Figure 10.1 shows the payoff profiles for buying a put and a call option for an underlying security struck at $100. Mathematically, the payoff at expiry is max(underlying – strike,0) for a call and max(strike – underlying,0) for a put. The payoff diagrams reflect the payment to the owner of the option at expiry and show the asymmetric nature of options. For an option seller, the situation is reversed, and the seller of either the call or the put faces the downside of asymmetry.

Although the variety of options is large, the right, but not the obligation, to enter the trade at expiry leads all options structures to have asymmetry in payoffs. The distinction can best be seen by considering the example of a stock versus a stock option. The payoff profiles of one unit of the stock and an option contract on one unit of stock *at expiry* are shown overlaid on Figure 10.1. For the stock, the payoff is a straight line as each $1 change in the stock price changes produces a $1 payoff change in either direction. For the call option struck at $100, the right but not the obligation to purchase presents a very different profile for the buyer; the buyer participates in all the upside since she would exercise the right to purchase at $100 if the stock was above $100 at expiry. However, if the stock was below $100, since there is no obligation to purchase, she would just let the option expire without exercising the right, leaving a zero payoff. To be sure, the market will not give away such a valuable right for free. In reality, an up-front payment called a premium is made for this right. We discuss the calculation of this premium shortly. The next few sections are a brief introduction to options in general before we discuss interest rate options in particular. For more on options, see Hull (2006).

OPTION PRICING AND FUNDAMENTALS

Given the asymmetric payoffs that exist in options, they are valuable instruments for expressing views or mitigating risks. The market charges for the asymmetric payoffs and the value of such payoffs depends on the market environment. This section explains how to deduce a fair price for an option and the factors that drive this fair value. To understand the logic behind pricing options, consider a situation where person A is presented with three boxes with variable quantities of money in each (including possibly with zero). Now assume someone offers A a call option on the boxes, which means that A gets the payoff of the box with the *maximum* amount of money of the three. Now suppose A is offered two possible situations in which to hold the option:

1. Each box can have only between $0 and $10, and the range of the three amounts (i.e., max − min) is $2.
2. Again, each box can have only between $0 and $10, but the range of the three amounts is $6.

Which of these two scenarios intuitively sounds better? Since person A receives the maximum amount of the three, the scenario with the higher range has a greater chance of having a greater payoff. Of course, the greater range also implies possibly lower payoffs than scenario 1, but for A, the downside is irrelevant in this case, and only the upside matters. This example highlights the importance of volatility in the underlying security (in this case, the three possible money amounts). In this simplistic example, we measured this variation by the range in payoffs, but as discussed in Chapter 1, the range is an inferior measure of volatility (i.e., variation) compared to the more commonly used standard deviation. We consider the importance of volatility in valuing options in the subsequent sections.

To understand option pricing, consider a simple option on a dice roll. This is a relatively common example used to demonstrate how option pricing works and helps set the foundation for some concepts used to price more complex, realistic options in the market. Suppose a trader can roll a fair die and earn a payoff equal to the number that appears on the die. In this case, there is a one-sixth chance of receiving $1 − $6, which means the expected value of the trade is $3.50, or $1/6 \times (1 + 2 + 3 + 4 + 5 + 6)$. This is a fairly simple transaction on the "underlying" security. Now suppose the trader is allowed to roll the die, witness the payoff, and has the *option* to roll the die once again. How much should the trader pay to own this option? A simple approach is to consider the optimal choices after the first roll. If the first roll is a 1, 2, or 3, the trader should roll once again since each of these three possibilities is lower than the expected value of the next roll ($3.50). If the first roll is 4, 5, or 6, then the trader should stay with the first roll and decline the option to roll again since each of those payoffs is higher than the expected value of the next roll ($3.50). Thus, if the roll is 1, 2, or 3 in the first roll, the result of the next roll results in an average of $3.50. If the roll is 4, 5, or 6, the payoff stays as it is. The overall average is therefore $1/6 \times (3.50 + 3.50 + 3.50 + 4 + 5 + 6) = \$4.25$. Without the option, the expected value is $3.50; with the option, the value is $4.25. Therefore, the fair value of the option is $\$4.25 - \$3.50 = \$0.75$.

This dice option is simplified by using just two steps. We can add more steps and repeat the process by working backward from the last option roll step and eliminating roll choices at each step. With more real-world options, two other factors come into play.

1. The payoffs being received are at different points in time, which requires discounting of payoffs.
2. The probabilities of different payoffs are not conveniently equal in the real world as in a dice roll.

For the payoff probabilities, we consider risk-neutral probabilities, described next. More complex options are priced using a method known as a binomial tree. For this process, conceptually the most common methods branch out a tree of possibilities and find the expected payoffs working backward along each branch, starting from the final day. The tree branch's spread implicitly incorporates the standard deviation of the underlying asset.

To better understand binomial trees, consider a contract whose price is based on a stock with a price of $97. To keep the scenario simple, assume the trader has a six-month option on the stock struck at $97. Thus, if the stock ends at $100 at the end of the period, the option's value is $3 at expiry; if the stock ends at $97 or lower, the option's value is just zero at expiry. Assume for simplicity that the stock can move only 10% up or 10% down. One way to value the fair price of this option is to use a binomial tree, which we outline in the next four steps. The binomial tree can have varying degrees of refinement. Here we choose to have two time periods for the tree, with each period being three months. Also assume that the annual risk-free rate for discounting purposes is 3%. Figure 10.2 shows the binomial tree of this security. A few points to note:

1. Each of the nodes displays the price of the stock after a certain path of the stock. For example, node (2,2) represents two up moves for the stock at step 2, which implies a price of $117.37 ($97 \times 1.1 \times 1.1$).

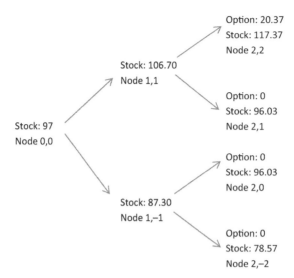

FIGURE 10.2 Simple Binomial Tree of a Stock Option

2. At termination, the payoffs are known from the payoff formula of the option: Max(S − X,0). Since we know value of the stock at each terminal node, we can calculate the payoff from this option at step 2.

3. After calculating the payoff at step 2 in each scenario, we are ready to employ backward induction, which is a sophisticated way to say that we are going to work backward.

4. For every two nodes where the payoff is known, the value at the node prior is its expected value: $P(A) \times \text{Payoff}_A + P(B) \times \text{Payoff}_B$, where $P(A)$ and $P(B)$ are probabilities of arriving at node A and node B.

Given these points, we are ready to proceed with the calculation of the option. Starting with the terminal nodes, we must calculate the expected value of each scenario. For example, the value of the option at node (1,1) in Figure 10.2 is the expected value of the value of the option on node (2,2) and node (2,1), as these stem from node (1,1). For expected value, the probability of up and down calculations is needed. One method is to use a risk-neutral probability that assumes the trader cares only about expected value rather than the riskiness of a transaction. In short, a risk-neutral trader is neither risk averse nor risk loving. Although we will not prove it here, it turns out that risk-neutral or real-world probabilities do not change the results of option pricing, but risk-neutral pricing tends to be simpler to formulate. In a risk-neutral framework, the expected value of a security should be equal to the risk-free rate, since there is no risk premium embedded in such a world. For the tree in Figure 10.2, from step 0 to step 1, the expected value of the stock is:

$$p \times 106.70 + (1 - p) \times 87.30 = 97 \times e^{0.03 \times 3/12}$$

The $97 \times e^{0.3 \times 3/12}$ is the expected return of the stock in a three-month period with a 3% annual risk-free rate and should equal the expected value of the two possible nodes of the stock. Here $p = 53.8\%$, which means in the risk-neutral world, the stock has a 53.8% chance of heading up. Note that this measure is not representative of the real world but just of the risk-neutral framework, which allows us to equate the expected value of the stock with the risk-free rate. Given the $\pm 10\%$ moves across the true and the static discount rate, the risk-neutral probability of the move up ends up being 53.8%. With this calculation, we can find the expected value of the option value. For node (1,1), the terminal values of the option stemming from this node are 20.37 and 0, which leads to an option expected value of $e^{-0.03 \times 3/12} \times [20.37 \times 0.538 + 0 \times (1 - 0.538)]$ (i.e., probability $\times$ payoff discounted back three months), which is \$10.88. In node (1,–1) the value of the option is zero since in both scenarios the option has zero value. Finally, for day 0 following the same process, the value of the option is $e^{-0.03 \times 3/12} \times$ $[\$10.88 \times 0.538 + 0 \times (1 - 0.538)] = \$5.81$.

To make the tree example more general and arrive at closed-form formulas for option prices, we have to make assumptions about how the underlying securities move. Although the tree method can be easily programmed into a computer, a closed-form formula for an option price is useful to understand the links between options and their risk parameters. For the stock, we assume that its returns are normally distributed, as the normal distribution stems from the mathematics of random motion under certain assumptions. For example, one such assumption is that one day's movement is independent from another day's, which is generally not too inaccurate. If the returns are distributed normally, and returns are essentially log(Δprice), then price is lognormally distributed in this case. For the stock, the standard deviation can be used as a common measure to assess the probability of up and down moves.

The Black-Scholes formula is a famous and widely used formula to price options (at least in the very simple cases). The formula essentially adds up the expected value for all possible underlying values above the strike for a call and below the strike for a put with the assumption of a lognormally distributed underlying. The Black-Scholes formula for the price of call and put options is:

$$C = S \times e^{(b-r) \times T} \times \Phi(d_1) - X \times e^{-r \times T} \times \Phi(d_2)$$
$$P = X \times e^{-r \times T} \times \Phi(-d_2) - S \times e^{(b-r) \times T} \times \Phi(-d_1)$$

where C = call price
         P = put price
         S = underlying asset price
         X = strike
         T = time to expiry in years
         b = cost of carry
         r = risk-free rate
         $d_1 = [\text{Log}(S/X) + (b + \sigma^2/2) \times T]/(\sigma \times \sqrt{T})$
         $d_2 = d_1 - \sigma \times \sqrt{T}$
         Φ = cumulative normal distribution function (see Chapter 1)

The formula can be thought of as somewhat akin to the tree methodology in a more compact version. There are a number of implicit assumptions behind the Black-Scholes formulation, such as constant volatility for the underlying asset and independent daily movement. For our purposes, the assumption of constant volatility will be an important one, as in reality volatility changes constantly and is traded as an asset class itself. The formula, while insightful, is less the point than the real purpose of Black-Scholes. The sigma term in the formula is volatility (i.e., standard deviation per year), and the chief use of the Black-Scholes formula is to link premium with volatility. The formula is not meant to be an authoritative trading price for an option, and memorizing it will not make someone an options trader. The formula's assumptions also lead to demonstrations showing the "failings" of Black-Scholes. There are numerous critiques of the constant volatility assumption and the fact that securities tend to show far more outliers than a normal distribution of returns would suggest, but most of these discussions miss the basic point: The Black-Scholes formula is merely a convenient way to convert premiums into volatility terms. This can be done by using the equation and, given a premium, reversing out an implied volatility (using a computer). The volatility derived from the Black-Scholes equation associated with a premium is known as the *implied volatility*. Few market practitioners would argue for using Black-Scholes for risk management; rather, the formula provides a simple transformation to compare options. This is a very similar idea to using duration to transform prices of bonds to yields, which allows for easy comparison of bonds with different maturities. Options have even more moving parts, such as strike and expiry. An out-of-the-money option will have a lower premium than an in-the-money one, but this difference in premium does not allow us to compare the time value in each option, because part of the price difference is just intrinsic value. The out-of-the-money option may be cheap relative to its chance of success; the presence of intrinsic value makes the premium difference difficult to judge. Implied volatility is one way, albeit an imperfect one, to compare options across strikes to judge how much underlying change they are implying in the asset versus what the actual changes have been recently. A similar dynamic occurs across expiries. A longer-dated option tends to have a higher premium than a shorter-dated one due to higher time value in the former (more time to have a chance for profit), but implied volatility provides a way to compare short- and long-dated options by accounting for the time difference. This makes it easier to calculate relative value across options.

MODIFICATIONS FOR THE INTEREST RATE MARKETS

The general principles just discussed hold for most options markets, but options on interest rates require a few modifications. Going back to the tree example, we assumed a constant 3% per year risk-free rate, which can be taken as a Treasury yield. However, if we are considering options on interest rates, an assumption of a constant discounting rate is not just impractical but inconsistent. To account for this assumption, we need a tree for the evolution of the discount rate itself using the volatility of the interest rate market. A tree of interest rates is used even in more accurate valuations of options on other assets.

Initial models for interest rates assumed that they moved in a lognormal fashion, as stock prices do. This distribution choice was driven partly by convenience, as lognormal distributions prevent negative rates and option pricing formulas can be derived for them relatively easily. Indeed, for the interest rate space, a common pricing formula is still the Black model:

$$C = e^{-r \times t} \times [F \times \Phi(d_1) - X \times \Phi(d_2)]$$
$$P = e^{-r \times t} \times [X \times \Phi(-d_2) - F \times \Phi(-d_1)]$$

where F = Forward rate
$d_1 = [\text{Log}\,(F/X) + \sigma^2 / 2 \times T] / (\sigma \times \sqrt{T})$
$d_2 = d_1 - \sigma \times \sqrt{T}$

The sigma here is in terms of percentage moves per year, as with the Black-Scholes model.

The similarity to the Black-Scholes model is not a coincidence; the Black model uses forward rates instead of the spot rate or current stock price used in the standard Black-Scholes. For interest rate options, the underlying is a forward rate starting at the expiry date and lasting for the underlying rate term. For example, an option on the 10-year swap rate that expires in three years is referred to as a 3Y × 10Y swaption. The underlying rate here is not the current 10-year rate, but instead the 10-year rate starting in three years, that is, the 3Y × 10Y forward swap rate. Unlike with stocks, the underlying here ages over time; after a year, the underlying asset will be the 2Y × 10Y forward swap rate. Like the Black-Scholes model, the Black model also assumes constant volatility and lognormal distribution for the underlying. The lognormal assumption of the underlying distribution is generally inappropriate for interest rates. Lognormality roughly implies that percentage moves in the asset have a similar distribution; in the interest rate space, this does not tend to be the case. For one thing, the Fed is likely to move in discrete 25-basis point (bp) increments, regardless of where rates are, rather than moving on the basis of the percentage of the interest rate. Another rough way to think about this is that prices of bonds are still likely lognormally distributed and since $P = e^{rt}$ in the limit of continuous compounding, r should be approximately normally distributed. These, of course, are not rigorous proofs, but they serve to develop intuition as to why interest rates are more likely normally distributed. The use of the normal model for the underlying originated prior to the Black-Scholes framework and was introduced by Bachelier in early twentieth century. As a result, the formulas are known as either the normal model or the Bachelier model. The prices under the normal model are

$$C = (S - X) \times \Phi(d_1) + \sigma \times \sqrt{T} \times \phi(d_1)$$

$$P = (X - S) \times \Phi(-d_1) + \sigma \times \sqrt{T} \times \phi(d_1)$$

where $d_1 = (S - X) / (\sigma \times \sqrt{T})$

ϕ = density function of the normal distribution

The formula is largely similar to the Black model with modifications to the log terms in the standard Black model. The sigma here is quoted in terms of *absolute* moves in the interest rate per year rather than a *percentage* move. Note that the put price can also be arrived at through put/call parity with an equivalent result. We discuss this difference in volatility quoting later.

Using a normal distribution for rates does lead to complications because now there is no restriction against zero rates, as there is with lognormal variables. Most of the time, the predicted chance of negative interest rates using the volatility of rates markets is minimal, but it does pose challenges when interest rates are near zero. In 2003 and from 2009 to 2010, when interest rates approached near–all-time lows, the distribution of rate movements needed to be adjusted toward lognormal, as assuming a normal distribution led to high chances of negative rates. For such environments, lognormal distributions also have issues since percentage moves can be enormous for small actual moves in rates. In general, such problems can be addressed by using more complex distributions, which have some features of normal and other features of lognormal distributions.

Finally, it is important to note that this discussion about normal underlying distributions applies mainly to swaptions, where the underlying directly is an interest rate. The depth and importance of the swaptions market makes it key to grasp the difference between normal and lognormal distributions, but sections of the market that trade on price terms tend to use lognormal distributions more frequently. In particular, the options markets on Treasury futures and Eurodollar futures continue to use lognormal distributions for underlying prices and quote volatility mostly in terms of the Black model.

QUOTING VOLATILITY

The reader may be wondering why a full section is needed to discuss quoting volatility. One reason is that the interest rate space has a multitude of different investor types, leading to a large variety of terminology. Also, over time, the rates market has migrated to using the normal distribution more widely than the lognormal distribution. As mentioned, the volatility input into the Black model is in terms of percentage moves per year while the normal model quotation is in terms of absolute moves per year. The quotation convention is also true for implied volatilities: An option premium can be fed into the Black model to arrive at a lognormal volatility or into the normal model price equation to arrive at a normal model. The rough conversion between the two implied volatility outputs can be reasoned out in this way: The lognormal volatility indicates how much the interest rate (or stock price) is expected to move as a percentage per year. To convert to an absolute move per year, we can take that percentage and multiply the current underlying value. For example, if IBM stock is at $80 and the lognormal volatility is 20%/year, the stock's expected 1 standard-deviation move in absolute terms is roughly 20% × 80 = $16/year. Although this method is rarely used as a quoted convention for stocks, it is very common in the rates space.

For interest rates, the underlying is a forward rate rather than a spot rate. For example, for an option on the 10-year rate that expires in one year, the underlying is the 1-year forward 10-year rate; therefore, to convert between lognormal and normal volatility in interest rates, the %/year volatility needs to be multiplied by the forward rate. If the forward rate is 4% and the lognormal volatility is 20%/year, the absolute change volatility is 20% × 4% = 0.80%, or 80 bps. The quotation is most often converted into bps and also is referred to as *abp*, which stands for annualized basis point volatility, since the quotation is in yearly terms. At times, a daily change measure is quoted instead of the annual measure; it can be arrived at by dividing the annual measure by $\sqrt{}$ (number of business days in 1 year) $= \sqrt{251} = 15.84$.

(251 is approximate; at times, 250 or 252 may be used.) For the option on the 10-year rate with 80 bp/year volatility, the daily volatility is approximately 80/15.84 = 5.1 bp/day. This quotation is referred to as the bp per day quotation or the daily bp vol.

The slew of quotation methods can be overwhelming at first, but the key concept to remember is that they convey the market's expectations of changes in the underlying over some reference time period, either as a percentage or in absolute terms. The Black model outputs an expected 1-standard-deviation move in terms of percentages of the underlying value, which tends to be appropriate for equities or commodities. For interest rates, the normal distribution model variant of the Black model also outputs the market's expectation of a 1-standard-deviation move in the underlying, but in absolute terms without reference to the current level. This method tends to be more appropriate for the interest rate world. As far as the time frame is concerned, that is mostly a matter of convenience and adoption, with annualized bp vol or daily bp vol both being common.

MEASURING RISKS IN OPTION POSITIONS

Due to their complex payoff nature, options are exposed to market variables in a multitude of ways. The risk exposures of options are generally expressed in terms of Greek letters (or Greek-sounding letters) leading to the colloquial name of "Greeks" for the risk parameters. For a bond, most of the risk is along one axis: the yield. If yields move, the impact on the price occurs through duration, convexity, and minute higher-order effects. Options can be thought of having risks along two axes: underlying asset and volatility of underlying asset. If the underlying asset is a swap or bond, then the option would have exposure not just to rates but also to rate volatility. To understand risks in options, one must understand the dynamic nature of risk parameters. As time passes or as the underlying moves, the risk parameters themselves evolve. Understanding these risks embedded in options and how they change over time is key to managing options positions and using them effectively to express views. The next section discusses these risk parameters with a focus on an intuitive understanding of their profiles rather than formulas.

Delta

Delta is defined as the change in the option premium for a unit change in the underlying. For a stock option, delta can be thought of as the change in the option premium for a $1 change in the stock; for an option on a bond, the delta might be expressed as the change in premium for a 1-bp change in the yield of the bond. Another approximate interpretation of delta is that it expresses the chances of the option ending up in the money. Note that in the rates world, then, delta is akin to the duration of a bond and indeed can qualify as the "duration" of an option. For an at-the-money option, delta is commonly 0.5, as the odds of ending up in the money are roughly 50%, although this is not always the case (discussed below). The probability interpretation, while not always accurate, does offer insight into evaluating likely effects on delta for *changes in other Greeks* (discussed later). Figure 10.3 shows the profile of delta for various underlying forwards. As the option goes deeper out of the money, delta approaches zero; as the option goes deeper in the money, the delta approaches 1. These moves should be intuitive, given the probability interpretation. Another line of reasoning is that for deep out-of-the-money options, the option becomes less sensitive to what the underlying is doing; for a deep in-the-money option, the option is itself essentially the underlying asset. Given that generally option transaction costs are higher than transacting in the underlying, buying deep in-the-money options is rarely fruitful, as traders basically are entering into positions in the underlying but paying more to do so. Figure 10.4 shows the delta profile of at-the-money, in-the-money, and out-of-the-money options. Instead of across the underlying, it shows the delta profile across time to maturity. As the option approaches expiry, the figure shows that the deltas essentially diverge. The in-the-money option delta heads toward 1 with increasing pace as the in-the-money option increasingly resembles exposure to the underlying. For example, a one-day option that is in the

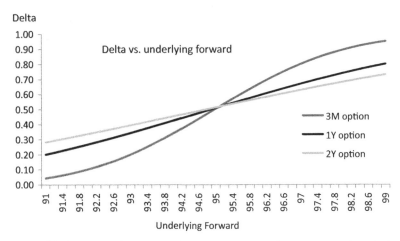

FIGURE 10.3 Delta of Options of Various Expiries for a Range of Underlying Prices

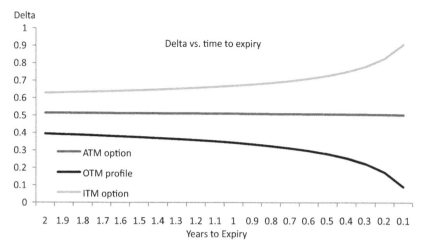

FIGURE 10.4   Delta of At-the-Money (ATM), Out-of-the-Money (OTM), and In-the-Money (ITM) Options for Different Times to Expiry

money will move very closely with the underlying since it is almost ready to be exercised, at which time the delta will be 1 (the underlying's delta is 1). An out-of-the-money option heads toward zero delta at an increasing pace as expiry approaches since at expiry the out-of-the-money option will be worthless. Finally, if the option is at the money, the delta will stay at 0.5 even as expiry approaches, as the option is on the edge of ending up in or out of the money.

The common way delta is quoted is in fractional form, such as 0.5, which implies that the option position is essentially equivalent to a 50% position in the underlying. For example, if a stock option has a delta of 0.30, this is equivalent to having a 30% position in the underlying stock for day-to-day moves. Delta for a call option is conventionally assigned a positive sign while delta for a put option is assigned a negative sign, since premium moves lower for a put option when the price of the underlying moves higher. The signs are reversed for a seller of an option.

Gamma

Option risk factors do not stay fixed when the market moves, and delta is no exception. As the underlying moves, the delta itself moves. Thus, for a stock option, a $1 change in the stock would move the premium but also move the delta. The moves in the delta become larger for larger moves in the underlying. Table 10.1 shows a hypothetical stock call option with a strike and stock price of $95 and volatility of 5%/year with deltas for

TABLE 10.1	Call Option Premium, Delta, and Gamma for Various Underlying Prices		
Underlying	**Premium**	**Delta**	**Gamma**
93.00	0.26	0.20	0.12
93.20	0.30	0.23	0.12
93.40	0.35	0.25	0.13
93.60	0.40	0.28	0.14
93.80	0.46	0.31	0.15
94.00	0.53	0.34	0.15
94.20	0.60	0.37	0.16
94.40	0.67	0.40	0.16
94.60	0.76	0.44	0.17
94.80	0.85	0.47	0.17
95.00	0.95	0.50	0.17
95.20	1.05	0.54	0.17
95.40	1.16	0.57	0.17
95.60	1.28	0.60	0.16
95.80	1.40	0.64	0.16
96.00	1.53	0.67	0.15
96.20	1.67	0.70	0.15
96.40	1.81	0.72	0.14
96.60	1.96	0.75	0.14
96.80	2.11	0.78	0.13
97.00	2.27	0.80	0.12

various scenarios of moves in the stock. As the price of the stock rises, the delta itself rises in increments of the gamma. This fact implies that an increasing stock value makes the option more sensitive to the stock; that is, for the owner of the call option, the position in the stock is rising as the market moves in the owner's favor. This concept should be familiar from Chapter 2's discussion of convexity. Indeed, as delta was akin to duration in the bond/swap space, gamma is the counterpart of convexity. In general, though, options are much more sensitive to this second-order effect than plain-vanilla bonds are to convexity.

Figure 10.5 shows the gamma profile of an option across underlying forwards. An at-the-money option has the highest gamma on the strike range since at-the-money options have the most uncertainty about leading to a profit at expiry. Deep out-of-the-money and in-the-money options have less uncertainty about where they will end up at expiry, which makes their delta less volatile as well. The figure also distinguishes between the gamma of a 3-month option, 1-year option, or 2-year option. Longer-dated options have a flatter gamma profile across strikes since moneyness is less

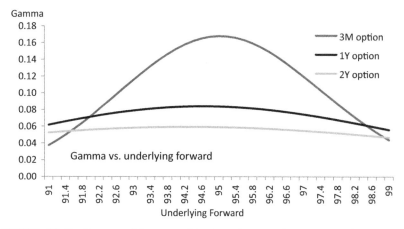

FIGURE 10.5 Gamma of Options of Various Expiries for a Range of Underlying Prices

relevant for longer-dated options—there is much time until expiry for the option to end up in the money. For shorter-dated options, though, time is of the essence, and being out of the money or in the money leads to a greater drop-off in gamma while an at-the-money short-dated option faces greater changes to its prospects. This phenomenon is explored in further detail in Figure 10.6, which shows the gamma profiles over time as expiry approaches. Overall, the gamma of an option increases as expiry approaches

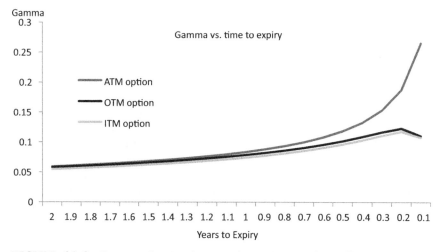

FIGURE 10.6 Gamma of ATM, OTM, and ITM Options for Different Times to Expiry

as small changes in the underlying stock price can result in greater risk of changes in moneyness. For example, if a stock is at $99 and the strike on the call option is $100, the less time to expiry, the more chance of a volatile move taking the stock in the money, which makes the delta very volatile. If there are years left to expiry, however, single-day moves will have less impact, and the delta will be less volatile. This effect is especially strong for at-the-money options; as such options reach expiry, the uncertainty of whether they will end up in or out of the money increases rapidly. Indeed, just before expiry, at-the-money options can end up either in the money with a delta of 1 or out of the money with a delta of zero, which implies a very large gamma. This leads to the gamma profile of Figure 10.5 for an at-the-money option. For out-of-the-money and in-the-money options, however, gammas do increase as expiry approaches, but after a certain point, as deltas get more "sure" to go toward zero or 1, the gamma increase tails off. The formula for the P/L arising from gamma is $1/2 \times$ gamma $\times$ (yield change)^2, or $1/2 \times$ gamma $\times$ (price change)^2 if the option trades on price terms such as Treasury future options. Notice the similarity of gamma P/L and convexity P/L of a bond, introduced in Chapter 2. This is not a coincidence; both gamma and convexity represent equivalent concepts, which is the asymmetry of gains versus losses.

The quotation method for gamma varies considerably. Gamma can be referred to in its fractional form; in this case, it is the change in the fractional delta for a unit change in the underlying. For gamma P/L, the dollar gamma is used, which is calculated as the dollar impact of the change in fractional gamma, which varies depending on the underlying contract. The buyer of an option is considered to be long gamma while the seller is short gamma. For a portfolio of options, if the net gamma is positive, the portfolio is referred to as long gamma; a negative net gamma is referred to as being short gamma.

Theta

Theta, otherwise known as time decay or theta decay, is the loss of option premium due to the passage of time. Because options are fixed expiry instruments, as time passes, the right to buy or sell the asset becomes less valuable for the owner, leading to a decline in the premium. The seller of an option waits until expiry in the hope that it stays out of the money, and benefits from the decline in premium on a daily basis. This is informally known as collecting theta, since theta describes the daily decline in premium. Figures 10.7 and 10.8 show the theta profile of an option across strikes and time. As with gamma, the theta for an at-the-money option is greatest in magnitude with a drop-off as the option moves in or out of the money. Theta also increases in magnitude as the time to expiry is reduced,

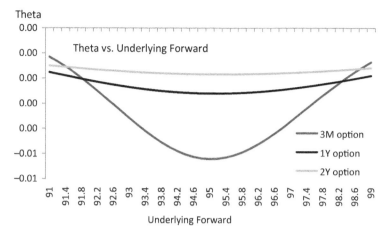

FIGURE 10.7 Theta of Options of Various Expiries for a Range of Underlying Prices

especially for at-the-money options. For example, returning to the example of the one-day at-the-money option, one day's passage here will have a very large effect on the premium, given the proximity to expiry. If five years were left to expiry, however, the passage of another day would mean very little in comparison.

The similarity between the theta and gamma profiles is not a coincidence. Theta can be interpreted as the cost of gamma spread out over time.

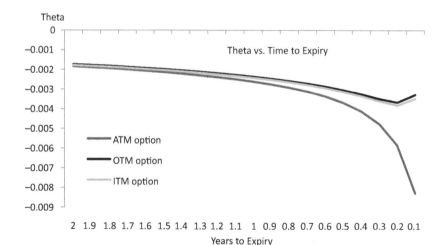

FIGURE 10.8 Theta of ATM, OTM, and ITM Options for Different Times to Expiry

The asymmetric nature of gamma is not provided for free; theta is the cost. For the seller of the option, the situation is reversed: Theta is the source of P/L as long as it overcomes the negative gamma P/L. Since theta has a negative impact on a long option position, it is generally denoted as a negative number. The formula for the P/L from theta is just the product of theta and the number of days that have passed (assuming theta is in days/year). Theta needs to be adjusted depending on whether "days" refers to calendar days or business days.

Vega

Vega is an option's risk factor along its other axis: implied volatility. Vega is the change in premium for a unit change in implied volatility. When using lognormal volatility, this unit change is generally 1%/year while for normal volatility in the rates space, it tends to be 1 bp/day. Unlike gamma, vega P/L is much more symmetric for up-and-down moves in implied volatility; it can be calculated as:

$$V \times \text{change in implied volatility}$$

where $V = $ vega of an option

   This formula is intuitively similar to the duration P/L formula for bonds with the underlying variable implied volatility instead of the interest rate.
   The vega profile for an option across strikes and across time is shown in Figures 10.9 and 10.10. Once again, the at-the-money option has the

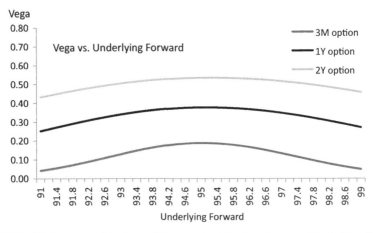

FIGURE 10.9 Vega of Options of Various Expiries for a Range of Underlying Prices

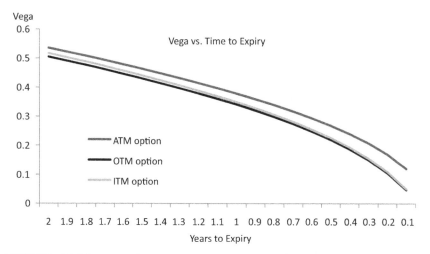

FIGURE 10.10 Vega of ATM, OTM, and ITM Options for Different Times to Expiry

highest vega, reflecting the general pattern of higher sensitivity to risk factors for at-the-money strikes. Vega is also higher for longer-dated options and declines steadily as expiry approaches. An intuitive reason for this is that implied volatility is the market's forward-looking expectation of volatility in the underlying, and a longer-dated option is likely to have heightened sensitivity to changes in forward expectations. In general, the market refers to trading vega as trading longer-dated options and trading gamma as trading shorter-dated options. Long vega is equated with owning a long-dated option; short vega is the reverse. A similar meaning is associated with being long or short gamma. This is certainly not to say that gamma/realized volatility is unimportant for longer-dated options or that vega/implied volatility is unimportant for shorter-dated options; instead, vega *tends to* form a larger portion of the P/L for a long-dated option while gamma *tends to* form the bulk of the P/L for a shorter-dated option. Not surprisingly, vega itself is not constant; it rises as strikes approach at the money or if implied volatility rises for non–at-the-money options, as shown in Figure 10.9. These second-order vega effects, stemming from changes in vega as the underlying changes for out-of-the-money options, can distort the simple formula for vega P/L. These adjustments are more important in exotic option structures or for large portfolios of options; for a single position, they generally are not major contributors to P/L.

As volatility quoting conventions vary for rates, so do vega quotation methods. In most markets, vega is quoted as the change in premium for each 1%/yr change in the implied volatility. However, given the interest rate market's use of the normal model, where volatility is represented in absolute changes, the vega is quoted in terms of change in premium for 1-bp/day change in volatility. These are just quotation conventions, and conversion from one to the other is relatively simple. For example, suppose we have a $100 million notional swaption with the underlying forward rate at 2.80%, implied volatility 32%, and 1%/yr vega at $70,000. A 1-bp/day change in implied volatility is equivalent to 15.84 bps/yr ($\sqrt{251}$), where 15.84 bps is equivalent to 15.84 bps/280 bps = 5.6% in percentage terms (2.80% underlying is 280 bps). Therefore, if the premium value changes $70,000 for each 1% move in implied volatility, it changes $70,000 × 5.6 = $392,000 for a 1-bp/day move in implied volatility, which is the 1-bp/day vega.

Rho

Rho is the sensitivity of an option to changes in the risk-free rate, which shows up in the discounting process of a binomial tree valuation or in the Black-Scholes formula. For longer-dated options in equities, for example, rho can be a significant determinant of P/L since option payoffs at expiry are being discounted over a long period of time. However, in the rate option world, rho is not a very meaningful concept, since the interest rate itself is the underlying, which confuses the rho with the delta. For this reason, rho is not a risk measure considered in the rates markets.

PUT/CALL PARITY

Put/call parity links the valuation of put options and call options *of the same strike* to the price of the underlying. To understand this relationship, consider a call option and put option on stock XYZ struck at $90 with the current price at $100. Now consider the payoff for an investor who buys the call and sells the put, both struck at $90. The payoffs for the individual options and the combination strategy are shown in Figure 10.11. The combination strategy's payoff ends up being a diagonal line and should be familiar—it is exactly the same payoff from buying the stock at $90. This fact is evident in the payoff diagrams of the individual options and in the combination strategy, which is a straight line resembling that of an equity purchase. This observation can be formalized as stipulating that the purchase of a call and sale of a put at the same strike equals the purchase of the underlying at the strike, or in mathematical form:

$$C - P = F - X$$

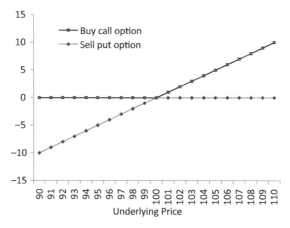

FIGURE 10.11 Combined Profile for Buying a Call Option and Selling a Put Option

where C = price of call option
P = price of put option
F = forward price
X = strike

The equation needs to be modified slightly if interest rates are not zero, since the call and put premia are settled up front while the $S - X$ payoff occurs in the future, bringing about the need for discounting. Thus, if the interest rate is r to the expiry of the option,

$$C - P = e^{-rt} \times (F - X)$$

The relation shown in the equation is known as the put/call parity and helps to link the prices of in-the-money call options with out-of-the-money put options or vice versa. For a market maker in options, making markets that adhere to put-call parity is one of the most basic lessons to grasp well. In today's markets, taking advantage of put/call parity violations is pretty much impossible after accounting for transaction costs.

Put/call parity allows replication of in-the-money options using out-of-the-money options. To replicate an in-the-money position in call (or put), which tends to be less liquid, one can purchase a matched strike put (or call) and use the underlying security to replicate the call (or put). Put/call parity also has implications for relationships between call option and put option Greeks. Since deltas are additive, one can write the relationship as:

$$\text{delta}(C) - \text{delta}(P) = \text{delta}[e^{-rt} \times (S - X)] = e^{-rt}$$

Recall that the delta of an underlying stock position is just 1; that is, it moves $1 for a $1 move in the stock. Hence the difference between the delta of a call and put struck at the same level is just $1 discounted back to today. For the other Greeks, the situation simplifies even more. The underlying stock does not have gamma, vega, or theta, as its sensitivity to the market does not change; nor does it face time decay or sensitivity to implied volatility. Since all these Greeks are additive for a portfolio, as discussed, we arrive at:

$$\text{gamma}(C) - \text{gamma}(P) = \text{gamma}(S - X) = 0$$

$$\text{vega}(C) - \text{vega}(P) = \text{vega}(S - X) = 0$$

$$\text{theta}(C) - \text{theta}(P) = \text{theta}(S - X) = 0$$

Thus, the gamma, vega, and theta of calls and puts are identical. An interesting corollary to this fact is that if the delta exposure is neutralized by trading the underlying, there is no difference left between a call and a put.

The standard put/call parity just discussed holds for plain-vanilla European options. American options, for example, do not adhere to put/call parity nor do a wide range of exotic options with more complex payoffs. For example, in Bermudan swaptions, which can be exercised on multiple dates known in advance, receivers (calls on rates) and payers (puts on rates) are not equivalent. In rates options, another issue arises with the assumption that the underlying has no gamma. Even plain swaptions, where the underlying asset is a swap, have underlyings with convexity. Convexity and gamma are equivalent concepts as discussed above. So while the vegas of a put and call are equal, the gammas are not because of the gamma (i.e., convexity) of the underlying swap. This difference can become quite extreme for swaptions with very long-dated forward swap/underlyings, such as 5-year × 10-year, for which the convexity is very large.

IMPLIED AND REALIZED VOLATILITY

The link between options and volatility has appeared repeatedly in the examples. When we discussed pricing options through a binomial tree, the movement of the underlying along the branch of the tree was directly linked to the volatility of the underlying asset. Volatility reappeared in the Black-Scholes framework as an input to arriving at an option's premium, and consequently, given an option's premium, we could derive the *implied* volatility. This implied volatility could be considered the market's expectation of volatility looking ahead, given the option premium in the market and the assumptions of the Black-Scholes framework, such as a lognormal distribution and constant volatility across strikes.

The P/L from owning an option is intimately linked to both implied and realized volatility. If implied volatility of the option is unchanged, the owner of a long option position receives net P/L from gamma and theta. Another way to visualize gamma is that it is the option's exposure to the volatility of the underlying asset. As the equation for gamma P/L shows, gamma P/L is proportional to the square of moves in the underlying; in other words, changes in price in either direction generate P/L. However, to overcome the constant loss from time decay, the moves in the underlying have to be sufficiently large. When the expressions for theta and gamma P/L are combined, it turns out that the P/L for an option is proportional to the difference between realized and implied volatility. This approximation gives insight into the drivers of option P/L. The net P/L for an option position from gamma and theta (leaving out delta and vega P/L here) is driven by differences in realized and implied volatility. For a long position, realized volatility needs to be greater than the implied volatility and vice versa for the seller. The buyer of the option aims to find assets whose standard deviation is likely to be more than the implied volatility while the seller aims to find assets where the standard deviation is less than the implied volatility. In this framework, the implied volatility is the *breakeven* amount by which the underlying has to move to generate enough gamma P/L to overcome negative theta P/L for the long position.

This framework kept delta and vega P/L out of the calculation. Most professional options traders remove the impact of delta through a process known as delta hedging, which we discuss later. Vega P/L is almost symmetric to changes in implied volatility; hence, changing implied volatility can add or subtract from the breakeven calculation. Thus, in options, P/L stems from a range of variables, such as realized volatility, implied volatility, and their relationship to the underlying variable (see the next section, "Skew"). Realized volatility, of course, is a backward-looking measure since standard deviation over a certain lookback is taken. For the options trader, the tricky part is to determine whether the past pattern of realized volatility will continue in the future when the trader owns the option. Realized volatility is itself notoriously volatile and can reverse direction rapidly, which makes backtesting model-driven strategies with realized volatility difficult. At the same time, implied volatility does not necessarily change in lockstep with realized volatility and can be sticky at times due to hedging flows.

SKEW

In the Black-Scholes framework, volatility is a fixed value used as an input to pricing an option regardless of its moneyness. Unfortunately, the market is not so simple. For example, in equity indices, such as the Standard & Poor's 500, lower strike prices tend to be associated with higher implied volatility as there is generally an expectation of higher realized volatility as the market declines. In rates, for example, the implied volatility may be higher for higher rate strikes as investors may expect more mortgage hedging activity at those higher rate levels, resulting in more volatility. The skew can be thought of as the difference between out-of-the-money implied volatility and at-the-money implied volatility. This statement may appear vague, but so is the concept of skew. Any mention of skew needs to be followed by clarification regarding which out-of-the-money option strikes are being referred to. The direction needs to be specified as well because out-of-the-money implied volatility on puts can differ from out-of-the-money implied volatility on calls. For example, the equity index skew just described would imply higher demand for out-of-the-money puts than for out-of-the-money calls, possibly because protection from deep crashes is more valuable than protection from sharp increases. The existence of skew alters the traditional Black-Scholes risk parameters. In particular, the delta of the option described earlier no longer gives the complete picture of the sensitivity to option premium versus the underlying. Instead, as the underlying moves, the implied volatility corresponding to its delta or strike level changes as well, which creates "extra" profit or loss from vega, not just the pure Black-Scholes delta.

DELTA HEDGING

The delta of an option exposes it to moves in the underlying. Occasionally, this can be an attractive feature to set up certain trades, such as conditional trades (discussed in Chapter 12). However, the main value from trading options stems from their exposure to volatility. Underlying assets, such as stocks or bonds, do not give exposure to implied volatility, and bond convexity is too small to give meaningful exposure to the volatility of the underlying asset. As discussed, options have exposure to both current and future expectations of volatility, which makes them useful for expressing views on an asset's volatility. To isolate this exposure, however, the exposure to the underlying asset itself needs to be removed. One way to think about this intuitively is that volatility trading involves isolating the "speed" of an asset without trading the "position" of the asset.

The basic process of removing the delta exposure of an option involves buying or selling the underlying asset. A useful thing to remember here is that a long position in the underlying asset has a delta of 1 (moves 1:1 with itself) and a short position in the underlying asset has delta of –1. Therefore, given the fractional deltas we discussed earlier, the hedge ratio is straightforward. For example, 100 call option contracts on Eurodollars with a delta of 0.5 would imply that the option position has long exposure to 50 Eurodollar contracts and thus would require selling 50 Eurodollar futures contracts to neutralize the delta. The sign convention described for delta is also useful here. For a put option with a negative exposure to the underlying, 100 put option contracts with a delta of –0.5 would require buying 50 underlying Eurodollar futures contracts to offset the delta. This position in the underlying to remove the delta is known as a delta hedge. The initial delta hedge is unlikely to stay adequate as markets move, given that option deltas keep changing due to gamma. Note that the changing delta and the need to dynamically offset it by changing the underlying hedge is akin to hedging mortgages, discussed in Chapter 8. This should not be surprising, since mortgages themselves have embedded option exposure. To remove the delta exposure of an option, the process is not as straightforward as with linear or quasi-linear assets, such as stocks and bonds. The delta hedge can be implemented on a daily basis or if and when the delta moves considerably. Delta and volatility will be calculated using the normal model since it is more appropriate for interest rates, as discussed.

The option we will delta hedge is a hypothetical 1-month at-the-money call option with 0.5 delta on a Eurodollar futures contract. The number of option contracts is 100. Other details have been omitted to avoid confusion. Recall that the Eurodollar futures contract has a change in value of $25 per bp change in its price. This convention holds for the option premium, too. The option is assumed to have a fixed 10-bp/day implied volatility throughout the time frame considered. Recall that in the normal model, volatility is quoted as an absolute change in the rate rather than as a percentage change. The example considers the P/L of a delta hedging strategy on three different scenarios of price movements:

1. Scenario 1 takes place over 10 days when the Eurodollar contract price trended lower daily.
2. Scenario 2 takes place over 10 days when the contract price trended higher daily.
3. Scenario 3 takes place over 10 days when the contract price witnesses large fluctuations but ends up at the same place.

Table 10.2 shows the P/L from delta hedging the call option in these three scenarios. In the table, the delta hedge is implemented daily. To explain the delta hedge, we consider the first couple days as an example. On day 1, we start out by selling 50 contracts in each scenario (100 × 0.5) to start out with zero delta. Notice that if we had sold the calls instead, the initial delta would have required *buying* 50 contracts since the delta of a short call option position is negative. The P/L on this position on any given day is calculated as a change in price of the contract multiplied by the number of hedge contracts at the prior day's close. In scenario 1 from day 1 to day 2, the price declines from 98 to 97.90, causing the delta of the option to go down from 0.5 to 0.45, since the option is farther out of the money. The initial 50-contract sale is now too large. Thus we buy back 5 contracts to arrive at the new appropriate delta hedge of 45 contracts. In scenario 2 from day 1 to day 2, the price actually goes up, thus increasing the delta (call option more in the money) from 0.50 to 0.55. Now the 50-contract sale is not enough, and if not adjusted, we will be left exposed to the market. Therefore, 5 more contracts are sold, leading to a delta hedge of short 55 contracts. Note that in this stylized example, the daily change in Eurodollar price in each scenario is 0.1% or 10 bps. The key point here is that even though a call option was purchased initially, each of the three cases end up with positive, and very similar, profits. By delta hedging, often the exposure to the underlying contracts is removed, leaving the call option with little dependence on the movement of the underlying price. In contrast, if a call option is just bought and held, the price needs to rise by expiry for the option to be profitable. If the delta exposure is hedged out frequently, the profit from an option position stems from the other Greek parameters: gamma (realized volatility), vega (implied volatility), and theta (time decay). In the simplified example shown here, implied volatility is unchanged, which means vega P/L is zero, leaving only gamma and theta P/L. Recall also that due to put/call parity, the gamma and theta of a call are identical, which would lead to identical gamma and theta P/L for the call option regardless of underlying direction. Indeed, in scenarios 1 and 2, with the contract increasing and decreasing by identical magnitude, the profit from the delta hedged call option is identical. For the third scenario, the profit is a bit lower due to some slippage from hedging only once a day while the contract keeps increasing and decreasing sharply. If delta hedging were more frequent, the profit here would catch up to that of the other two scenarios; even with just a once-a-day delta hedge, the profit is not significantly lower.

If the delta is not hedged, the option trade is merely a play on the underlying and much less benefit of volatility moves is captured. Scenario 1 with its declining prices would lead to a consistent loss, while scenario 2 with its increasing prices would lead to profits, because the option is a call.

TABLE 10.2 Different Scenarios for Delta Hedging

Inputs

Strike	98
Contracts	100
Volume (bp/day)	10
Expiry (days)	90

Scenario 1

Day	Days to Expiry	Price	Option Premium	Option P/L	Delta	Delta Hedge # Contracts	Hedge P/L	Net P/L
1	89	98	0.31		0.50	−50		
2	88	97.9	0.26	(12,299.22)	0.45	−45	12,500.00	200.78
3	87	97.8	0.22	(11,017.21)	0.40	−40	11,250.00	232.79
4	86	97.7	0.18	(9,745.37)	0.35	−35	10,000.00	254.63
5	85	97.6	0.15	(8,505.12)	0.30	−30	8,750.00	244.88
6	84	97.5	0.12	(7,316.99)	0.26	−26	7,500.00	183.01
7	83	97.4	0.09	(6,199.59)	0.21	−21	6,500.00	300.41
8	82	97.3	0.07	(5,168.56)	0.18	−18	5,250.00	81.44
9	81	97.2	0.05	(4,235.87)	0.14	−14	4,500.00	264.13
10	80	97.1	0.04	(3,409.28)	0.11	−11	3,500.00	90.72
							Total:	**1,852.79**

Scenario 2

Day	Days to Expiry	Price	Option Premium	Option P/L	Delta	Delta Hedge # Contracts	Hedge P/L	Net P/L
1	89	98	0.31		0.50	−50		
2	88	98.1	0.36	12,700.78	0.55	−55	(12,500.00)	200.78
3	87	98.2	0.42	13,982.79	0.60	−60	(13,750.00)	232.79
4	86	98.3	0.48	15,254.63	0.65	−65	(15,000.00)	254.63
5	85	98.4	0.55	16,494.88	0.70	−70	(16,250.00)	244.88
6	84	98.5	0.62	17,683.01	0.74	−74	(17,500.00)	183.01
7	83	98.6	0.69	18,800.41	0.79	−79	(18,500.00)	300.41
8	82	98.7	0.77	19,831.44	0.82	−82	(19,750.00)	81.44
9	81	98.8	0.85	20,764.13	0.86	−86	(20,500.00)	264.13
10	80	98.9	0.94	21,590.72	0.89	−89	(21,500.00)	90.72
							Total:	**1,852.79**

Scenario 3

Day	Days to Expiry	Price	Option Premium	Option P/L	Delta	Delta Hedge # Contracts	Hedge P/L	Net P/L
1	89	98	0.31		0.50	−50		
2	88	97.9	0.26	(12,299.22)	0.45	−45	12,500.00	200.78
3	87	98	0.31	11,417.71	0.50	−50	(11,250.00)	167.71
4	86	97.9	0.26	(12,296.89)	0.45	−45	12,500.00	203.11
5	85	98	0.30	11,405.19	0.50	−50	(11,250.00)	155.19
6	84	97.9	0.26	(12,294.47)	0.45	−45	12,500.00	205.53
7	83	98	0.30	11,392.22	0.50	−50	(11,250.00)	142.22
8	82	97.9	0.25	(12,291.97)	0.45	−45	12,500.00	208.03
9	81	98	0.30	11,378.79	0.50	−50	(11,250.00)	128.79
10	80	97.9	0.25	(12,289.38)	0.45	−45	12,500.00	210.62
							Total:	**1,621.98**

For scenario 3, because the underlying price shows little change after all the choppy volatility, the call option loses value due to time decay since there is little change in moneyness. Thus, delta hedging offers a way to take a view on volatility, which can be thought of as the speed of the underlying contract rather than the direction. The example, although stylized, shows how delta hedging monetizes volatility in the underlying price with minimal regard for the direction of movement.

How frequently should a trade be delta hedged? There is no one single answer to this question, and it depends on various factors. Because options are not symmetric instruments, different frequencies of delta hedging may be appropriate for opposing long and short positions of the same trade. Going back to the three scenarios, we can notice in the delta hedging example that the process constantly involves selling more securities at a higher price or buying more at a lower price. In scenario 1, as the price went lower, the delta on the call shrank, leading to a smaller need for the Eurodollar short position and thus *buying back contracts at a lower price*. In scenario 2, as the price went higher, the delta on the call increased, leading to more selling to keep the trade delta hedged and thus *selling contracts at a higher price*. The same logic works for a long put position, which the reader may like to verify. The long option position is therefore in a beneficial spot with regard to delta hedging, constantly buying low and selling high. The seller of the option, facing negative gamma, once again is left with the more painful side. In the call seller's case, the initial delta would have required buying the contracts. Subsequently, as the price moved lower, driving the delta toward zero, the seller would have needed to shed delta by selling contracts at successively lower prices. The seller of the option is indeed buying high and selling low.

For the long option position, the point is to maximize the realized volatility of the underlying series. For the short option position, the realized volatility needs to be minimized. Realized volatility is not a constant measure; instead it depends on the window of time being considered. Volatility can be very different when looking on a daily, weekly, or monthly basis. For example, in the three scenarios discussed, the daily magnitude of change is 10 bps for each. However, on a 10-day window, the third scenario has nearly zero volatility, since the price almost reverts to its initial level. The first two scenarios, however, have the price continually rising or falling, leaving a large volatility on the 10-day window. The idea of different volatilities for different windows of time offers guidelines for delta hedging frequency.

A mean-reverting series will have lower volatility over longer change periods, while trending markets have lower volatility over shorter change periods, and vice versa. In the example, scenario 3 is mean reverting while scenarios 1 and 2 are trending. For a short option position, delta hedges should therefore be less frequent in a mean-reverting market, as that market has lower volatility over longer time windows. In contrast, the long option position should hedge as frequently as possible in such a market to capture higher volatility over shorter time frames. The frequent hedging essentially allows more frequent buying low and selling high resulting in higher P/L; for the short option position, hedging less frequently prevents the option seller from buying high and selling low as frequently. With a trending market, the situation is reversed—a long option position should be hedged less frequently to capture higher volatility over longer time frames; for a short option position, a trending market can lead to higher losses.

Given the complex nature of option risks and the possible variability in delta hedging, our discussion merely presents a guideline rather than any hard formulas. For one thing, it is impossible to know whether markets will be trending or mean reverting in the near future. That said, the thought process behind the frequency of delta hedging should take into account the likelihood of a mean-reverting or trending market, both on an intraday and a multiweek scale. Second, delta hedging does not have to be at fixed time intervals; it can also be done on a threshold basis as and when the net delta of the option plus the underlying position crosses a certain threshold, such as 0.1. In reality, it is advisable to delta hedge with some guidelines based either on fixed time intervals (such as at close) or a fixed delta hedge threshold. Although these rules must be modified to prevent too-frequent delta hedging in volatile markets with high transaction costs, these guidelines do enforce discipline in trade management and should be a part of the overall delta hedging strategy. Third, transaction costs can make very frequent delta hedging a problem. This is a risk to consider especially for short option holders susceptible to large gaps in market moves.

INTEREST RATE OPTIONS

The principles of asymmetry, volatility, and delta hedging largely hold true for options across markets, including interest rates. From a pricing perspective, an interest rate option can be modeled with some modifications to the original Black-Scholes framework. The variety of options products in the rates markets does lead to various details that must be accounted for depending on the product and can result in a confusing introduction to the market. Stemming from the concept of convexity, equal increases and decreases in interest rates result in different magnitudes of price increases or decreases; with a rate increase, the price decrease is smaller in magnitude than the price increase if rates decline. The convexity in a plain-vanilla bond is generally a much smaller effect than the asymmetry in actual options, where an explicit right to buy or sell the security is the main feature. Nevertheless, the convexity idea is important in understanding option risk exposures. For bonds with more complicated structures, such as callables and mortgage bonds, which we introduced briefly in Chapter 3, embedded options play a much stronger role than convexity in plain-vanilla bonds. Thus it is important to understand options when trading callables and mortgage bonds.

Before we look at embedded options, we first consider stand-alone option structures in the rates markets. Doing this requires an introduction to a fair bit of jargon, which seems to permeate the entire fixed income space and can be especially confusing for new participants. The options space in the rates world can be thought of as separated into three distinct parts:

1. *Options on short-term rates.* This class is comprised of caps/floors, which are over the counter (OTC) (i.e., traded against a bank). There are also options on the Eurodollar futures contracts that are traded on the exchange.

2. *Options on longer-term rates.* This class is comprised of options on Treasury futures and swaps. The options on swaps, formally known as swaptions, give users the right to enter into a receiver or a payer swap, known as receiver or payer swaptions, respectively. Swaptions are OTC products and thus transacted against a bank. On the exchange side, options on Treasury futures give the buyer the right to buy or sell the futures contracts at expiry.

3. *Exotic/hybrid structures.* A range of exotic structures with embedded options tend to be less liquid than swaptions or Treasury futures options but offer investors the chance to earn higher yield or express more specific views. Due to the breadth of this space, we briefly consider a few structures that have tended to be popular with investors.

Although we have separated the options into various classes, this is merely for organizational purposes—the separations are rough, and sometimes an option may fit under more than one classification.

To build our discussion of rate options, we start with options on short-term rates, as these tend to be the simplest to analyze. First we need to make a point about notation: Although there is disagreement on the issue and usage varies, here we refer to any option that benefits from falling rates as a call option and any option that benefits from rising rates as a put option. In the rates space, "call" and "put" are terms used mainly for exchange-traded products; in the OTC space (such as swaptions and caps/floors), specific names are used, which we describe later.

As a first step, we consider the simplest option structure in the rates world: a caplet. A caplet can be thought of as an atom off of which more complex structures can be created. A caplet is an option on a short rate, such as three-month London Interbank Offered Rate (3M LIBOR), expiring at some point in the future. One example would be a call option on the 3M LIBOR rate one year from now struck at 1.00%. This caplet's profile at expiry would look similar to the payoff profile of a call with 3M LIBOR on the x-axis, with positive payoffs if 3M LIBOR settles above 1% on the expiry date one year from now and zero payoff otherwise. The term *caplets* is used specifically for structures benefitting from rising rates; *floorlet* is used for structures benefitting from lower rates. The reason for the "cap" and "floor" terms is that a caplet allows investors to cap interest rate exposure by offsetting any losses that may occur if rates rise, while a floorlet similarly puts a floor on losses from declining interest rates.

Caplets can be traded individually on an OTC basis—that is, versus a bank—rather than on an exchange. However, for many investors, their exposure to rates spans a longer tenor than the three-month rate. Therefore, options may be appropriate to protect against rising or falling interest rates, but it is unlikely a single caplet would suffice. To address this issue, caplets can be combined in chains to create caps or floors. A cap is just a series of caplets most commonly on 3M LIBOR. Each caplet is independent and expires prior to the start of the next consecutive caplet. Thus, the cap "looks" at the three-month rate every quarter. For each look, if the three-month rate at the time is higher than the strike, a payment is made; otherwise, there is zero payoff. Notice the similarity with the Eurodollar strip concept of stringing together short-term instruments to create longer-term instruments, but of course here the exposure at each point is only one-sided. The at-the-money strike for a cap is the average at-the-money strikes for the individual caplets. This makes the term "at the money" a bit misleading for a cap—because the strike is an average level, it can be the case that none of the individual caplets are at the money. A floor is similarly a chain of floorlets. Furthermore, the string of caplets does not have to start with the first 3M LIBOR rate; a cap that does so is called a spot-starting cap, and the first caplet starting later is known as a forward starting cap. As an example, consider a 1×3 cap struck at 2%. The "1×3" notation refers to a cap that starts in one year, with caplets strung for two years $(3 - 1)$. Finally, caps and floors can be modified to have underlying rates that differ from the very common 3M LIBOR case. Indeed, just about any floating interest rate will suffice, and even constant maturity swap (CMS) rates, which were introduced in Chapter 5. For example, one can have a spot starting 2-year cap on the 10-year CMS swap rate, which implies that the cap has a 2-year expiry and, every quarter (or some other interval), the option "looks" at the current 10-year swap rate and gives the investor a payoff if the CMS rate is above the cap. In general, CMS cap/floor structures are not very liquid, but at times they can offer interesting ways to take market views.

Caps and floors on 3M LIBOR are very liquid products especially at the short end of the curve, where they are used extensively by banks to manage interest rate exposure. However, their OTC nature does present counterparty risk and, at times, less transparency than the exchange. The exchange-traded counterparts to the forward rate agreements on 3M LIBOR are the Eurodollar contracts. It makes sense then that the counterpart to a caplet, an option on the 3M LIBOR rate, is an option on the Eurodollar contracts. Eurodollar contracts are on a quarterly schedule and the exchange provides options on each contract. These are known as the quarterly options. For example, EDU0, the Eurodollar contract expiring in September 2010 (see Chapter 4 for the symbols), has options expiring on September 13, 2010. The strikes are provided by the exchange in 0.125 increments; in interest rate terms, this is 12.5 bps. Note that the exchange uses prices as a reference for the strikes, but this is a minor issue since in Eurodollar contracts, the rate $= 100 -$ price. Of course, a strike of 100 would imply 0% interest rate strike, which is unlikely to be traded much. The premium is quoted as ticks on the exchange, with each tick being $25 in dollar premium. Therefore, an option that costs 8 ticks will cost $25 \times 8 = \$200$ for each option contract. Additionally, on the exchange, the convention reverts to using puts/calls instead of caps/floors, with a call on the Eurodollar price positioning for lower rates (higher prices). As with caplets, Eurodollar contracts can also be combined in chains to produce cap or floor structure, with a string of Eurodollar puts analogous to a cap and a string of Eurodollar calls analogous to a floor. (A minor difference is that Eurodollars are American options while caps/floors tend to be European.) The costs and benefits of Eurodollars versus caps/floors are similar to that of any exchange versus OTC product. Using Eurodollar options gives the user the transparency and counterparty protection of an exchange, but at the cost of flexibility. Eurodollar options exist only for preset dates; caps/floors, however, can be structured in a multitude of ways for any set of dates. Cap/floor structures can also be done for much longer tenors and forward starting dates, such as 5 × 10s; Eurodollar options are liquid generally out to two years. Also, the strikes for Eurodollar options occur at specific increments; for caps/floors, they can be chosen with any granularity.

The Eurodollar option space also provides an interesting set of options known as midcurves. Midcurve options are structures where, upon expiry, the reference rate is not the immediate contract but instead a contract farther forward. For example, the standard Eurodollar option on EDM0 would be expiring on May 17, 2010, and would settle on the EDM0 (i.e., 2010) rate at the time. However, a midcurve option would also expire on nearly the same day—May 14, 2010—but settle on the EDM1 rate, which is the 2011 rate. In general form, midcurves end up being options where the underlying at expiry is itself a forward rate rather than a current, spot security. Given that exchanges standardize their products, the Chicago Mercantile Exchange provides midcurves that expire with the first, second, or third Eurodollar contracts with the underlying rates one year forward or two years forward. Midcurves where the underlying rate at expiry is one year in the future are known as red midcurves; those with the underlying two years in the future are known as green midcurves. Midcurves are fairly liquid, especially in the red sector (one year out), and provide interesting ways to take views on longer-dated Eurodollars without using longer-dated options.

The set of caps/floors and Eurodollar options forms the liquid members of options on short-term rates. Now we can move on to options on longer-dated rate structures. The most liquid member of this class—and indeed, one of the most liquid options markets in the world—is the swaption. As with rates markets overall, it is important to keep track of terms to avoid confusion. Instead of calls or puts, swaptions use terminology such as receivers or payers. Receiver swaptions give the user the right, but not the obligation, to enter a receiving position in a spot-starting swap at expiry and therefore are structures to position for lower rates. Similarly, payer swaptions give the user the right, but not the obligation, to enter a payer swap position at expiry and therefore are profitable if rates increase. Unlike caps/floors, swaptions look only once, at expiry, at the underlying rate to decide whether the option is in or out of the money; with caps/floors, there is a package of caplets, and each takes a separate look at 3M LIBOR every quarter. The strike on the swaption is a swap rate; unlike the cap/floors, there is no averaging of multiple options. For this reason, structures like caps/floors are called multilooks while swaption-type structures are called single looks. The notation of the swaption is in the form of expiry × underlying; for example, a 1Y × 2Y swaption expires in one year and enters a two-year swap upon expiry. The one-year period to expiry is known as the expiry, while the underlying two-year rate is known as the tail. Note the contrast with the cap/floor notation, where the total period is referenced, not the underlying period (i.e., 1 × 3 versus 1Y × 2Y). Upon expiry, the standard swaption enters into the swap two business days afterward. At times this entry date can be modified. At expiry, if the swaption is exercised, the swap is entered at the strike, so the P/L stems from the difference between the strike and the current swap rate. The swaption notional is the notional amount of swap entered at expiry. The premium is generally quoted as an up-front bp of notional (% of notional × 100), which implies $10,000 payment for each bp of notional for $100 million notional.

The exercise is quoted as a yield for the underlying swap rate and not a price. Since swaptions are an OTC product, there are no restrictions on how much the strike can vary, although of course liquidity is not equal for all strikes.

Swaptions are extremely liquid for a wide range expiries and tails. Their depth and flexibility make them especially useful for a range of investors taking views on interest rates or for offsetting interest rate risk, as with caps/floors. A rough counterpart to swaptions in the Treasury space is the set of options on Treasury futures. As with options on Eurodollar futures, the options on Treasury futures are traded on an exchange, leading to very standardized maturity and strikes. The options are at quarterly intervals corresponding to the quarterly Treasury futures contracts, and expire in the second half of the month prior to the futures contract delivery month. For example, for the December 2010 10-year futures option, or TYZ0, the expiry of the option would be on November 26, 2010. Practically speaking, only options on the front contract have much liquidity. The strikes are also at fixed increments as with Eurodollar contracts. Currently the bond contract is at increments of one point and the other contracts are at increments of one-half point, with these specifications subject to change by the exchange. As with Eurodollars, Treasury futures options use the terms "calls" and "puts." A call gives the owner of the option the right to purchase a Treasury futures contract at the given strike, while the put gives the owner the right to sell a Treasury futures contract at the strike. The convention for quoting premia in Treasury futures is in 64ths, which is an extension of the 32nds convention for the underlying. Since the Treasury futures contract is $1,000 for each point, 1/64 of the point is $1,000/64 = \$15.625$. The quotation method is to quote a whole number and a fraction of 64th. For example, a premium of 1-02 in dollar terms is $1 \times 1,000 + 2 \times \$15.625 = \$1,031.25$, since each point is 1,000 and each fraction is 15.625. As with the futures, a "+" sign at the end indicates an extra half of the fraction; that is, 1-02+ means $1 \times 1,000 + 2.5 \times 15.625$ in dollar premium.

EMBEDDED OPTIONS AND HEDGING

So far, the options described in this chapter have been stand-alone structures for the most part. However, many rate options are not actually stand-alone but instead embedded into bondlike structures. Most often, these securities give the issuer the right to prepay or recall the security at the issuer's choosing at par value, with some possible restrictions in that choice. If the issuer has the choice to recall or prepay a security, the issuer is long an option on rates. This is because the issuer will prepay the debt only if it is optimal for the issuer—that is, if rates decline and new debt can be issued at a lower rate, the issuer will prepay the old debt, but if interest rates rise, the issuer will be happy with the old debt issued at a lower rate. More specifically, the issuer can be thought of as being long a call option on rates or, in other words, long a receiver swaption (technically, Bermudan receiver, which will be discussed later in the chapter). For the buyer of such a debt, the situation is reversed; the buyer is short the option on rates. If rates decline, the debt is prepaid by the issuer, and the buyer is left having to invest the prepaid funds at a lower interest rate in comparable assets. If interest rates rise, the value of this debt goes down, but there is scant hope of a prepay rescue from the issuer. This familiar asymmetry leads to the comparison with options.

The two largest groups of securities with embedded options in the fixed income world are fixed rate mortgages and Agency callable bonds. In fixed rate mortgages—which form the bulk of the mortgage market—the issuer is the homeowner, who has the right to refinance or prepay the mortgage to take advantage of lower rates at any time. If rates rise, no action needs to be taken since most mortgages have a fixed rate for 30 years. Certainly this option is not given for free; the fixed rate received by the general public on mortgages is higher than for mortgages with no refinancing option. Given the embedded options in mortgages, hedging their risk is more complex than for plain-vanilla bonds. We discussed dynamic hedging using swaps or Treasuries to offset the changing duration risk in Chapter 8. Given that mortgages have embedded optionality, hedging can also be approached using options. Technically, the mortgage bond has an American option embedded in it, although most often swaptions are used to hedge as an approximation. The other major source of embedded options, Agency callables, gives the issuer—in this case, Freddie Mac or Fannie Mae—the right to prepay and redeem the issue. With Agency callables, there is an initial period where the issuer has no option. Subsequent to that, the bond can be recalled only every six months, rather than at any time. As an example, Fannie Mae may issue a 3NC1 (pronounced 3 noncall 1), which is a 3-year bond where, in the first year, Fannie cannot redeem the bond and, subsequently, the bond can be recalled every six months. The option market equivalent of a 3NC1 would be approximately a $1Y \times 2Y$ swaption, which also expires in one year and has as the underlying rate the 2-year swap, as with the 3NC1. The yield on this 3NC1 will be higher than for a plain 3-year bond, given that the issuer will have to pay extra to have the option to prepay. The issuance of longer-dated callables has some effects on the volatility market, but most end users who purchase callables tend to hold onto them for the extra yield for being short the option rather than hedging the rate exposure.

The embedded options just described require additional methods to manage their interest rate risk. Not surprisingly, some concepts related to options help. We covered hedging standard rate instruments using interest rate products in Chapter 8. For the most part, hedging involves a calculation of the duration of the underlying portfolio as well as the instrument being used for hedging and matching the two. This method works when the duration of the security being hedged does not rapidly change as markets move. For assets with embedded options, such as mortgages and callable bonds, the duration does indeed change rapidly as markets move because the delta of the embedded option is sensitive to interest rates. To think about hedging these assets, the problem has to be broken down into hedging the underlying interest rate bond and the embedded option. The interest rate exposure from the underlying bond can be hedged in the same way by dollar value of one basis point (DV01) risk. For the option, there are two choices:

1. *Dynamic hedging.* Initiate interest rate hedge for the option and alter the rate hedge as the duration of the asset changes. This method is equivalent to delta hedging a stand-alone option described earlier. It is also equivalent to changing hedge sizes frequently for more complex instruments, such as mortgages, known informally as convexity hedging. For example, Chapter 8 discusses dynamically hedging mortgages and mortgage servicing assets as their duration exposures change. In essence, this type of dynamic hedging is equivalent to delta hedging an option.

2. *Hedging using another option.* Most commonly, given their liquidity, either swaptions or Treasury futures options are used to hedge embedded options. The principle here is similar to the hedging examples described in Chapter 8, but instead of matching durations, the gamma of the option being hedged and the swaption are matched. Most financial software packages can output the gamma of both swaptions and mortgages to accomplish this.

The upside of using options to hedge the short optionality in a mortgage, for example, is that the need for dynamic hedging is cut substantially, which can lower costs if markets become volatile and the need for dynamic hedging increases substantially. The downside is that up-front premium is required, and if markets do end up being less volatile than expected, the option cost can be too expensive in retrospect. This should not be surprising; buying an option is, after all, a long-volatility position.

MORE EXOTIC STRUCTURES

The products described in the previous section are some of the most liquid options structures across financial markets. For the interest rate markets, there exist numerous other products to hedge or take on more specific risks along different tiers of liquidity. The products described next can certainly be traded, but frequent, short-term trades are generally not common.

Bermudan Swaptions

Bermudan swaptions, like the island of Bermuda, fall in the middle of European and American options. Unlike American options, Bermudans can be exercised only at set expiry dates, generally spaced six months apart, although individual structures can vary substantially. As with American options, put/call parity does not hold for Bermudans, leading to different market forces driving receivers and payers. Bermudan options are generally created to hedge specific risks stemming from callable bonds. In most callable bonds, the issuer can prepay the bond only at specific intervals, generally around six months (near coupon payment dates). This makes a Bermudan option ideal for matching the embedded option in a callable bond.

Because Bermudan swaptions have multiple exercise dates, as interest rates move around, the likely exercise date changes as well. Due to the shifting optimal exercise dates, Bermudan swaptions can also have interesting gamma and vega profiles different than those of a simple option. For example, with a Bermudan receiver, if interest rates decline, the likely exercise date is closer to the present. This effectively makes the Bermudan a shorter expiry option and therefore the gamma of the option rises, but the vega declines. On the other hand, if interest rates increase, the receiver is further out of the money and the effective exercise date is further out, effectively making the option a longer expiry option. In this case, the Bermudan has increased vega and decreased gamma. A similar dynamic exists for payer swaptions.

Range Accrual Notes

Range accrual notes are present in a variety of forms but take the basic form of paying a coupon if an underlying variable is within a range. Two common types of range accrual notes are the LIBOR range accrual notes, which pay a coupon as long as 3M LIBOR remains in a certain range, and the yield curve spread notes, which pay a coupon as long as parts of the yield curve have a positive slope. In both cases, and with exotics in general, the parameters were chosen to arrive at an attractive yield for the end user. End users include a wide range of institutions and individuals from the United States to Asia seeking higher-yielding instruments.

These notes were popular enough that hedging activity from them affected the broader rates and rate options markets. In a LIBOR range accrual note, the dealer is essentially long a cap—if 3M LIBOR crosses a certain higher boundary, the dealer no longer has to pay a coupon and therefore witnesses a gain. The same is true for the floor side, although most of the lower boundaries tend to be at zero for such notes. After such a note has been issued, the dealer can hedge the exposure by doing the reverse, which is selling caps (and floors if necessary). Such hedging activity has effects on the liquid rate options market, which will be discussed later in the chapter.

YIELD CURVE SPREAD OPTIONS

Yield curve spread options (YCSOs), as the name may imply, are options on the *spread* of two yields rather than a single yield. An example of a yield curve spread option would be a 3M $\times$ 2s/10s call option struck at 1.5%. This option pays the buyer a certain amount based on notional for every percent that the difference between the 10-year and 2-year swap exceeds 1.5% after three months, which is the expiry of the option. For example, if the 2s/10s curve is 1.75% at expiry (in three months) and the trade is structured to have $1 million sensitivity for every 1% move in the curve, the investor would get paid $1 million $\times$ (1.75 − 1.5) = $250,000. If the 2s/10s curve ended lower than 1.5% at expiry, the investor would lose only the initial premium. An at-the-money strike on this spread option would be the current value of the three-month forward 2s/10s curve (i.e., 3M forward 10-year rate − 3M forward 2-year rate) with an adjustment, which we will discuss. A structure where the difference between the long and short rate rising benefits the buyer is known as a curve call; a curve put is the opposite structure. The call structure described in the example is a steepener (since 2s/10s steepening benefits the trade); a put spread option would be a flattener, but of course with the key benefit of asymmetry. As with rate options where caps are a multilook structure and swaptions are a single-look structure, yield curve spread options also have a curve cap counterpart. The 3M $\times$ 2s10s structure described in the previous paragraph was a single-look structure since P/L evaluation was done once at expiry. A curve cap would instead "look" at the 2s/10s curve every quarter (or at some other interval), and make payments if the 2s/10s curve at evaluation was steeper than the strike. In general, the cap structure tends to be more common, but because yield curve spread options are exotic structures, transaction costs can be an issue regardless of structure.

Apart from the fact that the underlying securities are different, there is another more subtle difference between swaptions and the example YCSO just described. In a swaption, the option can be exercised at expiry to enter into an actual swap; in this case, the P/L of the option is the difference in present value (PV) of the swap at market yield at expiry and the PV of the swap at the strike yield (assuming, of course, this is greater than zero, or else no exercise would have taken place). Given the present valuing, the swaption P/L is not just the change in swap yield $\times$ duration but has higher-order terms, such as convexity. In the case of the YCSO, the P/L on the option is cash settled and is indeed just a linear factor multiplied by the change in the yield spread. Hence the YCSO has no convexity and therefore is not directly analogous to a swap. Since the YCSO would be delta hedged using swaps, and swaps do have convexity, an adjustment is needed. To adjust for this lack of convexity, the strike on the YCSO is modified from the current forward curve, which would be the unadjusted at the money. This adjustment is referred to as a convexity adjustment and is necessary any time an instrument's payoff is a linear function of its yield, since for bonds and swaps, the payoff is a nonlinear function of yields. Recall that a similar concept applied to Eurodollar futures, where the linear payoff structure mismatches with the payoff profile of swaps and leads to a convexity bias. As in the case with Eurodollar futures, the convexity adjustment for YCSOs also depends on the volatility of the underlying rates.

FORWARD VOLATILITY

Forward volatility is a relatively new product in the rates space. As the name implies, forward volatility trades allow investors to take views on implied volatility in the future. The mechanism for this is a swaption, where the premium is paid up front but the swaption activates at some point in the future at the *at-the-money level on the forward date*. Thus, a 3M forward 1Y $\times$ 10Y swaption would require some premium at inception, and three months from the trade date, the buyer will enter into an at-the-money 1Y $\times$ 10Y option. Due to the floating strike, forward swaptions are exposed purely to implied volatility, and the contract requires no delta hedging. Currently, the transaction costs are high with this product. Over time, if liquidity improves, forward volatility could prove to be a convenient instrument to take views on volatility without cumbersome delta hedging.

VOLATILITY TRADING

Delta hedging allows the investor to take a view on the volatility of the asset while offsetting most of the risk of the underlying moving asset. With delta hedging, the volatility of the asset becomes an asset class in itself. The act of trading volatility, as described in the "Delta Hedging" section, essentially involves taking a view on the spread between implied volatility and realized volatility of the underlying forward rate. Trading volatility can be a source of uncorrelated returns to trading underlying. The nuances of trading volatility as an asset class are numerous and detailed; here we will map out some broad principles that drive rate volatility, including the participants and behavior of different sectors of the market.

For most participants, the starting point for trading volatility is to look for mismatches in realized versus implied volatility and for interest rate points where the mismatch is large. The idea behind this was mentioned earlier: The net P/L from gamma and theta (known as gamma P/L) is approximately the difference between the implied and the realized volatility. Since delta hedging supposedly removes the delta P/L from the trade, the risk factors that produce P/L are gamma, theta, and vega, reflecting realized volatility of the underlying interest rate, passage of time, and changes in implied volatility. (We also ignore other smaller higher-order risks.) For a long volatility position, then, the ideal conditions would be a higher realized volatility than implied volatility, which would result in a high gamma P/L as well as rising implied volatility, which adds to vega P/L (see "Measuring Risks in Option Positions" for more details). For a short volatility position, the situation is reversed. In general, then, trading volatility entails forming a view on what the trader's *expected* realized volatility for the interest rate market and the particular underlying is. In addition, a corresponding view on implied volatility needs to be developed. Finally, these two views are combined in determining whether implied volatility is headed higher and, if it is realized, whether it is likely to stay above or below implied volatility.

Unfortunately, trading volatility is not as straightforward as the previous paragraph may make it seem. As we explain, trading volatility as a way to capture only the variation in movement of a security rather than its direction is just an approximation. In reality, there are numerous other effects to consider. Merely finding securities with high realized volatility versus implied volatility or trading using a chart of implied volatility is a recipe for disaster when trading volatility. Often concepts that may be applicable in underlying, mostly linear markets are not applicable in options markets (or other asset classes), given their asymmetric nature. It is important to remember that, with options, many approximations and errors tend to grow rapidly and result in unanticipated sources of loss (or profit).

The reality of delta hedging involves appreciating a range of complications that arise in markets and cannot be considered merely extreme cases. These complications stem from the nature of constantly changing risks along multiple fronts for options, some of which are even assumed away in the familiar Black-Scholes framework to simplify the mathematics. However, simple and elegant equations such as Black-Scholes should mainly be used to understand markets in terms of understandable metrics, such as volatility, rather than as a trading mechanism. Markets are unfortunately neither elegant nor simple in their behavior, and any attempts to impose such constraints lead to very large losses when markets inevitably break. Three features of delta hedging, and thus trading volatility in general, to remember are:

1. *No assumption of smooth delta hedging.* This is a common criticism of the Black-Scholes framework, which assumes the ability to continuously delta hedge with zero transaction costs. Of course, neither assumption is valid, but in "normal" times, delta hedging with liquid, low-cost underlying securities such as Treasury futures can be a close approximation to the Black-Scholes framework. However, the assumption of underlying markets being around all the time to delta hedge with can be an incomplete one even with the most liquid underlyings. When markets become very volatile or illiquid, it can be difficult to delta hedge frequently. This situation can result in P/L that differs from the usual gamma, vega, and theta P/L approximations. Illiquid markets in particular carry gap risk, where the underlying price may go through discontinuous jumps resulting in large variations in delta and gamma P/L from the textbook formulas. These risks especially grow for short volatility positions, given the already negative asymmetry present in such positions.

2. *No assumption of constant volatility across strikes.* Black-Scholes assumes a single sigma variable regardless of where the underlying security might be. Unlike the formula, though, skew tends to exist across markets where implied volatility changes as the underlying itself moves. For example, if the interest rate market anticipates a spike in hedging activity by servicers if rates rise, the options market may reflect higher implied volatility for higher strikes than the at-the-money volatility. For a delta hedger, this situation introduces complications as changes in the underlying security bring about changes in implied volatility as the at-the-money strike moves, which in turn introduces vega P/L, not just the usual gamma and theta P/Ls from textbook delta hedging. In cases of steep skew, the delta may need to be adjusted to account for the vega P/L that stems from the underlying security moving.

3. *Path dependency of delta-hedged P/L.* Just as volatility is not constant over time, neither are the Greek risk parameters, across either strikes or time. As the underlying moves, the vega, gamma, and theta are also changing along with the delta, and the same is true as the option ages. These changes in risk parameters make even the delta-hedged P/L of an option dependent on the path the underlying security takes: The notion of "volatility trading" capturing the difference between realized and implied volatility is only an approximation. For example, consider the example of buying an at-the-money Eurodollar option and daily delta hedging the option. Now suppose after a very slow and steady climb, the Eurodollar price is over 100 bps above the fixed strike of the option that was bought. If the realized volatility of this move has been less than the implied volatility at which the option was purchased, the buyer encounters a loss. Now assume that the Eurodollar contract suddenly becomes extremely volatile around its new point at +100 bps from the original strike. Although this is welcome news for the buyer, at +100 bps from the original strike, the vega and gamma of the option are much lower than at the original point, leading to far lower gains from this increase in volatility. It would have been much more profitable if the *same* increase in volatility occurred around the original strike; even though the increase in implied and realized volatility may be the same, the path the security takes does matter. This is just one example of path dependency. Many more complex scenarios can be constructed to generate a wide range of P/Ls for the same levels of implied and realized volatility on a delta-hedged options trade. To counter some unintended effects of unexpected decays in risk parameters, a wider range of strikes can be bought, but overall dependency on the path of the security is unfortunately a risk any delta hedger bears.

Although these points introduce the complications any participant in the volatility markets must keep in mind, the dominant source of P/L remains the difference between realized and implied volatility. Thus, having a grasp of the drivers of realized and implied volatility in the interest rate market is essential for any rate options market investor. The ebb and flow of implied volatilities is first and foremost driven by realized volatility—as markets go through periods of stress and calm, implied volatilities are driven along with them. Realized volatility in the interest rate market stems from the interaction of Fed monetary policy with the future expected path of the economy and inflation. As would be intuitive, when there is a great deal of uncertainty about the direction of the economy, realized volatility in the rates space is higher. Another source of uncertainty for the rates market tends to be the question of how the Fed may respond to conflicts in its mandates to maintain maximum employment and stable prices.

Furthermore, the time period over which these uncertain views are likely to play out contributes to the *structure* of volatility in the market. For example, if the Fed is likely to stay on hold for at least a year but the direction of the economy is very uncertain after two to five years, this situation will be reflected in higher volatility for intermediate rates rather than for very short rates. Uncertainty about the fiscal situation and in particular about the sustainability of government spending with regard to inflation may push volatility even farther out toward 10-year and 30-year rates. This assessment of sources of uncertainty in the broad economy and Fed policy as well as the likely tenor of these uncertainties forms the starting point about taking a structural view on interest rate volatility.

Another source of volatility, both realized and implied, is the shape of the curve. In general, a steep curve is conducive to higher volatility. The reasons for this are difficult to prove empirically, but some possible reasons are that steeper curves incorporate more uncertainty as part of term premium, in addition to incorporating higher rates in the future, which adds to expected volatility. Flat curves, however, have little term premium and incorporate expectations of steady rates in the future. Such environments tend to be relatively steady, as witnessed by the fact that investors need little compensation for lending out for longer terms. Finally, on the other side, sharply inverted curves (i.e., long rates far lower than short rates) can be volatile once again as such a term structure of rates tends to predict future economic slowdown (see Chapter 6).

To most participants, the economic and monetary policy sources of volatility are probably the first ones that come to mind as drivers of volatility. However, one factor that is often missed is liquidity. *Liquidity* refers to the ease of doing trades (i.e., the trade volumes the market can digest without resulting in large price adjustments). For very liquid markets such as swaps, extremely large trades can be conducted without a significant impact on prices; for markets such as illiquid exotic options, a single trade may result in significant movement. Although some markets are more liquid than others, a single market itself can go through periods of high or low liquidity. Some of these shifts may be time-period dependent—for example, liquidity for the U.S. swaps market would be much lower during U.S. nighttime than U.S. daytime, and liquidity tends to be lower around major holidays compared to regular weekdays. These incidences of low liquidity are generally expected. However, liquidity can vanish during stress periods, which can be systemic or contained within a particular market. For example, if a very large hedge fund in a particular market closes down due to heavy losses, the expected deluge of asset sales could make other participants afraid to trade and therefore lower trading volume and liquidity. To be sure, systemic events, such as the Lehman Brothers bankruptcy or the Long-Term Capital Management collapse in 1998, can add considerable uncertainty to all markets, and liquidity retreats from nearly all asset markets if such an event occurs. Other nonfinancial events, such as 9/11, can also result in almost no liquidity for a number of trading days. Symptoms of lower liquidity include low trading sizes and very high bid/offer spreads that greatly increase transaction costs. Abundant liquidity acts as a dampener of volatility, given the market's ability to absorb large trading sizes. The situation reverses sharply when liquidity is unexpectedly withdrawn due to financial market stress. In such situations, similar trading sizes to prior environments now move markets a great deal more than previously as the market has more difficulty handling the same size trades. For example, in liquid times, a $100 million trade on 10-year swaps would be easily doable; in a stress event, though, dealers would be unwilling to do the whole transaction at once. In such situations, bid/offer spreads tend to be much wider, and larger trades need to be chopped up into smaller ones, two factors that raise transaction costs. The market's difficulty in digesting trade volume in turn raises realized volatility as the market moves a larger amount to adjust to incoming trades. High transaction costs also raise the cost of delta hedging, which in turn raises the fair value of implied volatility by making options more expensive. Lower liquidity certainly does not mean an automatic buying of options—both realized and implied volatilities head higher, and the implied volatility market may already reflect the expected impact—but it is certainly a factor to consider when taking a view on volatility.

Beyond the structure of the underlying rates market, the interest rate volatility market can also be thought of as an asset class of its own. It has structural sources of supply and demand that drive implied volatilities relative to realized volatilities. The most important structural source of demand for rate volatility stems from the mortgage market. Specifically, this market can be broken down into the mortgage portfolio of the government-sponsored enterprises (GSEs) and the hedging needs of the mortgage servicers. A mortgage asset is inherently short volatility because the homeowner holds the option to refinance. The more volatile interest rates are, the more valuable is the choice to be able to refinance the mortgage. Conversely for the mortgage loan owner, this volatility leads to decline in the value of the mortgage holdings.

Currently, the structure of the U.S. mortgage market includes GSEs, such as Freddie Mac and Fannie Mae, which provide guarantees to mortgages and also hold very large mortgage portfolios. Hedging the volatility exposure of this portfolio requires purchasing options and, in particular, swaptions, given their variety and liquidity. Due to the mortgage asset's long-dated tenor, hedging its exposure to volatility on a forward basis requires the purchase of long-expiry options in the middle of the volatility surface, such as $3Y \times 10Y$ swaptions. Although it is difficult to isolate specific expiries and tails of purchase, the large hedging demand tends to show itself especially in longer-dated options. There are two reasons for this:

1. Longer-dated options are less affected by realized volatility and more by implied volatility (see "Vega" section), making structural hedging needs more important.
2. The relative illiquidity of longer-dated options makes them more susceptible to large hedging flows than shorter-dated ones are.

To be sure, the need to purchase options rises and falls with market movements and with regulatory changes over time, making it difficult to quantitatively pinpoint volatility demand, but it is a key factor to model before beginning trading rate options, especially longer-dated ones. At the time of this writing, the conservatorship of the GSEs adds a great deal of uncertainty about the future direction of the interest rate volatility market as these major players may scale back on hedging compared to previous years. Given their massive size, any changes with regard to GSEs are likely to be implemented slowly, making them important players to track when trading rate volatility.

Mortgage servicers, which were described in Chapter 3, are another large contingent of volatility demand. Although their underlying asset is different from the mortgage assets of the GSEs, they still have a similar short volatility exposure. The mortgage servicing asset consists of a small section of the interest payment in mortgages. Therefore, a full or partial prepayment of the mortgage by a homeowner terminates all or part of their payment stream in the future. This sensitivity to prepayments makes the duration of the mortgage servicer portfolio very susceptible to changes as interest rates move and prepayments/refinancings become more or less attractive. Although part of mortgage servicer hedging is done via dynamic hedging, which involves changing interest rate hedges as the duration of the portfolio changes, this can be a very expensive endeavor when the market is volatile and liquidity is low. Therefore, part of the portfolio is hedged by options. Even though options may be a more expensive route at times, they can help the hedger be better prepared for sudden spikes in volatility. Furthermore, by reducing the need to dynamically hedge during illiquid and volatile times, options can be well worth the cost. It is not surprising then that servicers tend to be large buyers of interest rate options to manage their volatility exposure.

From a rates perspective, a major risk to a servicer portfolio is lower mortgage rates, which can subsequently lead to higher prepayments. Consequently, mortgage servicers at times hedge by buying mortgages directly, especially if the relationship between swaps and mortgages has been weak. Since a mortgage-backed security is itself negatively convex and short volatility, hedging with mortgages only adds to the short-volatility exposure of the underlying servicing asset. To offset this, demand for short-dated interest rate options in the 5- to 10-year sector is likely to go up, given that the short-volatility exposure leaves mortgage servicers very exposed to large moves in interest rates. Such hedging demand can cause implied volatility to trade well above realized volatility and cause other dislocations across the volatility surface. Consequently, watching the behavior of mortgage servicers and empirically tracking their hedge composition can be useful in understanding the factors driving implied volatility for intermediate rates.

The GSEs and mortgage servicers are generally drivers of intermediate-rate volatility, that is, from 1-year to 5-year expiries of options on 5- to 10-year rates. Farther out on the curve, the structural flows generally stem from the exotics desks. These flows are very difficult to generalize and tend to depend on the types of structured notes currently popular with end users/retail investors. If these structures are sufficiently long-dated or explicitly involve longer-dated rates, the dealers will tend to offload this risk in the longer-dated volatility markets. A crucial piece of analysis before trading longer-dated volatility is to analyze current risk in the popular structured notes and deduce the risks dealers are likely to hedge. For trading volatility on longer-dated rates, such as 30 years, and especially in longer expiries past one year, an understanding of the exotics flows is a must.

So far we have considered sources of demand for volatility from the GSEs and servicers as well as the ambiguous effect of the exotics desk at the longer end of the volatility surface. Now we consider *supply of volatility* in different parts of the surface. The chief source of supply to the volatility market stems from the issuance of callable structures. Callable debt or callable structured notes leave the issuer with a long option position—the option to redeem the security. Callability was discussed earlier in reference to embedded options in fixed income instruments. If a callable instrument is issued, and neither the issuer nor the purchaser hedges volatility exposure, there is no net effect on the market. Similarly, if both parties hedge their exposure, one will be selling options while the other will be buying options, leaving no net effect. However, for most option-embedded structures, the response is not symmetric. Earlier we discussed above how many purchasers of mortgage-backed securities, which are themselves a type of callable instrument with the option to call (or refinance in the hands of the homeowner), tend to hedge their short-volatility exposure in the market, making them a source of volatility demand. For callable debt issued by the agencies, banks, or other structured notes, the buyers are rarely active hedgers of the optionality; instead, they tend to purchase the callable bonds precisely to earn the extra yield that the short option position offers. Indeed, for these types of issues, more often it is either the issuers or dealers (sometimes the same thing) that offset the option to call back the bond by selling options into the market. This statement does not apply to all situations, and each type of callable debt has issuers or intermediaries with different propensities to offset the optionality exposure. The desire to hedge by issuers or the desire to even issue the types of debt being discussed here also shifts as the regulatory winds shift. One example is the trust-preferred notes market, which banks used to issue prior to the credit crunch; these notes had extremely long maturities, ranging from 20 years to perpetual (i.e., infinite) and in general were not callable for the first 5 to 10 years. Such notes were issued mainly to fund banks in regulatory-friendly ways. In many cases, the issuing banks offset their long volatility exposure by selling 5Y × 30Y swaptions and similar structures that approximately matched the debt profile. Tracking the issuance of trust preferreds was key in such periods as large issuance programs could depress longer-dated volatility significantly. The credit crunch put a large dent in the issuance of such hybrid notes as risk aversion on both buyer and issuer sides set in, especially in an environment of regulatory uncertainty. Instead of trust preferreds, at other times, the callable issuances of note were zero-coupon callable bonds issued for investors seeking yield. The main point of these examples is to recognize that the volatility market sources of demand and supply are constantly changing. This is especially true when trading longer-expiry options in the rates space, where the effects of structural supply and demand changes are magnified. Many investors not directly involved in the interest rate markets will often transact in longer-dated options to take broad macro views on rates, but it is important to remember the myriad influences on longer-dated volatility from structural demand and supply sources.

INTEREST RATE SKEW

The term *skew*, as mentioned, refers to the difference between out-of-the-money and at-the-money implied volatility for an option. The term itself is ambiguous (as usual); in general, it has to be specified which out-of-the-money strike is being referenced to calculate the difference. The skew in essence displays the market's expectation of the directionality of implied volatilities with the underlying interest rate. In the interest rate market, this directionality itself depends on the *level of rates*. To clarify, consider the case of a 6M × 1Y swaption (i.e., 6-month expiry option on the 1-year rate).

The underlying rate here is the 6M × 1Y rate (i.e., 6M forward 1Y swap rate). Now consider the two extreme cases of the rate being at 0.5% and 12%. In the 0.5% case, the interest cannot go below zero (or at least much below zero), which severely limits the *absolute* volatility of the option on the receiver side. If a trader bought a 0% receiver, there is not much hope for volatility at that level, and so the volatility at the 0% rate level should be almost zero. The volatility on the higher end of rates, however, is likely to be at more normal levels, making the out-of-the-money put/payer volatilities much higher. In this case, the market is just implying that as rates go lower, it expects volatility to head lower, and vice versa. At the 12% level, though, the skew would likely be more symmetric as one could expect sufficient volatility on either end. On the whole, skew trading in rates is difficult for smaller option portfolios to monetize, and often the skew trades do not have enough potential profit for reasonable position sizes. Not surprisingly, dealer desks, with large options portfolios and the benefit of few or no transaction costs, are in a much better position to trade the skew.

A concept related to the skew often mentioned in the market is the risk reversal. One common risk reversal is the 25 delta risk reversal, which represents the difference between the implied volatility of a 25 delta call (out-of-the-money strike with delta = 0.25 for a call option) and the 25 delta put (out-of-the-money strike with delta = 25 for a put option). The risk reversal is so named because if the call is sold and put is bought, the gamma of the position changes sign as the underlying moves. As the underlying rate moves toward the call strike, the position becomes short gamma since the call option has been sold; if the underlying rate moves toward the put option strike, the gamma becomes increasingly positive as this option has been bought and we are moving closer to the at-the-money level. The risk reversal can also sell the put and buy the call to reverse its exposure, and even the convention of quoting risk reversals can at times be either call volatility minus put volatility or vice versa.

VOLATILITY SPREAD TRADES

As with curve trades in the rates market, volatility spread trades involve trading volatility of one option relative to another. In general, the trades tend to take advantage of relative value mispricings between implied and realized volatilities of pairs of options. The spreads tend to be across expiry or across tails, known as expiry switches or tail switches. Expiry switches are trades between options on the same interest rate *at expiry* but with different expiries. Tail switches have the same expiry but different tails (i.e., underlying interest rates). An example of an expiry switch would be buying 6M × 2Y swaptions (6-month expiry swaptions on 2-year rates) and selling 3Y × 2Y swaptions (3-year expiry swaptions on 2-year rates). Note that in this expiry switch, the rate at expiry is the same but, at inception, the underlyings are different. In the case of the 6M × 2Y swaption, the 6M × 2Y forward rate is the underlying. In the 3Y × 2Y swaption, the underlying is the 3Y × 2Y forward rate. An example of a tail switch would be buying the 6M × 2Y swaption and selling the 6M × 10Y swaption. Here the expiries are identical, but the interest rates at expiry are different.

Weighting tail switches or expiry switches resembles the idea behind weighting interest rate curve trades. In the rate space, the weighting of the two legs of a curve trade relies on equating the DV01 of the two components; in this way, the trade is not affected by parallel shifts in interest rates. For volatility spread trades, the concept is the same. We want the volatility spread trade to be unaffected by parallel shifts in *volatility* since that is the underlying variable being traded here; instead, the aim of a volatility spread trade is to take advantage of differences in volatility of one option versus another. In the case of options, however, one can control for two different volatilities: realized or implied volatility. If the volatility spread trade P/L needs to be immune to parallel shifts in implied volatility, then the vega of the two legs of the trade needs to be equated. For example, suppose the 6M × 2Y versus 6M × 10Y tail switch has $87,433 vega per $100 million notional per 1 bp/day volatility move for the 6M × 2Y swaption and $392,000 vega per $100 million for 1 bp/day volatility move for the 6M × 10Y swaption. Recall that this means the 6M × 2Y incurs a profit or loss of $87,433 per 1 bp/day move in implied volatility of the 6M × 2Y option, while the 6M × 10Y incurs a profit or loss of $392,000 per 1 bp/day move in implied volatility of the 6M × 10Y option. Therefore, if $22.3 million of the 6M × 10Y is sold for each $100 million bought of the 6M × 2Y option, the vega of the two legs is exactly offset. This way, the P/L from an equal move in implied volatility of the 6M × 2Y and 6M × 10Y legs results in exactly offsetting P/L (since vega P/L = vega × change in implied volatility). In this case, the volatility spread trade will witness a profit if the implied volatility of the 6M × 2Y option increases more (or declines less) than the implied volatility of the 6M × 10Y option. In other words, the profit/loss of this trade will roughly track the 6M × 2Y implied volatility − 6M × 10Y implied volatility. Notice the similarity here with a curve trade in rates. To be sure, the volatility spread trade could also be based on taking advantage of different realized volatility in the two options. Hedging for equal realized volatility in the two option legs is more difficult to grasp intuitively, but the main concept is equating the total gamma of the two legs of the trade instead of the vega. In market jargon, equating the vegas of the option legs is referred to as a vega-neutral spread trade and equating the gammas is known as a gamma-neutral spread trade. Notice again the similarity to rates where curve trades are duration neutral. In general, the term that is neutral is the one for which parallel shifts do not impact P/L. The vega-neutral switch just described attempts to take a view on the difference in implied volatility between two options. The same switch can be done as a gamma-neutral switch. In this case, instead of choosing notionals to equate the vegas, we choose notionals to equate the gamma exposure of each leg, which again is the same principle as duration hedging for bonds. As vega-neutral spreads take a view on implied volatility spreads, the gamma-neutral spreads take a view on realized volatility spreads.

If the expiries are the same, then the gamma and vega hedges are roughly similar. For expiry switches, however, gamma neutrality and vega neutrality result in very different trades. Consider buying a 6M × 10Y swaption and selling a 3Y × 10Y swaption. With a vega-neutral switch, the 3Y × 10Y swaption has much larger vega than the 6M × 2Y swaption vega. A 6M × 10Y swaption has a much higher gamma than the 3Y × 10Y swaption. With a vega-neutral switch, for a given amount of 3Y × 10Y swaption sold, a larger amount of 6M × 10Y swaption needs to be bought since the 6M × 10Y has less vega. This switch then ends up being long gamma since the 6M × 10Y gamma is larger than the 3Y × 10Y gamma. Thus, being vega neutral leads to being long gamma in this case. Now consider the case where the trade was gamma neutral instead. Now the 3Y × 10Y notional needs to be larger than the 6M × 10Y notional to equate the gammas since 3Y × 10Y has less gamma than the 6M × 10Y. Given that the 3Y × 10Y swaption has larger vega than the 6M × 10Y and that we are selling the 3Y × 10Y swaption, the gamma-neutral trade ends up being short vega. These changes in risks stem from the fact that short-dated options have more gamma than vega and longer-dated options have more vega than gamma. When an expiry switch is made gamma neutral, a large amount of the long-dated option needs to be used to equate the gamma of the short-dated option; if the long-dated option is being sold, its vega overwhelms the short-dated option's vega. However, if the expiry switch is made vega neutral, a large amount of the short-dated option needs to be traded to equate the vegas, leaving the gamma unbalanced. When setting up switches, it is important to keep track of all the risk parameters. At times, the volatility spread between two different expiries may appear very attractive to initiate, but care must be taken to make sure that the gamma exposure in the switch is desirable as well to avoid unexpected losses.

Volatility spread trades can be attractive because they express a more specific view than an outright trade. This can make the chance of success higher, as the trade is less exposed to the broad factors that may drive an outright trade and can capture relative effects between sectors. Some of the same principles of doing curve trades in rates to express more specific views related to flows apply to volatility spread trades. For example, at times volatility spread trades may have structural factors, such as hedging demand from servicers or exotic desks, that affect some sectors but not others. For example, a 6M × 2Y versus 6M × 10Y swaption tail switch where the 6M × 10Y is bought can allow an investor to take advantage of anticipated mortgage servicer hedging, which tends to affect intermediate volatility more than shorter-dated volatility. The reverse trade may be more appropriate if the trader believes that the Fed is likely to begin a rapid easing program in response to financial market stress; here, the 6M × 2Y rate is likely to be more volatile, as it is nearer to the Fed's action. In both these cases, an outright trade, such as 6M × 10Y or 6M × 2Y buying, would be at the mercy of overall levels of volatility, which could decline if anticipated mortgage hedging or Fed activity happens later than expected; a spread trade provides more staying power by having less volatility in P/L of the trade. Expiry switches can have different sector-driven rationales; in market stress situations, for example, short-expiry volatility rises much faster than long-expiry volatility as investors expect more realized volatility over the near term.

CAPS VERSUS SWAPTIONS

As described, caps and swaptions are two forms of options on interest rates. A swaption can be thought of as a one-look option on a single rate while a cap can be thought of as a multilook structure as a portfolio of options. When comparing caps/floors with swaptions, it is common to look at approximately matched structures; thus, a 1Y × 2Y swaption would be compared to a 1 × 3 cap/floor (since both expire on the same date; see earlier discussion for more details). The differences between the structures of the two products and sector-specific flows lead to differences in their implied volatilities. Given the cap's portfolio construction, the cap's volatility can be thought of as the average volatility of the underlying 3M LIBOR rates. For a swaption, however, there is only a single option on a swap rate, which itself is akin to an average of 3M LIBOR forwards. Thus, a swaption's volatility can be conceptualized as the volatility of the average of underlying forward rates instead of the average volatility. This difference, of course, brings in correlation; recall from Chapter 1 that the volatility of a sum of two variables is composed of both the sum of volatilities and a correlation component. Therefore, it is no surprise that the spread between the volatility of a swaption and cap/floor structure is dependent on the correlation between forward rates. However, this correlation is very difficult to monetize, since each caplet's expiry does not match each swaption's. In practice, the primary driver of the cap/swaption trade's P/L ends up being the shape of the volatility surface; when compared to the same matched swaption, a cap has a longer expiry (as its caplets expire at successive three-month intervals) but a shorter tail (three-month underlying) than the swaption, and movements in the volatility surface with regard to short tails versus long tails and short expiry versus long expiry are the primary drivers in the spread.

Beyond the differences that stem from their structure, caps also differ from swaptions through the effects of structured note flows. One such structured note is the LIBOR range accrual note, which pays the investor a coupon if 3M LIBOR is within a certain range. Although the details of the structure vary depending on the financial environment and investor demand, most of these structures result in the dealer being long caps/floors (or just caps if the lower threshold for 3M LIBOR is zero) since 3M LIBOR crossing these barriers means that the dealer will not have to pay a coupon. The hedging activity of dealers then leads them to sell caps, which lowers cap volatility versus swaption volatility. Thus issuance of these structured notes is key to track when taking a view on the swaption/cap volatility spread. To be sure, this dynamic certainly is not a permanent one, but it serves as an example of the wide variety of factors that must be tracked when trading rate option spreads.

SUMMARY

This chapter introduced a large number of concepts relating to options. Due to their asymmetric nature, options add a new set of tools for investors to take views and manage risk in many markets. Interest rate options markets are some of the largest in the world and share many basic principles with options from other markets, such as equities. However, as the chapter showed, there are some big differences as well in both the way underlying rates are assumed to move and the types of options products available. Furthermore, interest rate markets are cluttered with a large set of products where options are embedded for either the issuer or investor. Generally these products are best understood as some combination of bonds and interest rate options. Finally, options offer investors the ability to trade the volatility of rates, which can provide diverse sources of return for a fixed income portfolio.

CHAPTER 11

Treasury Futures Basis and Rolls

T his chapter considers the Treasury futures market in more detail. Treasury futures are, on one level, a simple way to take a view on Treasury yields. However, there is much more depth to the product due to the range of choices presented to the seller of the futures with regard to the bond and timing of delivery. In markets, choices are never presented for free. The valuation of these choices can be traded as well and can be viewed as a type of embedded option of the type presented in Chapter 10. The embedded option forms an important component of the Treasury futures basis, which is one of the common relative value trades in the fixed income space. The basis incorporates the relative richness or cheapness of a Treasury futures contract versus members of its deliverable basket. Chapter 4 discussed the mechanics of Treasury futures contracts and some metrics to measure the relative value of the futures contracts versus similar Treasury bonds, such as the basis net of carry (BNOC). The BNOC, also known as the net basis, incorporates the value of the option to deliver any member of the delivery basket. It is this optionality that separates the Treasury futures basis from other forward/spot differences. The reader is advised to review Chapter 4 in detail to better understand the concepts outlined in this chapter.

THE FUTURES DELIVERY OPTION

In Chapter 4, we defined the gross basis as bond price – futures price × conversion factor. Trading the basis involves buying or selling a Treasury bond (known informally as a cash Treasury) and doing the reverse trade with the Treasury futures contract. Since it is the difference between a forward price and a spot price, the gross basis incorporates the carry of the bond until delivery date. As carry can be locked in using term repurchase agreements (repo), we can subtract carry of the bond from the gross basis and arrive at the BNOC. This chapter considers the reasons for and thought process behind trading the Treasury futures net basis. Although the underlying concept is simple and involves trading bonds versus futures, there are numerous nuances because of the delivery basket structure of the futures contract. As discussed in Chapter 4, the gross basis is the sum of the carry and delivery option value. After subtracting carry, the net basis represents the delivery option value. Trading the net basis essentially is equivalent to trading the delivery option value and combines many of the concepts of both options and futures. In practice, instead of doing two transactions, the gross basis can be traded as an entity of its own. Dealers will give a bid and offer on the basis itself. Conventions regarding direction with the basis follow the Treasury bond part; hence, *going long*, or *buying the basis*, refers to buying the Treasury bond and selling the futures contract, whereas *going short*, or *selling the basis*, refers to selling the Treasury bond and buying the futures contract. Borrowing from the spreads convention, if the basis value increases, it is said to be getting wider, and a basis value getting smaller (or more negative) is said to be getting narrower. On a gross basis trade, if the repo rate is locked in for a certain period, it becomes a net basis trade since the carry is locked in. When discussing the term "basis" in this chapter, we are referring to the net basis. In the case that we mean gross basis, we will clarify in the text.

To understand the delivery option value, suppose we take the deliverable basket of the futures contract and rank the bonds by duration. Recall that on the last delivery date, the futures contract needs to converge to the final cheapest-to-deliver (CTD) bond; if it does not, a trader could immediately trade the futures contract versus the CTD bond and earn risk-free profit. Note that the convergence between CTD and futures price is only guaranteed at the time when the futures contract is about to expire. Prior to this date, the valuation of a contract and its CTD bond can differ due to the chance of a switch to a different CTD. Consider a situation where the CTD bond is the lowest-duration bond in the basket. Also assume the basis net of carry for the CTD bond is currently zero. Table 11.1 shows this base case scenario including the yields, prices, and bases for three bonds in the basket. The futures price for this and other scenarios will be the minimum of the forward bond prices divided by the conversion factor, as discussed in Chapter 4. If yields change, we can recalculate the change in the state of the basket. Table 11.2 shows one such scenario, when yields for the three bonds all rise by 100 basis points (bps) (1%), and the

TABLE 11.1 Base Case Scenario for a Treasury Futures Contract with Three Deliverable Bonds

Base Case Scenario

Contract	Sep 10Y
Last Deliv	9/30/2010
Tsy Repo	0.22
Yld shift (bp)	0.00

	Coupon	Maturity	Yrs to Mat	Duration	Yield	Curr Price	Carry	Fwd Price	C. Factor	Fwd Price/ Factor	Gross Basis	BNOC
Bond1	6.000	2/15/2026	15.5	10.8	3.614	128.12	22.5	127.42	0.9999	127.43	23	0.0
Bond2	6.125	8/15/2029	19.0	12.3	3.772	131.71	23.0	130.99	1.0138	129.21	81	57.6
Bond3	4.375	5/15/2040	29.8	16.8	4.018	106.16	16.3	105.65	0.7765	136.06	231	214.3
Futures Px	**127.43**											

*Highlighted bond indicates CTD bond.

TABLE 11.2 Treasury Futures Contract Basket for a Yield Shift Higher

Higher-Yield Scenario

Contract	Sep 10Y
Last Deliv	9/30/2010
Tsy Repo	0.22
Yld shift (bp)	100

	Coupon	Maturity	Yrs to Mat	Duration	Yield	Curr Price	Carry	Fwd Price	C. Factor	Fwd Price/ Factor	Gross Basis	BNOC
Bond1	6.000	2/15/2026	15.5	10.4	4.614	115.22	22.7	114.52	0.9999	114.53	24.4	1.7
Bond2	6.125	8/15/2029	19.0	11.8	4.772	116.78	23.1	116.05	1.0138	114.48	23.1	0.0
Bond3	4.375	5/15/2040	29.8	15.6	5.018	90.11	16.5	89.60	0.7765	115.39	39.1	22.7
Futures Px	114.48											

*Highlighted bond indicates CTD bond.

corresponding changes to the net bases and other variables in the basket. Note that once again, the futures price in this scenario is the minimum of the forward bond prices divided by the conversion factor. To understand the nature of the net basis of each bond, it is useful to consider changes in each bond's net basis in a large range of yield scenarios. Table 11.3 condenses the calculations of the last two scenario tables for a range of parallel yield shifts across the three bonds by calculating the forward prices, the futures price, and net bases in each scenario. Note that the conversion factors are unchanged throughout this process. Figure 11.1 shows the net bases across different yield shifts for bond1, bond2, and bond3, which are in increasing order by duration. When yields head lower, the other bonds with higher duration in the basket witness a greater rise in the price (i.e., the conversion factor adjusted price) compared to the CTD bond. This is because as the shortest-duration bond in the basket, the CTD here undergoes the least amount of richening in the basket and therefore remains CTD as yields fall. In this case, the net basis of this bond converges to zero at the last delivery date. If yields rise, though, as in Table 11.2, the current CTD declines in price at the slowest pace, given its low duration, while prices of higher-duration bonds (bond2 and bond3) decline faster. At some point, the varied speed of price declines leads to a change in the CTD to bond2 from the original CTD, bond1. Further yield increases lower the price of the highest-duration bond, bond3, further, and at some point, the CTD bond switches to bond3. Note that once the CTD switches away from bond1, its basis is no longer zero, since by definition it is not the cheapest bond in the basket any longer. The net basis profiles at expiry for these bonds resemble option payoff profiles. For the buyer of the net basis of bond1, the net basis at expiry stays at zero as yields decline. However, if yields increase past a certain point, the bond1 net basis at expiry is greater than zero. Thus, the expiry profile of the net basis of bond1, a low-duration bond, thus resembles a call option on yields. For bond2, the medium-duration bond, there is a range of yield changes where the expiry BNOC is zero. For yields outside this range, the net basis at expiry rises into positive territory. Here, for a long-basis position, the position resembles a straddle on yields. Finally, if bond3, the highest duration bond, is CTD, then as yields increase, the net basis of the bond stays at zero at expiry. However, if yields decrease, the net basis rises. Thus, the bond3 net basis resembles a put option on yields. In sum, trading the net basis resembles trading an option on yields.

Since the holder of the short position in the futures contract delivers the bond at expiry, the short futures contract holds the delivery option (i.e., can make choice to deliver a bond of his or her choosing). The short futures position having the option is also consistent with our terminology, where "long basis" equates to buying a bond and selling the futures contract, thus retaining the delivery optionality. In contrast, the buyer of a

TABLE 11.3 Net Bases for Parallel Yield Shifts (bps)

	Base Yield	−100	−80	−60	−40	−20	0	20	40	60	80	100	120	140	160	180	200
Bond1	**3.614**	0.0	0.0	0.0	0.0	0.0	0.0	0.0	0.0	0.0	0.0	1.7	11.3	46.9	79.7	109.7	137.2
Bond2	**3.772**	139.2	120.8	103.5	87.2	72.0	57.6	44.1	31.5	19.7	8.6	0.0	0.0	27.2	52.0	74.6	95.2
Bond3	**4.018**	498.1	432.6	371.7	315.2	262.9	214.3	169.4	127.9	89.5	54.0	22.7	0.0	0.0	0.0	0.0	0.0

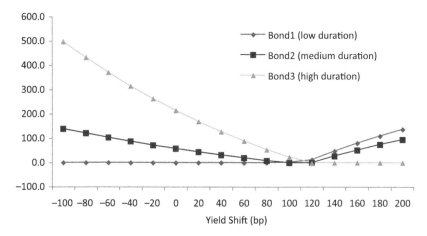

FIGURE 11.1 Net Bases for Three Bonds in a Basket for Different Yield Shifts

Treasury futures contract is short the delivery option, as the long position has no choice as to which bond will be delivered. Figure 11.2 shows the price profile of a Treasury futures contract and prices of the three bonds in the basket. As expected, the price of the futures contract tracks the lowest-priced bond in the basket and thus has more limited price appreciation in each scenario. The profile does not resemble the convex-up shape of a regular bond but instead is convex-down. This limited upside profile stems from the short delivery option position of the buyer of the futures contract.

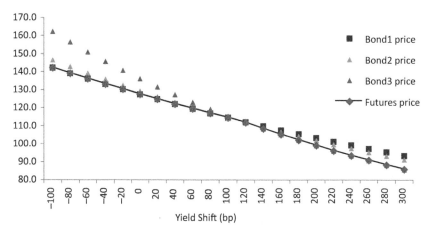

FIGURE 11.2 Bond and Futures Prices for Different Yield Shifts

The stylized example in Figure 11.2 points to the option nature of trading the basis. Although the theoretical concept behind trading the basis is relatively simple, basis trading is all about the details. The biggest pitfalls in basis trading stem from the assumptions in the stylized examples, which do not always hold in the real market. Many of these assumptions are rarely violated and may seem minor, but their violation can lead to the largest losses due to complacency. We consider these assumptions next, starting with some obvious assumptions and then exploring more subtle ones.

In the examples just given, the assumption is that the CTD bond starts off with BNOC of zero. Another way to think of the assumption here is that the delivery option is being offered for free; in our stylized example, if the BNOC is at zero at inception of the trade, then the trade has no downside since at the last delivery date, the BNOC of the current CTD can be either zero if it remains CTD or higher if there is a switch. The assumption of a zero BNOC on the CTD is generally not realistic. The BNOC of the CTD should be thought of as a premium for the option to switch the choice of bond to deliver. Most of the time, the market is unlikely to offer the switch option for free, although often values are close to zero if a switch is very unlikely. For a nonzero BNOC on the CTD bond, the trader with a long basis position stands to lose those ticks if there is no switch. For example, if the net basis of the CTD is three ticks, a buyer of the basis is hoping for a CTD switch, which presumably will drive the BNOC higher. However, with a nonzero net basis, the decision is more complicated. Going into last delivery date, if the net basis has not switched, the net basis of this bond decays to zero, causing a loss of three ticks. Note the similarity of the BNOC decay to theta decay of an option. Indeed, even a switch could take place. If it is a minor switch, where the bonds are both close to being CTD, the BNOC still may decay to a lesser number, such as one tick. The key takeaway here is that the BNOC of the CTD is the market's estimation of the delivery option's worth; this value needs to be compared with the trader's own estimation of the option's worth. Thus, to make a decision about buying or selling the basis, the trader must compare his or her valuation of the delivery option with the BNOC of the CTD bond. The idea behind estimating the delivery option value is outlined subsequently. In some cases, it may be attractive to sell the basis, which would benefit from the net basis decaying to zero as long as there is no large CTD shift. Selling the basis, therefore, is a way to sell optionality on yields and benefits if yields do not change much. Indeed, selling the basis was, and to a lesser extent remains, an effective way for basis traders to enhance returns since the market *tends* to overvalue the delivery option. This is by no means a blanket statement, however, as selling the basis can be an incredibly challenging and painful trade if markets enter a volatile phase, as was the case in 2008.

The previous paragraph considered the situation where the CTD net basis does not trade at zero in the market. Another, more subtle, assumption in the simplified example is that a zero net basis indeed implies no downside at expiry. A zero net basis having no downside is generally the case in reality. However, some nuances in the market can cause rather large losses if certain risk is not carefully managed. To understand the issues that may arise, assume there is one month until last delivery date and once again assume a zero net basis for the CTD. To truly capture the no-downside feature, a few conditions must be met. If the bond is being borrowed from the repo market, it must be held in a secure manner. In the repo market, at times, a party to a trade may fail to honor the obligation to repurchase or resell the bond as previously agreed. Such an event is known as a repo fail and generally incurs a penalty on the failing party. For a typical repo transaction, a bond may be borrowed or lent several times among various parties, and even a single party failing to honor its obligation can create a chain of repo fails. One method for preventing a bond being lent out multiple times is a triparty repo, where an agreement is made to "box" the bond, which essentially means securing the bond such that it is not exposed to repo fails. Boxing the bond ensures that the bond is indeed ready when delivery approaches. If this precaution is not taken, a squeeze could take place on the bond, which would entail too little supply of the bond to deliver, or repo fails may occur for a variety of other reasons. For the seller of the contract, although failing on a repo transaction does incur a penalty, failing to deliver a bond to the exchange tends to be considerably more expensive. Therefore, the repo fail penalty is not a big enough deterrent to guarantee a short futures position holder can access the bond at delivery time. Issue scarcity leading to squeezes or fails is less common now due to more stringent regulatory oversight of repo markets and generally larger issue sizes, but is still a possibility that deserves careful management. Essentially, for a short futures position holder, the closer the delivery of bonds is going to be made to the last delivery date, the greater the care that must be taken to ensure the desired CTD bond will be available.

Another key assumption associated with *any* net basis calculation is that of a termed-out repo. *Term repos* refer to a fixed financing rate offered by a counterparty for a certain length of time. Although repo markets tend to be concentrated around the overnight to one-week tenors, longer term repos are also available in the market. For example, a three-month term repo would fix a repo rate for three months, allowing an exact carry calculation for a three-month period. Recall that to calculate the net basis, we subtract the futures price $\times$ conversion factor and carry from the cash price of the bond. This carry calculation in turn assumes a constant repo rate for the period from trade date to last delivery date. At times it can be difficult to secure term repos, or it may be cheaper to continuously roll overnight repos, especially if the front end is seen as stable with the Fed on hold. However, rolling repos overnight, especially for the basis seller, can be a very dangerous proposition. This is because repo rates can be extremely volatile if conditions change. If there is a flight to quality or a similar stress event, the rush into safer assets, such as Treasuries, brings significant liquidity to the Treasury financing market, causing repo rates to collapse. If the stress events are serious enough, Fed expectations of an easing can set in, further driving repos lower. Sharply lower repos can increase carry costs considerably for short positions in bonds, such as for a basis seller. Futures prices decline as well from declining financing rates, since the opportunity cost of holding futures, which offer no coupon payments, increases (also recall that forward price = spot price − carry). August 2007 presented an empirical example of the risks stemming from repo markets. Instead of a quiet summer, sellers of the basis without termed-out repo rates faced financing rates that plunged hundreds of basis points as a liquidity squeeze led to a flight into Treasuries. The plunge in financing rates resulted in sharp losses for short basis positions where repos were not termed out.

These points should impress upon the reader the importance of details when trading the basis. Basis trading involves mostly collecting small ticks, cycle after cycle, but at certain times, seemingly minute factors can cause extraordinary amounts of volatility. The term versus rolling repo issue from August 2007 is one such example. The credit crunch was instructive for futures markets in that it pointed out the importance of systemic factors that can make seemingly low-volatility variables, such as the basis, behave unpredictably. The credit crunch was characterized by a sharp scarcity of balance sheet capacity. For basis traders, balance sheet capacity is a key hidden input in the attractiveness of a trade. In simple terms, the balance sheet can be thought of as the size of trades an investor can initiate comfortably. Having a large balance sheet is especially important for trading the basis because generally selling the basis and waiting for convergence to the CTD price is the profitable trade. Such short basis trades tend to make a small number of ticks, which leads to the need for very large trades to earn a reasonable profit in absolute dollar terms. As banks pulled back from risk taking in 2008 and as the interest rate market became increasingly volatile, basis traders who were short the basis rapidly unwound positions. These unwinds required buying back the basis (i.e., buying cash bonds and selling futures), which led to further increases in the basis. The lack of balance sheet and the volatility also prevented new traders and investors from stepping in and selling the basis, even when BNOCs on 10-year Treasury futures went into the low twenties (prior to 2008, a basis of five ticks would have been rather large). On the other side of this reluctance was a stampede to sell futures as a hedge for cash assets, such as Treasury bonds, and other fixed income instruments, such as corporates and mortgage-backed securities (see also Chapter 8). The usual method of hedging with Treasury bonds or futures opportunistically was not practical, given the numerous problems in Treasury repo and overall volatility of financing markets. In short, futures continued to cheapen, driven by the spiral of hedging activity on one side and basis position unwinds on the other side. Any model that worked during the "normal" years would have indicated that futures were extremely cheap, but for basis traders, market flows dominated most delivery option value considerations.

Although the dynamic just described drove 10-year BNOCs to extremely wide levels, a very different dynamic was occurring with the 30-year futures. This divergence further highlighted the importance of understanding flows in each part of the curve when trading the basis. Unlike the 5-to-10-year sectors, the 30-year sector was characterized by a structural demand for longer-end fixed income assets, which arose as equity values contracted sharply. The contraction led to sharp shortfalls for pension funds, which needed to increase fixed income exposure and reduce equity exposure. Since selling equities rapidly would have been impractical and undesirable, pension funds proceeded to increase fixed income exposure synthetically using derivatives, where, in general, up-front payments are not required in large size and transactions are relatively straightforward. Although long-end swaps felt the greatest effect (see Chapter 9), there were spillover effects on Treasury futures, which offer another derivative method to get exposure to the long end of the fixed income space. As this took place, Treasury futures richened significantly with respect to cash Treasury bonds; in particular, the BNOC of the CTD traded at negative levels even near delivery. For those lucky enough to have spare capital in such an environment, buying the basis and terming out the repo provided nearly risk-free money as the basis trended toward zero on the final day.

CALCULATING THE DELIVERY OPTION VALUE

So far we have stressed that the BNOC should be seen as an option premium and going long or short the basis depends on the trader's assessment of the delivery option premium versus the market's. The calculation of the delivery option value is similar to pricing other options using a tree model with some modifications to account for the basket of underlying securities. The valuation of the delivery option involves six general steps:

1. Determine the forward yields of each bond in the basket to the last delivery date.
2. Create a set of outcome possibilities (i.e., a tree) of possible yields at delivery (more on this later).
3. In each possible scenario, calculate the futures price.
   a. Since all the forward yields are known, we can determine the bond with the lowest forward price/conversion factor.
   b. The bond with lowest forward price/conversion factor is the CTD on the last date and the forward price/conversion factor of this bond is the futures price.
4. Assign a probability to each outcome of yields. This can be done using a normal distribution framework. The volatility to use can be interpolated for last delivery date from the futures options market.
5. Calculate the expected value of the futures price using the futures price in each scenario and the probability of each scenario occurring. This can be thought of as the fair value of the futures contract.
6. For the value of the switch option, we need to calculate the difference between the fair value of the futures price and the expected value of the current CTD. In other words, delivery option value = EVal Current CTD/conversion factor – fair futures price. Recall that anytime we compare a bond price to a futures price, the conversion factor adjustment is required.

This procedure outlines how to calculate a fair futures price and the delivery option value. However, the steps require modeling outcome scenarios for each bond in the basket separately, which is computationally intensive and not necessary. Bonds in the same sector of the yield curve tend to be very highly correlated. Instead of modeling each bond separately, we can model just a few factors that explain most of the yield movements in the basket. One common way to approach this is to consider yield outcome possibilities in step 2 as arising from two factors: changes in the average yield of the bonds in the basket and changes in spread between the highest- and lowest-maturity bonds in the basket. For changes in the average yield, we can approximate the increments using implied volatility from the futures options market, interpolated to the last delivery date. For yield spreads, which do not have a liquid options market, we can estimate the increments using a recent historical standard, deviations of spread changes. Suppose we have a futures contract with three bonds in its basket: bond1, bond2, and bond3. We can create a simple table of outcome scenarios where each cell represents the intersection of a specific basket average yield and basket yield spread (between bond3 and bond1). For each outcome, then, we can determine the yields of the bonds in the basket by determining the parallel shift in the basket yields to arrive at the particular average yield and then maturity-weighted increments to ensure that the particular yield spread is preserved.

The calculation of the delivery option value leaves ample room for incorporating more subtle modifications. Instead of using average yield and yield spread, the first and second principal components analysis could be used to distill the yield curve into simpler factors, adding to the robustness of the model. Also, instead of just assuming a parallel shift as the first factor, we can incorporate a regression beta between the changes in yields of the bonds in the basket. For example, in the bond futures basket, the span of the basket in maturity terms is 15 years; in this case, bonds in the 15-year sector rarely move parallel to the 30-year sector, and a beta of yield changes between the 30-year and 15-year sector could be assumed instead of a parallel shift. However, adding this layer of complexity can at times make the model unstable, since betas are by definition backward-looking measures. In times of high volatility, betas can misrepresent yield curve moves as relationships between yield curve sectors can become unstable.

OPTION-ADJUSTED AND EMPIRICAL DURATION

Given the importance of Treasury futures for hedging risks for a wide range of fixed income assets, the futures contract duration and dollar value of one basis point (DV01) are important quantities to compute accurately. The simplest way to determine the futures contract DV01 is through the current CTD DV01/conversion factor. Although simple, this calculation is inaccurate because it does not account for the chance of a CTD shift. Specifically, if markets become volatile and the chance of a CTD shift to a higher or lower duration bond arises, the CTD DV01/conversion factor can leave the futures contract user unhedged and exposed to the market. The delivery option valuation procedure can also be used to arrive at an option-adjusted duration and DV01 for the futures contract. As the futures contract follows a basket of bonds, the general convention is to base the DV01 on changes in the on-the-run bond yield for that sector, since most hedgers look to the on-the-run Treasuries on a daily basis rather than the more obscure CTD issue. If only parallel moves are assumed (i.e., no yield betas), then the point is somewhat moot as a 1-bp change in the on-the-run Treasuries would alter the other bonds by the same amount. When betas are included, it is important to have a clear reference point for the DV01.

For a futures contract, the duration is not as straightforward as that for a bond. In a plain-vanilla bond, the cash flows are known in advance, making it relatively straightforward to use time-weighted discounting to calculate the sensitivity of a bond to changes in its yield. For futures contracts, the main complicating factor is that the contracts track a basket of bonds rather than a single bond. Since the basket nature of the underlying asset complicates the issue of yields, as discussed earlier, it becomes difficult to even define DV01, which is the sensitivity of the contract to a 1-bp change in its yield. For a futures contract, DV01 is generally taken with reference to the on-the-run yield in the basket since futures often are used as hedges for on-the-run maturity instruments. For example, for a 10-year futures contract, we may be interested in the sensitivity of the contract price to changes in the 10-year on-the-run yield. Other bonds, including the CTD, can also be used as reference bonds for DV01, but the on-the-run bond is used most commonly. The most direct way to calculate the sensitivity of a futures contract to yields is to shift yields of the underlying bond basket and calculate the impact on the futures price based on the delivery option calculation described earlier. Futures contract prices do not display positive convexity as regular bonds do. In a regular bond, an increase in yields results in a smaller price decrease in magnitude than the magnitude of price increase if yields decline. In a futures contract, the basket nature of the underlying alters this dynamic. As yields rise, the CTD shifts to a higher-duration bond, which removes the positive convexity benefit of a regular bond; a decline in yields reduces the duration of the CTD bond, which also curtails the upside on the futures contract price. Thus, the duration of the futures contract increases as yields increase and declines as yields decrease. The direct method here requires setting up a futures delivery option valuation model. If that is not feasible, a simpler method to determine the futures contract risk is to use empirical data. Since we wish to calculate the change in futures price for a unit change in the on-the-run bond in the delivery basket, we can use a regression to calculate the sensitivity. Specifically, if we regress the daily change in the futures price and regress against the change in the on-the-run yield (or any yield in the basket), the beta of the regression is the DV01 we seek. Figure 11.3 shows the futures price regressed against bond1's yield in the example described earlier. The beta of the regression shows that a 1% rise in yields reduces the futures price by 14, or 0.14 for every 1-bp change in bond1's yield. This DV01 can in turn allow hedging of other fixed income instruments versus Treasuries. Note that in our simplified example, the DV01 is being calculated with respect to bond1 instead of an on-the-run yield, but the procedure is the same with any bond as a reference.

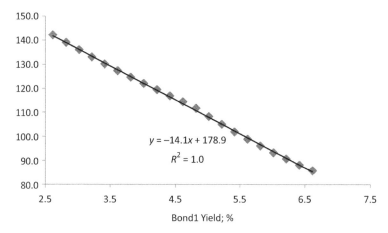

$y = -14.1x + 178.9$

$R^2 = 1.0$

Bond1 Yield; %

FIGURE 11.3 Futures Price Regressed on the Yield of a Bond in the Basket

TREASURY FUTURES ROLLS

For most participants in the Treasury futures markets, the delivery period is largely avoided and instead the contract is rolled forward into the next front month. Since Treasury futures contracts are quarterly, the term "rolling contracts" refers to selling (or buying) the current contract prior to expiry and buying (or selling) the next quarter's contract. For example, if the current date is February 15, 2010 and trader A is long 250 TYH0 contracts (March 2010 10-year contracts), the rolling procedure would involve selling 250 TYH0 contracts and simultaneously purchasing 250 TYM0 contracts (June 2010 10-year contracts). In this way, the trader has replicated the same directional position in the June contract as she had in the March one. The March contract, or the prompt one, is usually referred to as the front contract while the next contract is referred to as the back contract. Many institutions, including various portfolio managers, are not allowed to go through the delivery process even if they wish to, due to logistical or regulatory hurdles; indeed, the majority of Treasury futures holders never enter the delivery month of the contract and avoid the delivery process altogether. In such cases, the roll needs to take place before first notice day for long positions in the futures contract; otherwise there is a risk of taking delivery.

Many participants in the Treasury futures market see the roll largely as an administrative affair. For certain institutions, the roll even takes place at the same time each quarter. Such a mechanical approach to the roll can leave behind a source of return enhancement or, at the very least, cause unnecessary losses. By adjusting the timing of the roll period based on market conditions, a portfolio manager can extract more value from a futures portfolio. For larger institutions, liquidity can be a major constraint when it comes to changing the time of the rolls; there needs to be enough volume trading in the back contract to avoid paying excessive transaction costs when exiting the front contract and entering the back contract. Even for institutions with large positions and a mandate to avoid the delivery month, there is approximately a 1.5- to 2-week period prior to first notice day where there is sufficient flexibility to at least begin partial rolls. The futures roll dynamics to be discussed focus on this 1.5- to 2-week period prior to first notice date after which the open interest in the contract declines and roll dynamics fade as a major effect. Consequently, in the next sections, an *early roll* refers to starting the roll about 1.5 to 2 weeks prior to first notice date; a *late roll* refers to rolling positions a few days prior to first notice date. For traders who do venture into the delivery month, the game centers around the basis and extracting the decay of the BNOC of the CTD and other basis trading technicals.

Future rolls have a fair bit of terminology associated with them, and understanding some of the jargon is likely to help avoid confusion later on. Mathematically, the "roll" refers to the front contract price – back contract price, which is referred to as the *calendar spread*. A wider calendar spread implies a higher front contract price relative to the back contract price. At times, a widening view on the calendar spread is equivalent to having a bullish view. Conversely, a bearish view on the calendar spread is equivalent to a narrowing view, which entails the front contract price declining more than the back contract view. To make the example clearer, we consider rolling from TYH0 (March 2010 10-year contract) to the TYM0 (June 2010 10-year contract). A widening calendar roll implies TYH0 – TYM0 price spread increases, which means TYH0 outperforms TYM0. Thus, a short position in TYH0 should roll early in the roll period if the view is for the roll to widen. An investor long the TYH0 contract should hold on as long as possible, given TYH0's expected outperformance. Conversely, a narrowing calendar roll implies that the short position should roll late and the long position should roll early.

To understand the likely behavior of calendar spreads, we need to first formulate views on their main drivers. Calendar spreads are driven by:

- Yield levels
- Financing rates
- Positions
- Front contract CTD versus back contract CTD
- Relative value of each contract

Even though the roll involves moving from one quarter to the next in the same contract, yield levels do impact the calendar spreads because the DV01s of the two contracts tend to be different if they have different CTDs, each with a distinct duration. For example, suppose TYH0 and TYM0 CTDs are 2.75% Nov-16 and 4.625% Feb-17, and their DV01s are $607/bp and $666/bp (for $1 million notional). For a 1-bp move in the yield curve, then, the price of TYH0 CTD changes by $607, and the price of TYM0 CTD changes by $666. Thus, for a parallel move in the yield curve, the value of TYM0 changes by 1.1 times the value of TYH0 ($666/$607). When rolling from TYH0 to TYM0, a portfolio manager using Treasury futures to manage yield exposure or speculate on yield movements will tend to keep the DV01 of the portfolio constant; if not, the portfolio would become increasingly mismatched in duration after each roll. For example, assume a portfolio manager owns 1,000 TYH0 contracts with a DV01 of $75 per contract and wants to roll into TYM0 at $80 per contract. To maintain the same DV01 for the futures portfolio, the number of TYM0 contracts to buy is $75/$80 × 1,000 = 938. It is easily verifiable that the futures portfolio sensitivity to rates has remained the same ($75 × 1,000 = 938 × $80). Note that if the CTD of the two contracts was the same, their DV01s would be very similar; however, frequently, by entering a new quarter, some low-maturity bonds in the front contract basket drop out from the back contract basket. Due to this need to adjust the number of back contracts and broad yield effects on the calendar spread, we consider the *weighted calendar spread*, which takes into account DV01 differences. For the TYH0/TYM0 example, the weighted calendar spread would be TYH0 price – $75/$80 × TYM0 price, in contrast to the unweighted calendar spread (TYH0 price – TYM0 price). The weighted calendar spread, although used less frequently, allows us to consider the true roll impact on the portfolio by keeping DV01 constant. In practice, due to ease of transaction, rolling the position will consist of trading the unweighted calendar spread and then offsetting any extra back contract exposure. In the next sections, when we mention the calendar spread, we are referring to the weighted calendar spread; we refer to the more common calendar spread as the unweighted spread.

Once overall yield effects are taken into account by weighting the calendar spread, other effects need to be considered to determine the likely direction of the spread. When volatile, financing rates can be some of the most significant factors to consider when deciding the roll. When discussing financing rates, we refer both to general collateral Treasury repo rates and to issue-specific repos of the front and back contract CTDs. Why should financing rates affect the calendar spread? Recall that any forward price, including that of a Treasury futures contract, accounts for the carry cost between the current date and the forward date. The longer the forward date, the more a buyer of the forward contract forgoes by not having income from holding the spot asset during the interim period. In the case of the roll, the back contract undergoes greater adjustment with regard to carry than the front contract. In particular, if all Treasury repo rates decline, the carry on both the front and back contract CTDs rises. However, the increase in carry for the front and back CTDs lowers the back contract price more than the front contract price as the owner of the back contract forgoes greater amount of carry until back contract expiry than with the front contract expiry. Thus, lower financing rates richen the calendar spread; that is, they increase the front contract price *relative to* the back contract price. The reverse effect takes place if overall financing costs rise. If there is scope for volatility in financing rates, the impact of financing rates on the roll needs to be carefully managed. For example, during the early stages of the credit crunch in 2007, financing rates dropped sharply as stress conditions led investors to Treasuries and increased the expectations of numerous Federal Reserve easings. Such a drop in front-end rates led to sharply wider weighted calendar rolls in 10-year futures, for example, where weighted rolls widened orders of magnitude more than their pre-crisis movement in some cycles. For hedgers with short positions in futures contracts, the widening of the roll (i.e., richening of the front contract) meant incurring heavy losses for each day's delay during the roll cycle.

Although the most common scenario for financing rate movement is changes in the general collateral repo rate, issue-specific repo rates also rise or fall depending on a particular issue's scarcity. The issue-specific financing rate tends to be a factor especially if one of the CTD issue sizes is small, resulting in greater risk of repo fails.

After financing rates, positioning is probably the second most important factor driving calendar rolls. During cycles when the Fed is on hold and front-end rates are stable, positioning takes on increased importance for the rolls. Chapter 4 discussed the data provided by the Commodity Futures Trading Commission (CFTC) on commercial and noncommercial positions in Treasury and Eurodollar futures. Note that over time the CFTC has added further categories to its breakdown of market participant types, but the discussion below still applies. For the rolls, commercial positions tend to be of more interest for two reasons:

1. Commercial positions tend to be the bulk of the outstanding contracts for Treasury futures.
2. More importantly, many commercial accounts are mandated to roll futures contracts prior to delivery month. This is because as hedgers, they use the futures contracts to offset risk and generally are not set up logistically or legally to participate in the delivery process.

Due to these common mandates to roll prior to delivery month and liquidity constraints to rolling over two weeks prior to delivery, many commercial accounts have a small window for rolling. The restricted window for commercials provides important insight into the likely direction of the roll. For example, suppose commercial accounts are long futures in large size in the bond contract. We know that these longs have to roll sometime in the two-week period prior to delivery month. As these longs roll, *they sell the front contract and purchase the back contract*, which drives the weighted calendar spread narrower (i.e., cheapening of the front versus the back). For long positions in the contract, then, rolling early is advisable to avoid the risk of losing money as the front cheapens. The converse is true if commercial accounts are net short. Noncommercial accounts can affect the roll as well but these effects are more difficult to pinpoint since such accounts have the flexibility to wait and roll during the delivery month or even participate in the delivery process. Finally, the CFTC breakdown between commercial and noncommercial accounts is not a perfect one; nonetheless, monitoring positioning is a key exercise in deciphering the Treasury roll.

If the CTD securities of the front and back contracts are different, the spread between the CTD issues can affect the roll as well. This spread is also referred to as the CTD curve, and mathematically it represents back CTD bond yield minus front CTD bond yield. A steepening of the CTD curve implies the back CTD yield rises more than the front CTD yield, and vice versa for a flattening. A steepening of the CTD curve, all else being equal, would widen the calendar spread as a higher back CTD bond yield equates to a lower back CTD bond price and thus a lower back contract futures price. If the CTD curve is expected to flatten, however, the calendar spread can be expected to narrow, barring other effects. Therefore, if the CTD curve appears sharply dislocated, any reversion to the normal level can have implications for the calendar spread itself. Care needs to be taken for two reasons when evaluating the impact of this factor.

First, because in most cycles the successive CTDs tend to be bonds very near each other in maturity, there generally needs to be a fairly large dislocation in the CTD curve for it to manifest itself in the calendar spread in a material way.

Second, often, dislocations in the CTD curve occur *because of* futures roll dynamics rather than because of any effects from the bond market. Furthermore, even if the CTD curve is dislocated due to effects related specifically to the Treasury bond market, the reversion needs to take place in the two-week period of the roll for it to have a material impact on the calendar spread. Even if reversion back to the norm may be expected, the timing of such reversion is generally difficult to pinpoint. In sum, the CTD curve should be seen as a marginal factor for evaluating the roll rather than a primary driver.

Finally, a factor often cited but in general of limited value is the relative value difference between the front and back contract. By *relative value*, we mean each contract's richness or cheapness (i.e., the difference between the trader's estimation of the BNOC versus the market's). As with the CTD curve, the relative value difference between the contracts can be a marginal factor at times. Often, relative value differences can persist for structural reasons well beyond the short roll window time period. For example, during 2008, large mispricings between the front and back contracts persisted in 10-year futures well into the delivery month. These mispricings persisted because of a structural need to use the contracts as hedges by a wide range of market participants during a time when other markets were difficult to access. The rolling activity of these hedgers led to persistent mispricings of the back versus front contract that made relative value an unreliable factor in taking a view on the roll.

SUMMARY

As the concepts in this chapter show, many details about Treasury futures are not apparent at a cursory glance. The fact that a basket of bonds, rather than a single bond, underlies each contract presents the seller of the futures contract with a range of options. By trading Treasury futures and the underlying Treasury bonds, some of the value in these delivery options can be captured. However, with the Treasury basis, assumptions can be very dangerous, and small details, if left unmonitored, can lead to large losses. Some of these complexities regarding the futures contract also need to be accounted for when rolling the contract from one quarter to the next. It is important to keep in mind that although rolling a contract may seem like a mundane exercise, it can be a valuable source of return for a portfolio manager.

CHAPTER 12

Conditional
Trades

I n previous chapters we went through the thought process for taking views on the curve as well as swap spreads. For all these quantities, numerous factors drive them and at different times, the magnitudes of the factors vary, adding to the difficulty in trading. One factor common in both the curve and spreads is the level of interest rates, with both being directional to interest rates at times. This link to the level of rates can be in either direction depending on the environment; at times, for example, the curve may flatten as interest rates rise, but other times the curve may steepen with similar yield moves. Swap spreads can display similar directionality with regard to interest rates, especially during mortgage duration extension episodes. This chapter considers a common class of trades in the fixed income markets known as conditional trades, which combine concepts from the underlying rates and options market to express views on the directionality of either spreads or curves with rates.

As we mentioned earlier, one of the keys to trading rates is to structure trades that take as specific a view as possible and hedge out remaining, unwanted risks. Doing this reduces the possibility of unforeseen effects influencing profit and loss (P/L); given the multitude of factors that drive interest rates, an unexpected factor is never far away. Conditional trades use options to take views on the curve or swap spreads only in certain interest rate scenarios and expire worthless in others. Conditional trades are a mixture of underlying rates concepts and options and utilize details of both to take a specific view. Therefore, a thorough knowledge of both rates market trades and options is required to understand this chapter.

319

CONDITIONAL CURVE TRADES

Due to its nature as an options trade that takes a view on the underlying, the setup of a conditional trade can be intricate and requires care. Without proper hedge ratios, the trade may be left unhedged and expose the investor to unexpected market movements. As mentioned, there are two basic categories of conditional trades in rate space: conditional curve or butterfly trades and conditional spread trades. We consider examples of both conditional curve and spread trades since each type has its own nuances when it comes to weighting the trade. For conditional trades on the yield curve—that is, curve or butterfly—the underlying premise for both is similar, although the butterfly trade adds a further layer of complexity.

Often in fixed income markets, curve trades can become highly directional with yield movements. This tends to happen when one end of the curve is anchored or when a certain set of flows that affect yields are likely to be focused on a specific part of the curve. The most likely reason for an anchored part of the curve is a Fed firmly on hold, which reduces chances of short-end rates, such as 2-year Treasury yields, moving much; in these cases, if yields do rise, the intermediate-sector yields, such as 5-year and 10-year rates, are likely to lead the way. One way this can happen is if mortgage servicer hedging flows enter the market in size in intermediate rates, driving up both yields and the curve. Figure 12.1 shows this phenomenon empirically from the summer of 2003, when the curve and yields rose in tandem as the Fed was on hold with low rates, keeping the front end anchored, while mortgage hedging drove both 10-year rates and the 2s10s

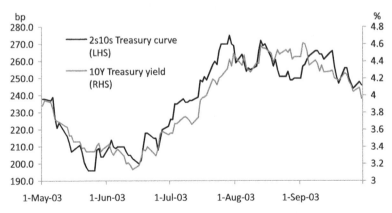

FIGURE 12.1 2s10s Treasury Curve and 10-Year Treasury Yield during Mortgage Extension in 2003
Source: Board of Governors of the Federal Reserve.

curve along with it. For a numerical example, consider an investor who believes the 2s/10s swap curve will steepen in a selloff; in other words, if rates rise overall, the 10-year rate will rise faster than the 2-year rate. One possibility is to initiate a standard curve trade (i.e., pay in 10-year swaps and receive in 2-year swaps with duration neutral weights). However, this outright trade leaves the investor exposed to scenarios where interest rates decline. For example, when it comes to mortgage hedging, if rates fall, mortgage hedgers may instead receive in swaps and generally receive more in intermediate maturities, such as 10 years, due to the duration characteristics of mortgages. This reverse situation may indeed leave the curve flatter in a decline in rates and cause the investor losses. As explained previously, one of the ways to improve risk-adjusted return in trading is to take views more specifically based on the processes driving the markets. In this case, the investor's view on the curve is dependent on the scenario where rates rise overall, given the driving factors behind mortgage hedging.

To take the view that the curve will steepen in a selloff, the investor can use a conditional curve steepener using payer swaptions. To initiate this trade, we would sell payer swaptions on 2-year swaps and buy payer swaptions on 10-year rates. The sale of the payer swaption on 2-year rates brings in a premium, which can be then used to finance the purchase of the 10-year swaption. Both swaptions should have the same expiry date, and the notionals should be duration weighted; we explain the choices of trade characteristics later. Before the details, it is important to understand the motivations behind selling the 2-year payer and buying the 10-year payer. Since both legs are payer swaptions, a decline in rates leaves both options worthless at expiry, thus giving meaning to the "conditional" nature of the trade. If instead rates have risen, the options would be exercised, leaving the investor short a payer swap in 2-year swaps and long a payer position in 10-year swaps. Thus, the purchase of the 10-year payer results in positive P/L at expiry if rates rise. For the sold payer swaption on 2-year swaps, a rise in rates results in negative P/L. If we choose the notionals correctly, *we would want to have zero P/L if both 2-year and 10-year rates rise by an equal amount.* This is because we want to make money if the curve steepens and, of course, if both rates rise an equal amount, there is no change in the curve steepness; therefore, such a scenario should produce no P/L. If, however, 10-year rates rise more than 2-year rates, the purchased payer swaption on 10-year rates makes more money than the loss of P/L on the sold payer swaption on the 2-year rate. Note that if the reverse happens—if 10-year rates rise less than 2-year rates, or, in other words, the curve flattens in a rate increase—the trade loses money.

This line of reasoning gives an idea of why the payer swaption trade results in conditional exposure to curve steepening. Now we can consider the numerous details that go into setting up such a trade. The three main details to consider are swaption expiry, swaption notionals, and swaption strikes. The first thing to do is to decide on the expiry of the swaptions. The main guiding factor here is that conditional trades are almost always set up with eventual exercise of the swaptions in mind. The goal is that the options will be exercised (the purchased option exercised by us and the sold option exercised by the buyer) if they are in the money. For this reason, most conditional trades are initiated with less than three months to expiry since, in the worst case, such a trade would be held for three months. Investors with longer trade horizons can use longer expiries, but this is rare since curve directionality with yields can be quite volatile. It is certainly possible that the conditional trade may be in the money before expiry and one can indeed sell the options to take profits, but, in general, that should not be the main goal of the trade as it may not retain its conditional nature in the meantime. For example, in our example of the sale of 2-year payer swaption and purchase of 10-year payer swaption, rates may decline prior to expiry. If rates decline prior to expiry, the investor may have negative P/L as the premia of the swaptions decline relative to the at-the-money (ATM) levels. The key point to remember is that the options expire worthless *at expiry* if rates decline, but in the meantime, one can be exposed to changes in time value of money stemming from rate changes or even changes in volatility prior to expiry (see Chapter 10). Therefore, we would prefer an expiry for the conditional trade for a period that we can be sure to hold the trade, depending on trading horizon and limitations of funding, which ends up being one to three months for most investors.

The second detail regarding a conditional trade is deciding how much notional to put on each leg. Once again, the main thing to remember here is that we want to be exercised in a 2s/10s steepener at expiry, assuming the options are in the money. Recall from Chapter 2 that a trade on the 2s/10s curve relies on taking a view on the spread between 10-year yields and 2-year yields, which means that the notionals should be duration adjusted. In particular, the total dollar value of one basis point (DV01) of the 2-year leg should be equal to the total DV01 on the 10-year. Therefore, the weightings of the option notionals should also be DV01 weighted since if we exercise the trades, we enter into a DV01 neutral curve. For example, suppose the DV01 of the 10-year swap is $850. If we buy $100 million of the payer swaption in 10-year swaps, we have $85,000 of DV01 per basis point (bp) on the 10-year swap position if it gets exercised. Now, if the 2-year swap has a DV01 of $190 per million per bp, we would need $447.3 million notional ($85,000/$190) of options on the 2-year swap so that, at expiry, an exercise would leave us entered into a DV01 neutral curve trade. The DV01 neutrality, as explained earlier, keeps us in "yield space" and ensures that equal yield moves in 2-year and 10-year swaps leave us with zero profit at expiry, as described in the condition above.

Before we get to the final detail about choosing the strikes for the two options, we need to discuss premium neutrality. We mentioned earlier that the sale of the payer swaption in the 2-year sector is meant to pay for the sale of the swaption in the 10-year sector. However, at times, the DV01 neutral ratio of swaptions sold in 2-year swaps and bought in 10-year swaps may leave some out-of-pocket premium to be paid. At other times, a premium may be paid to the investor instead if 10-year swaptions are trading cheaper than 2-year swaptions. A premium-neutral trade, as might be guessed, is one in which the premium collected from selling the swaption and the cost of the swaption purchased is equal. For the most part, we will not complain if premium is being handed to us, but when conditional trades require a premium to be paid, strikes may need to be adjusted to keep the trade premium neutral so we do not have to pay out cash at inception to enter the trade. There is a way to deduce whether a particular conditional trade is likely to be premium neutral or have an intake or payout of premium. This is done using the implied volatilities of the options used in the curve trade. If the option being bought has a higher implied volatility than the option being sold, the conditional trade will require a net premium payment at inception. If the implied volatility of the option being sold is higher, the conditional trade will pay out a premium at inception. This link between implied volatility and premium neutrality stems from the implied volatility being a proxy for price.

Many conditional trades are done with both swaptions at-the-money-forward (ATMF) at inception. When one makes a premium-neutral trade, the term used is doing the trade "at the forwards." To see why, consider the example of the 2-year/10-year conditional trade. Suppose the ATMF rate for the 2-year swap is 1.2% and the 10-year ATMF rate is 3.70% for 3-month swaptions. The conditional trade is attempting to express a widening view of the forward curve here (i.e., larger rise in 10-year rate versus 2-year rate) from a current level of 2.5% (3.7% − 1.2%). If we enter a conditional trade at expiry, we initiate a 2-year swap struck at 1.2% and 10-year swap at 3.70%. If the trade had no output or input of premium, the strikes do not need an adjustment and so, at expiry, we start the swap trade at exactly where forwards were today; hence the term "at the forwards." However, if the trade requires an input of money at inception, then the strikes need to be adjusted until the trade is premium neutral. The ATMF strikes discussed are 1.20% and 3.70%, which implies a 2s/10s curve of 150 bps. If the trade is not premium neutral, we can keep the 2-year strike still at 1.20% but the 10-year strike can be moved to make the trade premium neutral. Recall that we are selling the 2-year payer swaption and buying the 10-year payer swaption. If the trade was net positive premium intake at inception, the 10-year strike can be lowered to increase its premium until the trade is premium neutral (payer swaption implies lower strike = higher premium). If the trade was net premium payout at inception, the 10-year strike can be increased to lower the buy premium (payer swaption implies higher strike = lower premium). To illustrate with a simple example using convenient rather than accurate numbers, suppose that the 6M × 2Y swaption has a premium of 20 bps and the 6M × 10Y has premium of 90 bps, and also assume that the DV01 neutral ratio is 4.5 between the two. Here, selling 4.5x the quantity on 6M × 2Y swaption and buying the 6M × 10Y swaption is premium neutral. Now suppose the 6M × 10Y premium is 100 bps. The trader is now paying 10 bps in premium for the conditional trade; to match the premium, the strike on the 6M 10Y can be moved to, say, 3.80%. Here, the implied curve is 3.80% – 1.20% at expiry, which is 10 bps steeper than the ATMF curve; in other words, it is 10 bps "worse than forwards" since we are initiating steepeners. If the strike on the 6M × 10Y was increased 20 bps, then the trade would be 20 bps worse than forwards since we are now initiating a steepener at a level steeper than the current market. In general, if a trade requires payment of up-front premium, it is worse than forwards, while a trade receiving an up-front premium is better than forwards. This is why premium neutrality or premium receipt up front is attractive since it means the trade is at or better than forwards. If a trade is being done worse than forwards, then almost always just the outright trade should be done even if the option trade appears safer.

CONDITIONAL SPREAD TRADES

Conditional trades do not have to be limited to the curve. Swap spread trades can also be expressed in a conditional manner since both the Treasury futures market and swaps have liquid options markets. Conditional spread trades allow an investor to express a spread widening or narrowing view *only in the case of a yield decline or yield increase*. The concept is similar to the conditional curve trade, where a steepening or flattening view is taken only if the underlying yields decline or increase. Why express conditional spread views? One example is to take advantage of anticipated mortgage market hedging. If yields rise, hedging activity of mortgages tends to lead to paying in swaps rather than Treasuries, causing swap spreads to generally widen, as described in Chapter 9. This is certainly no hard-and-fast rule, but if an investor anticipates that the mortgage factor is likely to dominate swap spreads in the near term, a conditional view may be more appropriate than an outright one. In case of spread widening driven by the mortgage market, for example, a decline in yields may lead swap spreads to narrow or stay unchanged. Expressing a conditional view allows the trader to reduce risks from extraneous factors.

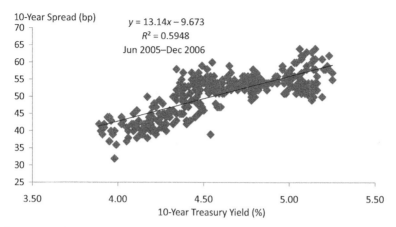

FIGURE 12.2 10-Year Swap Spread Regressed against the 10-Year Treasury Yield during 2005–2006
Source: Board of Governors of the Federal Reserve.

Wider swap spreads do not necessarily coincide with higher yields. One example of a situation where swap spreads may narrow instead of widen during a yield increase is if mortgage portfolios and servicers have few hedging needs but heavy Treasury supply raises Treasury yields. Other situations when swap spreads narrow as yields rise are when the swap spreads are retracing back narrower after periods of flight to quality. As the safety demand recedes, investors head back to riskier assets, causing liquid fixed income rates to rise and swap spreads to narrow. Figures 12.2 and 12.3 show the 10-year swap spread regressed against the 10-year

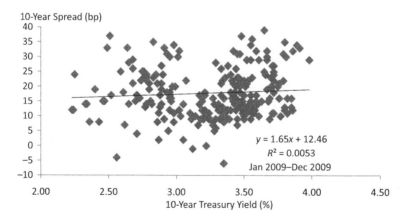

FIGURE 12.3 10-Year Swap Spread Regressed against the 10-Year Treasury Yield during 2009
Source: Board of Governors of the Federal Reserve.

Treasury yield during two distinct periods, one in 2005 to 2006 and the other in 2009. In the more stable markets of 2006, swap spreads indeed tended to widen as yields rose. At times, the swap spread widens as interest rates rise driven by mortgage hedging flows, but in 2009, as the market was recovering from the 2008 credit crunch, yields rose as risk appetite returned and swap spreads narrowed as bank credit concerns receded. Initiating conditional wideners or narrowers therefore requires careful evaluation of the factors likely to drive swap spreads, including tracking aggregate duration exposure of servicers and mortgage portfolios.

To take advantage of widening or narrowing swap spreads in certain yield movement scenarios, a conditional swap spread trade relies on using payer/receiver swaptions and Treasury futures option puts/calls. For a conditional spread widener in a rising yield environment, the investor would buy a payer swaption and sell a duration-matched amount of Treasury futures puts to pay for the trade. We discuss the details of the trade setup later; for now, the key point is to understand why these combinations of trades lead to a conditional spread exposure. When a trader buys a payer swaption and sells a duration-matched amount of Treasury futures puts, any decline in yields will leave both options worthless at expiry. This way, the trader is only exposed to scenarios where yields in the maturity sector of the options rise. Next, since a payer swaption is purchased and a Treasury put is sold, the trade will be profitable if the payer swaption produces more profit than the loss on selling the Treasury put—that is, the swap rate underlying the swaption needs to rise *more than* the Treasury yield underlying the futures contract. Thus, to make money, we need the swap spread to widen (or in other words, swap rate rises more than the Treasury rate) if interest rates increase. If instead swap spreads narrowed when interest rates rose, the swap spread would rise less than the corresponding Treasury rate, and the loss on the Treasury put sale would outweigh the gain on the payer swaption purchase.

A spread widener is just one of the various combinations of conditional trades that can be initiated. If a trader's view was that swap spreads were likely to narrow as yields fell, the trade to express this view would be to buy a receiver swaption and sell a Treasury futures call. Given the receiver and call legs, if interest rates increased, both options would expire worthless, leaving no exposure to the trader. If yields decreased, a greater decline in the swap rate relative to the corresponding Treasury rate would lead to a gain (i.e., spread narrowing in a yield decline). The setup here should be familiar from the conditional curve trade setup, but instead of two points on the swap maturity curve, here the two legs are a swap and Treasury leg on the same maturity point.

Setting up the conditional spread trade requires carefully choosing hedge ratios between the Treasury futures option and swaption. As with conditional curve trades, we choose option notionals on both legs such that the trade is DV01 neutral if the options are exercised. The setup of the trade is somewhat more involved than the curve trade, mainly due to differing units in the futures and swap markets as well as the complications stemming from futures duration. Suppose we take the example of a FVZ9 contract (5-year Treasury futures expiring in December 2009) with a futures DV01 of \$49/contract per 1bp move in the on-the-run 5-year contract (see Chapter 11 for more details). The example will set up a puts-payers trade, which is a trade using a put option and a payer swaption. Such a trade attempts to provide exposure to widening of swap spreads only when yields rise. If yields decline, the trade is supposed to expire worthless.

A base amount of FVZ9 is chosen, such as 1,000 contracts. The total DV01 of the FVZ9 contract is \$49,000. Assume the current price of the contract is 119-29 and the strike of the put option is 120. The payer swaption needs to be chosen to match the characteristics of the futures contract. Suppose the cheapest-to-deliver (CTD) bond of the contract is 2.25% Feb-14, with a maturity of February 15, 2014. The last delivery date of the contract is January 4, 2010. The matched swap in this case is a forward starting swap with forward start of January 4, 2010 and maturity of February 15, 2014. The FVZ9 put option expires prior to the delivery month, say November 20, 2009. In that case, the matched payer swaption has an expiry of November 20, 2009, but the underlying swap here is 1/4/2010 × 2/14/2014. Notice that here the underlying swap is not a spot-starting one at expiry but instead a forward-starting one, which is similar to the midcurve structure discussed in Chapter 10. Given the short time difference between expiry and the forward start date, there is not much transaction cost penalty. Suppose the payer swaption has a DV01 of \$460/million. Then the payer swaption notional required is \$49,000/\$460 = \$106.5 million.

Once the matched payer is chosen and the DV01-neutral notional is calculated, as with the conditional curve trade, the matched strike needs to be found. Unlike the conditional curve case, the matched strike here is a more difficult proposition since Treasury futures do not have continuous strikes, as do swaptions. The strike on the swaption should be an equivalent distance from the ATM strike in yield terms as the Treasury futures put is from its ATM in price terms. In the example, the futures put is 3/32 out of the money, or 0.09375% in price terms. To convert to yield terms, the price bps need to be divided by the duration of the futures contract. The duration here is 4.9 years (technically, a forward duration should be used, but we use spot duration as an approximation). Therefore, in yield terms, the difference is 0.09375%/4.9 = 0.019%, or 1.9 bps. Thus, the payer swaption needs to be 1.9 bps out of the money. If the ATM payer swaption strike is 2.5%, the strike of the payer will be approximately 2.52%. After the strikes have been matched, the net premium can be calculated by calculating the total premium of the Treasury and swaption legs. If the premium of the FVZ9 option is 12 ticks, for example, the total premium is 12 × 15.625 × 1,000, since each option tick is 1/64 and therefore equals $15.625 in dollar terms.

Premium neutrality in the conditional spread trade encompasses a similar concept to that in the conditional curve trade. Here also, if the implied volatility of the payer swaption being bought is higher than that of the Treasury futures option, the trade has a net premium payout; in the reverse case, there is a net premium intake. The implied forward swap spread of the trade is the difference between the strike of the swaption and Treasury futures option (in yield terms). As with the conditional curve trade, the trade is done at a spread level worse than forwards if there is a premium payout at inception and better than forwards if there is a premium intake at inception.

SUMMARY

As seen from the examples, conditional trades combine concepts from both options and the underlying markets to create trades that take specific views in more efficient ways. Conditional trades are one of many possible ways to combine the instruments and concepts discussed in this book to take views on rates in more intelligent ways than just outright buying and selling Treasuries. At times, the outright trade may be the best one, but many times controlling for extraneous risk factors that do not form part of the view results in higher risk-adjusted returns. It is important for investors to be on the lookout for interesting ways to structure trades that are efficient from a carry, relative value, or risk perspective while still maintaining the original intended view of the trade.

References

Bank of Japan. www.boj.or.jp/en.

Bloomberg L.P. Bloomberg Database. New York.

Board of Governors of the Federal Reserve System. *The Federal Reserve System: Purposes and Functions.* Washington, DC: Federal Reserve Staff Publication Committee, 2005.

Burghardt, Galen. *The Eurodollar Futures and Options Handbook.* New York: McGraw-Hill, 2003.

Carnes, Stansbury W., and Stephen D. Slifer. *The Atlas of Economic Indicators.* New York: HarperCollins, 1991.

"Federal Reserve." Board of Governors of the Federal Reserve System. www.federalreserve.gov.

Garbade, Kenneth D., and Jeffrey F. Ingber. "The Treasury Auction Process: Objectives, Structure, and Recent Adaptations," *Current Issues in Economics and Finance: Federal Reserve Bank of New York* 11, no. 2 (February 2005), www.newyorkfed.org/research/current_issues.

Härdle, Wolfgang, and Simar Leopold. *Applied Multivariate Statistical Analysis.* Berlin: Springer Science, 2003.

Hull, John C. *Options, Futures, and Other Derivatives.* Upper Saddle River, NJ: Prentice Hall, 2006.

Securities Industry and Financial Markets Association. www.sifma.org.

"St. Louis Fed: Economic Research." Federal Reserve Bank of St. Louis. http://research.stlouisfed.org.

U.S. Bureau of Economic Analysis (BEA). www.bea.gov.

U.S. Commodities Futures Trading Commission. CFTC Large Trader Reporting Program. www.cftc.gov/MarketReports/CommitmentsofTraders/HistoricalCompressed/index.htm.

About the Author

Siddhartha Jha graduated from Harvard University with a bachelor's degree in applied mathematics and economics and a master's degree in statistics. He worked at a top-tier investment bank in fixed income strategy, covering a range of markets, including municipal bonds, Treasury bonds, swaps, futures, and options. Mr. Jha's focus was on analyzing markets and finding trade ideas for institutional clients across the financial industry with an emphasis on intuitive explanations rather than equations. Mr. Jha also presented in numerous client teaching seminars and taught parts of the bank's incoming analyst and associate fixed income training programs. He currently works as a senior analyst at a hedge fund.

About the Web Site

This book includes a companion web site, which can be found at www.wiley.com/go/jhainterestrate.

The web site is intended to provide further details on the topics discussed in the book. It allows readers to view step-by-step calculations of concepts introduced in the book relating to cash and derivatives products in the rates markets.

Index

A

Agency-backed mortgages, 73–74
Agency bonds
  Agency bullets, 78
  Agency callables, 79, 276, 281
Agency debt
  Fed ownership, 152
  market description, 77–79
Agricultural futures, 86
Alpha, 7
Asset liability management,
  156–157
At-the-money option
  definition, 247
  delta of, 258
  gamma of, 260, 262
  theta of, 262–263
  vega of, 265
Average, 3

B

Backtesting, 16–17
Banking system, 60–61, 118, 133,
  230
Bank run, 62
Banks
  banking system. *See* Banking
    system
  crisis in unsecured lending, 103
  fixed income demand, 154–155
  interbank market, 90–92
  issuance of callables, 292–293

regulation, 133
  Treasury demand, 133, 154
Base symbol (futures), 88–89
Basis net of carry (BNOC),
  100–101, 209–210, 299–300,
  306
Basis point, 21–22
Basis point value (BPV), 34
Basis swaps
  constant maturity, 119–120
  cross-currency, 119
  description, 117
  fed funds, 117–118
  one-month/three-month, 119
  SIFMA/LIBOR, 120–123
  three-month/six-month, 119
Bear flattener, 53–54
Bear steepener, 53–54
Benchmark maturity
  bid/offer, 45
  risk-free rate, 70
  in Treasury auctions, 72
  in Treasury futures, 95
  versus swaps, 114
Bermudan options, 248, 268, 283
Beta
  interpretation, 7–8
  partial, 9
  regression, 7–11
Bid/offer, 45, 112, 290
Bills (Treasuries), 68
Black model, 254–257

Black-Scholes model, 252–254
BMA/LIBOR swaps. *See*
    SIFMA/LIBOR swaps
BNOC. *See* Basis net of carry
    (BNOC)
Bond futures. *See* Treasury futures
Bonds
    basics, 19–22
    convexity. *See* Convexity
    credit risk. *See* Credit risk
    duration. *See* Duration
    face value, 21
    inflation risk. *See* Inflation risk
    interest rate risk. *See* Interest
        rate risk
    liquidity risk. *See* Liquidity risk
    Macaulay duration, 34–35
    modified duration. *See* Duration
    notional, 20
    pricing, 28–32
    regulatory risk. *See* Regulatory
        risk
    types of risks, 22–27
    yield to maturity, 30–31
Bootstrapping. *See* Swaps
BPV. *See* Basis point value (BPV)
Breakeven
    in bond P/L, 52
    in options, 269
    in TIPS, 72
Brownian motion, 15
Budget deficit
    cyclical deficit, 141–143, 232
    structural deficit, 129–130,
        141–143, 232–233
Bull flattener, 53–54
Bull steepener, 53–54
Bureau of Labor Statistics, 160
Butterfly trade
    basic structure, 55–56
    curve and level neutral, 190
    relative value example, 185–189

C
C-STRIPS. *See* Coupon STRIPS
    (C-STRIPS)
Callable bonds
    Agencies. *See* Agency bonds
    municipals, 82
Capacity utilization, 162
Caplets, 276–278
Caps
    dealer hedging, 284
    structure, 276–279
    versus swaptions, 297–298
Carry
    basic concept, 45–47
    pitfalls, 178–181
    trades, 173–175
    trade setup, 175–178
Carry-efficient trades, 182–183
Carry-to-volatility ratio, 176–179
Carry trades
    motivation, 173–175
    pitfalls, 178–180
    setup, 175–178
Cash-settled futures, 89–90
Census Bureau, 163
CFTC. *See* Commodity Futures
    Trading Commission (CFTC)
Chained dollars, 163
Cheapest to deliver (CTD)
    calculation, 98–101
    convergence to futures price,
        300
    definition, 97–98
    setting up conditional spread
        trade, 327
Chicago Mercantile Exchange
    (CME), 88, 279
Clearinghouse
    definition, 87
    for swaps, 115
CME. *See* Chicago Mercantile
    Exchange (CME)

CMS swap. *See* Constant maturity swap (CMS)
Commercial accounts
description, 104
futures rolls, 317
Commodity Futures Trading Commission (CFTC), 104, 316–317
Competitive bid, 69
Conditional trades
conditional curve trade, 320–324
conditional spread trade, 324–328
important past periods, 320, 325
motivation, 319
Constant maturity swap (CMS), 119–120, 277
Consumer price index (CPI)
data release, 162
use with inflation swaps, 123
use with TIPS, 72
Consumption
causing inflation, 129–131
in emerging markets, 149–151
future consumption, 27
gross domestic product component, 164
housing market, 164
Conversion factor
definition, 97
delivery option value calculation, 303, 310
example, 98–99
need for, 98
rule of thumb DV01, 214–215, 311
use in calculating gross basis, 100
Convexity
bias, 92–93
bonds, 37–41
effect on bond P/L, 40
example from stocks, 38
formula, 41
hedging. *See* Convexity hedging
interest rate swaps, 111–112
Convexity bias, 92–93
Convexity hedging
example, 220–221
mortgages, 218–222
servicer, 222–223
using options, 282
Core CPI
definition, 163
Fed policy, 165
Core PCE, 163
Corporate bonds
credit risk, 24
hedging, 211–214
interest rate risk, 23
investment grade, 80
issuance. *See* Corporate supply
market description, 79–81
mutual funds, 153
percentage of fixed/floating rate, 81
ratings, 80
risk breakdown, 201
Corporate supply
drivers, 147
effect on fixed income markets, 146
effect on swap spreads, 235, 237–238
effect on yields, 158, 168
long-end supply, 156
Correlation
between forward rates, 297
description, 11
effect on Sharpe ratio, 16
formula, 11
in carry-efficient trades, 182
in carry trades, 181
regression goodness-of-fit, 11
stationary variables, 13

Counterparty risk
  description, 87, 115
  with clearinghouse, 115
  in futures market, 87
  with OTC markets, 115
Coupon, 21
Coupon STRIPS (C-STRIPS),
  71
Coupon switches, 193–194
CPI. *See* Consumer Price Index
  (CPI)
Credit risk
  Agencies, 79
  banks, 205
  debt/GDP ratio, 144
  description of bond credit risk,
    23–24
  issue-specific, 201
  municipals, 84
  U.S. government, 24
Cross-currency basis swap, 119
Crowded trades
  behavior, 181
  example, 105
CTD. *See* Cheapest to deliver
  (CTD)
CTD spread, 317–318
Curve trade, 53–55

D
Deliverable basket, 95–96
Delivery option value
  calculation, 310–311
  definition, 100–101
  description, 300–304
Delivery specifications, 95–96
Delta
  call versus put, 267
  hedging. *See* Delta hedging
  option risk parameter, 258–259
Delta hedging
  assumptions, 287–288
  constant volatility, 287

definition, 270
  example, 270–273
  frequency, 274
  link to liquidity, 289–290
  path dependency, 288
  price smoothness, 287
  procedure, 272–273
Dice, 4, 249–250
Discounting, 27–28, 252
Dollar value of '01 (DV01)
  bonds, 34
  swaps, 111
  swap spreads, 228
Drawdown, 16–17
Durable goods, 162, 164
Durable goods orders, 162
Duration
  bonds, 34–37
  Macaulay, 34–35
  modified, 35
  Treasury futures option
    adjusted, 311–312
  Treasury futures rule of thumb,
    214–215
  swaps, 111–112
Dutch auction, 69
DV01. *See* Dollar value of '01
  (DV01)
Dynamic hedging, 221–222, 282

E
Effective federal funds rate
  dislocation from federal funds
    rate, 103
  Federal Reserve, 65
  fed funds basis swaps, 117–118
  fed funds futures, 101
Embedded options, 280–282
Empirical duration, 311–312
Establishment survey, 159–160
Eurodollar bundles
  definition, 94
  hedging with, 214

Eurodollar futures
  basics, 89–90
  bundles. *See* Eurodollar bundles
  codes, 88–89
  convexity/financing bias,
    92–93
  creating longer-dated assets
    with, 93–94
  example, 91
  fair value, 92
  option. *See* Eurodollar futures
    option
  packs, 94
  strip. *See* Eurodollar strip
Eurodollar futures option
  comparison with caps/floors,
    278
  delta hedging example, 288
  description, 278–279
  midcurves, 278–279
Eurodollar packs, 94
Eurodollar strip
  definition, 93–94
  hedging with, 210
  strip rate, 93
Excess reserve rate, 64, 66, 103
Excess reserves
  definition, 64
  interest rate, 64, 66, 103
  trading by banks, 101
Exchange (futures), 86, 88
Existing Home Sales, 164
Exotic securities
  definition, 170, 238
  hedging. *See* Exotics hedging
Exotics hedging
  description, 238
  effect on swap spreads,
    238–239
  effect on yields, 158, 170–171
Expectations hypothesis, 34
Expected value, 3–5, 249–251
Explicit guarantee, 144–145

F
Federal funds basis swap, 117–118
Federal funds futures
  description, 101–103
  forecasting front-end yields,
    135–136
  futures codes, 89
  implied Fed probability, 102
  term premium, 103
  trading banking crises, 103–104
  underlying, 101
Federal funds rate. *See* Effective
  federal funds rate
Federal funds target rate
  description, 65–66
  link to short-end rates, 12
Federal Open Market Committee
  (FOMC), 63, 165
Federal Reserve
  functions, 63–66
  history, 61–63
  mandate, 63–64
  purpose, 61–63
  structure, 62–63
  tools available, 64–65
Fed speak, 165–166
Financing bias. *See* Convexity bias
Financing rate. *See* On-the-run
  Treasury
Flattener, 53–54
Flight to quality
  breakdown of hedging, 205
  effect on swap spreads, 231, 240,
    325
  effect on Treasury futures rolls,
    308
  mutual fund ownership, 153
  repo market, 44
  short-term yield driver, 158,
    166–168
Floating rate bonds
  definition, 23
  link to swaps, 109

Floor, 276–280
FOMC. *See* Federal Open Market
    Committee (FOMC)
Foreigner holdings, 148–151
Forward rate, 47–51
Forward rate agreement (FRA), 91,
    93
Forward trade, 85
Forward volatility, 285
FRA. *See* Forward rate agreement
    (FRA)
Futures
    asset swaps, 241–243
    basic principles, 85–89
    basis. *See* Treasury futures basis
    Eurodollar futures. *See*
        Eurodollar futures
    Treasury futures. *See* Treasury
        futures

G
Gamma
    calls versus puts, 268
    link to bond convexity, 262
    option risk parameter, 259–262
Government spending
    components of GDP, 159
    deficit. *See* Budget deficit
    effect on interest rates, 129–130

H
Hedge ratio, 210–213
Hedging
    breakdown in, 204–205
    calculating hedge ratio, 210–213
    choices, 203
    convexity hedging, 218–223
    mortgages, 169–170
    principles, 198–202
    swaps versus Treasuries,
        205–206
    with yield betas, 215–218
High-yield bonds, 80

Households
    employment surveys, 159–160
    fixed income demand, 157
    as part of leverage cycle, 127,
        130–131
Household survey, 159–160
Housing starts, 164
Humphrey Hawkins, 166

I
Implicit guarantee
    description, 74
    implications for Agencies,
        78–79
Implied forward yield,
    calculating, 99
    futures asset swaps, 242
Implied repo, 99–100
Implied volatility
    across strikes, 270
    calculation, 253–254
    link to option P/L, 269
    quotation, 256–257
    sensitivity of option price to,
        264–266
    spreads, 294–297
    view on implied volatility,
        286–287
Industrial production (IP)
    economic data, 161–163
    link to yields, 127
Inflation
    data releases, 162–163
    expectations, 126–127, 128–130
    interplay with growth, 129–130,
        134–135
    link with Federal Reserve, 152
    link to money supply, 65
    link to TIPS. *See* Inflation risk
    risk associated with bonds. *See*
        Inflation risk
    swaps, 123–124

Inflation risk
    definition, 22, 24–25
    link to inflation swaps, 123
    link to TIPS, 71–72
Inflation swaps, 123–124
Institute for Supply Management
    (ISM), 127, 161
Insurance companies, 239–240
Intercept, 7
Interest-Only security, 76–77,
    222–223
Interest rate risk
    in bonds, 22–23
    managing with swaps, 114
    in mortgages, 76–77
International Swap Dealer
    Association (ISDA), 115
In-the-money option
    definition, 247
    delta of, 258, 259
    gamma of, 260–262
    in put/call parity, 267
    versus out-of-the-money option,
    253
Intragovernment debt, 67
Investment (GDP component),
    159
Investment-grade bonds, 80–81
Invoice price (futures), 97,
    99–100
IP. *See* Industrial production (IP)
ISDA. *See* International Swap
    Dealer Association (ISDA)
ISM. *See* Institute for Supply
    Management (ISM)
ISM manufacturing,
    data release, 161–162
    link to yields, 127–128
ISM nonmanufacturing, 161–162
Issue-specific risk
    credit risk, 201
    Treasury bonds, 191–192,
    200

L
Labor force, 159–160
LIBOR, 3, 89–90
LIBOR panel, 90
Liquidity
    in Agency markets, 79
    during credit crunch, 103
    enhancement programs by the
    Fed, 152
    link with Fed operations, 65
    link to Treasury demand, 167
    link with volatility markets,
    289–290
    risk stemming from. *See*
    Liquidity risk
    in swap markets, 116
    timing of futures rolls, 314
Liquidity risk, 22, 25–26
Lognormal distribution, 254–256
Lognormal volatility, 256, 264
London Interbank Offered Rate, 3,
    89–90

M
M1, 63
M2, 63
M3, 63
Macaulay duration, 34–35
Marketable debt, 67, 69
Mark-to-market P/L, 45, 174, 178
Matched-maturity spreads. *See*
    Swap spreads
MBS. *See* Mortgage-backed
    security (MBS)
Mean, 3
Midcurves. *See* Eurodollar futures
    option
Modified duration, 34–36, 38
Monetary policy, 62–66
Money supply, 63–65, 134, 234
Mortgage-backed security (MBS),
    73–77

Mortgage hedging, 169–170
Mortgage issuance, 147
Mortgage market, 73–77
Mortgage servicing assets, 76–77, 222–223
Mortgage supply, 147–148
Municipal bonds
   comparison with SIFMA/LIBOR swaps, 122–123
   description, 26, 82–83
   hedging, 199–200, 205
Mutual funds, 153

N
Net exports, 159
Net issuance (Treasuries), 67
New Home Sales, 164
Noncommercial accounts
   description, 104
   futures rolls, 317
Noncompetitive bids, 69
Nonfarm payroll, 160
Nonmarketable debt, 67
Nonstationary variables, 13
Normal distribution
   description, 4–5
   scaling through time, 15
Normal volatility, 256–257
Notes (Treasury), 68
Notional, 20

O
OIS. *See* Overnight index swap (OIS)
OIS rate, 101
Off-the-run Treasury, 22
On-the-run Treasury
   definition, 22
   reference for futures duration, 311–312
   repo rate, 44
   swap spread, 226–227

OPEC. *See* Organization of Petroleum Exporting Countries (OPEC)
Open market operations, 63–66, 69, 152
Options
   basics, 247–248
   Bermudan, 283
   delta. *See* Delta
   delta hedging. *See* Delta hedging
   embedded options, 280–282
   gamma. *See* Gamma
   interest rate options, 275–280
   interest rate skew, 293–294
   pricing of options, 250–254
   risk parameters, 257–266
   skew, 270, 293–294
   swaptions. *See* Swaptions
   theta. *See* Theta
   vega. *See* Vega
   volatility. *See* Volatility
   yield curve spread options, 284–285
Option-adjusted duration
   futures, 311–312
   mortgages, 168–170, 220
Option expiry switch. *See* Volatility spread trades
Option tail switch. *See* Volatility spread trades
Organization of Petroleum Exporting Countries (OPEC), 149
OTC. *See* Over-the-counter (OTC)
Out-of-the-money option
   definition, 247
   delta of, 258, 259
   gamma of, 260, 261
   in put/call parity, 267
   skew, 270
   theta of, 262
   vega of, 265
   versus in-the-money option, 253

Over-the-counter (OTC), 108, 115
Overnight index swap (OIS), 116
   rate, 101

P
PCA. *See* Principal components
   analysis (PCA)
PCE. *See* Personal consumption
   expenditure (PCE)
Pension funds
   fixed income demand, 155–157
   link to futures markets, 309
   link to swap spreads, 234–235
   STRIPS demand, 71
Personal consumption
   expenditure (PCE), 163
Physical settled contracts, 94
Principal components analysis
   (PCA), 14–15
Principal-Only security, 76
Principal STRIPS (P-STRIPS), 71,
   194
Present value (of swap). *See* Swaps
Primary dealers, 65, 69
Probability distribution
   continuous, 4
   discrete, 4
Producer Price Index, 162–163
P-STRIPS. *See* Principal STRIPS
   (P-STRIPS)
Public debt, 67, 72, 231
Put/call parity
   for American options, 268
   for Bermudan options, 268, 283
   description, 266–268
   for option Greeks, 268

Q
Quantitative easing
   in Japan, 66
   in United States, 137–138,
   152

R
Range accrual notes, 283–284
Ratio swaps. *See* SIFMA/LIBOR
   swaps
Realized volatility
   backtesting strategies, 269
   link with gamma, 265, 272
   link with path dependency,
   288
   link with skew, 270
   link with trading volatility, 274
   in longer-dated options, 291
   versus implied volatility,
   268–269, 286–287
   in volatility spread trades,
   295–297
Real yield, 72
Reference rate (Eurodollars),
   89–91
Refinancing, 74–77, 147–149,
   219–220
Refinancing index, 236–237
Regression
   correlation, 11–12
   error, 7–8
   fundamentals, 6–11
   goodness of fit, 11–14
   multiple, 8–9
   partial, 9
   polynomial, 9–11
   residual, 7–8
   standard error, 11
Regulatory risk, 22, 26–27, 133
Relative value
Repos. *See* Repurchase
   agreements
Repurchase agreements, 42–44
Required reserves, 64, 101
Reserve ratio requirement, 64–65
Residual, 8
Retail sales, 164–165
Retail sales ex autos, 164–165
Rho, 266

Risk
  counterparty. *See* Counterparty
    risk
  credit. *See* Credit risk
  inflation. *See* Inflation risk
  interest rate. *See* Interest rate
    risk
  issue-specific. *See* Issue-specific
    risk
  liquidity, 22, 25–26
  regulatory, 22, 26–27, 133
  tax, 22, 26, 84, 199
  types of risks, 22–27
Risk aversion
  household Treasury buying, 157
  link with corporate issuance,
    147
  link with term premium, 33–34
Risk-free rate, 43, 70, 251–252, 266
Rolldown, 51–53, 175–176
R-squared, 11–12

S

Savings rate, 131–133, 155, 157
Scaling (Brownian motion), 15
Seasonality
  SIFMA, 122
  Treasuries, 171–172
Segmentation (yield curve), 33–34
Separate Trading of Registered
    Interest and Principal
    Securities (STRIPS)
  definition, 70–71
  liquidity differences, 194
  relative value, 193–194
Serials (Eurodollar), 90
Sharpe ratio, 16–17, 244
SIFMA/LIBOR swaps
  curve properties, 122–123
  description, 120–121
  link to tax rates, 122
  ratio, 121–123
  swapping to fixed, 121–122

Skew
  description, 270
  interest rate, 293–294
Slide. *See* Rolldown
Standard deviation, 2–5, 15–16
Standard error, 8, 11
Stationary variables, 13
Steepener, 53–54
STRIPS. *See* Separate Trading of
    Registered Interest and
    Principal Securities (STRIPS)
Swaps
  basic principles, 108–111
  basis swaps. *See* Basis swaps
  bootstrapping, 110–111
  counterparty risk. *See*
    Counterparty risk
  fed funds. *See* Federal funds
    basis swap
  fixed rate, 108
  floating rate, 108
  inflation swaps. *See* Inflation
    swaps
  one-month/three-month, 119
  OTC. *See* Over-the-counter
    (OTC)
  payer, 107
  present value, 109–110
  pricing, 109–110
  receiver, 107
  SIFMA/LIBOR. *See*
    SIFMA/LIBOR swaps
  three-month/six-month, 119
Swap spread curve, 243–245
Swap spreads
  and bank health, 230–231
  and budget deficits, 232–233
  curve, 243–245
  directionality, 240–241
  drivers, 230–235
  headline, 227
  matched-maturity, 113–114
  narrower, 226

purpose, 230–234
setup, 227–229
wideners, 226
Swaptions, 256, 276, 279–281

T
Tax risk, 22, 26, 84, 199
Term premium
in fed funds futures. *See* Federal
funds futures
link to volatility, 289
in municipal bonds, 84
in yield curve, 33–34
Theta
calls versus puts, 268
link to delta hedging, 272
option risk parameter, 262–264
similarity to BNOC, 306
TIPS. *See* Treasury Inflation
Protected Securities (TIPS)
Trade weights
in butterfly trades, 56
in carry-efficient trades, 182
in conditional trades, 321
in relative value trades, 188–191
Treasury debt auctions, 68–70
Treasury futures
basis. *See* Treasury futures basis
basis net of carry. *See* Basis net
of carry (BNOC)
cheapest to deliver. *See*
Cheapest to deliver (CTD)
codes, 89
contract notionals, 96
conversion factors. *See*
Conversion factor
deliverable baskets, 95
delivery option value, 100–101
delivery process, 97
empirical duration, 311–313
implied repo. *See* Implied repo
invoice price. *See* Invoice price
(futures)

option-adjusted risk measures,
311–313
options. *See* Treasury futures
options
rolls, 313–317
Treasury futures basis
assumptions in trading, 306–308
basis net of carry. *See* Basis net
of carry (BNOC)
delivery option value. *See*
Delivery option value
gross basis, 100
link to balance sheet size,
308–309
link to term repos, 307–308
in yield shifts, 300–305
Treasury futures options
description, 280
use in conditional swap spread
trades, 326–328
Treasury futures rolls, 313–317
Treasury Inflation Protected
Securities (TIPS), 24–25,
71–72
Treasury par curve, 191–193
Treasury supply
auctions. *See* Treasury debt
auctions
basics, 141–143
link with budget deficit, 231–233
link with other fixed income
markets, 146
Trust-preferred securities, 293

U
Ultra-long futures, 85, 95–97, 208
Unemployment insurance, 142, 160
Unemployment rate
economic data releases, 160–161
link with inflation expectations,
156
regression versus inflation, 6

Vega
  calls versus puts, 268
  converting between lognormal
    and normal, 266
  option risk parameter, 264–266
Vega P/L
  formula, 264
  link to skew, 287
  symmetry, 269
Volatility
  implied. *See* Implied volatility
  quoting, 256–257
  realized. *See* Realized volatility
Volatility spread trades
  expiry switches, 294–296
  motivation, 296–297
  tail switches, 294–296
  weighting, 295–296
Volatility trading
  assumptions in, 286–287
  asymmetry in, 286–287
  importance of GSEs, 290–293
  link to delta hedging. *See* Delta
    hedging
  link with Fed policy, 288–289
  link with mortgage servicing,
    291
  longer-dated options, 290–293
  P/L from, 286

structural factors in, 288–290
  volatility spreads. *See* Volatility
    spread trades
YCSO. *See* Yield curve spread
    option (YCSO)
Yield
  bond, 30–31
  spreads. *See* Yield spreads
  Treasury futures. *See* Implied
    forward yield
Yield betas, 215–218
Yield butterfly. *See* Butterfly trade
Yield curve
  definition, 32–33
  explanations of shape, 34
Yield spreads
  in futures basket, 310–311
  relative value example, 184
  underlying YCSO, 285
Yield curve spread option (YCSO),
    284–285

Z
Zero-coupon bonds
  bond pricing, 29–30
  inflation swaps, 123
  link with STRIPS, 70–71
  zero-coupon callables, 293

Printed and bound by CPI Group (UK) Ltd, Croydon, CR0 4YY

23/04/2025

14660919-0003